Honda 360/600/Z Owners Workshop Manual

by J H Haynes
Associate Member of the Guild of Motoring Writers
and Peter Strasman
MISTC

Models covered

UK: 360 Saloon and Estate, 354cc
600 Saloon, 599cc
600 Coupe Z, 599cc

USA: 360 Sedan and Wagon, 21.5 cu in
600 Sedan, 35.5 cu in
600 Coupe, 35.5 cu in

ISBN 0 85696 138 8

ABCDE 138
FGHIJ
KLMNO
PQRST

Printed in England

HAYNES PUBLISHING GROUP
SPARKFORD YEOVIL SOMERSET ENGLAND
distributed in the USA by
HAYNES PUBLICATIONS INC
861 LAWRENCE DRIVE
NEWBURY PARK
CALIFORNIA 91320
USA

Acknowledgements

Our thanks must go to Honda (UK) Limited, for the use of some of their technical illustrations, to Castrol Limited for advice on lubrication, and to the Champion Sparking Plug Company for the illustrations showing the spark plug conditions. The bodywork repair photographs used in this manual were provided by Lloyds Industries Limited who supply 'Turtle Wax', 'Dupli-color Holts', and other Holts range products.

Brian Horsfall carried out the mechanical work and Les Brazier took the photographs. George Magnus made several useful contributions to the fault finding charts, incorporated in this book.

About this manual

Its arrangement

This book is divided into 12 Chapters. Each Chapter is divided into Sections. The Sections contain serially numbered paragraphs.

All the illustrations carry a caption. When the illustration is designed as a figure the reference number consists of the Chapter number, followed by a sequence number; the sequence starting afresh for every Chapter. Photographs have a reference number in the caption this reference number pinpoints the Section and paragraph in that Chapter to which the photograph refers. Almost invariably the existence of this photo is indicated in the paragraph by direct reference in the text, or the words "photo" or "see photo" in brackets.

Note: All photographs refer are of a Honda 600 Saloon/Sedan model. These pictures will apply to the 600 (2) Coupe and the 600 Estate/Wagon. The 360 series components are similar in most respect, with the exception of the generator, which is of combined dynamo/starter type.

When the left-hand side or right-hand side of a car or component is mentioned, this is to be taken as if the viewer was looking in the forward direction of travel and the component normally fitted in the car.

Getting the best from your manual

Before starting a job, read all the relevant parts of the manual and indeed any irrelevant parts which you think might be useful. As well as providing information, it will help you to check that you have all the tools, and all the spares that you will need. The ideal time to do this is on the Friday night if you are going to do the job over the weekend - not the Friday night before you start but the previous Friday night. This will allow you a full week to get all of the materials which will be needed. Obviously this manual will be used as the actual work is carried out: in order to make on the spot references. When the manual is being put to this use, it is a good idea to cover the open pages with polythene or a sheet of glass to prevent item from becoming stained with oil or grease.

The tools for the job

You will see from this book that you can do almost anything if you possess a set of open-ended spanners and a set of cranked ring spanners.

Torque wrenches, puller and other specialised tools are pricey items - therefore, you will not find them easy to borrow. However, one possible source should not be overlooked - many local car clubs lend tools to their members, and it could well be that a subscription to such a club would cost you less than buying a torque wrench.

One most useful 'tool' which we hope you have already bought or are about to buy is the Haynes Owners Workshop Manual for your car.

Contents

Honda 600 Series Sedan/Saloon

Honda Tourer

Honda Coupe Z

Buying spare parts and vehicle identifcation numbers

Buying spare parts

Spare parts are available from many sources, for example: garages, other garages and accessory shops, and motor factors. Our advice regarding spare part sources is as follows:

Location of engine number

Officially appointed Honda garages - This is the best source of parts which are peculiar to your car and are otherwise not generally available (eg complete cylinder heads, internal gearbox components, badges, interior trim etc). It is also the only place at which you should buy parts if your car is still under warranty non-Honda components may invalidate the warranty. To be sure of obtaining the correct parts it will always be necessary to give the storeman your car's engine and chassis number, and if possible, to take the 'old' part along for positive identification. Remember that many parts are available on a factory exchange scheme - any parts returned should always be clean! It obviously makes good sense to go straight to the specialists on your car for this type of part for they are best equipped to supply you.

Other garages and accessory shops - These are often very good places to buy materials and components needed for the maintenance of your car (eg oil filters, sparks plugs, bulbs, fan belts, oils and greases, touch-up paint, filler paste etc). They also sell general accessories, usually have convenient opening hours, charge lower prices and can often be found not far from home.

Motor factors - Good factors will stock all of the more important components which wear out relatively quickly (eg clutch components, pistons, valves, exhaust systems, brake cylinders/pipes/-hoses/seals/shoes and pads etc). Motor factors will often provide new or reconditioned components on a part exchange basis - this can save a considerable amount of money.

Vehicle identification numbers

The *engine number* is located on the left-hand side of the crankcase (photo).

An *identification plate* is fixed to right-hand engine compartment bulkhead.

Body numbers are stamped on both the engine rear bulkhead and the upper surface of the fascia panel within the vehicle.

Routine maintenance

Maintenance is essential to ensure safety and is desirable for the well being of the car and preservation of its resale value. Although the oil can and grease gun have largely been rendered obsolescant by pre-packed bearings and automatic lubrication, the need for routine cleaning and careful inspection is even more necessary if the twin destructive agents, rust and mechanical wear are to be kept at bay.

In the summary given a suggested routine of essential maintenance is given. The items in bold type affect the owner's safety and are vital, the others are designed to combat depreciation.

All nuts and bolts are metric sizes.

Filling the engine with recommended lubricant

600 miles (1000 km)

Steering

Check tyre pressures
Examine tyres for wear

Brakes

Try an emergency stop
Check the handbrake on a steep incline
Check the level of hydraulic fluid in the reservoir

Lights and electrical components

Are all the lights working properly?
Do the direction indicators work properly?
Do the brake stop lights work?
Is the windscreen wiper and washer working correctly?
Does the horn work?

Engine compartment

Check the level of oil in the crankcase.
Check the battery electrolyte level.
Check the transmission fluid level (automatic transmission only)

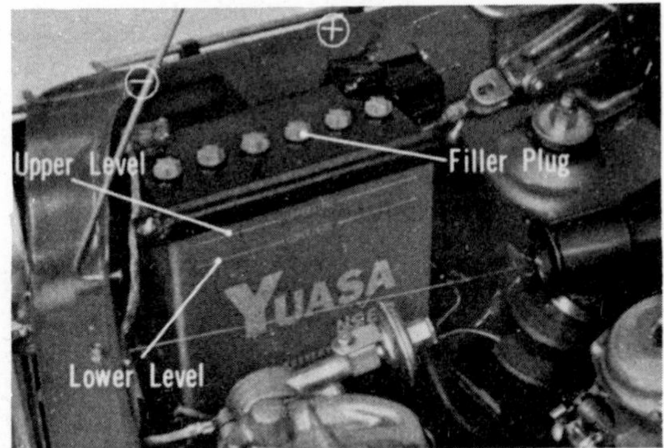

RM.1. Battery electrolyte levels

3000 miles (5000 km)

Steering

Check for free play at steering wheel
Rotate - the position of the road wheels (include spare)

Brakes

Check wear of disc pads or drum linings.
Adjust drumstype brakes and handbrake.
Check hydraulic pipes and unions for leaks.

Engine

Change engine oil
Check fan belt tension
Check carburettor adjustments.

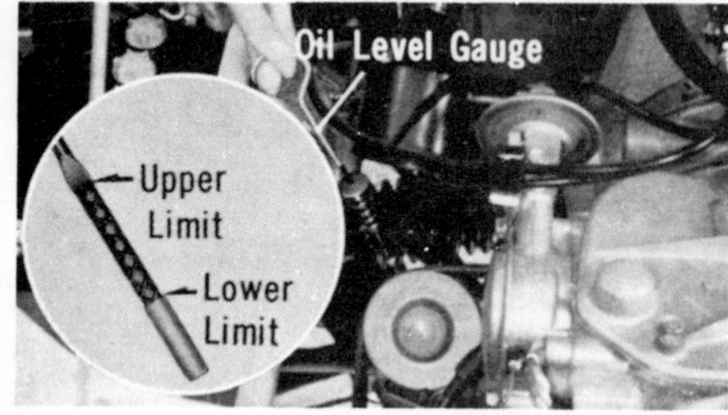

RM.2. Crankcase oil level dipstick

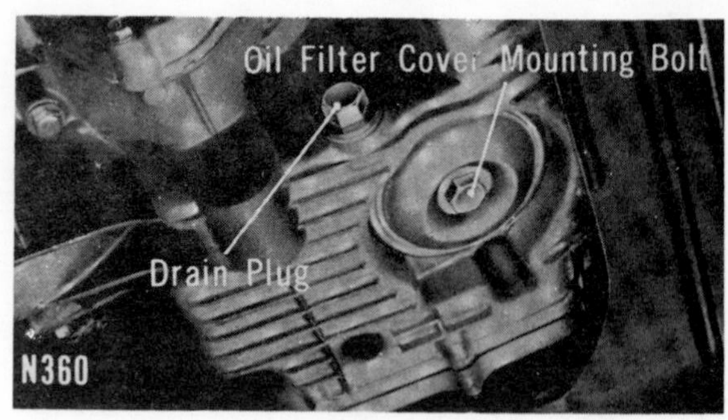

RM.3. Crankcase oil drain plug and filter mounting

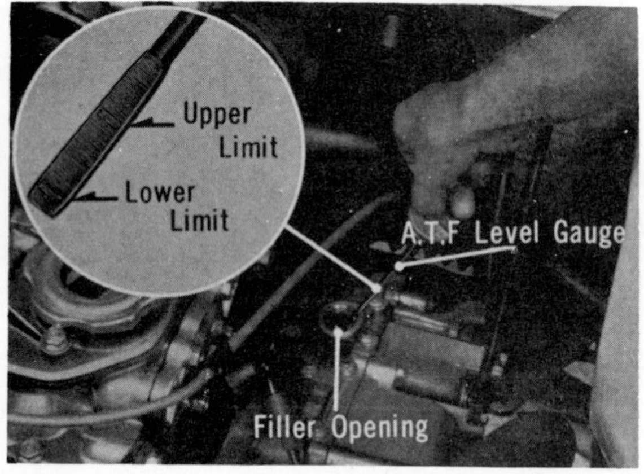

RM.4. Automatic transmission fluid combined dipstick and filler plug

RM.5. Crankcase and automatic transmission drain plugs

RM.6. Brake reservoir fluid level

RM.7. Air cleaner oil residue drain plug (North America only)

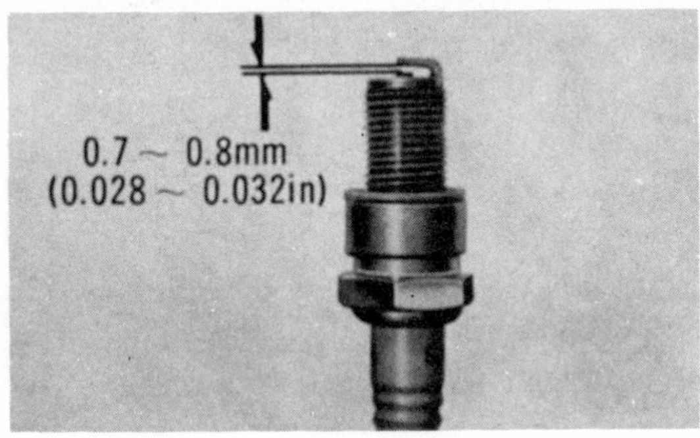

RM.8. Correct spark plug gap

RM.9. Adjusting valve clearance

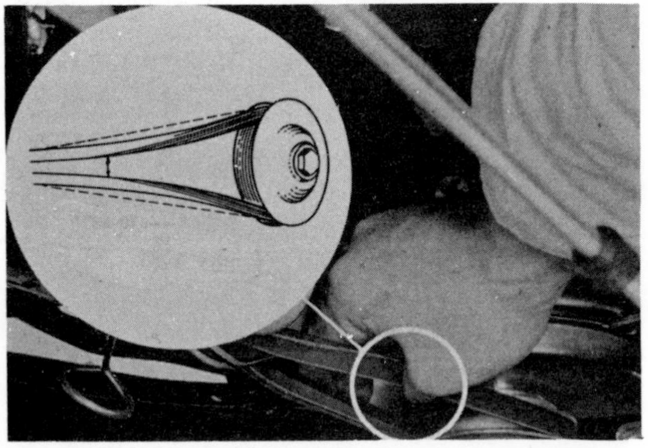

RM.10. Checking cooling fan drive belt tension (½ to ¾ in. - 12 to 20 mm)

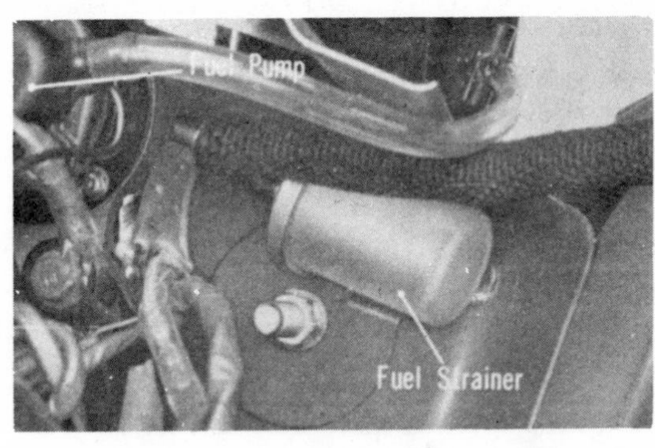

RM.11. Location of fuel filter/strainer

RM.12. Steering box grease nipple

RM.13. Brake vacuum servo air filter

Check valve clearance.
Check contact breaker gap and ignition timing.

6000 miles (10000 km)

Steering
Check front wheel alignment

Brakes
Clean vacuum servo filter (if fitted) in fuel and dry.

Engine
Renew engine oil filter.
Clean air cleaner element and drain oil residue.

Clean and adjust spark plugs.
Check security of all nuts and bolts

Clutch
Check and adjust free movement

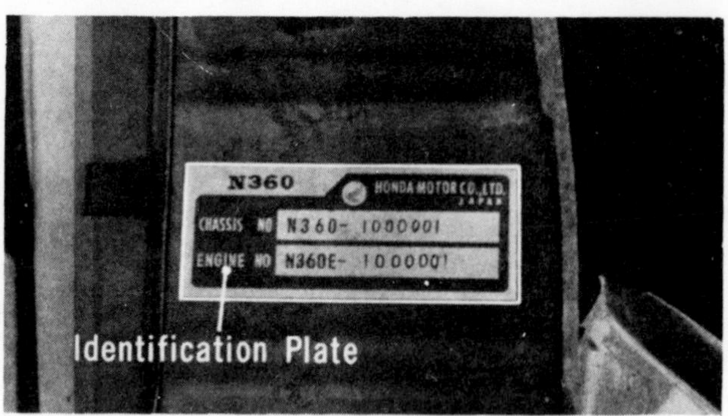

RM.14. Location of vehicle identification numbers

12000 miles (20000 km)

Steering
Grease steering box and inspect condition of bellows

Engine
Renew fuel filter
Renew spark plugs
Renew air cleaner element

Automatic transmission
Change transmission fluid.
Check and adjust shift lever control cables.

Electrical
Check starter motor/generator brushes (360 cc models only)

Suspension, driveshafts and front hubs
Check security of all bolts and nuts.
Check condition of rubber bellows.
Check operation and resistance of shock absorbers.
Check rear springs for cracked leaves.

Body
Check security and condition of safety belts.

Examine underbody for rust, particularly where the rear suspension is anchored.

Oil locks and hinges.
Fit new wiper blade rubber inserts.

Exhaust system
Check for leaks and signs of heavy rusting, replace before leaks occur.

24000 miles (40000 km)

Brakes
Change hydraulic fluid and bleed system

Steering
Check steering column flexible joint for deterioration

48000 miles (77000 km)

Brakes
Renew all seals in master and slave cylinders and calipers.
Check operation of vacuum servo unit.

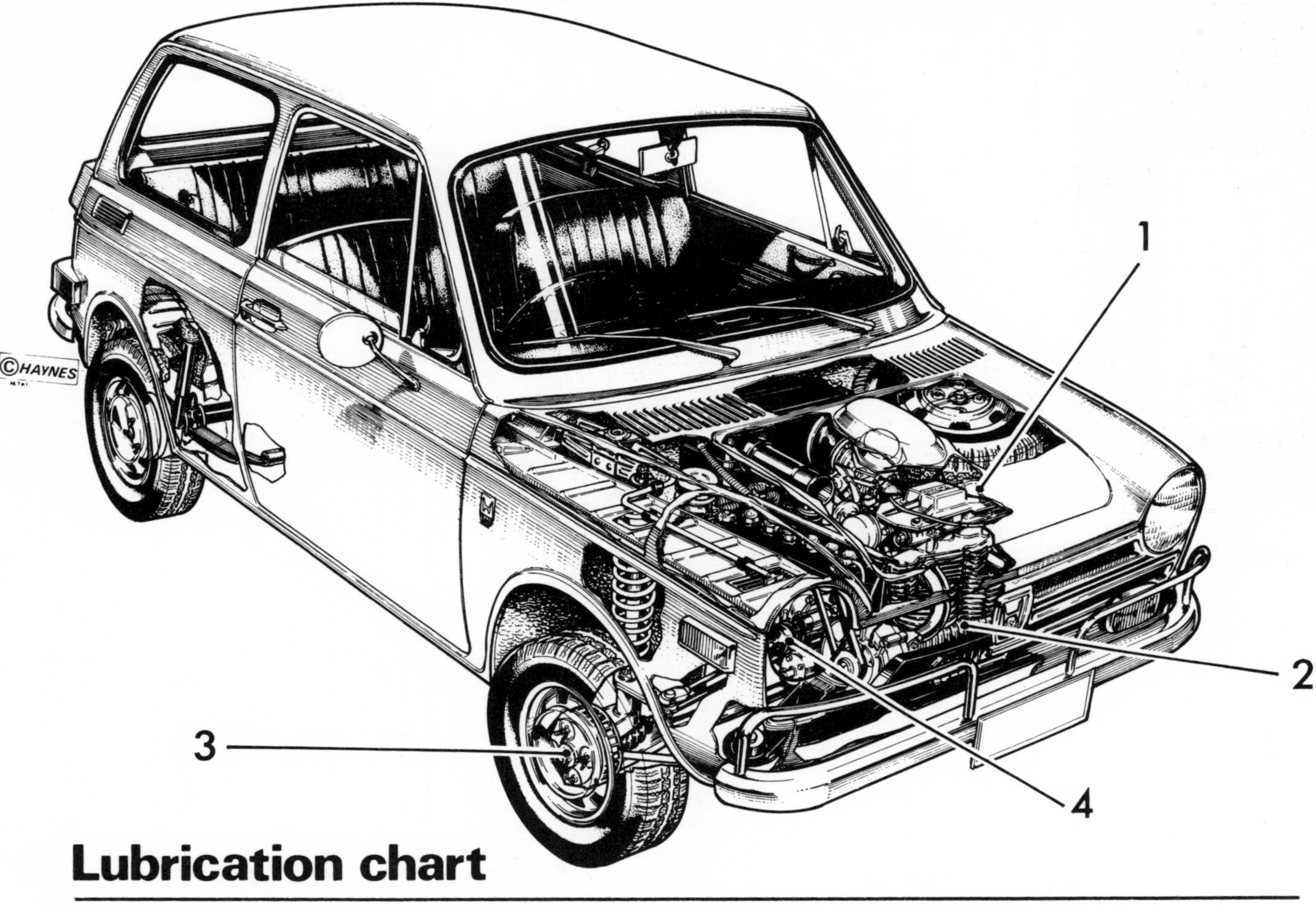

Lubrication chart

1	Engine/Manual gearbox/final drive	Castrol GTX
2	Automatic transmission	Castrol TQF
3	Front wheel bearings	Castrol LM Grease
4	Rack and pinion unit and inner joints of tie-rods	Castrol LM Grease

Note: this is a general recommendation. Different operating conditions require different lubricants - consult the handbook supplied with the car

Chapter 1 Engine

Contents

Specifications

Engine general:

Type	Four stroke, air-cooled
Number of cylinders	2
Bore and stroke:	
360 cc/21.5 cu in.	2.46 x 2.28 in (62.5 x 57.8 mm)
600 cc/35.5 cu in.	2.91 x 2.74 in (74.0 x 69.6 mm)
Displacement:	
360 series	354 cc (21.5 cu in.)
600 series	598.4 cc (35.5 cu in.)
Compression ratio:	
360 cc/21.5 cu in.	8.6 : 1
600 cc/35.5 cu in.	8.3 : 1 (Z Coupe' 8.5 : 1)
Maximum power output:	
360 cc/21.5 cu in.	31 bhp at 8,500 rev/min
600 cc/35.5 cu in.	45 bhp at 7000 rev/min
600 cc/35.5 cu in. (USA)	36 bhp at 6000 rev/min
Maximum torque:	
360 cc/21.5 cu in.	21.7 lb/ft at 5,500 rev/min (3.0 kg/m at 5,500 rev/min)
600 cc/35.5 cu in.	37.6 lb/ft at 5,000 rev/min (5.2 kg/m at 5,000 rev/min)
600 cc/35.5 cu in. (USA)	31.8 lb/ft at 4,000 rev/min (4.4 kg/m at 4,000 rev/min)

Crankshaft and connecting rods:

Type	Four bearing, press fitted assembly with connecting rods and

	camshaft sprocket, cannot be dismantled except for outer bearings
Connecting rod axial endfloat (maximum)	0.0193 in. (0.49 mm)
Big-end play (maximum)	0.004 in. (0.010 mm)

Cylinder block:

Standard bore diameter	
360 cc/21.5 cu in.	2.4606 to 2.4610 in. (62.50 to 62.51 mm)
600 cc/35.5 cu in.	2.9134 to 2.9138 in. (74.00 to 74.01 mm)
Maximum bore diameter before rebore necessary *	
360 cc/21.5 cu in.	2.4646 in. (62.60 mm)
600 cc/35.5 cu in.	2.9173 in. (74.10 mm)

* *Oversize pistons are available in increments of 0.0098 in. (0.25 mm).*

Pistons:

	360 cc/21.5 cu in.	**600 cc/35.5 cu in.**
Top diameter	2.439 to 2.441 in. (61.95 to 62.00 mm)	2.890 to 2.891 in. (73.40 to 73.45 mm)
Skirt diameter	2.458 to 2.459 in. (62.45 to 62.47 mm)	2.911 to 2.912 in. (73.95 to 73.97 mm)
Gudgeon pin bore diameter	0.6694 to 0.6696 in. (17.002 to 17.008 mm)	
Piston ring groove clearance:		
Top	0.0018 to 0.0030 in. (0.045 to 0.075 mm)	
Second and oil control	0.0006 to 0.0018 in. (0.015 to 0.045 mm)	
Piston ring end gap	0.008 to 0.015 in. (0.2 to 0.4 mm)	

Gudgeon pins:

Diameter	0.6691 to 0.6693 in. (16.994 to 17.000 mm)
Maximum inside diameter of connecting rod small end	0.6709 in. (17.043 mm)

Camshaft and rocker gear:

Journals, minimum diameter due to wear	0.941 in. (23.9 mm)
Maximum inside diameter, due to wear, of camshaft journal holder	0.9468 in. (24.05 mm)
Camshaft housing rocker shaft bush maximum bore diameter, due to wear	0.474 in. (12.05 mm)
Camshaft lobe, minimum overall length, due to wear:	
360 cc/21.5 cu in. inlet cam	1.563 in. (39.70 mm)
360 cc/21.5 cu in. exhaust cam	1.583 in. (40.22 mm)
600 cc/35.5 cu in. inlet cam	1.621 in. (41.18 mm)
600 cc/35.5 cu in. exhaust cam	1.602 in. (40.70 mm)

Valves:

Stem diameter:	
Inlet	0.2591 to 0.2594 in. (6.58 to 6.59 mm)
Exhaust	0.2579 to 0.2583 in. (6.55 to 6.56 mm)
Head thickness:	
Inlet	0.0350 to 0.0433 in. (0.9 to 1.1 mm)
Exhaust	0.0550 to 0.0630 in. (1.4 to 1.6 mm)
Stem to guide clearance:	
Inlet	0.0004 to 0.0016 in. (0.01 to 0.04 mm)
Exhaust	0.0016 to 0.0028 in. (0.04 to 0.07 mm)
Spring free length:	
Inner	1.65 in. (42.0 mm)
Outer	1.76 in. (44.8 mm)
Valve clearances (cold)	0.003 to 0.005 in. (0.08 to 0.12 mm)

Primary drive:

Driven sprocket endfloat	0.0039 to 0.0118 in. (0.1 to 0.3 mm)
Drive sprocket endfloat	0 to 0.0078 in. (0 to 0.2 mm)
Maximum primary drive backlash	0.00071 to 0.00209 in. (0.018 to 0.053 mm)

Maximum difference in length between two primary chains (manual gearbox)	0.0118 in. (0.3 mm)

Lubrication system:

Type	Pressure and splash feed
Oil pump	
Manual gearbox	Plunger type
Automatic transmission	Rotor type
Oil filter	Disposable element type
Oil capacity:	
With manual gearbox fitted, crankcase oil also lubricates gearbox and differential unit	5.3 Imperial pints (3 litres)
With automatic gearbox fitted, crankcase oil also lubricates differential	4.4 Imperial pints (2.5 litres)

Torque wrench settings:

	lb/ft	kg/m
Crankshaft centre bearing bolts	28	3.871
Crankshaft pulley retaining bolt	35	4.838
Crankshaft right-hand bearing retainer bolts	8	1.106
Crankcase bolts (small)	8	1.106
Crankcase bolts (large)	20	2.765
Camshaft housing domed nuts	23	3.179
Camshaft housing standard nuts	9	1.244
Primary drive sprocket bolt	18	2.488
Rocker arm lock bolt	28	3.871
Engine mounting strut to subframe bolts	25	3.456
Engine to mounting strut bolts	18	2.488
Engine rear mounting to subframe bolts	18	2.488
Engine rear mounting insulator to bracket	8	1.106
Stub axle carrier clamp bolt	35	4.838
Driveshaft to differential bolts	24	3.318
Exhaust pipe clamp bolt	18	2.488
Exhaust pipe flange to engine bolts	18	2.488

1 General description

The engine fitted to the range of vehicles covered by this manual is of air-cooled, vertical twin cylinder overhead camshaft type. Series 360 models have an engine capacity of 354 cc (21.5 cu in) and series 600 models have an engine capacity of 594 cc (35.5 cu in) as has also the (Z) Coupe. The saloon versions are available with optional automatic transmission.

Both sizes of engine are of similar design and construction but differ in certain component details. The procedure described in this Chapter applies to all models and engine capacities.

The cylinder block is of alloy construction, generously finned with cast-iron sleever pressed in. The pistons are aluminium with fully floating gudgeon pins. The overhead camshaft is driven by a single roller chain directly fron the crankshaft.

The crankshaft is an assembly which incorporates the connection rods, bearings and camshaft chain drive sprocket. The connection rod big-end bearings are of needle roller type as are also the crankshaft main bearings. The crankshaft can only be serviced as a complete assembly.

The splined end of the crankshaft is fitted with a drive sprocket (rubber clamped on 600 cc (35.5 cu in) models) from which power is transmitted to the transmission mainshaft through two singe roller chains equipped with a tensioner device.

A pressurised lubrication system and oil filter provide adequate oil feed to all engine components; full details are given in Section 12, of this Chapter.

2 Major operations possible with engine in vehicle

1 All servicing work can be carried out without removing the engine except where attention is required to components within the crankcase and to the crankshaft itself.

2 The following items can be removed and replaced without removing the power unit from its mountings.

Camshaft gear (Section 8).
Cylinder head and valves (Section 8).
Cylinder block, pistons and gudgeon pins (Section 17).
Air cooling and fan assembly (Chapter 2).
Primary drive chains and sprockets (Sections 14 or 15).
Carburettor (Chapter 3).
Oil filter and oil pump (Sections 13,14 or 15.
Generator (Chapter 11).
Contact breaker (Chapter 4).

3 Method of engine removal

1 The engine, gearbox (or automatic transmission) and differential are constructed as a single unit and are removed in a similar manner, as one unit.

2 It is recommended that the power/transmission unit is removed together with the front sub-frame, drive shafts and hubs as described in the next two sections.

3 Before commencing operations, provide axle stands and a trolley type jack.

4 Engine/manual transmission - removal

1 Drain the engine oil and disconnect the cable from the battery negative - terminal. Remove the bonnet.

2 Remove the exhaust type vehicle interior heater (if fitted) as described in chapter 12.

3 Disconnect the engine earth strap from the bodyframe.

4 Disconnect the following electrical leads:

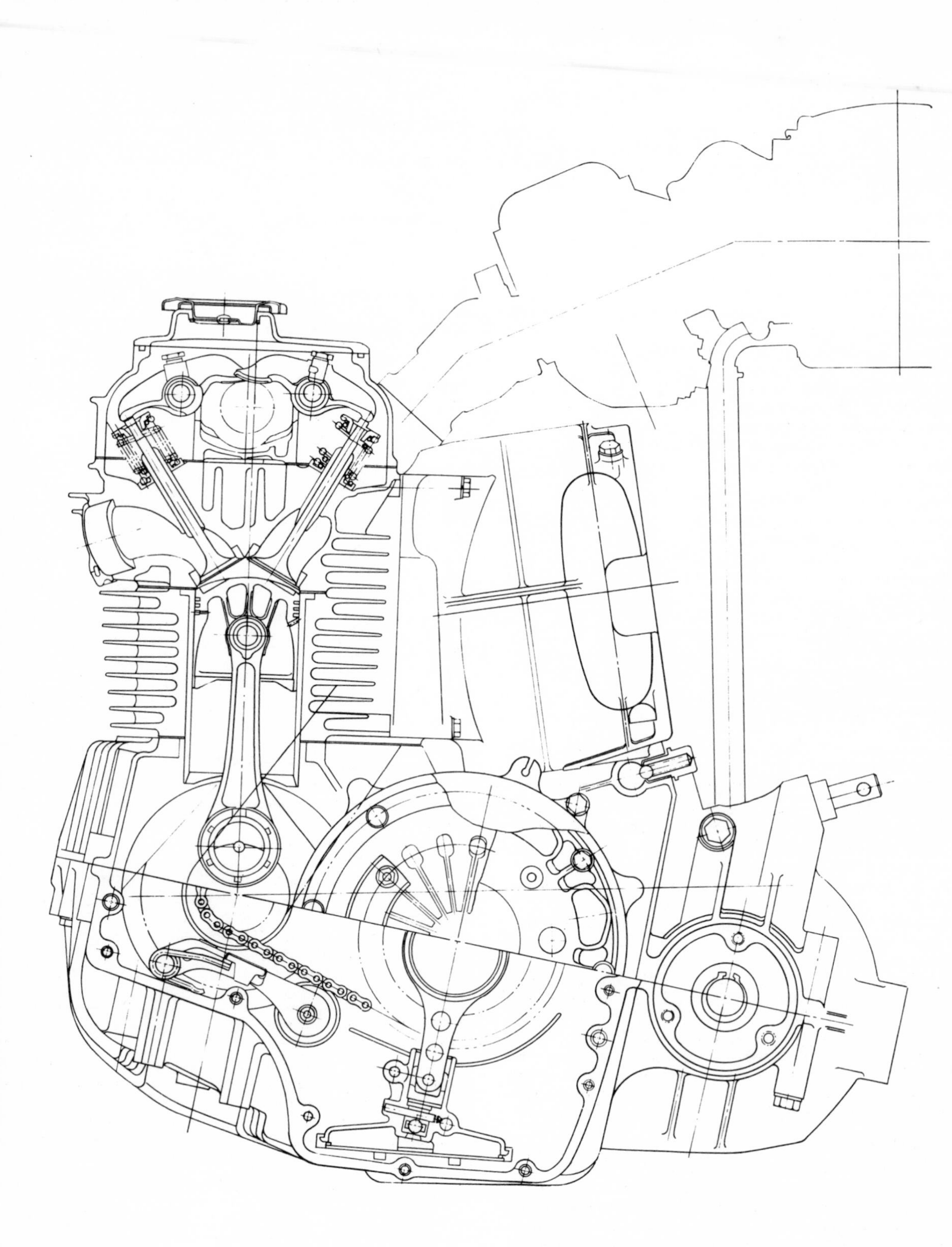

Fig. 1.1. Cross-sectional view of the engine (manual transmission)

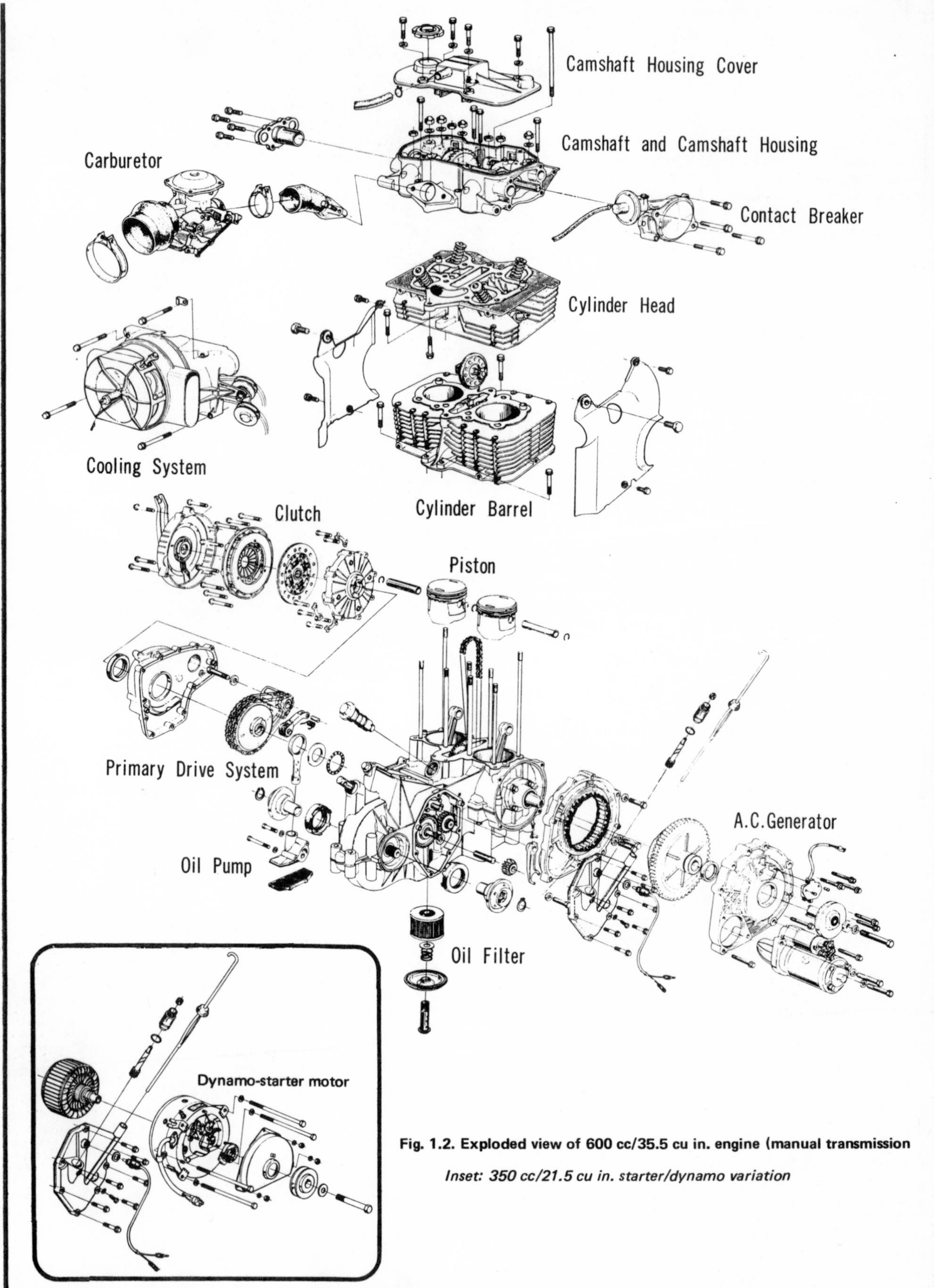

Fig. 1.2. Exploded view of 600 cc/35.5 cu in. engine (manual transmission

Inset: 350 cc/21.5 cu in. starter/dynamo variation

Coil ignition LT lead to contact breaker unit.
Coil ignition HT lead to contact breaker unit.
Fuel solenoid valve.
Reversing lamp switch.
Generator.
Starter motor.

5 Disconnect the clutch operating cable as described in Chapter 5 and detach the speedometer drive cable at its union on the gearbox housing.(photo).

6 Disconnect the choke and accelerator cables from the carburettor.

7 Pull off the vacuum tube from the contact breaker unit and detach the breather tube from the camshaft housing cover. (photo).

8 Loosen the securing clamp which retains the flexible carburettor intake hose to the air cleaner. (photo).

9 Detach the fuel line from the carburettor.

10 Remove the two inlet flange mounting bolts and from the camshaft housing, lift away the insulator/flange, carburettor and bellows. Retain the sealing 'O' ring.

11 *On vehicles equipped with engine warmth heaters;* Loosen the air duct clamps (photo) and detach them from the cooling fan housing. Pull out the heater control connection pin (photo) and push the control rod into the vehicle interior.

12 *On vehicles equipped with fascia mounted gearshift;* Remove the floor cover and drift out the connection tension pin to separate the column and shift-rods. Push the shift-rod towards the engine.(photo)
(photo).

13 *On vehicles equipped with floor mounted gearshift levers:* Remove the two handbrake lever flange mounting bolts and incline the lever to one side. Unscrew the control lever knob and remove the console securing screws. Withdraw the console and shift lever bellows. Unscrew and remove the gearshift lever bracket.

14 Disconnect the flasher direction indicator cable connectors which are located just behind the front grille.

15 *On 360 series vehicles:* Remove the front grille and screen (five screws).

16 *On 600 series vehicles:* Detach the flasher indicator lenses and remove the front grille securing bolts and screws.

17 Loosen the exhaust pipe clamps and detach them fom engine support front crossmember. (photo).

18 Unscrew and remove the exhaust flange nuts at the cylinder head and slip the flanges down the pipes. (photo).

19 One of two methods may now be used to remove the power train from the car.

(A)Removal without disconnecting brake hydraulic circuit

20 Loosen the stub axle and road wheel nuts and then jack up the front of the vehicle by placing a jack under the front crossmember. When the front bumper is at least 30 in (762 mm) from the ground, place axle stands under the bodyframe sidemembers and remove the jack.

21 Remove the roadwheels and stub axle nuts from both front hubs and withdraw the brake drums using a suitable extractor.

22 Remove the four bolts which secure each brake backplate to the stub axle carrier and tie the brake backplate assembly up so that its weight will not strain the flexible pipe.

(B) To remove by disconnecting hydraulic front brake lines

The advantage of this method is that the front brake/hub assemblies do not have to be dismantled. Disconnect each underwing brake hose at its banjo connection and plug the fluid line to prevent ingress of dirt and loss of fluid.

23 Whichever of the two suggested methods is chosen, proceed by removing the pinch bolts from the clamps which secure the stub axle carriers to the front suspension leg. These bolts act as cotter pins and locate in the groove at the base of the suspension leg. They must be fully withdrawn before the stub axle carrier can be tapped downwards off the suspension leg. (photo).

24 Remove the left and right-hand splash guards (fitted with engine warmth heaters only) and locate a trolley type jack under the crankcase. Use a piece of wood as an insulator to prevent damaging the ribbed surface of the crankcase.

25 Unscrew and remove the front and rear subframe mounting bolts. (photo).

26 Remove the bolt from the exhaust silencer mounting bracket.

27 Lower the jack very slowly and check for any wires or cables which may become hooked up and then withdraw the complete engine/transmission unit from below the front of the vehicle. (photo).

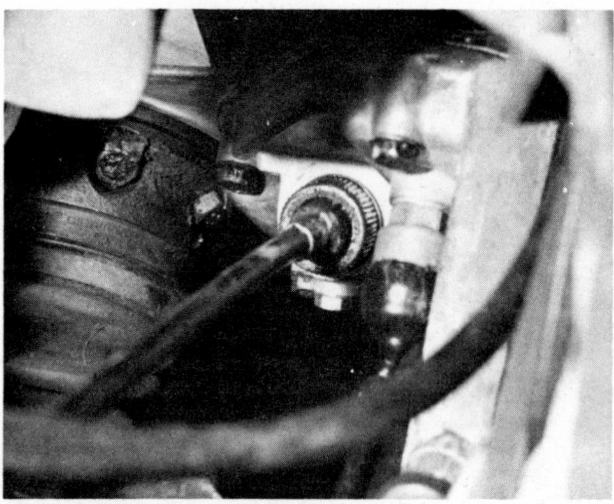

4.5 Speedometer drive connection

4.7 Rocker cover fume extraction tube

4.8 Disconnecting air cleaner

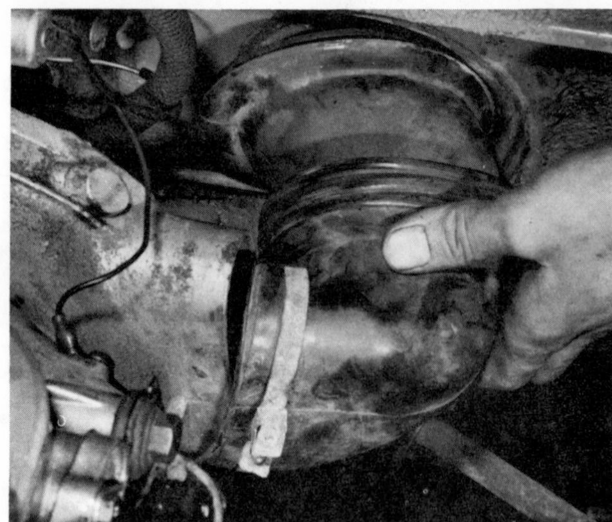
4.11a Disconnecting flexible heater duct

4.11b Heater control rod connection

4.12 Gearshift rod connecting tension pin

4.17 Exhaust pipe bracket

4.18 Detaching exhaust flanges

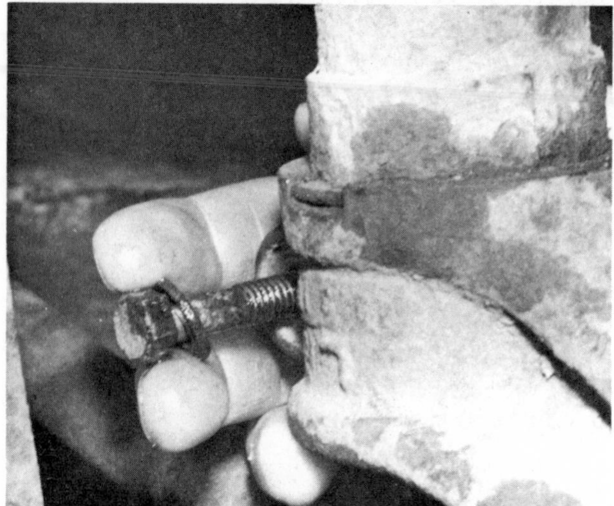
4.23a Front suspension leg cotter bolt

4.23b Detaching stub axle carrier from front suspension leg

4.25a Unscrewing a front mounting bolt

4.25b Unscrewing a rear mounting bolt from inside the car

4.27 Removing the engine from below the bodyframe

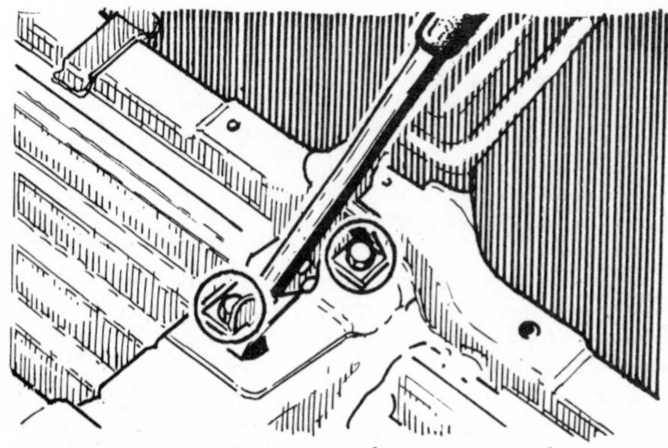
Fig. 1.3. Handbrake control lever mounting bracket bolts

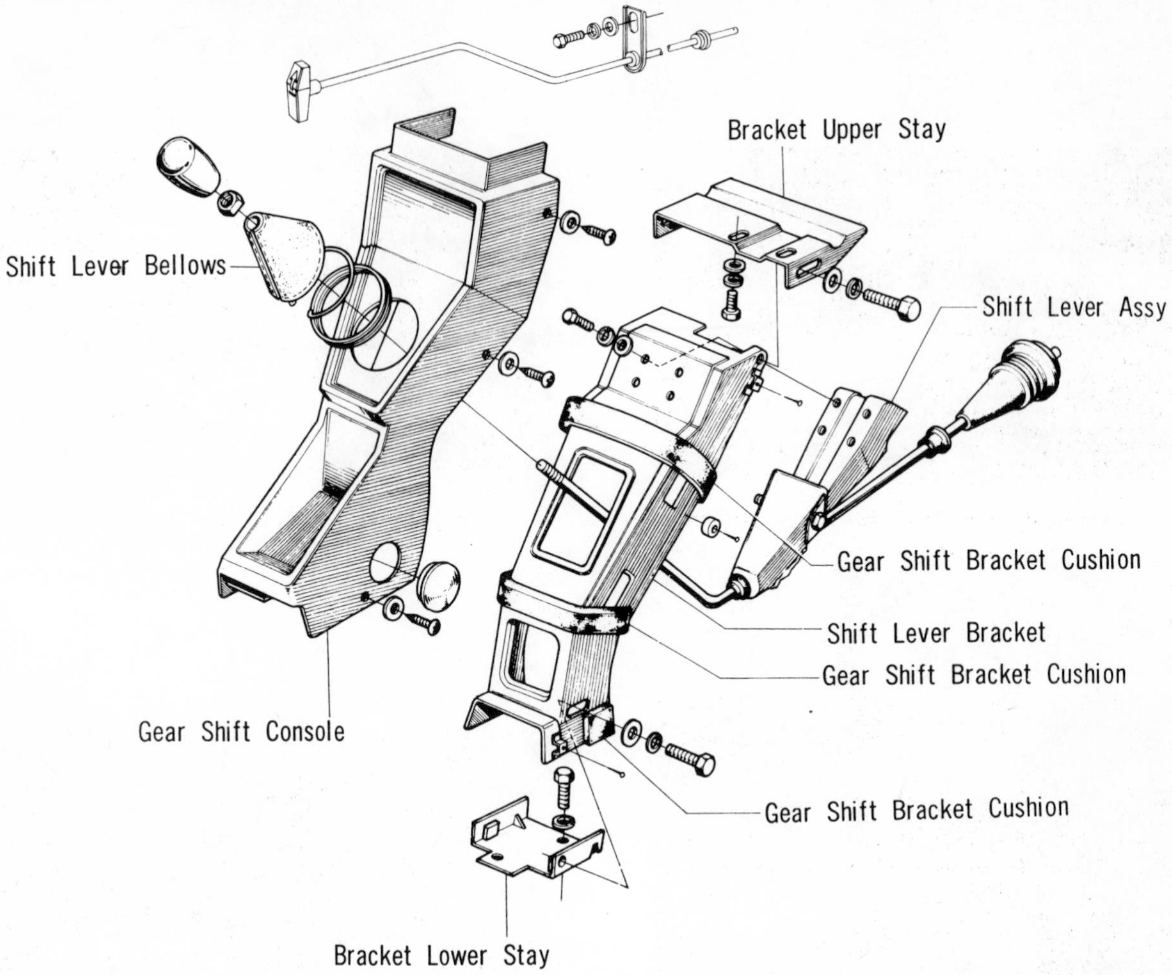

Bracket Upper Stay
Shift Lever Bellows
Shift Lever Assy
Gear Shift Bracket Cushion
Shift Lever Bracket
Gear Shift Bracket Cushion
Gear Shift Console
Gear Shift Bracket Cushion
Bracket Lower Stay

Fig. 1.4. Components of floor mounted type gearshift lever

5 Engine/automatic transmission - removal

1 Unscrew the locknut on the accelerator secondary cable at the carburettor and also the lock nuts on the cables "A" and "B". Disconnect the cable-end balls from the selector strap arm, Figs. 1.5 and 1.6.
2 Disconnect the selector cables from the manual control lever.
3 Release the exhaust pipe clamps from the torque convertor case cover. Drain and retain the transmission fluid.
4 Detach the automatic transmission fluid cooler from behind the front engine bulkhead.
5 Carry out all the operations described in the preceding Section (4), except paragraphs 5, 12 and 13.

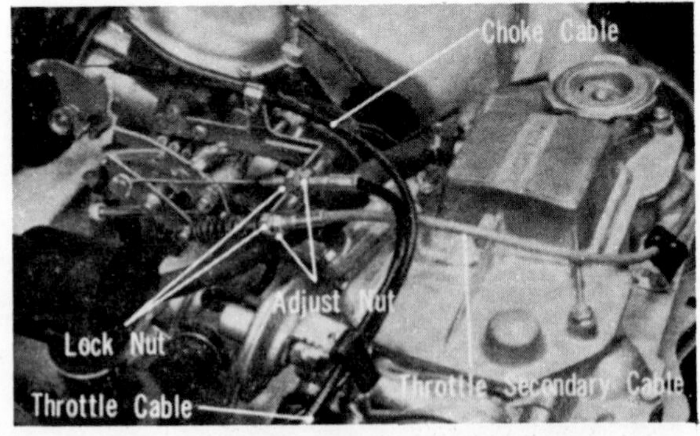

Fig. 1.5. Location of throttle secondary cable locknut (automatic transmission)

6 Engine dismantling - general

1 It is best to mount the engine on a dismantling stand but if one is not available, then stand the engine on a strong bench so as to be at a comfortable working height. Failing this, the engine can be stripped down on the floor.
2 During the dismantling process the greatest care should be taken to keep the exposed parts free from dirt. As an aid to achieving this, it is a sound scheme to thoroughly clean down the outside of the engine, removing all traces of oil and congealed dirt.
3 Use paraffin or a good grease solvent such as 'Gunk'. The later compound will make the job much easier, as, after the solvent has been applied and allowed to stand for a time, a

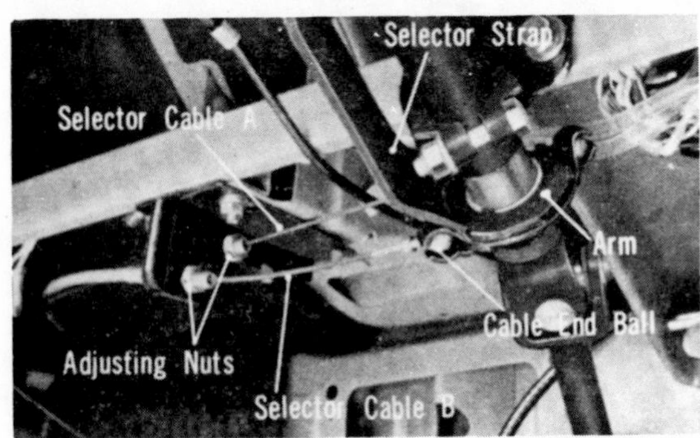

Fig. 1.6. Location of speed selector cables (automatic transmission)

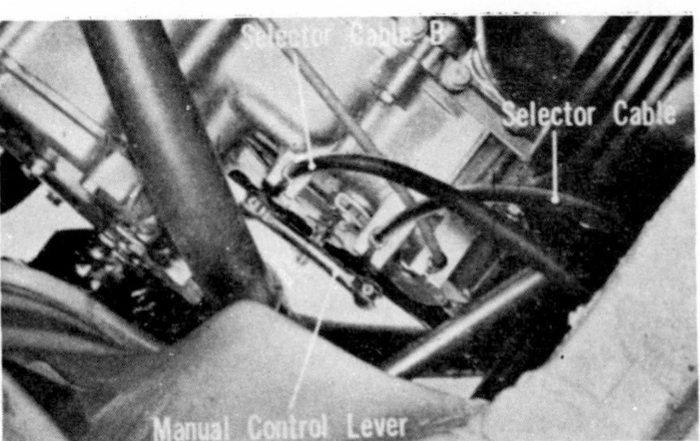

Fig. 1.7. Attachment of selector cables to manual control lever (automatic transmission)

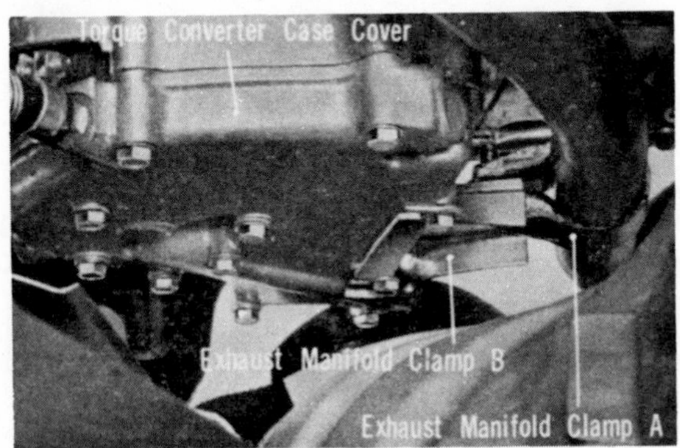

Fig. 1.8. Location of exhaust pipe clamps on torque convertor case (automatic transmission)

Fig. 1.9. Location of oil cooler (automatic transmission)

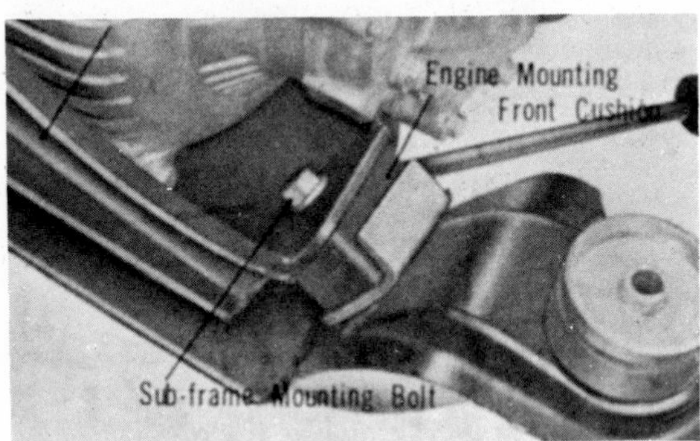

Fig. 1.10. An engine front mounting

vigorous jet of water will wash off the solvent and all the grease and filth. If the dirt is thick and deeply embedded, work the solvent into it with a wire brush.

4 Finally wipe down the exterior of the engine with a rag and only then, when it is quite clean should the dismantling process begin. As the engine is stripped, clean each part in a bath of paraffin or petrol.

5 Never immerse parts with oilways in paraffin, i.e. the crankshaft but to clean, wipe down carefully with a petrol dampened rag. Oilways can be cleaned out with pipe cleaners. If an air line is present all parts can be blown dry and the oilways blown through as an added precaution.

6 Re-use of old engine gaskets is false economy and can give rise to oil or compression leaks. Always use new gaskets at a major overhaul.

7 Do not throw old gaskets away immediately as they may prove useful as templates if a replacement is not available and one has to cut a gasket from sheet jointing.

8 To strip the engine, work to the suggested sequence. Wherever possible, replace nuts, washers and bolts finger tight to avoid loss and muddle later on during reassembly.

7 Engine external components - removal

1 From the right-hand side of the engine, remove the starter motor and alternator (series 60 and (Z) Coupe) or the starter/dynamo (series 360) as described in Chapter 12. (photo).
2 Remove the driveshafts by bending back the locking tabs and unscrewing the driveshaft inner joint bolts. (photo).
3 Detach the engine front mounting strut first from the engine and then from the sub frame. (photo).
4 Detach the engine rear mounting bolts and separate the exhaust manifolds.
5 Remove the contact breaker unit (Chapter 4) (photo) and withdraw the dipstick(s).

8 Camshaft, rocker gear and cylinder head - removal

1 Remove the engine cooling fan assembly and drive belt as described in Chapter 2. Remove the spark plugs.
2 Remove the hydraulic chain tensioner from the base of the cylinder block. (photo). Remove the rocker box cover.
3 Remove the two securing bolts from the right-hand camshaft holder, withdraw the holder complete with engine earthing strap.
4 Release the lock bolt from the inlet valve rocker arm/shaft and withdraw the shaft and rocker arm, noting particularly carefully the location of the spring or rubber type spacers fitted to the rocker shaft.
5 In a similar manner remove the exhaust valve rocker arm and shaft and then remove the left-hand camshaft holder and withdraw the inlet and exhaust rocker arms and shafts from the left-hand side. (photos).
6 Pull the camshaft chain upwards so that the camshaft sprocket can be disengaged and the camshaft withdrawn. (photo).
7 Detach the air distribution shrouds from the cylinder block (see Chapter 2) and then remove the bolts which secure the camshaft housing to the cylinder block. Unscrew the bolts a turn at a time in the sequence shown in Fig. 1.12. Lift off the camshaft housing. (photo).
8 Remove the exhaust pipes from the cylinder head outlets (if the engine is still in the car then the front grille will have to be removed).
9 Unscrew the bolt which is located below the inlet manifold and lift the cylinder head from the cylinder block. If it is stuck, do not attempt to lever it off against the fins or they will break off. Squirt a little penetrating oil down the studs and bolt holes and tap the head at both sides using a plastic faced or wooden mallet only. (photo).

9 Valves - removal

1 Remove the four valves from the cylinder head by using a valve spring compressor to enable the retaining collets and spring retainer to be withdrawn.
2 It is essential that the valves are kept in their correct sequence unless they are so badly worn that they are to be renewed. If they are going to be kept and used again, place them in a sheet of card having four holes numbered 1 to 4 corresponding with the relative positions the valves were in when fitted. Also keep the valve springs, (inner and outer) washers etc in the correct order.

10 Lubrication system, oil pump and oil filter (manual, gearbox) - description

1 On vehicles fitted with a manual gearbox, the engine oil is contained in the crankcase and also supplies the lubricating requirements of the gearbox and differential.
2 The oil is pressurised by a plunger type pump which is actuated by an eccentric cam on the engine driven sprocket. A

7.1 Removing the starter

7.2 Unscrewing a driveshaft bolt

7.3 Unscrewing an engine to crossmember bolt

7.5 Removing contact breaker/camshaft holder unit

8.2 Removing camshaft chain hydraulic tensioner

8.5a Removing left-hand camshaft holder

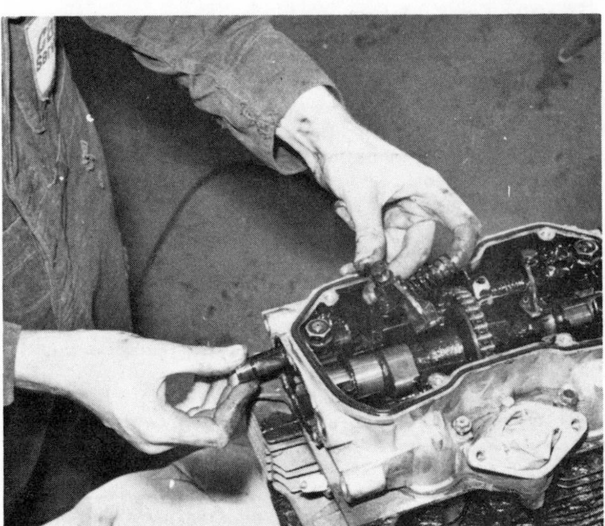
8.5b Removing an exhaust rocker shaft

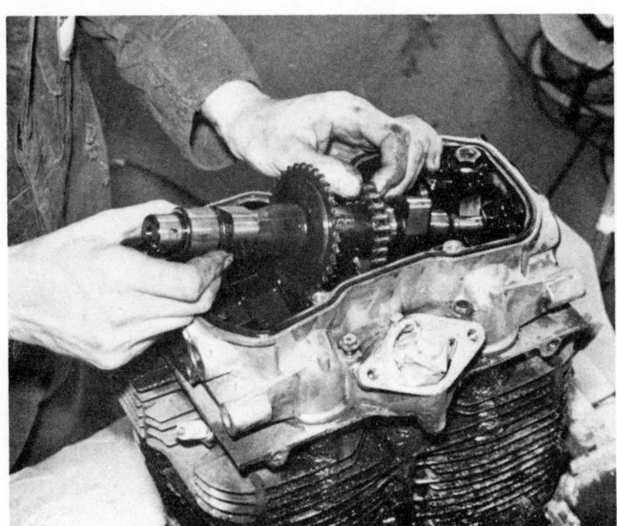
8.6 Removing the camshaft

8.7 Removing camshaft housing

pressure relief valve is incorporated in the oil pump body.

3 Oil pumped by the oil pump passes through a paper element type filter which is screwed into the base of the crankcase. The filter is provided with non-return valves so that in the event of the element becoming clogged, the oil will bypass the filter and flow directly to all lubrication points.

11 Oil filter (manual gearbox) - servicing

1 The oil filter element should be renewed every 3000 miles (5000km). To do this, simply unscrew the central mounting bolt, discard the old element and fit the new one. Install a new cover gasket (supplied with the new element), tighten the mounting bolt (do not overtighten), run the engine and check for leaks.

12 Primary drive and oil pump (manual gearbox) - removal

1 These components may be removed with the engine still in the car.

2 Remove the clutch as described in Chapter 5.

3 Remove the left side cover from the engine, jacking-up the crankcase slightly will facilitate withdrawal of the lower bolts if the engine is still in the vehicle.

4 Remove the circlip from the now exposed driven sprocket (photo) and the washer from the mainshaft. Remove the drive sprocket retaining bolt (photo) and washer and the two oil pump securing bolts. (photo).

5 Withdraw the drive and driven sprockets, double chain and oil pump assembly simultaneously; at the same time depressing the chain tensioner. (photo).

6 Note the location of the thrust washer behind the drive sprocket and the thrust washer and bearing ring behind the driven sprocket (photos).

7 Dismantle the oil pump by removing the plunger pin and pulling off the strainer gauze.

8 Clean and examine all components of the oil pump and renew any which are worn or scored. Remove the chain tensioner if necessary. photo).

13 Lubrication system. primary drive, oil pump and filter - automatic transmission - description, removal and servicing

1 On vehicles fitted with automatic transmission, the engine oil also lubricates the differential. Lubrication and operation of the automatic transmission depends upon an entirely separate oil supply and pump within that unit. (Chapter 6, part2).

2 Removal and servicing of the engine oil filter is carried out in exactly the same way as described in the preceding Section (13) for manual gearbox type cars.

3 The oil pump fitted to cars with automatic transmission is of rotor type and is driven by the crankshaft.

4 To gain access to the oil pump first remove the following components all as described in Chapter 6, part 3:

Torque converter case cover.
Regulator valve.
Pressure pump and regulator valve drive arm.
Torque connecter case.
Torque converter.
Main timing valve body.

Then remove the left side cover from the engine noting carefully the location of the thrust washer (either on the transmission mainshaft or stuck to the bearing race inside the engine cover. Remove the drive sprocket, and the driven sprocket/primary clutch mechanism complete with single chain as an assembly simultaneously whilst depressing the chain tensioner. Remove the oil pump drive gear from the crankshaft splines.

5 Unscrew and remove the pump cover bolts and detach the cover.

9.8 Removing cylinder head

11.1a Removing oil filter

11.1b Fitting a new oil filter element

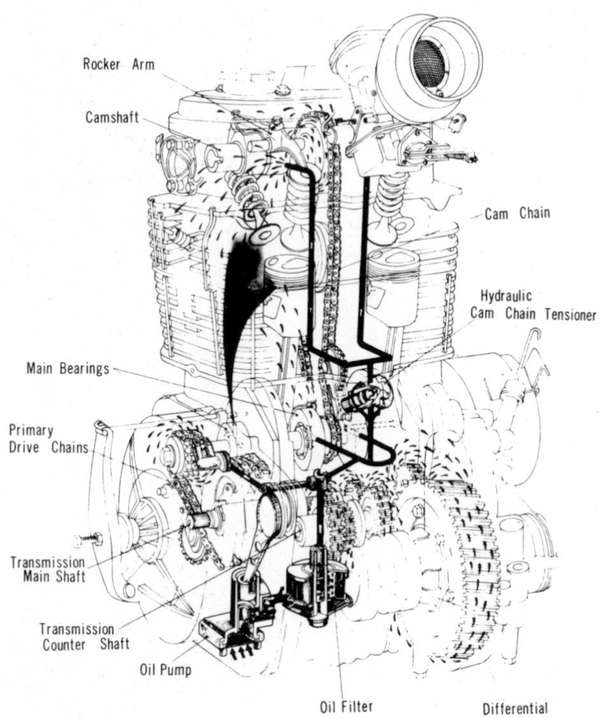

Fig. 1.14. Engine and transmission lubrication system (manual gearbox)

Fig. 1.12. Loosening sequence diagram for camshaft housing bolts

Two domed nuts (12 and 14) only are used on 600 cc/ 35.5 cu in. engine

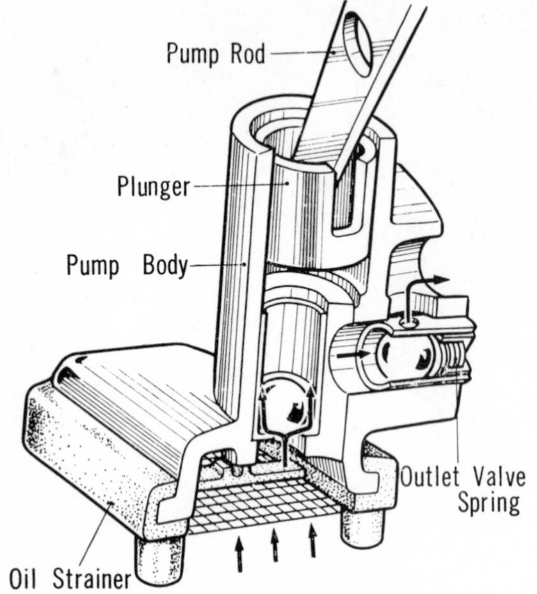

Fig. 1.15. Cutaway view of oil pump (manual transmission)

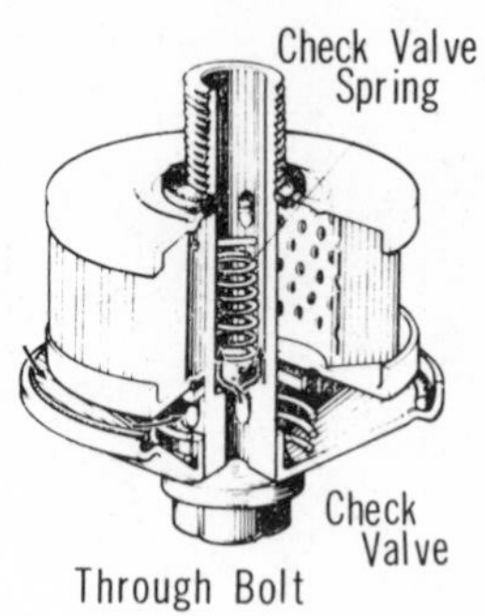

Fig. 1.16. Cutaway view of oil filter

Fig. 1.19. Primary driven sprocket showing oil pump eccentric cam

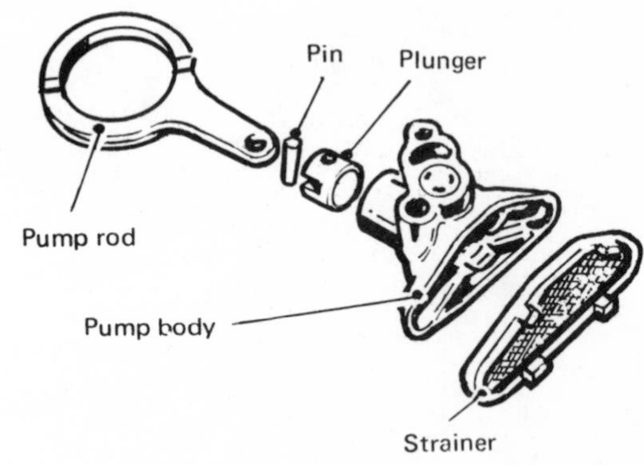

Fig. 1.18. Components of oil pump (manual transmission)

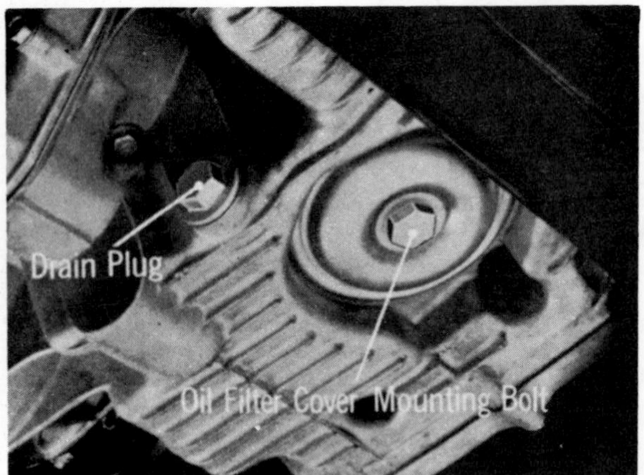

Fig. 1.17. Location of crankcase drain plug and filter (manual gearbox)

12.4a Removing driven sprocket circlip

12.4b Removing drive sprocket bolt

12.4c Removing oil pump bolts

12.5 Removing primary drive gear and oil pump

12.6a Drive sprocket thrust washer

12.6b Driven sprocket thrust washer and bearing ring

12.8 Removing primary chain tensioner

6 Unscrew and remove the oil pump mounting bolts which are accessible through the apertures in the oil pump driven sprocket and then withdraw the oil pump.
7 If necessary detach the oil strainer by prising off its rubber seal.
8 Inspect all components for wear or scoring. Use a feeler gauge to check the clearance between the tip of the inner rotar and a high point of the outer rotor cam. This should not exceed 0.010in (0.25mm).
9 Check the clearence between the outer rotor and the oil housing. Test at several different positions, the clearance should not exceed 0.0118 in (0.3mm).
10 Finally check that the surfaces of both rotors is not more than 0.0118 in (0.3 mm) below the surface of the oil pump housing in which they are located.
11 Use a tubular drift to renew the oil pump housing oil seal.

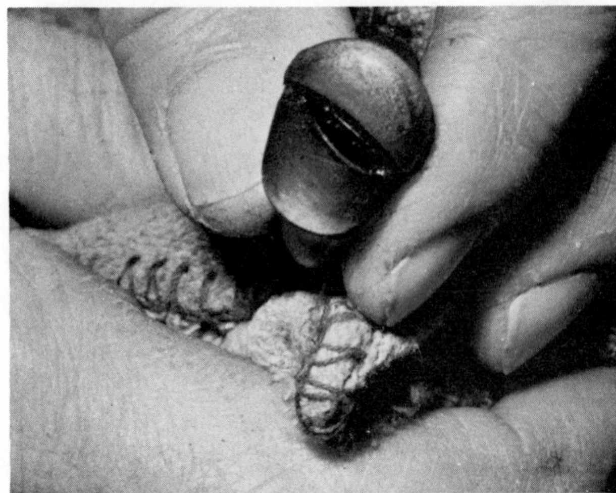
14.1 Crankcase vapour self ejecting tube

14 Crankcase ventilation system

1 The system simply comprises a breather and drain tube. Oil vapour and crankcase blow-by gas is conducted from the camshaft housing cover to the air cleaner casing where the gas is drawn into the inlet manifold and burnt in the normal process of internal combustion while the oil vapour condenses and is disposed of through a drain tube.(photo). No maintenance is required except to occasionally check the condition and security of the hoses.
2 Vehicles destined for operation in North America are fitted with a drain plug instead of a drain tube. This must be removed periodically and accumulated oil drained off into a container.
15 Cylinder block, pistons and rings - removal

15.2 Camshaft idler wheel

15 Cylinder block, pistons and rings - removal

1 Remove the cylinder head as described in Section 8.
2 Remove the camshaft chain idler from its location in the top of the cylinder block. Tie or wire-up the camshaft chain to prevent it dropping into the crankcase when the idler is removed. (photo).
3 Remove the three cylinder mounting bolts, Fig. 1.24.
4 Carefully pull the cylinder block upwards and draw it off the pistons. If it is stuck to the crankcase, top it gently with a plastic faced or wooden mallet. (photo).
5 Cover the crankcase opening with rag to prevent anything dropping in.
6 Remove the circlip from each end of the gudgeon pin and push the gudgeon pin out of the piston and connection rod with finger. (photo).
7 Each piston is fitted with two compression rings and an oil control ring at the bottom. Remove them very carefully to avoid breakage. Start with the top ring and slide two or three feeler gauges or strips of tin behind it at equidistant points. These will help to make the ring slide off the piston and in the case of the lower rings, prevent them dropping into an empty groove as they ride over the piston lands.

15.4 Removing cylinder block

16 Crankshaft - removal

1 Remove the camshaft and cylinder head (Section 8).
2 Remove the cvlinder block and pistons (Section 17)
3 Remove the crankshaft pulley from the right-hand side of the engine and then remove the starter/dynamo (350cc) (21.5 cu in) or the starter motor and alternator (600cc) (35.5 cu in) both as fully described in chapter 11. In the case of 600cc 35.5 cu in engines, also remove the flywheel housing from the engine crank-case.
4 Unscrew and remove the four bolts which secure the crank-

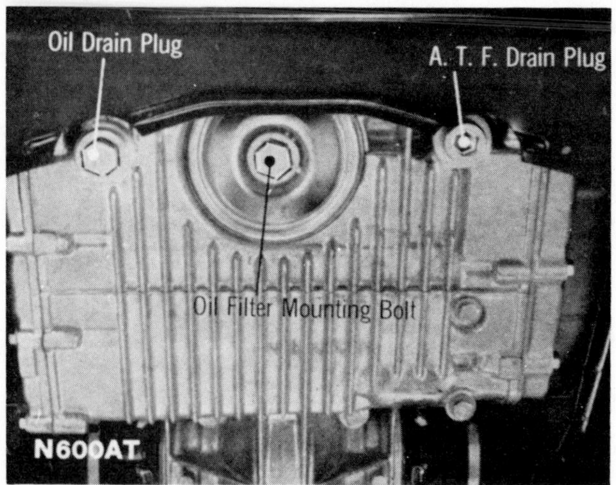

Fig. 1.20. Crankcase engine oil and automatic transmission fluid (ATF) drain plugs locations

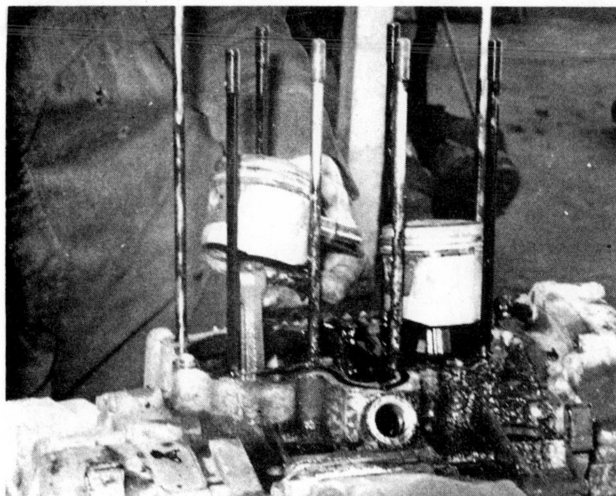

15.6 Removing a gudgeon pin

shaft right-hand main roller bearing retainer.

5 Remove the clutch (Chapter 5) from the left-hand side of the engine;

6 Remove the cover from the left side of the engine crankcase and then remove the primary drive mechanism (described in Sections 14 or 15 according to type of transmission) together with the oil pump.

7 Unscrew and remove the mounting bolt (Fig. 1.27) and retain the aluminium washer.

8 Invert the engine but do not allow its weight to rest on the gear selector rod.

9 Remove the bolts which secure the reverse selector mechanism cover to the right-hand side of the crankcase and tap off the cover. Remove the reverse gear shift fork from the selector shaft. (photo).

10 Unscrew and remove the bolts which secure the two halves of the crankcase together (8 large, 10 small).

11 Lift the lower half of the casing away to leave the transmission and differential lying in position in the upper half.(photo).

12 Unbolt and remove the crankshaft centre bearing cap with the camshaft chain tensioner attached to it . (photo).

13 Lift the crankshaft assembly complete with connecting rods and bearings from the crackcase. (photo).

14 Detach the endless chain from the drive sprocket of the crankshaft.

15 For the vehicles equipped with automatic transmission, also refer to Chapter 6, Sections 17 and 18.

16 The flexible oil channels should only be removed from the crankcase if they have cracked or hardened and require renewal. (photo).

17 The flexible chain oiler sprout should not be removed unless it has deteriorated and requires renewal.

17 Crankshaft assembly - examination and renovation

1 Apart from renewal of the end bearings, the crankshaft cannot be dismantled. Wear cannot be checked without the use of a dial gauge, micrometer and V blocks so that checking must be limited to visual inspection,

2 Check the teeth of the camshaft chain sprocket for wear or a 'hooked' appearance.

3 Rotate the centre bearings and check for noisy operation or slackness.

4 Test the fit of the gudgeon pin in the connection rod small end and check for play in the big-end bearings moving the connecting rod round the journal and testing at several different positions.

5 Where there is evidence of any of the foregoing, the complete crankshaft assembly must be renewed.

18 Cylinder bores - examination and renovation

1 The bores must be checked for ovality, scoring, scratching and pitting. Starting from the top, look for a ridge where the top piston ring reaches the limit of its upward travel. The depth of this ridge will give a good indication of the degree of wear and can be checked with the engine in the car and the cylinder head removed. Other indications are excessive oil consumption and a smoky exhaust.

2 Measure the bore diameter across the block and just below any ridge. This can be done with an internal micrometer of a Mercer gauge. Compare this with the diameter of the bottom of the bore, which is not subject to wear. If no micrometer measuring instruments are available, use a piston from which the rings have been removed and measure the gap between it and the cylinder wall with a feeler gauge.

3 If the difference in bore diameters at top and bottom is .010 inch (0.2540 mm) or more, then the cylinders need reboring. If less that .010 inch (0.2540 mm) then the fitting of new and special rings to the pistons can cure the trouble.

4 Oversize pistons are available in increments of 0.0098in (0.25 mm).

19 Pistons and rings - examination and renovation

19 Pistons and rings - examination and renovation

1 Examine the pistons for signs of damage on the crown and around the top edge. If any of the piston rings have broken there could be quite noticeable damage to the grooves, in which case the piston must be renewed. Deep scores in the piston walls also call for renewal. If the cylinders are being rebored new oversize pistons and rings will be needed anyway. If the cylinders do not need reboring and the pistons are in good condition only the rings need to be checked.

2 To check the existing rings, place them in the cylinder bore and press each one down in turn to the bottom of the stroke. In this case a distance of 2½ inches (64 mm) from the top of the cylinder will be satisfactory. Use an inverted piston to press them down square. With a feeler gauge measure the gap for each ring.

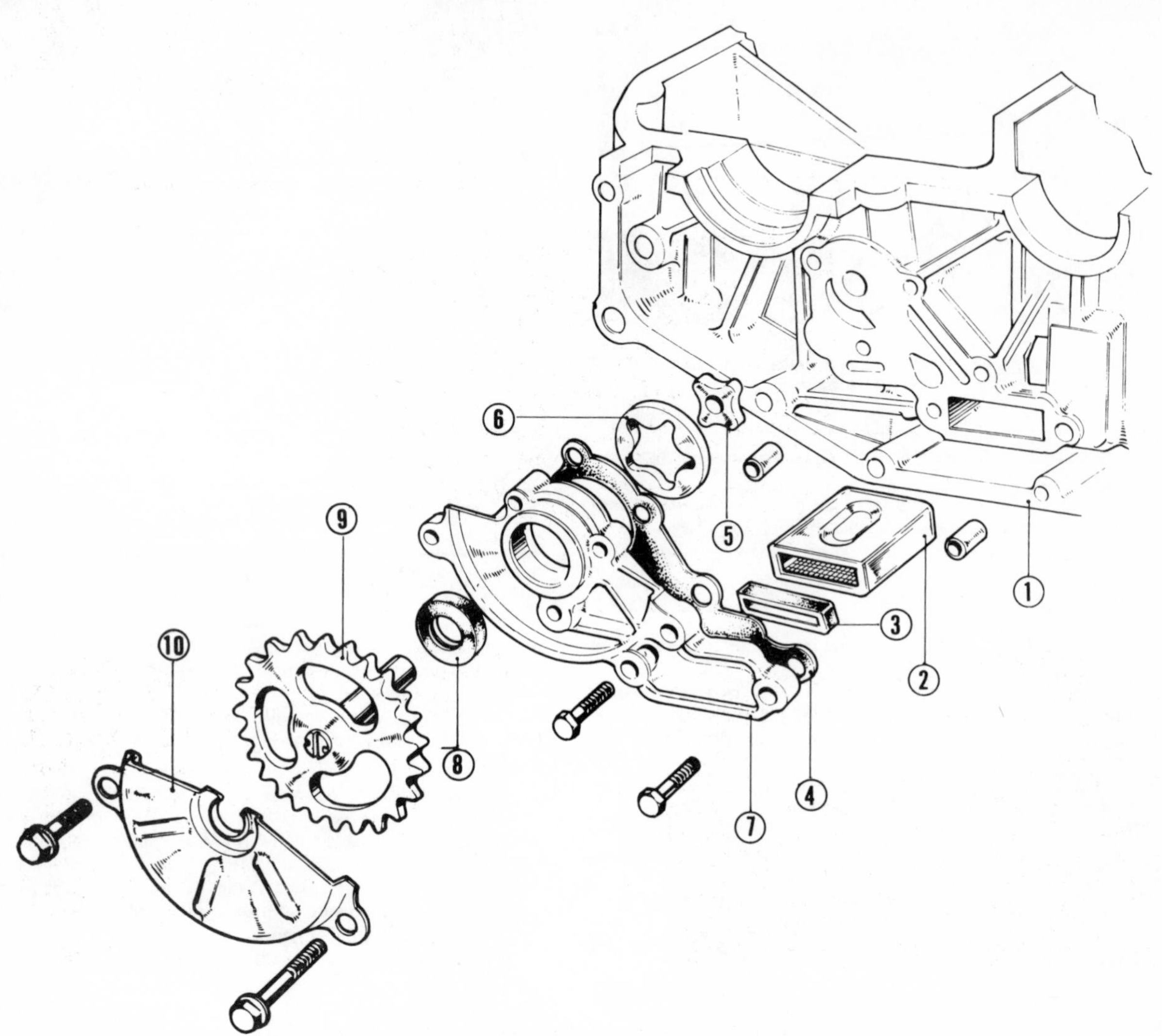

Fig. 1.21. Exploded view of the engine oil pump (automatic transmission)

1 Lower half of crankcase
2 Oil strainer
3 Rubber seal
4 Gasket
5 Inner rotor
6 Outer rotor
7 Housing
8 Oil seal
9 Driven gear
10 Cover

Fig. 1.22. Crankshaft oil pump drive and driven sprockets (automatic transmission)

Fig. 1.23. Oil pump bolts exposed (automatic transmission)

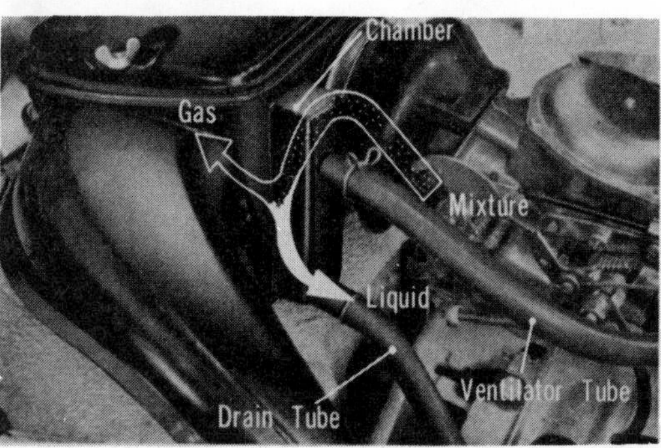

Fig. 1.23a Crankcase ventilation system (for North American cars see Routine Maintenance)

Fig. 1.24. Front and rear cylinder block locating bolts

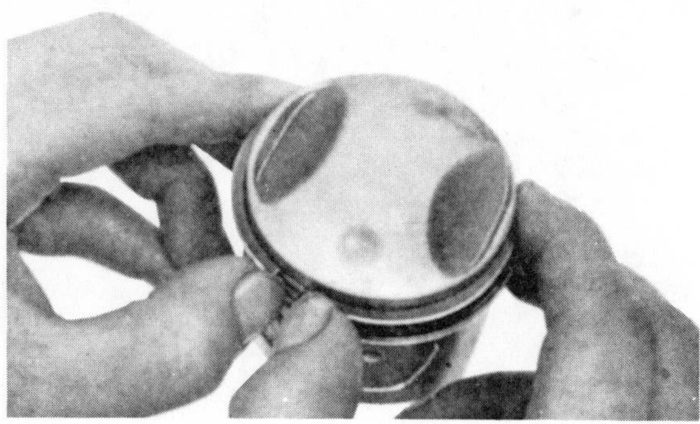

Fig. 1.25. Removing piston rings

Fig. 1.27. Crankcase halves upper securing bolt

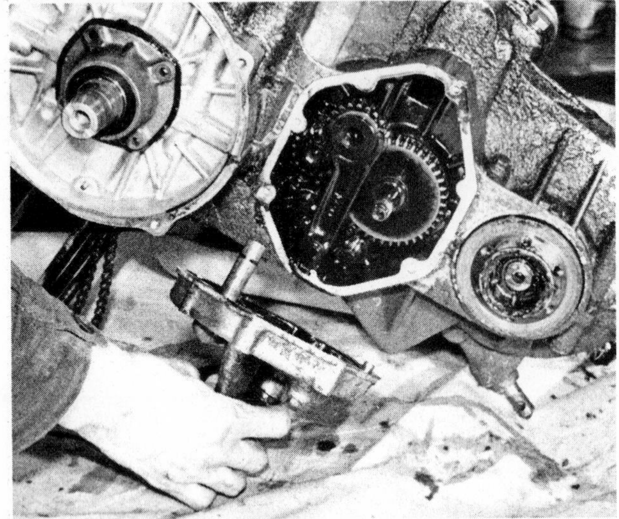

16.9 Removing reverse shift fork cover

16.11 Transmission and final drive (differential)

16.12 Removing the crankshaft centre bearing

16.13 Lifting the crankshaft from the crankcase

16.16 Crankcase oil flow channel

16.17 Primary chain oiler nozzle

The gap should not exceed 0.0413 in (0.105mm) otherwise renew the ring.

3 Check the clearance of each ring in its piston groove. Use a feeler gauge and measure the clearance at four equidistant points. It should not exceed 0.0413 in (0.105 mm) otherwise the ring will have to be renewed or the grooves widened by a specialist to receive thicker ones. If new pistons and rings are being obtained it will be necessary to have the ridge ground away from the top of each cylinder bore. If specialist oil control rings are being obtained from an independent supplier the ridge removal will not be necessary as the top rings will be stepped to provide the necessary clearance. If the top ring of a new set is not stepped it will hit the ridge made by the former ring and break.

4 The new rings should be placed in the bores as described in paragraph 2 and the gap checked. Any gaps which are too small should be increased by filing one end of the ring with a fine file. Be careful not to break the ring as they are brittle (and expensive). On no account make the gap less than specification. If the gap should close when under normal operating temperatures the ring will break.

5 The groove clearance of new rings in old pistons should be within the specified tolerances. If it is not enough, the rings could stick in the piston grooves causing loss of compression.

20 Camshaft chain and tensioner - examination and renovation

1 If the camshaft drive chain becomes noisy, it can cause damage to the cylinder head and block. The noise is due to slackness and may indicate the failure of the hydraulic tensioner or wear of the idler wheel or even of the chain itself.

2 Check the teeth of the chain tensioner guide roller and renew the roller if they are worn.

3 Examine the contact face of the idler wheel and if it appears worn or cut, renew it.

4 Test the plunger of the hydraulic tensioner and if faulty, renew it. Replacement hydraulic plunger units are only available as sealed components and cannot be dismantled. The chain tensioner is mounted on the crankshaft centre bearing cap and on some models an additional slipper is fitted within the cylinder block chain aperture to reduce chain whip even further. In the case of the 360cc (21.5cu in) engine, this slipper is secured with one pin while on the larger engine it is held by two pins, Fig. 1.28. On the slipper fitted to the larger engine, the shorter retaining pin locates in the centre hole of the slipper and the longer pin in the groove at the top of the cylinder barrel.

5 Finally, check the chain for wear in its links and rollers. A simple test is to hold it horizontally (rollers vertical) whilst supporting it at both ends. Observe the extent to which the chain bows towards the ground. The greater the deflection the greater the wear.

21 Camshaft and housing - examination and renovation

1 Using a micrometer, check the cam lobes for wear. Referring to the following table, renew the camshaft if outside the specified tolerances.

Model	*Minimum overall cam lobe dimension*
360cc/21.5 cu in inlet cam	1.563 in (39.70 mm)
360cc/21.5 cu in exhaust cam	1.583 in (40.22 mm)
600cc/35.5 cu in inlet cam	1.621 in (41.18 mm)
600cc/35.5 cu in inlet cam	1.602 in (40.70 mm)

2 Check the camshaft journals and if below 0.941 in (23.9 mm) in diameter, renew the camshaft.

3 Check the camshaft chain sprocket for wear.

4 Using an internal type micrometer test the bores of the camshaft holders. Take two measurements at 90° to each other, and if the diameter is greater than 0.9468 in (24.05mm) renew the holder.

5 Check the bore of the rocker shaft bosses in the camshaft housing. If the bore diameters exceed 0.671 in (17.05mm) renew the housing.

6 Test the camshaft housing for warp on a piece of plate glass. Any minor warping, scratches or scoring may be removed by rubbing the surfaces with an oilstone using a circular motion.

22 Rocker gear - examination and renovation

1 Examine the contact faces of the rocker arms. Any wear marks can be removed on an oilstone only if of a minor nature. If the wear is severe, renew the arm.

2 Check the rocker shafts for scoring and see that the lock bolts are in good condition without burred heads or stripped threads.

23 Primary drive - examination and renovation

1 Check the oiler nozzle. This is made of rubber and if it has deteriorated, renew it.

2 Check the condition of the rubber content of the drive and driven sprockets. If soft, sticky or perished, renew the damper rubber inserts as described later in this Section.

3 Check the tension of the chain tensioner spring. Attach a spring balance and read off the force required to pull it down until the tensioner almost touches the crankcase. The correct tension should be:

36occ (21.5 cu in)	3.74 to 4.63lbs (1.7 to 2.1 kg)	manual
600cc (35.5 cu in)	5.07 to 6.39lbs (2.3 to 2.9 kg)	gearbox
360cc (21.5 cu in)	Automatic transmission	1.2 to 1.3 lbs
600cc (35.5cu in)	(single chain)	(540 to 660g)

If the tension is incorrect renew the tensioner spring.

4 Examine the surface of the tensioner rubber roller and renew it if cut or badly grooved.

5 Depress the upper run of both primary chains (manual gearbox) and check for equal deflection. Where this is not so, it may be due to uneven wear or deteriorated rubber inserts in the driven sprocket. Check the chains for wear as described in Section 22, paragraph 5

6 Rubber damped primary drive sprockets are only fitted to 600cc (35.5 cu in) model vehicles. If deterioration cannot be detected by observation, temporarily refit the sprocket to the crankshaft. Place a chain over the sprocket teeth and hold the chain at the same time as the sprocket retaining bolt is turned in a clockwise direction with a socket wrench. When maximum torque is effected, the clearance between both sectors of the sprocket should be between 0.1378 and 0.1969 in (3.5 and 5.0 mm).

7 When reassembling the drive sprocket, grease the rubber inserts and use a vice if necessary.

8 The rubber damped driven sprocket (fitted to all models) is simply dismantled by pulling the two sprocket halves apart. The two sprocket halves are interchangeable.

9 Install the new rubber inserts into their recesses so that their point or "Y" marks are uppermost. Grease the rubbers to facilitate fitting.

10 With all models except those manufactured in 1970, mate the alignment marks and fit the two sprocket sections together. On 1970 model cars, the alignmant marks must be positioned 180° apart and the teeth staggered as shown in Fig. 1.33 and 34.

11 The set plate should be fitted to the drive sprocket with the centre hole chamfer towards the sprocket.

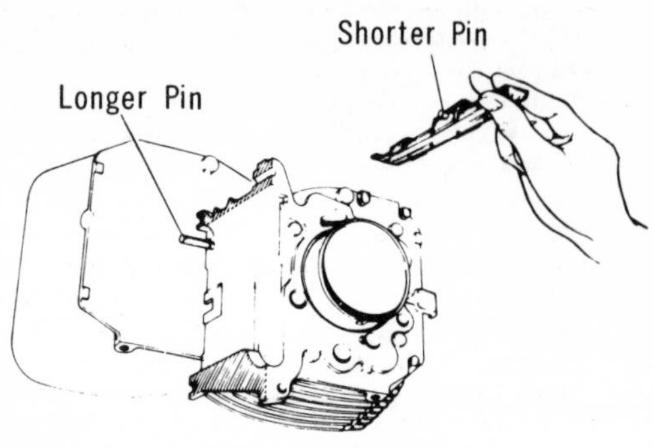

Fig. 1.28. Fitting of camshaft chain slipper (600 cc/35.5 cu in. engine)

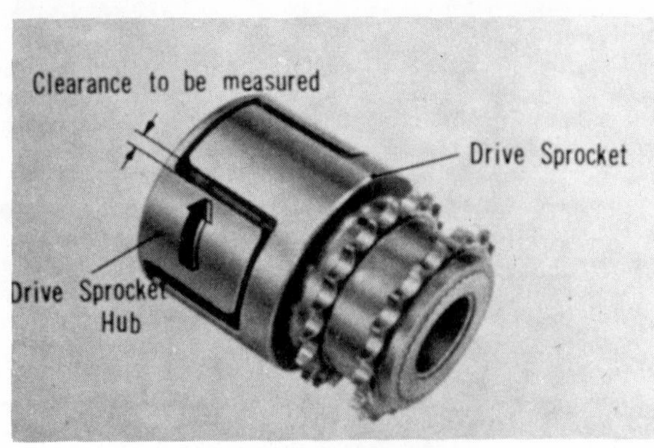

Fig. 1.30. Primary drive sprocket and damper efficiency diagram

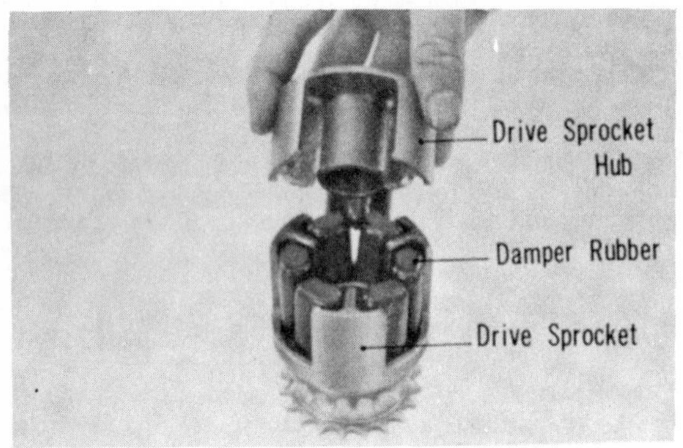

Fig. 1.31. Assembling primary drive sprocket

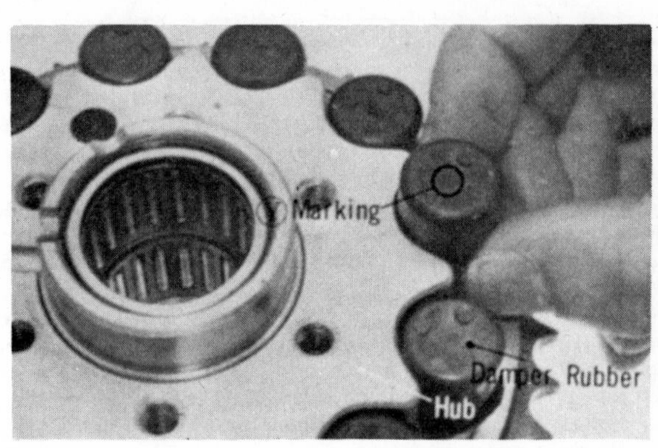

Fig. 1.32. Fitting driven sprocket inserts

Fig. 1.33. Fitting two halves of driven sprocket together (except 1970 cars)

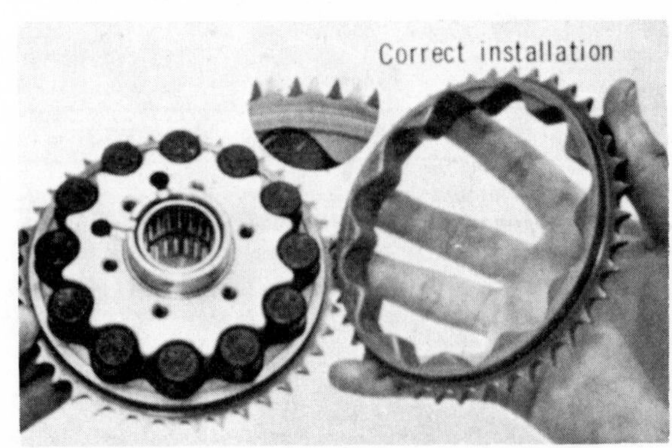

Fig. 1.34. Fitting two halves of driven sprocket together (1970 models only)

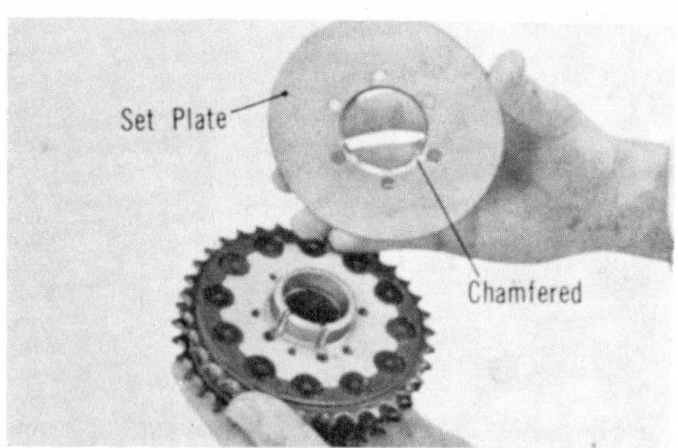

Fig. 1.35. Correct fitting of driven sprocket set plate

24 Cylinder head - decarbonising, examination and renovation

1 This can be carried out with the engine either in or out of the car. With the cylinder head off, carefully remove with a wire brush and blunt scraper all traces of carbon deposits from the combustion spaces and the ports. The valve head stems and valve guides should also be freed from any carbon deposits. Wash the combustion spaces and ports down with petrol and scrape the cylinder head surface free of any foreign matter with the side of a steel rule, or a similar article.

2 Clean the pistons and areas near the tops of the two cylinder bores. If the cylinder block has not been withdrawn and the pistons are still in their bores, it is essential that great care is taken to ensure that no carbon gets into the cylinder bores as this could scratch the cylinder walls or cause damage to the piston and rings. To preclude this happening, rotate the crankshaft so that the pistons are at the tops of their bores.

3 Press a little grease into the gap between the cylinder walls and the pistons then remove all trace of carbon from the piston crowns using a blunt scraper. Take care not to scratch the aluminium surface of the piston.

4 Also scrape away the carbon from the surrounding lip of the cylinder wall. When all carbon has been removed, scrape away the grease which will now be contaminated with carbon particles, taking care not to press any into the bores. To assist prevention of carbon build-up the piston crown can be polished with a metal polish.

5 Wipe away all trace of carbon particles and dress the mating face of the cylinder head with an oilstone to remove any pieces of old gasket or burrs.

6 Check the valve guides for wear. This is best done by inserting a new valve into each of them in turn.The specified maximum clearance between the valve stem and the guide is inlet 0.0032 in (0.08 mm); exhaust 0.0043 in (0.11 mm). Wear is very difficult to measure but if the valve stem rocks appreciably in the guide then the guide clip must be removed and the guide drifted out of the cylinder head, New valve guides can be drifted into position but they require reaming after fitting and it will probably be preferable to leave this work to a service station.

25 Valves and valve seats - examination and renovation

1 Examine the heads of the valves for pitting, splits, and burning, especially the heads of the exhaust valves. The valve seatings should be examined at the same time. If the pitting on valve and seat is very slight the marks can be removed by grinding the seats and valves together with coarse, and then fine, valve grinding paste.

2 Where bad pitting has occurred to the valve seats it will be necessary to recut them and fit new valves. If the valve seats are so worn that they cannot be recut, then it will be necessary to fit new valve seat inserts. These latter two jobs should be entrusted to the local HONDA agent or engineering works. In practice it is very seldom that the seats are so badly worn that they require renewal. Normally, it is the valve that is too badly worn for replacement, and the owner can easily purchase a new set of valves and match them to the seats by valve grinding.

3 Valve grinding is carried out as follows. Smear a trace of coarse carborundum paste on the seat face and apply a suction grinder tool to the valve head. With a semi-rotary motion, grind the valve head to its seat, lifting the valve occasionally to redistribute the grinding valve seat and the valve, then wipe off the paste and repeat the process with fine carborundum paste, lifting and turning the valve to redistribute the paste as before. A light spring placed under the valve head will greatly ease this operation. When a smooth unbroken ring of light grey matt finish is produced, on both valve and valve seat faces, the grinding operation is completed.

4 Scrape away all carbon from the valve head and the valve stem. Carefully clean away every trace of grinding compound, taking great care to leave none in the ports or in the valve guides. Clean the valves and valve seats with a paraffin soaked rag then with a clean rag, and finally, if an air line is available, blow the valves, valve guides and valve ports clean.

5 Obtain a set of new valve springs if the original ones have been in operation for more than 20,000 miles (32.000km). There is an inner and outer spring for each valve.

Fig. 1.36. Drifting out a valve guide

26 Engine reassembly - general

1 All components of the engine must be cleaned of oil sludge and old gaskets and the working ares should also be cleared and clean. In addition to the normal range of good quality socket spanners and general tools which are essential, the following must be available before reassembly begins:-

1) Complete set of new gaskets.
2) Supply of clean rags.
3) Clean oil can full of clean engine oil.
4) Torque spanner.
5) All new spare parts as necessary.

27 Crankshaft - reassembly

1 Fit the camshaft chain to the sprocket on the crankshaft. (photo).

2 Lower the crankshaft into position in the upper half of the crankcase ensuring that the three dowels engage correctly. (photo). Make sure that the oil return holes on the right-hand bearing and retainer are in alignment. (photo). Renew the oil seal retainer if required. (photo).
3 Locate the crankshaft centre bearing cap and tighten the bolts evenly to a torque of 28lb/ft (3.871 kg/m) (photo).
4 Smear the mating places of the two crankcase halves with gasket cement and ensure that the two alignment dowels are in position. (photo). Insert the securing bolts and tighten to a torque for the smaller bolts 8lb/ft (1.106kg/m) and for the larger bolts, 20lb/ft (2.765 kg/m). Note the location of the aluminium washers. (photo).
5 Insert the bolts into the right-hand bearing retainer and tighten them to a torque of 8lb/ft (1.106 kg/m) (photo).
6 Should the rollers have become disassembled from the bearing track then they should be retained in position using some thick grease. (photo).
7 Refit the starter/ generator (360cc) 21.5 cu in or the flywheel/generator (600cc) 35.5 cu in as described in Chapter 12.
8 To the right hand side of the engine fit the reverse gear shift fork to the selector shaft (photo).
9 Using a new gasket, refit the cover. (photo)

27.1 Installing crankshaft

28 Pistons and rings - reassembly

1 Install the piston rings into their grooves by using feeler blades as guides as used for their removal (Section 17). Fit the lower oil control ring first, followed by the two compression rings. Ensure that the side of the ring which has a reference mark on it faces upwards.
2 Stagger the piston ring gaps at three equidistant points of a circle so that the gaps do not align vertically to cause gas blow-by under operating conditions.
3 Locate the piston on the connection rod so that the "IN" mark on the piston crown is nearer to the inlet manifold. (photo).
4 Push in the gudgeon pins, using fingers only. (photo).
5 Insert new circlips in the grooves at each end of the gudgeon pin. (photo).

27.2a Crankshaft alignment dowel

29 Cylinder block - refitting

1 Turn the crankshaft so that both pistons are at the tops of their stroke. Oil the piston rings liberally with engine oil and fit piston ring clamps.
2 Give a final wipe to the mating surfaces of the cylinder block and crankcase and locate a new gasket on the crankcase.
3 If the help of as assistant is available, he will be able to keep the two pistons perfectly level as the cylinder block is lowered over them. If such help is not available then the base of each piston must be supported squarely on two flat strips or bars.
4 Position the cylinder block on the tops of the studs and with a piece of hooked wire, pull the camshaft chain through the aperture in the cylinder block.
5 Lower the cylinder block slowly onto the pistons so that the piston ring clamps are pushed off the rings as the rings enter the cylinder bores. (photo).
6 Push the cylinder block fully home and check that it seats squarely on the new gasket and alignment dowels.
7 Fit the camshaft chain guide roller to prevent the chain dropping into the crankcase when the hooked lifting wire is removed. (photo).
8 Refit the mounting bolts at the base of the block. (photo).
9 Check the security and condition of the rubber anti-resonance strips which are pressed into recesses in the external finning of the cylinder block. If they are hard or perished, renew them.

27.2b Crankshaft main bearing oil hole and gasket alignment

27.2c Fitting new oil seal to crankshaft bearing retainer

27.3a Fitting crankshaft centre bearing

27.3b Tightening crankshaft centre bearing bolts

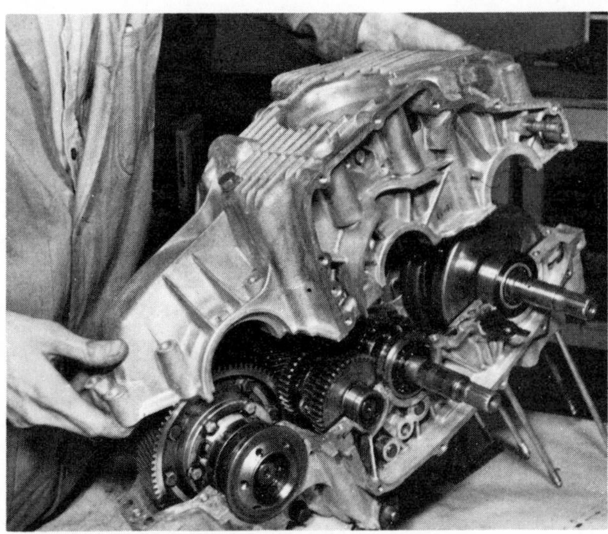
27.4a Installing crankcase half housing

27.4b Tightening crankcase bolts

27.5 Tightening bearing retainer bolts

27.6 Assembling crankshaft main bearing

27.8 Fitting reverse selector

27.9 Fitting reverse selector engine cover

28.3 Piston fitting mark

28.4 Fitting gudgeon pin

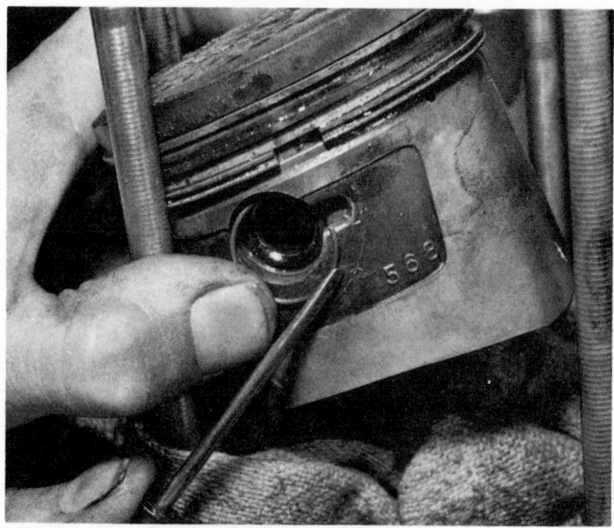

28.5 Fitting gudgeon pin circlip

29.5 Installing cylinder block

29.7 Fitting camshaft chain idler wheel

29.8 Fitting cylinder block lower bolts

30 Cylinder head - reassembly and refitting

1 Lubricate each valve stem and insert it into the guide from which it was removed. (photo).
2 Fit the double valve springs and plate, compressing the springs until the split cotters can be slipped into their recess in the valve stem. (photos).
3 Fit a new gasket to the top of the cylinder block and check that the two hollow dowel pins are in position.
4 Lower the cylinder head into position at the same time pulling the camshaft chain through the aperture in the head. Retain the chain in position by passing a rod under its loop.(photo).

31 Camshaft housing, camshaft and rocker gear - reassembly

1 Fit a new gasket to the cylinder head surface and locate the camshaft housing. Pull the camshaft chain through the housing aperture and again retain it in position by passing a screwdriver or rod through its loop. (photo).
2 Screw on the nuts finger tight, ensuring that the domed type nuts are positioned exactly as shown in Fig. 1.35 otherwise oil leaks will occur. Tighten the nuts to a torque of 23 lb/ft (3.179 kg/m) for the domed nuts and 9 lb/ft (1.244 kg/m) for the standard ones. (photo). Tighten in the reverse sequence to that shown in Fig. 1.36 starting with number 14 and not overlooking number 1.
3 Lift the camshaft chain, remove the screwdriver and install the camshaft. (photo).
4 Rotate the crankshaft, (by temporarily inserting the pulley bolt and applying a spanner to it), until both pistons are at tdc This position may be established by observing the piston crowns through the spark plug holes or by inserting a length or wire. Remove the crankshaft pulley bolt and fit the pulley so that the notch on the pulley is in perfect alignment with the "T" mark on the generator cover. **Unless this procedure is followed it is possible to time the engine 180° out due to the fact that the crankshaft pulley has two locating cut-outs and can be fitted in one of two positons, 180° apart.** (photo).
Lift the chain from the camshaft sprocket and turn the camshaft until the line engraved on the sprocket is absolutely parallel to the top face of the camshaft housing. Re-engage the chain with the camshaft sprocket without moving the sprocket and checking to see that the chain has not disengaged from the sprocket on the crankshaft.
6 Screw the hydraulic chain tensioner into position in the side of the crankcase. (photo). Check that the timing marks have not moved.
7 Fit the rocker shafts to the right-hand side of the engine first, so that the punch marks on their end faces will be uppermost. Insert the right-hand exhaust rocker shaft (the one nearer the leading face of the engine) from outside the camshaft housing and as it projects into the interior of the housing fit a rocker arm (marked R) followed by a coil spring.(photo). It is important to note that it is possible to select a rocker shaft which after fitting will have its adjustment holes masked by the housing bearing support. Check the shaft for adjustment-hole accessibility before installation.
8 Insert the right-hand inlet rocker shaft and as it passes into the interior of the camshaft housing, fit a rocker arm (marked R).
9 Fit the coilsprings (600cc 135.5 cu in engine) or rubber spacers (360cc 121.5 cu in engine) to the rocker shaft end recesses on the right-had side, noting that the lighter springs fit into the exhaust rocker shaft recesses. (photo). Install and bolt up the right-hand camshaft holder using a new gasket and having renewed the holder oil seal if required. Note the earth strap connected to the camshaft holder bolt. (photo).
11 Fit and bolt up the left-hand camshaft holder, using a new gasket and having renewed the holder oil seal if necessary.

Fig. 1.37. Camshaft timing mark

30.1 Installing a valve

30.2a Valve springs and retaining components

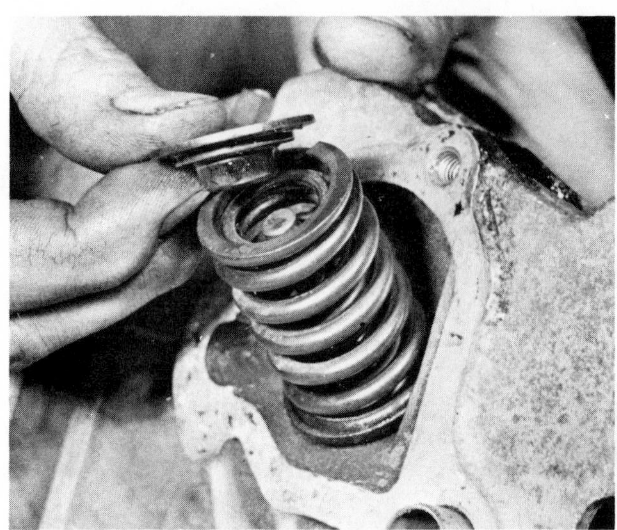

30.2b Fitting a valve spring retaining plate

30.2c Compressing a valve spring

30.4 Lowering cylinder head into position

31.1 Fitting camshaft housing

31.2 Tightening engine bolts

31.3 Installing camshaft

31.4 Camshaft setting timing marks (generator cover and pulley)

31.6 Installing hydraulic chain tensioner

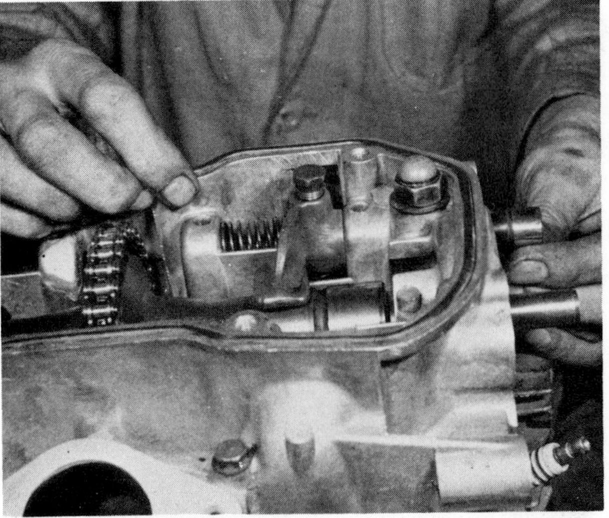
31.7 Fitting an exhaust rocker shaft

31.9a Exhaust (right) and inlet rocker shaft end springs

31.9b Installing contact breaker/camshaft holder assembly

31.11 Fitting left-hand camshaft holder

(photo). Check the valve clearances as described in the next Section.

32 Valve clearances - adjustment

1 Carry out the checking and adjustment only when the engine is cold.
2 Using a spanner on the crankshaft pulley bolt, rotate the crankshaft until the left-hand inlet valve and the right-hand exhaust valve rocker arms are fully raised and in balance.
3 Using a feeler gauge check the clearance between the heels of the rocker arms of the opposing valves (left-exhaust; right- inlet) and the camshaft lobes. The correct clearance should be between 0.003 and 0.005 in (0.08 and 0.12 mm).(photo).
4 If the clearance is incorrect, loosen the locking bolts on the rocker arms and using a thin rod or drift rotate the rocker shafts in either direction until the feeler is a stiff sliding fit. Tighten the locking bolts to a torque of 29lb/ft (4.009kg/m). Re-check the clearances.
5 Rotate the crankshaft until the right-hand inlet valve and the left-hand exhaust valve rocker arms are fully raised and in balance and check the clearances of the opposing valves in a similar manner to that already described.

33 Primary drive and oil pump (manual gearbox) - refitting

1 Locate the oil pump needle roller bearing and thrust plate onto the transmission mainshaft bearing outer track. (photo).
2 Install the oil pump rod/plunger onto the driven sprocket so that the oil grooves of the pump rod face the sprocket. (photo).
3 Fit the oil pump, drive and driven sprockets complete with chains, as one assembly, to the crankshaft and transmission mainshaft simultaneously. Note that the thrust washer which fits behind the drive sprocket has its grooves facing outwards. (photo).
4 Insert and tighten the two oil pump bolts.
5 Fit the thrust washer to the front of the driven sprocket so that its tongue locates in the sprocket hub. Secure with a new circlip. (photo).
6 Tighten the drive sprocket securing bolt to a torque of 18 lb/ft (2.488 kg/m). Check for endfloat (Fig. 1.39a) changing the rear thrust washer if more than 0.0078 in (0.2 mm)
7 Fit the primary chain tensioner and the engine cover, checking that the two hollow dowels are in postion and installing a new gasket and cover oil seal. (photo).
8 Refit and adjust the clutch as described in Chapter 5.

34 Primary drive and oil pump (automatic transmission) - refitting

1 This is a reversal of the removal procedure described in Section 15. but make sure that the thrust washer is fitted to the face of the primary clutch. Fig. 1.40.
2 When locating the left-hand engine cover, check that the thrust washer is correctly positioned between the end of the mainshaft and the face of the primary drive cover bearing.
3 Refitting of the automatic transmission components is as described in Chapter 6, part 3.

35 Engine - preparation for installation

1 With the engine now fully assembled and adjusted, fit the remaining external components which include:

The starter motor (600cc 135.5cu in only).
The camshaft housing cover.
The spark plugs.
The contact breaker assembly (Chapter 4).

Fig. 1.39a Checking primary drive sprocket for endfloat

Fig. 1.40. Fitting thrust washer to face of primary clutch (automatic transmission)

32.3 Checking and adjusting a valve clearance

33.1 Locating oil pump needle roller bearing

33.2 Assembling oil pump to driven sprocket eccentric

33.3 Correct fitting of drive sprocket thrust washer

33.5 Fitting driven sprocket retaining circlip

33.7a Primary drive chain tensioner

33.7b Fitting new oil seal to engine left-hand cover

33.7c Fitting engine left-hand cover

The cylinder block cooling shrouds.
The oil dipstick.
The engine cooling fan assembly and drive belt (Chapter 2).

2 Reconnect the engine front mounting strut and the sub frame. Attach the engine rear mounting bolts.

3 Connect the driveshafts to the differential unit by screwing in the driveshaft inner joint bolts and bending over the locking tabs.

4 The engine/transmission unit mounted on the front suspension subframe is now ready for installation.

36 Engine - installation

1 This is a reversal of the removal procedure described in Section 4 or 5 (according to the type of transmission fitted).

2 Carefully note the fitting arrangement of the front and rear mountings, Figs. 1.41 and 1.42 (photos).

3 Connect all electrical leads correctly according to their colour cooling. Check that the engine earth strap is connected.

4 Ensure that the 'O' ring seal is in position at the inlet manifold flange connection.

5 Check the front wheel alignment (toe-in) as described in Chapter 8.

6 With automatic transmission vehicles check the adjustment of

Fig. 1.41. Assembling subframe front mounting

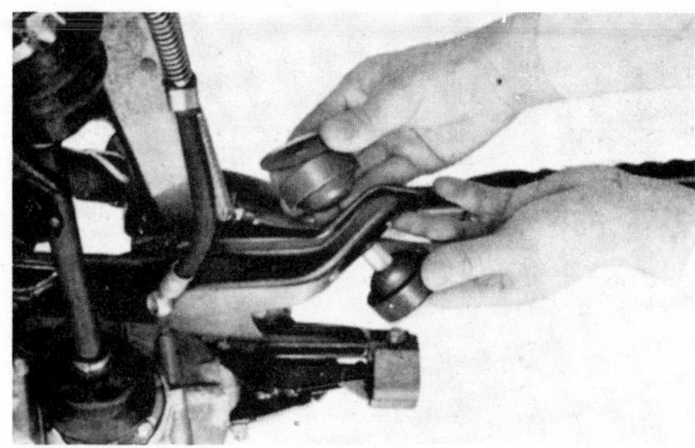

Fig. 1.42. Assembling subframe rear mounting

36.2a Subframe mounting

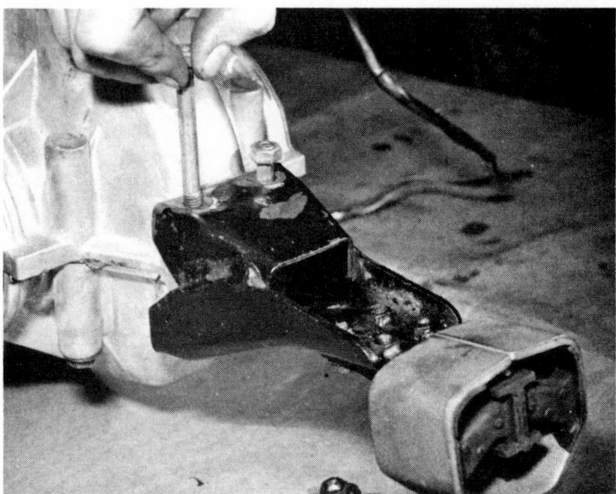

36.2b Engine/Transmission rear mounting

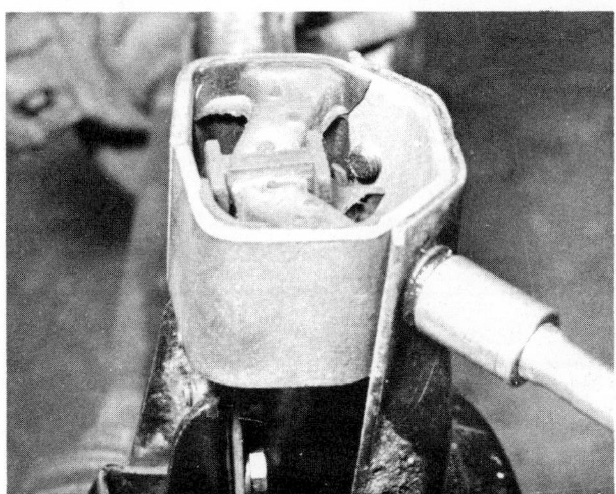

36.2c Fitting rear mounting to extension bracket

all selector cables and controls as described in Chapter 6, part 2.
7 Fill the engine with the correct grade and quantity of oil and refill the automatic transmission unit.

37 Engine operation after major overhaul

1 Start the engine and run at a fast idling speed. Watch for oil leaks and exhaust leaks and rectify.

2 When the engine has reached normal operating temperature, adjust the carburettor as described in Chapter 3.
3 Check the ignition timing as described in Chapter 4.
4 After 500 miles (800km) check the torque of the camshaft housing bolts and the valve clearances-both with the engine cold.
5 If new major internal components have been fitted, change the engine oil after the first 500 miles (800 km) while it is still hot after a run.

38 Engine - fault diagnosis

Symptom	Cause	Remedy
Engine will not turn over when starter switch is operated	Flat battery Bad battery connections Bad connections at solenoid switch and/or starter motor	Check that battery is fully charged and that all connections are clean and tight.
	Defective solenoid	Remove and check solenoid.
	Starter motor defective	Remove starter and overhaul.
Engine turns over normally but fails to fire and run	No spark at plugs	Check ignition system according to procedures given in Chapter 4.
	No fuel reaching engine	Check fuel system according to procedures

		given in Chapter 3.
	Too much fuel reaching the engine (flooding)	Check fuel system if necessary as described in Chapter 3.
Engine starts but runs unevenly and misfires	Ignition and/or fuel system faults	Check the ignition and fuel systems as though the engine had failed to start.
	Incorrect valve clearances	Check and reset clearances.
	Burnt out valves	Remove cylinder head and examine and overhaul as necessary.
Lack of power	Ignition and/or fuel system faults	Check the ignition and fuel systems for correct ignition timing and carburettor settings.
	Incorrect valve clearances	Check and reset the clearances.
	Burnt out valves	Remove cylinder head and examine and overhaul as necessary.
	Worn out piston or cylinder bores	Remove cylinder head and examine pistons and cylinder bores. Overhaul as necessary.
Excessive oil consumption	Oil leaks from crankshaft oil seal, camshaft cover gasket, drain plug gasket, sump plug washer	Identify source of leak and repair as appropriate.
	Worn piston rings or cylinder bores resulting in oil being burnt by engine Smoky exhaust is an indication	Fit new rings or rebore cylinders and fit new pistons, depending on degree of wear.
	Worn valve guides and/or defective valve stem seals	Remove cylinder head and recondition valve guides and valves and seals as necessary.
Excessive mechanical noise from engine	Wrong valve to rocker clearances	Adjust valve clearances.
	Worn crankshaft bearings Worn cylinders (piston slap)	Inspect and overhaul where necessary.
Unusual vibration	Misfiring on one cylinder	Check ignition system.
	Loose mounting bolts	Check tightness of bolts and condition of flexible mountings.

Note: When investigating starting and uneven running faults do not be tempted into snap diagnosis. Start from the beginning of the check procedure and follow it through. It will take less time in the long run. Poor performance from an engine in terms of power and economy is not normally diagnosed quickly. In any event the ignition and fuel systems must be checked first before assuming any further investigation needs to be made.

Chapter 2 Cooling system

Contents

1 General description

The engine cooling system consists of an air intake at the front of the engine through which air is forced by the ram effect of the forward motion of the car and the suction of the belt driven fan. The air is conducted round the fins on the exterior surfaces of the cylinder block by shrouds and the warmed air is then exhausted by the fan assembly mounted at the rear of the engine.

With some model vehicles, the fan assembly embodies a heater drum and the warmed air from the engine is dispersed into the vehicle interior by means of a variable hand control.

Whether this type of heater unit or an axhaust type heater is fitted, reference should be made to Chapter 12 where both types are fully described.

2 Cooling shrouds - removal and refitting

1 The cooling shrouds are fitted to both sides of the cylinder block with cutouts for access to the two spark plugs.
2 The shrouds are bolted into position and have a rubber insulator located on each side at the bolt mounting points on each side of the camshaft housing.
3 Removal is carried out by removing the two bolts and withdrawing the shroud in an upward direction. (photo).
4 Refitting is a reversal of removalbut ensure that the insulators are correctly positioned and have not hardened or previously been over compressed.

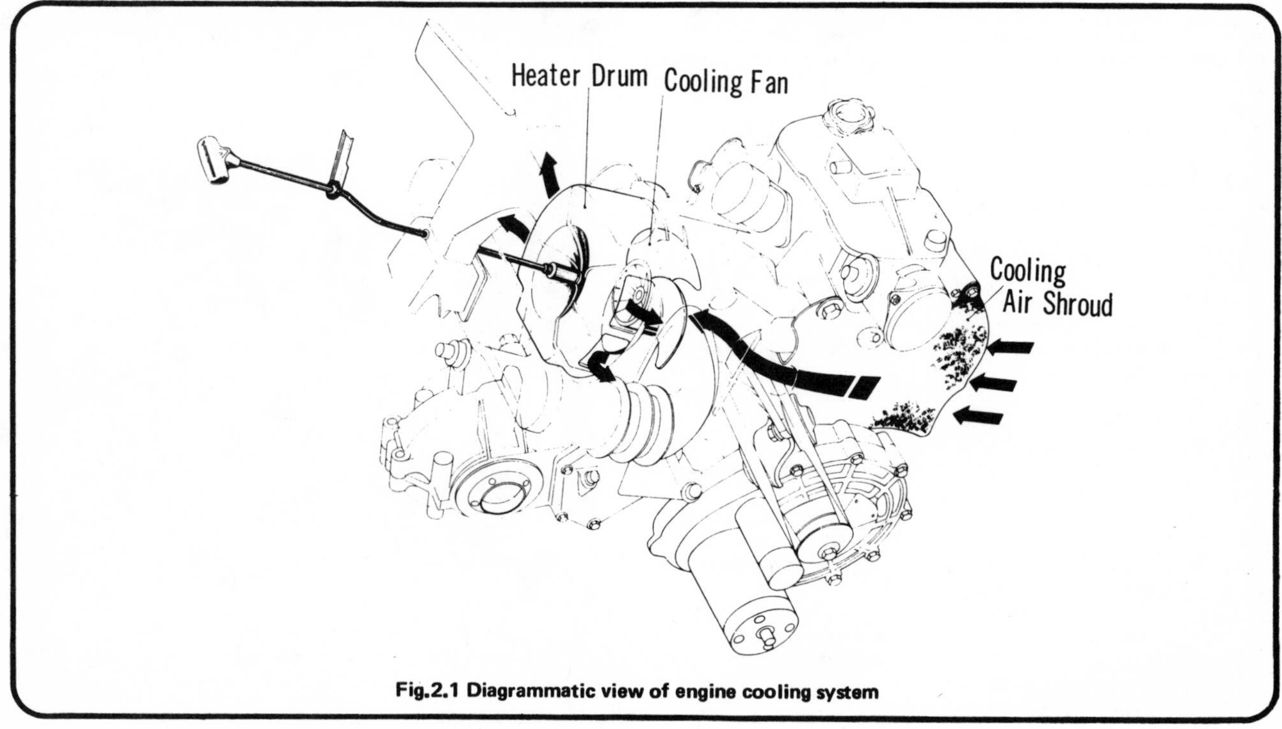

Fig.2.1 Diagrammatic view of engine cooling system

Fig. 2.2 Location of engine cooling shrouds

2.3 Removing an engine air deflector plate

3 Cooling fan drivebelt - removal, refitting and adjustment

1 Loosen the adjusting nut which is located immediately below the idler pulley. (photo).
2 Press the tension adjusting pulley towards the engine as far as it will go and remove the belt by slipping it off the crankshaft pulley using the fingers only.
3 Now detach the drive belt from the pulley within the fan housing.
4 Pull the tension adjusting pulley to the end of its adjusting slot as far from the engine as possible. This will then provide sufficient clearance for the belt to be withdrawn completely. (photo).
5 Refitting is a reversal of the removal procedure.
6 Once the belt has been fitted to all four pulleys, adjust its tension by pinching the belt together at the centre of its run between the crankshaft pulley and the ajusting and idler pulleys. The distance between the two runs of the belt should be between ½ and ¾ in (12 and 20 mm).

When adjustment is correct, fully tighten the adjusting nut.

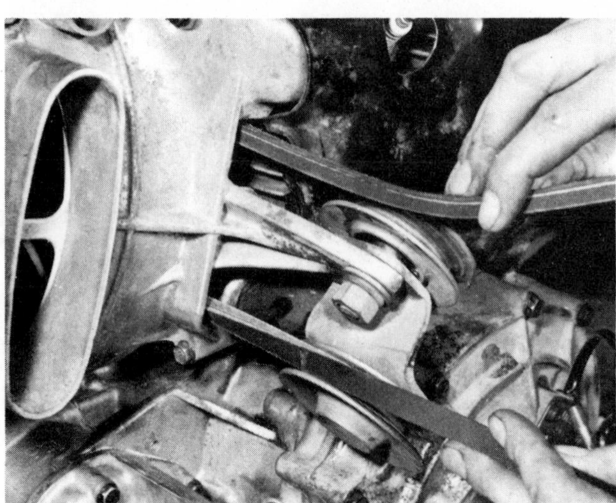

3.1 Adjusting tensioner pulley

4 Cooling fan assembly - removal, servicing and refitting

1 Withdraw the pin which connects the heater control rod to the heater drum. Push the control rod towards the vehicle interior.
2 Unscrew and remove the four bolts which secure the cooling fan assembly to the rear of the engine block. Withdraw the assembly. (photo).
3 Detach the heater drum from the fan housing by removing the two mounting bolts from the spring steel brackets.
4 Rotate the cooling fan by hand and check for noisy or slack bearings. Where these are evident, remove the fan pulley using an extractor.
5 Withdraw the fan/shaft assembly (this cannot be dismantled) and drift out the two bearings. Take great care during this operation to support the bearing housing otherwise the supporting webs may be cracked or broken.
6 Press in the new bearings and fan/shaft assembly. The pulley must be discarded and a new one pressed onto the shaft. The pulley is an interference fit on the shaft and its removal will render it unsuitable for further use.
7 Refitting is a reversal of removal.

3.4 Method of engaging or disengaging drive belt and fan pulley

4.2 Removing the fan cooling assembly

Fig. 2.3 Preparing to detach the drive belt from the crankshaft pulley

Fig. 2.5 Testing the tension of the fan drive belt

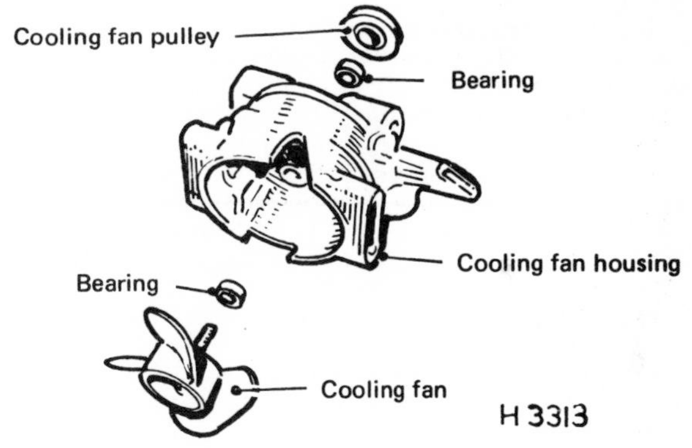

Fig. 2.6 Components of the fan assembly

5 Cooling system - fault diagnosis

Symptom	Cause	Remedy
Engine overheats	Slack drivebelt	Adjust tension.
	Broken drivebelt	Renew.
	Shrouds not fitted or displaced	Fit or adjust.
	Ignition retarded	Adjust timing.
	Weak mixture	Adjust carburettor.
	Air intake obstructed	Clear.
Noisy operation	Fan housing bearings worn	Renew.
	Pulley bearings worn	Renew pulley assemblies.

Chapter 3 Carburation, fuel and exhaust systems

Contents

Specifications

Fuel pump:

Type	Electric
Minimum operating voltage	Less than 9 volts
Current	Less than 0.6 amp
Discharge capacity	220 to 250 cc/min

Carburettor:

Type	Variable choke with accelerator pump
Make	Keihin
Idling speed	1100/1200 rev/min

Carburettor data (360 series):

Carb. Index Mark	Secondary Main Jet No.	Primary Main Jet No.	Secondary Air Jet No.	Primary Air Jet No.	Needle Jet No.	Slow Jet No.	Float Level "h" mm	Accelerator Pump Stroke (mm)	Slow Air Jet No.
NE	145	80	90	50	223302	35	17	2.4 ± 0.5	90
NF	145	80	90	50	223302	35	17	2.4 ± 0.5	80
NH	135	82	90	50	223303	35	17	1.6 ± 0.5	80
NI	135	82	90	50	223303	35	17	2.3 ± 0.5	80
NJ	135	82	90	50	223303	35	17	2.3 ± 0.5	100

Carburettor data (600 series):

Carb. Index Mark	Secondary Main Jet No.	Primary Main Jet No.	Secondary Air Jet No.	Primary Air Jet No.	Needle Jet No.	Slow Jet No.	Float Level "h" mm	Accelerator Pump Stroke (mm)	Slow Air Jet No.
N6B	150	85	70	70	234301	35	16	1.6 ± 0.5	120
N6C	140	88	50	50	234002	35	16	2.8 ± 0.5	120
N6D	140	88	50	50	234003	35	16	1.6 ± 0.5	120
N6D1	140	88	50	50	234003	35	22	2.3 ± 0.5	120
N6D2	140	88	50	50	234003	35	22	2.3 ± 0.5	120
6NM	135	92	90	50	234003	6	23.5	2.3 ± 0.5	130

Fuel tank:

Fuel tank capacity ... ... 5.7 gallons (6.9 US gallons) 26 litres

Torque wrench settings:

	lb/ft	kg/m
Exhaust flange to cylinder head bolts	20	2.765
Rear silencer mounting bolts	17	2.349
Exhaust pipe clamp bolts	17	2.349

1 General description

The fuel system comprises a rear mounted tank, an electrically operated pump, a variable choke carburettor and a disposable dry element type air cleaner.

2 Air cleaner - removal, servicing, refitting

1 The air cleaner is mounted on the engine compartment rear bulkhead.

2 Normal cleaning of the element with compressed air or renewal of the unit is carried out by removing the two air cleaner cover wing-nuts and detaching the retainer spring (photo).

3 When refitting the cover ensure that the rubber washers are correctly positioned.

4 To remove the air cleaner assembly complete, remove the clamping clip which secures the rubber connection bellows to the air cleaner case (photo). Disconnect the breather tube and the warm air inlet tube from the engine cooling fan housing.

5 Unscrew and remove the mounting bolts (or supports) and rubber insulators.

6 Refitting is a reversal of removal.

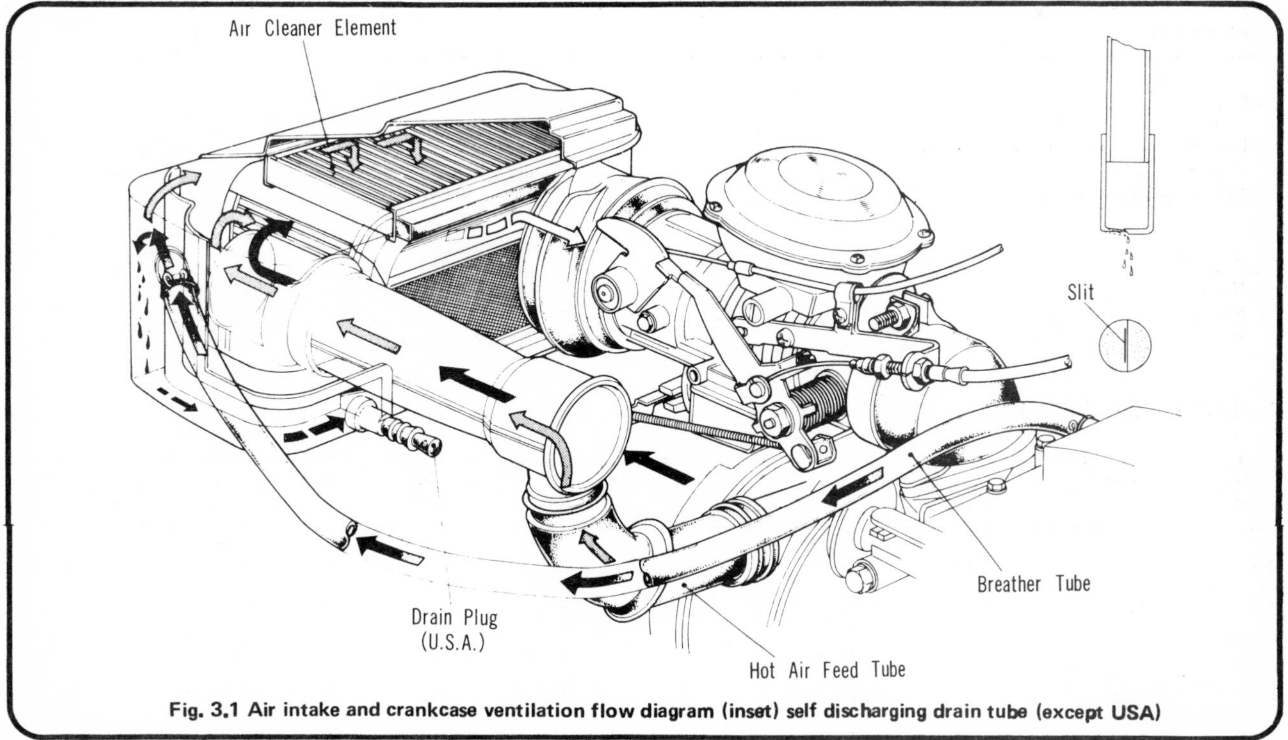

Fig. 3.1 Air intake and crankcase ventilation flow diagram (inset) self discharging drain tube (except USA)

Fig. 3.2 Air cleaner cover wing nuts

Fig. 3.3 Air cleaner support bracket (early models were secured with internally fitted bolts)

2.2 Air cleaner showing element and forward pressure spring

2.4 Carburettor air duct disconnected from air cleaner

3 Fuel pump - description and testing

1 The fuel pump is of electromagnetic type mounted on the left-handside of the engine compartment. Adjacent to it is a fuel filter which must be renewed at the specified intervals (see Routine Maintenance Section).

2 The cause of fuel pump failure may be established by carrying out the following checks.

First, check the pump earth connection for tightness and feeedom from rust or corrosion.

3 Disconnect the outlet pipe from the fuel pump nozzle. Switch on the ignition, when a consistent, well defined, flow of fuel should be observed. If it is only a trickle, check for a clogged filter. If there is no operating noise from the pump at all, carry out the other tests described in this Section and renew the pump if necessary. (Section 4).

4 Connect a voltmeter between the pump positive (+) terminal and the pump body. Switch on the ignition and measure the pump terminal voltage. If 12 volts are not indicated, check the condition of the battery or look for an open circuit, due probably to a wiring insulation fault.

5 Disconnect the snap connector at the pump positive (+) terminal and connect an ohmmeter between the positive (+) terminal of the pump and the pump body. A reading of 5 ohms should be indicated.

6 If these tests prove negative, do not attempt to dismantle the pump but renew it on a factory reconditioned exchange basis.

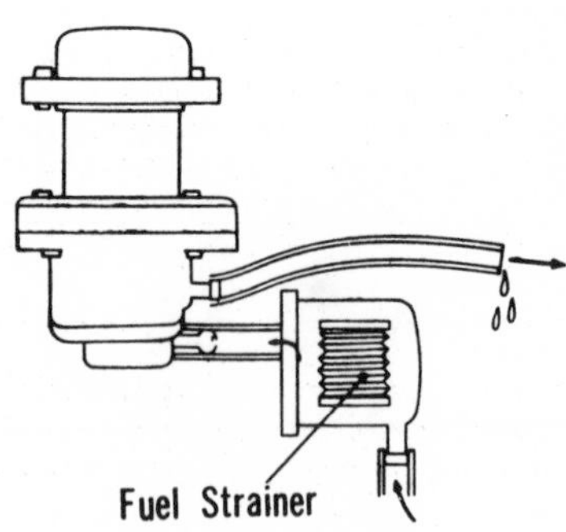

Fig. 3.4 Fuel flow diagram .

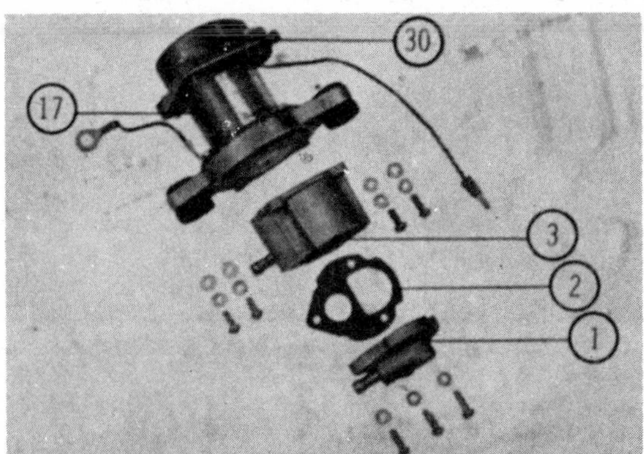

Fig. 3.5 Exploded view of the fuel pump
1 Cap *17 Main body*
2 Gasket *30 Cover*
3 Valve chamber

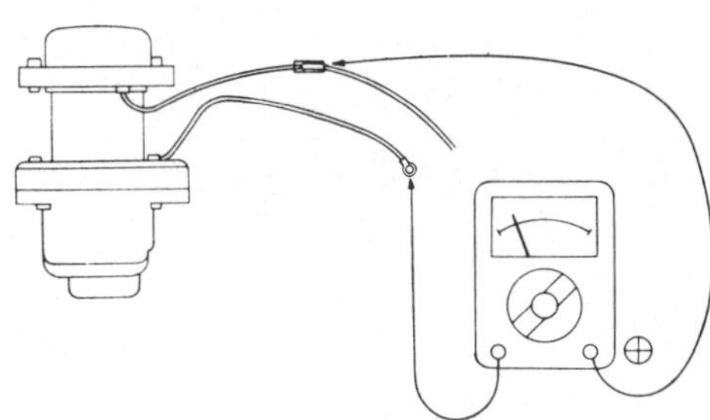

Fig. 3.6 Measuring fuel pump terminal voltage

4 Fuel pump - removal and refittings

1 Disconnect the elctrical cable snap connectors.
2 Disconnect the inlet and outlet fuel hoses from the pump, plug the fuel hose from the tank.
3 Unscrew and remove the two pump mounting bolts.
4 Installation is a reversal of removal.

5 Fuel tank - removal and refitting

1 Before removing the fuel tank, unscrew the drain plug and drain the fuel. It is a good plan to periodically let the fuel level fall very low and drain any sediment or water with the remaining fuel. This action will prevent the tank rusting and prolong the life of the fuel filter.
2 Remove the interior right-hand door tidy and disconnect the fuel gauge wires at their snap connectors.
3 Disconnect the tank to filler neck flexible hose (two clips) and the handbrake cable guide (one bolt).
4 Remove the short piece of flexible hose which joins the tank outlet pipe to the main fuel line running the length of the car.
5 Unscrew and remove the four tank mounting bolts and lower the tank sufficiently to be able to pull off the breather tube.
6 Refitting the fuel tank is a reversal of removal but before bolting it up, ensure that the breather tubes are not trapped between the top of the tank, and the under surface of the body.

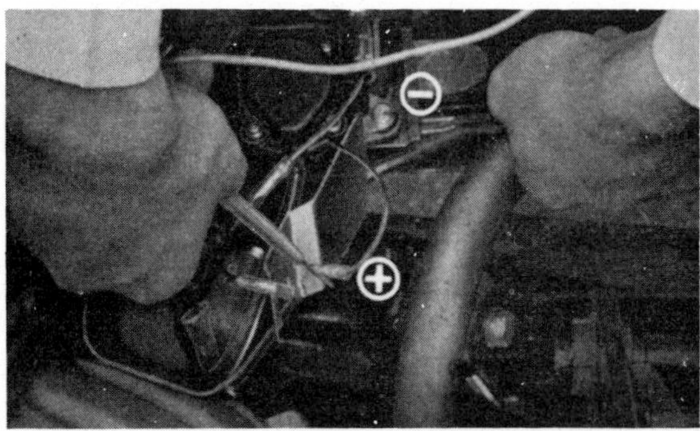

Fig. 3.7 Testing resistance of fuel pump coil

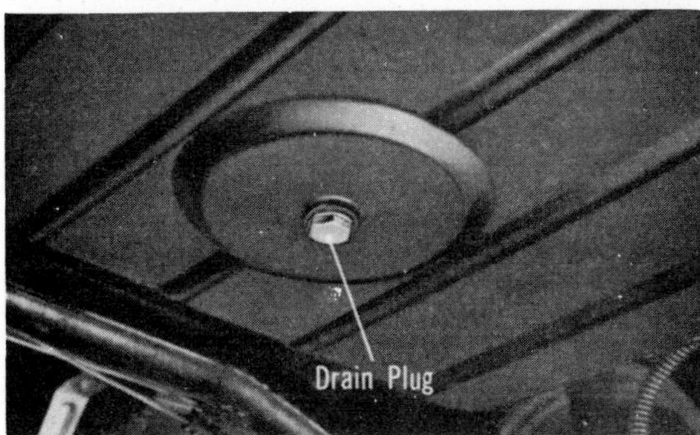

Fig. 3.8 Location of fuel tank drain plug

6 Fuel tank - servicing

1 On no account attempt to solder or weld a leak or hole in a fuel tank. This is a most dangerous operation and should be left to a specialist repairer.
2 Due to the need to render the tank free of fuel vapour and the length of time taken to do it, a new tank will probably prove less expensive than a repair in any event.
3 Application of a reliable brand of undersealing compound to the exterior surfaces of the tank will do much to prevent perforation by rust or stones.

7 Fuel contents gauge and sender unit - testing, removal and refitting

1 Failure of the fuel contents gauge to register even though the tank is well filled may be due to a faulty gauge or sender unit.
2 Disconnect the wires from the fuel gauge terminals and connect an ohmmeter in their place. A reading of less than 100 ohms shows the gauge to be in good order but if the resistance

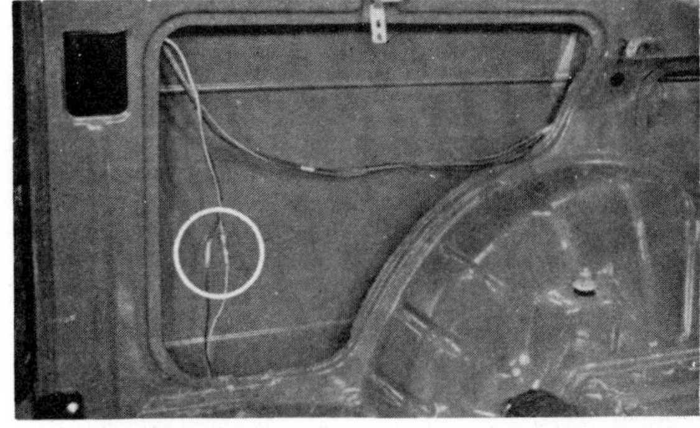

Fig. 3.9 Location of fuel tank sender unit cable connectors

exceeds this figure - renew the gauge.
3 Next, connect the ohmmeter to the sender unit cables. The indicated resistance should be between 30 and 34 ohms. If the reading is not as specified, loosen the sender unit flange securing screws and rotate the flange slightly in case the float arm is making contact with the fuel tank anti-surge baffle plate.
4 Check the sender unit to gauge connection wiring for breaks or faulty insulation.
5 Where the sender unit fails to respond to the foregoing tests, it must be renewed.
6 Remove the sender unit flange screws and withdraw the unit with a twisting motion so that the float and float arm will negotiate the locating hole.
7 Fitting the new unit is a reversal of removal but check that the float is not touching the tank baffle plate before tightening the flange securing screws.
8 Apply gasket cement to both sides of the sealing gasket and to the threads of the securing screws.

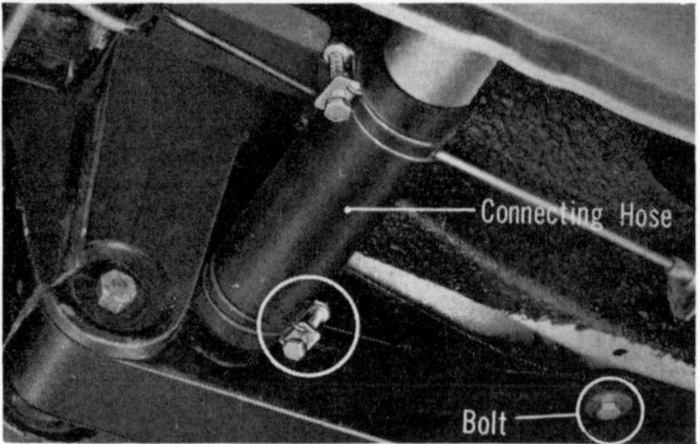

Fig. 3.10 Fuel tank flexible filler hose

8 Carburettor - general description

1 The variable choke type carburettor embodies an accelerator pump and a manually operated strangler. A fuel solenoid valve is included in the fuel inlet part of the carburettor to ensure immediate fuel cut-off once the ignition switch is turned off.
2 Operation of the carburettor is similar to all conventional diaphragm-vacuum piston carburettors and provided the idling and mixture settings are adjusted correctly, the unit will give the correct fuel/air mixture over the whole vehicle operating range.
3 A large number or variations to jet and setting specifications have been made and whenever the carburettor is dismantled or new parts ordered, the index mark on the unit should be compared with the table in the specifications Section at the begining of this chapter.

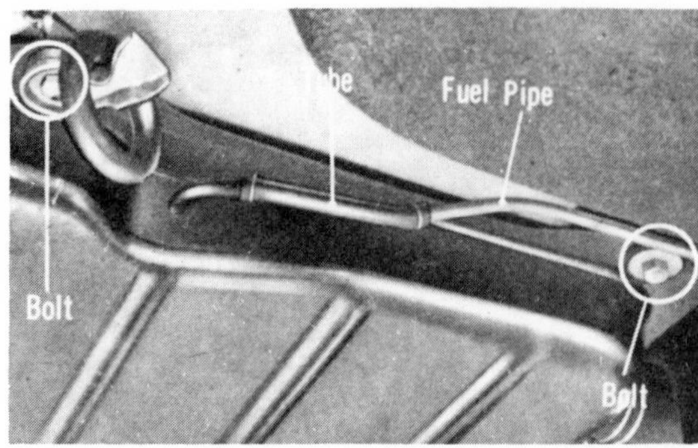

Fig. 3.11 Fuel tank outlet pipe and flexible connecting tube

9 Carburettor - choke and fast idle adjustments

1 The choke outer cable is clamped to the carburettor body.
2 Check that the fascia mounted choke control is pushed fully 'home'.
3 Check that the choke fast idle cam is pushed fully forward (open) and adjust the cable clamp so that the cable does not exert any pull on the cam and on the other hand has no slack in it.
4 The fast idle setting is the amount by which the throttle is opened when the fast idle cam is operated by the action of the choke cable. To make the correct adjustment, slacken the throttle stop screw right off. Now bend the throttle lever slipper so that it will just start to lift at the punch mark on the cam.
5 Re-set the throttle screw as described in Section 12.
10 Carburettor - throttle cable adjustment

10 Carburettor - throttle cable adjustment

1 Have an assistant depress the accelerator pedal fully.
2 Check that the throttle lever at the carburettor is in the fully open position. If not, loosen the two outer cable adjusting units and rotate them until the correct setting is obtained.
3 Never set the cable so that it is being strained when the pedal is fully depressed.

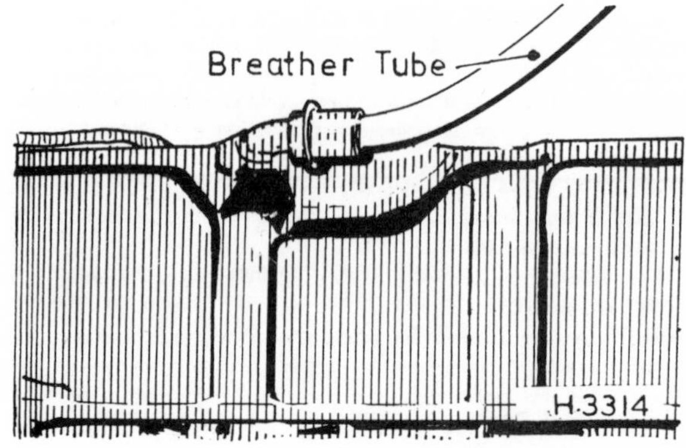

Fig. 3.12 Fuel tank breather tube

11 Carburettor - accelerator pump adjustment

1 This is carried out by varying the position of the split pin or lock nuts (according to type) on the pump operating rod to give the correct stroke in accordance with that specified for the index number of the particular carburettor (see table, specifications Section, at the begining of this Chapter).

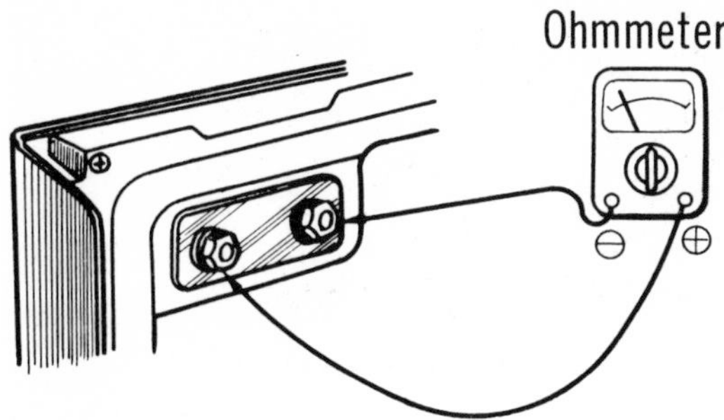

Fig. 3.13 Checking fuel gauge with an ohmmeter

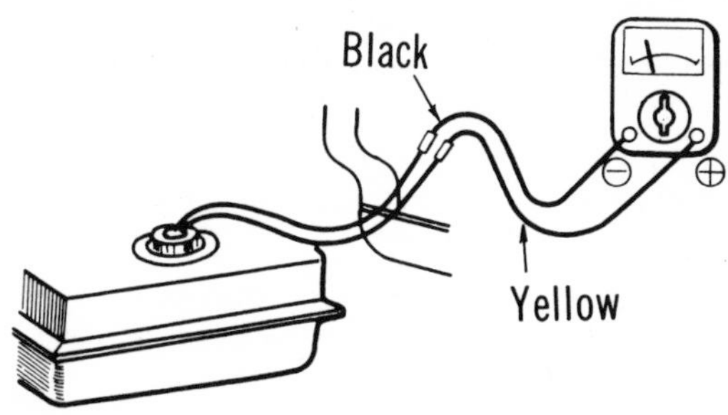

Fig. 3.14 Testing fuel tank sender unit with an ohmmeter

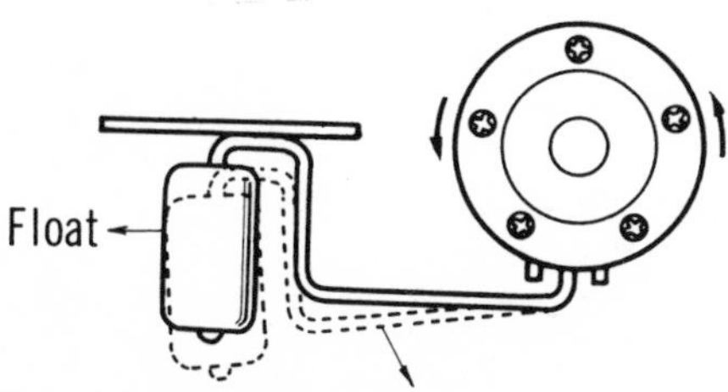

Fig. 3.15 Fuel tank float arm adjustment to prevent contact with baffle plate

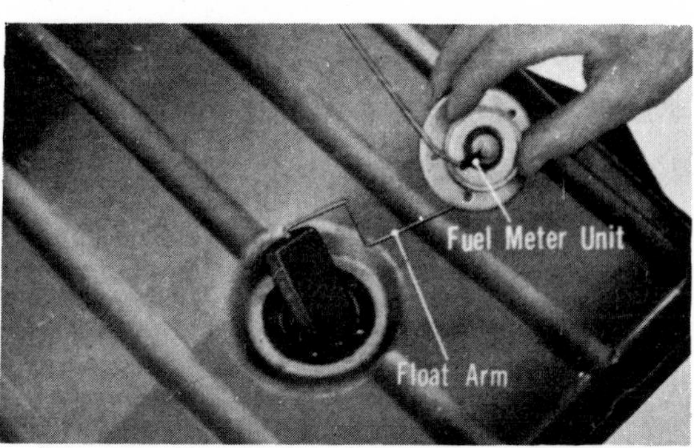

Fig. 3.16 Removing fuel tank sender unit and float assembly

12 Carburettor - slow running and mixture adjustment

1 It is preferable to make these adjustments using a vacuum gauge, exhaust gas analyser or 'Colortune'.
2 Where these are not available however, run the engine to normal operating temperature and ensure that the valve clearances and ignition system are in good order and correctly adjusted.
3 Set the mixture (pilot) screw in accordance with the following, from the fully closed position (do not force the screw home but just tighten until it seats:

360cc 121.5 cu in engine 5/8 of a turn unscrewed.

600cc 135.5 cu in engine (all carburettors except series D1/2) 1¼ turns unscrewed.

600cc 135.5 cu in engine (series D1/2 carburettor) 2 1/8 turns unscrewed.

4 With the engine running at a fast idle, turn the mixture screw first in one direction, and then the other, until the point smoothest of idling is obtained.
5 Now adjust the throttle stop screw until the ignition warning light on the fascia panel is almost extinguishing.
6 Re-adjust the mixture control screw if necessary.

13 Carburettor - removal and refitting

1 Pull off the fuel inlet pipe from the carburettor. (photo)
2 Disconnect the choke cable clamp screw and the outer cable clip.
3 Disconnect the throttle cable. To do this, slacken the two locknuts at the carburettor support brackets and pass the inner cable through the slots in the bracket eyes.
4 Disconnect the snap connector on the lead to the fuel solenoid valve and remove the earth lead.
5 Pull off the short vacuum hose which runs between the contact breaker capsule and the carburettor body.
6 On vehicles fitted with automatic transmission disconnect the throttle secondary cable from the carburettor extended support bracket.
7 Release the circular clamp which secures the rubber duct to the air cleaner body. Pull the duct off the air cleaner, do not attempt to pull it from the carburettor as it is retained by internal screws.
8 Unscrew and remove the two bolts from the inlet manifold flange and withdraw the carburettor, noting the location of the inlet manifold sealing 'O' ring.
9 Refitting is a reversal of removal.

14 Carburettor - dismantling and inspection

1 It is not recommended that the carburettor is completely dismantled as a part of routine overhaul. In fact the choke and throttle valve should only be dismantled if absolutely essential and if there is wear in the valve operating shafts or body bores

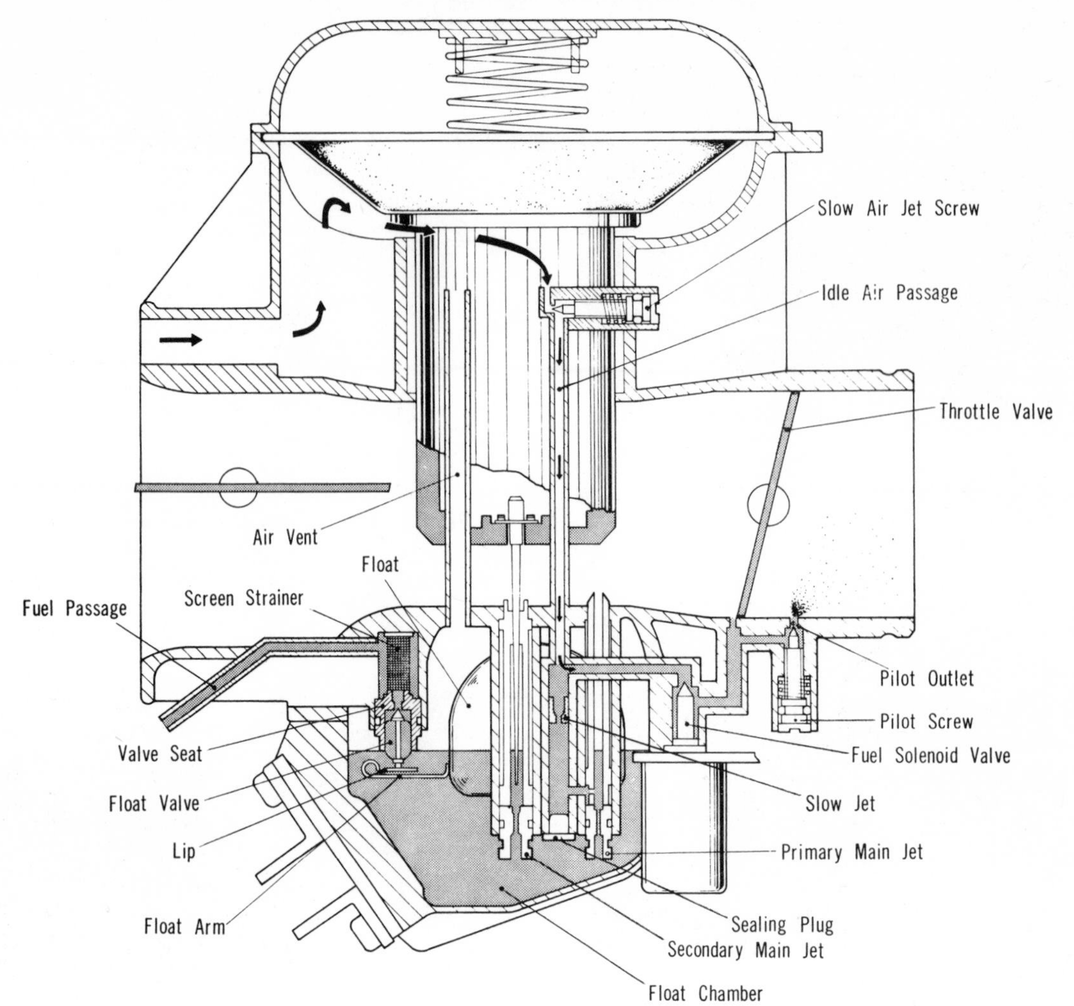

Fig. 3.17 Cross sectional view of carburettor (in idling mode)

Fig. 3.18 Location of carburettor index mark

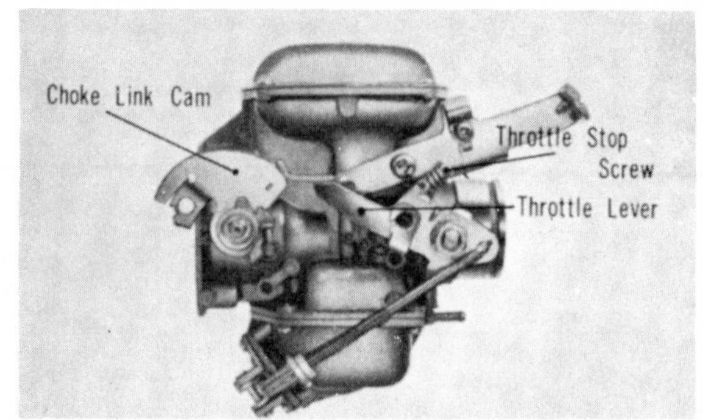

Fig. 3.19 Location of choke cam, throttle stop screw and throttle lever

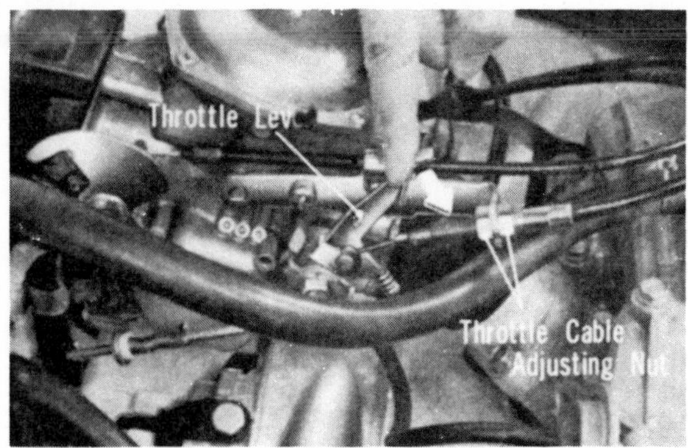

Fig. 3.20 Adjusting the throttle cable

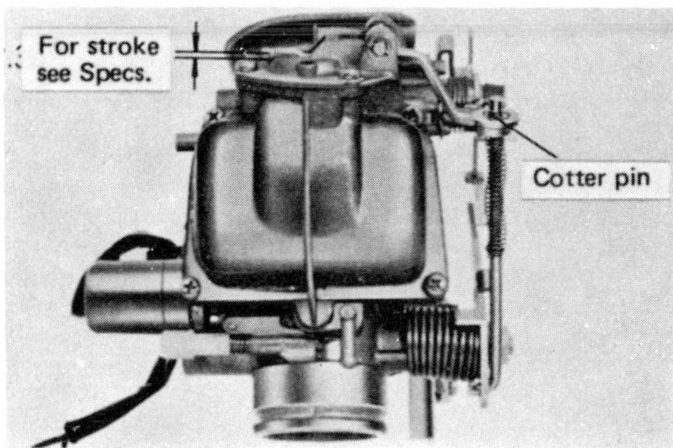

Fig. 3.21 Accelerator pump operating rod stroke

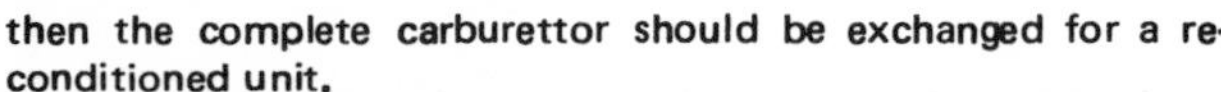
Fig. 3.22 Location of throttle stop and mixture control screws

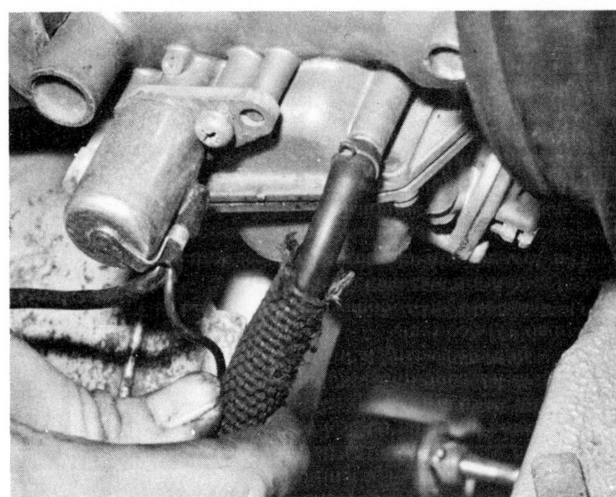

13.1 Fuel inlet pipe and solenoid shut-off valve on carburettor

then the complete carburettor should be exchanged for a reconditioned unit.

The primary and secondary main air jets are force fitted and cannot be removed. The non-return valve collar of the accelerator pump cannot be extracted and should be treated carefully.

2 From inside the air cleaner connection bellows, remove the air funnel and then withdraw the bellows from the carburettor.

3 From the other side of the carburettor remove the intake manifold.

4 Remove the carburettor cap screws, lift off the cap and withdraw the piston spring and the diaphragm/vacuum piston assembly (photo).

5 Extract the jet needle retainer from the vacuum piston and remove the shims and needle.

6 Invert the carburettor and disconnect the accelerator pump drive-rod. Remove the four screws which secure the float chamber bowl in position and lift off the float chamber and seal.

7 Withdraw the pivot pin and lift off the float assembly. Now remove the fuel inlet valve, valve seat retainers, valve seat and filter screen.

8 Dismantle the accelerator pump from the float chamber bowl by removing the lever assembly screws.

9 The primary and secondary jets and nozzles are accessible after withdrawing the main jet retainer.

10 The fuel solenoid valve is held to the carburettor body by a single screw.

11 If the choke and throttle linkage and shafts have to be dismantled, the arrangement of the components is shown in Fig. 3.23.

12 Wash all components in clean fuel and blow dry with air from a tyre pump. Never attempt to probe jets or nozzles with wire but clear them with compressed air only.

13 Check all rubber seals, diaphragms and gaskets for deformation, cut, tears or hardening, and renew as necessary after obtaining a carburettor repair kit.

14 Examine the fuel inlet valve and accelerator pump valve faces and seats for wear or scoring and renew these components if thers is evidence of deterioration.

15 Check the calibraion markings on jets and other components with those listed in the specifications Section of this chapter .

15 Carburettor - reassembly and adjustment

1 Reassembly is a reversal of dismantling but the following fitting details and adjustments must be carried out.

2 Make sure that the fuel inlet valve seat retainer is fitted with the bend as shown in Fig. 3.25.

3 Check the float level. To do this, set the carburettor on its side and position the float operating arm so that it is barely making contact with spring loaded plunger of the inlet valve. Measure the distance "L" shown in Fig. 3.28 and compare the measurement with that specified for the particular carburettor (see specifications Section). Adjust if necessary by bending the float operating arm.

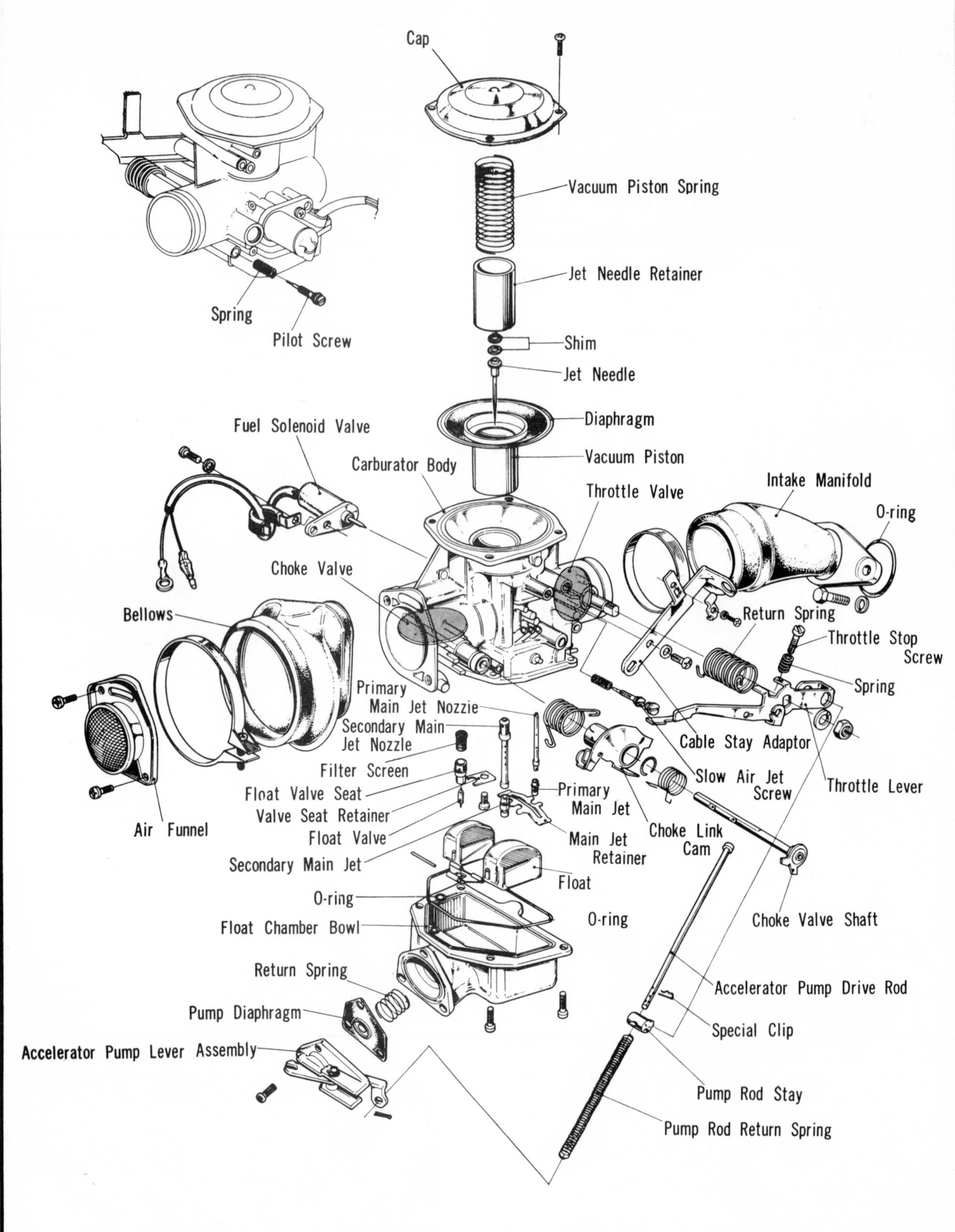

Fig. 3.23 Exploded view of carburettor (type N6D)

14.4 Carburettor cap removed showing diaphragm and spring

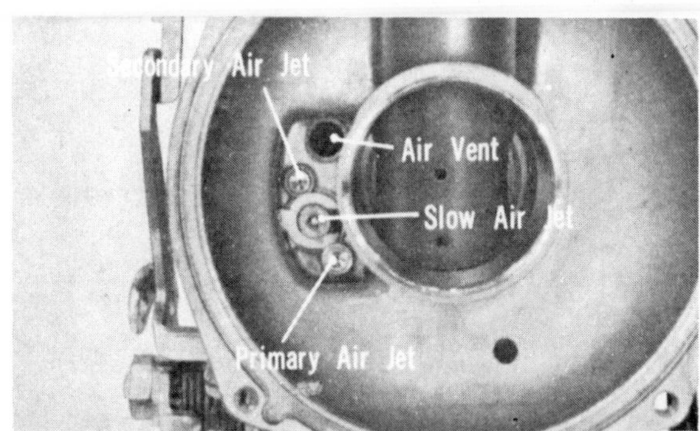

Fig. 3.24 Location of slow air jet (detachable) and primary and secondary air jets (non-detachable)

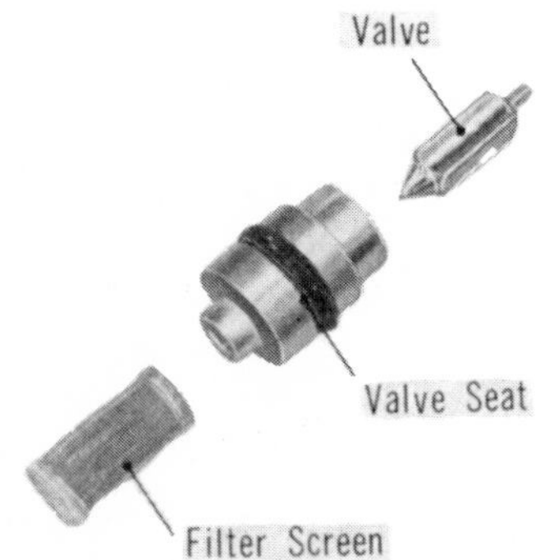

Fig. 3.25. Components of the fuel inlet valve

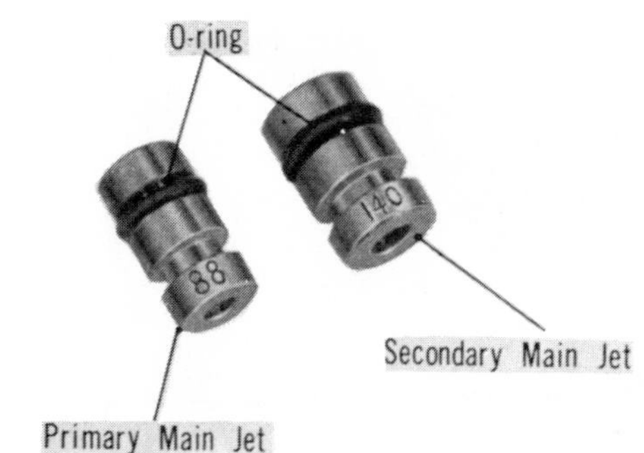

Fig. 3.26. Primary and secondary main jets showing calibration marks

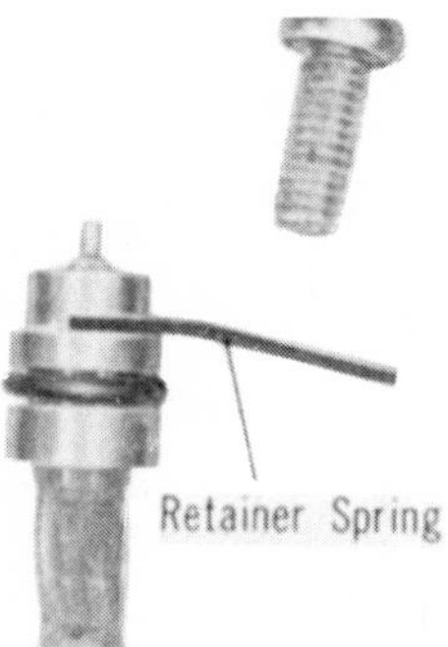

Fig. 3.27. Correct orientation of fuel inlet valve seat retainer

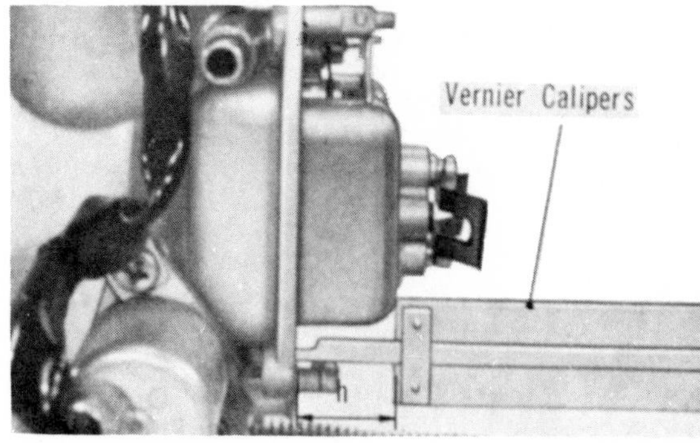

Fig. 3.28. Checking float adjustment (for dimension 'h' see table in Specifications Section)

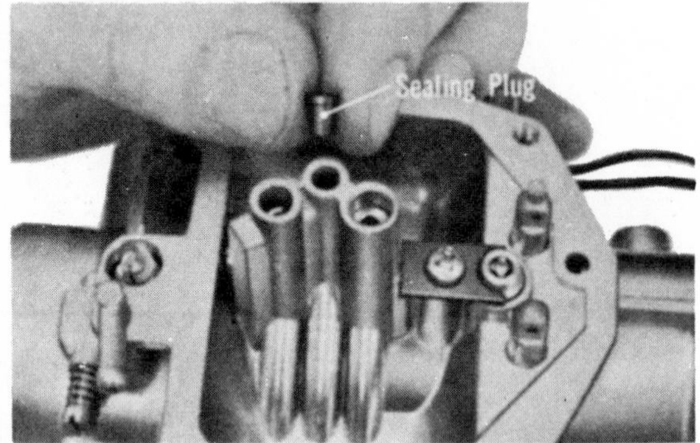

Fig. 3.29. Slow jet sealing plug

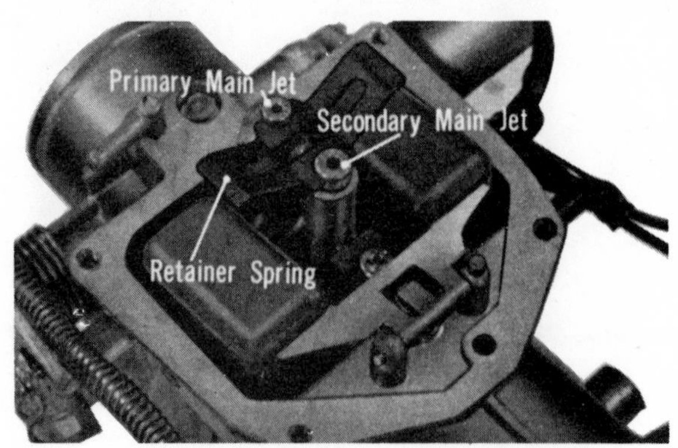

Fig. 3.30. Correct orientation of main jets retainer

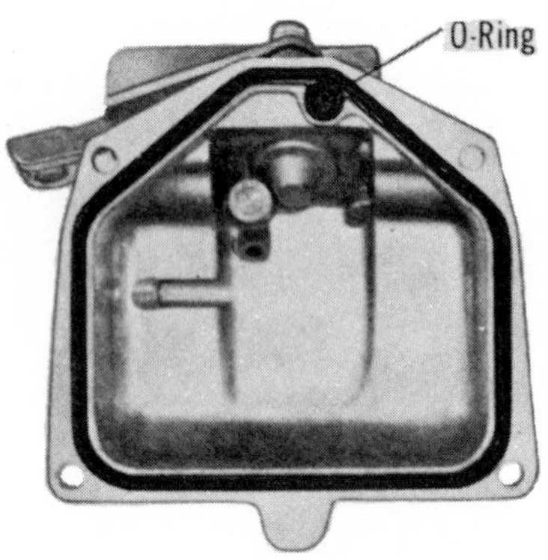

Fig. 3.31. Location of accelerator pump outlet port 'O' ring

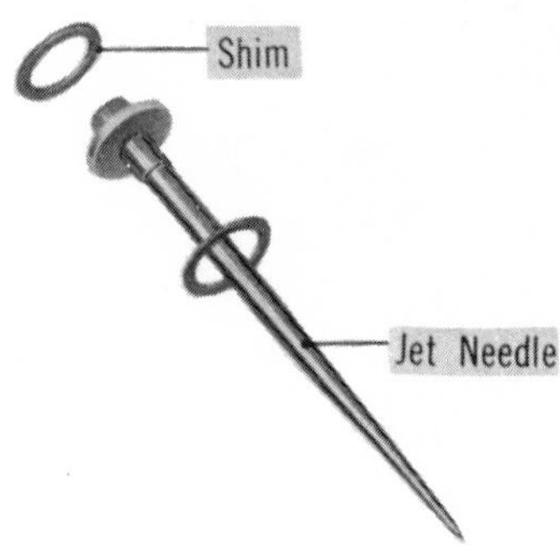

Fig. 3.32. Needle jet and shims

Fig. 3.33. Inserting needle jet retainer into vacuum piston

Fig. 3.34. Flexible diaphragm locating tab

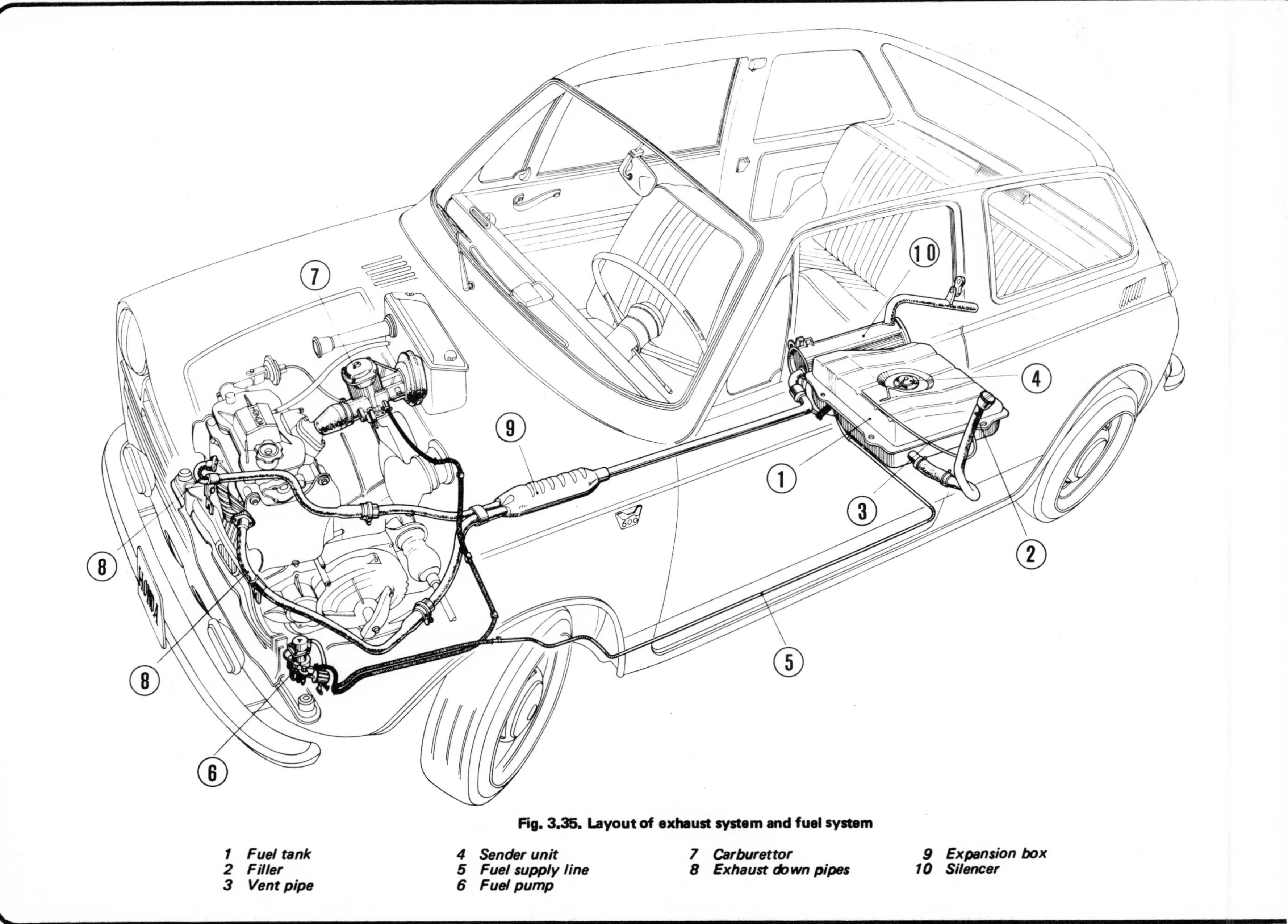

Fig. 3.35. Layout of exhaust system and fuel system

1 *Fuel tank*
2 *Filler*
3 *Vent pipe*
4 *Sender unit*
5 *Fuel supply line*
6 *Fuel pump*
7 *Carburettor*
8 *Exhaust down pipes*
9 *Expansion box*
10 *Silencer*

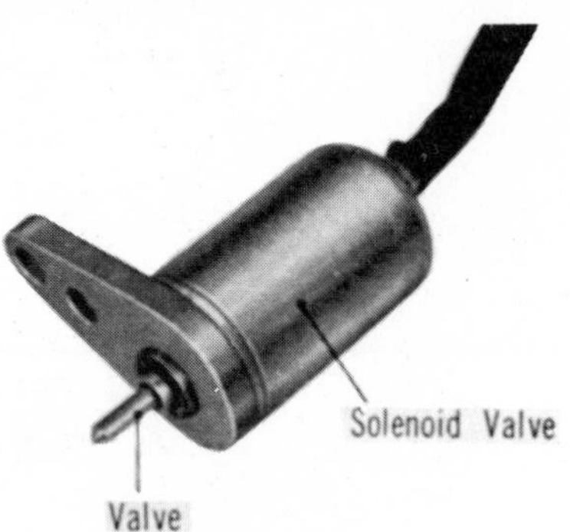

Fig. 3.36. Fuel cut-off solenoid valve

Fig. 3.37. Exhaust pipe flange gaskets at cylinder head

4 Securely install the slow jet sealing plug and ensure that the main jets retainer spring is fitted correctly.

5 Remember to fit the accelerator pump passage 'O' ring into the float chamber bowl.

6 The shims fitted to the flange at the upper end of the needle jet are normally located one each side of the flange but for operation in cold climates or at high altitudes they should both be positioned below the flange of the needle.

7 Note the locating tab on the periphery of the flexible diaphragm. This must engage in the recess in the carburettor body to ensure the correct installation of the vacuum piston. Check that the vacuum piston slides freely under its own weight in the carburettor bore.

8 Check the operation of the fuel cut-off solenoid valve by connection its leads directly to the battery. When the valve is energised, the needle is withdrawn. If at anytime the valve developes a fault then it will be impossible to start the engine. As a temporary measure, withdraw the solenoid securing flange slightly and insert a strip of flat metal such as a feeler blade to keep the valve plunger depressed within the solenoid valve body. This action will keep the fuel channel open for starting and idling circuits to function.

9 When the carburettor has been completely reassembled, carry out all the checks and adjustments described in Sections 9 to 12 inclusive, of this chapter.

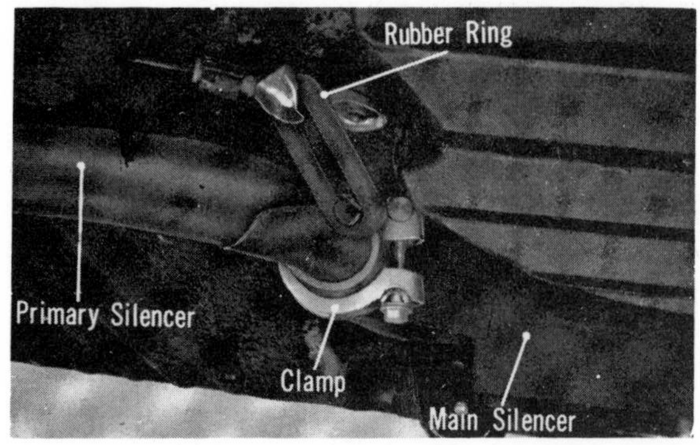

Fig. 3.38. Exhaust system suspension ring

16 Exhaust system - description and renewal

1 The system comprises separate down pipes, one from each cylinder which then enter an expansion box located beneath the differential unit.

2 From the expansion box a single pipe runs to the rear mounted, perforated-baffle type silencer.

3 The rear section of the system is suspended on rubber rings and links.

4 Renewal of the exhaust system may be carried out in sections which can be detached at the pipe connections after removal of the pipe clamps. Apply freeing fluid liberally at the joints and drive a blade up into each of the slots which are cut in the overlapping sections of the pipe. This will have the effect of widening the inside diameter of the larger pipe end will facilitate its removal.

5 When renewing sections of an exhaust system, use new gaskets at the cylinder head flanges and new pipe joint clamps. Inspect the rubber mountings for deterioration and renew if necessary.

Fig. 3.39. Exhaust mounting on rear road spring bracket

Fig. 3.40. Exhaust tailpipe suspension link

17 Carburation, fuel and exhaust systems - fault diagnosis

Symptom	Cause	Remedy
Failure to start	Empty fuel tank	Refill.
	Incorrect choke adjustment	Adjust (Section 9).
	Incorrect fast idle adjustment	Adjust (Section 9).
	Faulty solenoid cut-off valve	Renew.
	Blocked fuel filter	Renew.
	Faulty fuel pump	Test and renew if necessary (Section 3).
Excessive fuel consumption	Air cleaner element choked	Renew.
	Leaks in system	Rectify.
	Incorrect carburettor bowl fuel level	Adjust (Section 15).
	Incorrect carburettor adjustment	Adjust (Section 12).
	Loose slow-running jet	Tighten plug.
	Incorrect location of needle jet shims	Re-position (Section 15).
	Loose fuel inlet valve retainer	Secure (Section 15).

In addition to the above, heavy fuel consumption can be caused by ignition faults, dragging brakes and under-inflated tyres.

Symptom	Cause	Remedy
Weak mixture or lack of fuel	Tank vent blocked	Rectify.
	Blocked fuel filter	Renew.
	Faulty fuel pump	Test and renew.
	Fuel inlet valve in carburettor stuck	Release and clean.
	Inlet manifold 'O' ring seal leaking	Renew seal.
	Incorrect mixture adjustment	Adjust (Section 12).
Defective idling	Incorrect carburettor adjustment	Adjust (Section 12).
	Faulty solenoid valve	Renew.
	Solenoid 'O' ring deteriorated	Renew.
	Perforated or detached vacuum capsule tube (carburettor to contact breaker)	Renew or connect.
	Slow-running jet clogged or loose	Clear or tighten plug.
	Incorrect carburettor fuel level	Adjust (Section 15).
Poor acceleration and reduced high speeds	Incorrect accelerator pump rod adjustment	Adjust (Section 11).
	Sticky carburettor vacuum piston	Clean.
	Perforated carburettor flexible diaphragm	Renew.
	Needle jet incorrectly fitted	Reassemble (Section 15).
	Incorrect fuel level in carburettor bowl	Adjust (Section 15).
	Clogged or loose jets	Clear and tighten.
	Deteriorated main jet 'O' rings	Renew.

Chapter 4 Ignition system

Contents

Specifications

Type	Battery, coil, contact breaker
Timing (dynamic)	10º btdc at 1600 rev/min 30º btdc at 4000 rev/min
Contact breaker points gap	0.012 to 0.016 in. (0.3 to 0.4 mm)
Spark plug type	NGK B-8ES or SENSO W 24 ES
Spark plug gap	0.028 to 0.032 in. (0.7 ro 0.8 mm)

1 General description

The contact breaker assembly is mounted within the right-hand camshaft holder and is driven directly by the camshaft.

In order that the engine may run correctly it is necessary for an electrical spark to ignite the fuel/air mixture in the combustion chamber at exactly the right moment in relation to engine speed and load. The ignition system is based on supplying low tension voltage from the battery to the ignition coil, where it is converted into high tension voltage. The high tension voltage is powerful enough to jump the spark plug gap in the cylinders many times a second under high compression pressure, providing that the ignition system is in good working order and that all adjustments are correct.

The ignition system comprises two individual circuits known as the low tension and high tension circuits.

The low tension circuit (sometimes known as the primary circuit) comprises the battery lead to the ignition switch, to the low tension or primary coil windings (terminal SW) and the lead from the low tension coil windings (terminal CB) to the contact breaker points and condenser in the contact breaker unit.

The high tension (HT) secondary circuit comprises the secondary coil windings and the heavily insulated HT leads, from the coil to the two spark plugs.

The complete ignition system operation is as follows: Low tension voltage from the battery is changed within the ignition coil to high tension voltage by the opening and closing of the contact breaker points in the low tension circuit. High tension voltage is then fed to the spark plugs where it jumps the gap between the spark plug electrodes, one of which is connected to earth through the contact of its body and the cylinder head.
Both spark plugs fire simultaneously at each opening of the contact breaker points (each revolution of the breaker cam) but as the pistons are on different strokes then only the one on the compression stroke will cause ignition.

The ignition timing is advanced and retarded automatically to ensure the spark occurs at just the right instant for the particular load at the prevailing engine speed.

The ignition advance is controlled by a mechanical and vacuum operated system. The mechanical governor mechanism comprises two weights which move out under centrifugal force from the central shaft as the engine speed rises. As they move outwards they rotate the cam relative to the shaft, and so advance the spark. The weights are held in position by two springs, and it is the tension of the springs which is largely responsible for correct spark advancement.

The vacuum control comprises a diaphragm, one side of which is connected via a small bore tube to the carburettor, and the other side to the contact breaker plate. Depression in the induction manifold and carburettor, which varies with engine speed and throttle opening, causes the diaphragm to move, so moving the contact breaker plate and advancing or retarding the spark.

A condenser (capacitor) is fitted inside the contact breaker housing and is connected between the moving contact breaker and earth to prevent excessive arcing and pitting of the contact breaker points.

The actual point of ignition of the fuel/air mixture which occurs a few degrees before top-dead-centre is determined by correct static setting of the ignition timing as described in Section 6.

2 Contact breaker - adjustment of points gap

1 Remove the cover from the contact breaker unit. (photo).
2 Apply a spanner to the crankshaft pulley bolt and turn the crankshaft until the heel of the flexible contact breaker arm is at the centre of the highest point of the cam lobe.
3 Check the gap between the two points with a feeler gauge. The gap is correct when a blade of between 0.012 and 0.016 in (0.3 and 0.4 mm) is a sliding fit.
4 If adjustment is required, loosen the two lockscrews and move the rigid arm by engaging a screwdriver in its leverage slot. Retighten the screws.

2.1 Removing contact breaker cover

3 Contact breaker points - removal and refitting

1 Remove the cover from the contact breaker unit.
2 Unscrew the bolt at the terminal on the baseplate noting carefully the relative positions of the flexible contact breaker arm and the condenser lead also the location of the insulating washers all as shown in Figs. 4.5 and 4.6 (photo).
3 Pull off the contact breaker flexible arm.
4 Unscrew and remove the two screws which secure the rigid arm to the baseplate and lift the arm away.
5 Examine the points. After a period of operation, one contact face should have a pip and the other a crater caused by arcing. This is a normal condition which should be removed by dressing the faces squarely on an oilstone.
6 Excessive pitting of the contact points may be caused by operation with an incorrect gap, the voltage regulator setting too high, faulty or wrong type of condenser or coil fitted, poor earth connections to condenser, baseplate or battery.
7 Where contact breaker points are so badly worn or the pitting so deep that excessive rubbing would be required to eliminate it, then they should be renewed.
8 Refitting is a reversal of removal but check most carefully the fitting of the LT terminal insulators.
9 Adjust the points gap as described in Section 2.

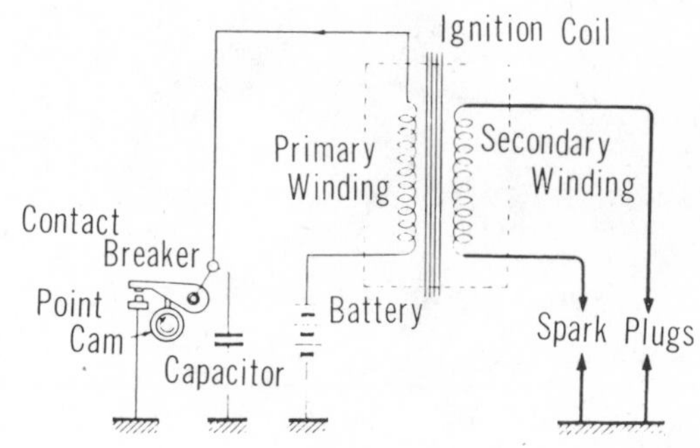

Fig. 4.1. The ignition circuit

4 Condenser (capacitor) - removal, testing and refitting

1 The condenser ensures that with the contact breaker points open, the sparking between them is not excessive to cause severe pitting. The condenser is fitted in parallel and its failure will automatically cause failure of the ignition system as the points will be prevented from interrupting the low tension circuit.
2 Testing for an unserviceable condenser may be effected by switching on the ignition and separating the contact points by hand. If this action is accompanied by a blue flash then condenser failure is indicated. Difficult starting, missing ot the engine after several miles running or badly pitted points are other indications of a faulty condenser.
3 The surest test is by substitution of a new unit.
4 Removal of the condenser is by means of withdrawing the screw which retains it to the baseplate and detaching the lead. Replacement is a reversal of this procedure.

3.2 Details of contact breaker unit

5 Contact breaker unit - removal, servicing, refitting

1 Remove the cover from the unit and disconnect the LT lead at its connector and pull off the vacum tube.

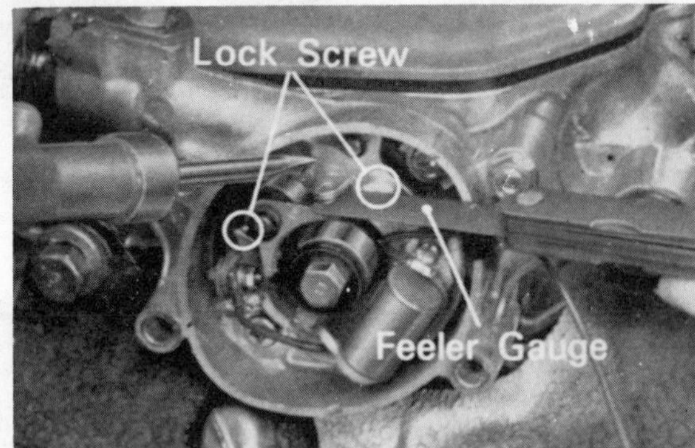

Fig. 4.2. Checking contact breaker points gap

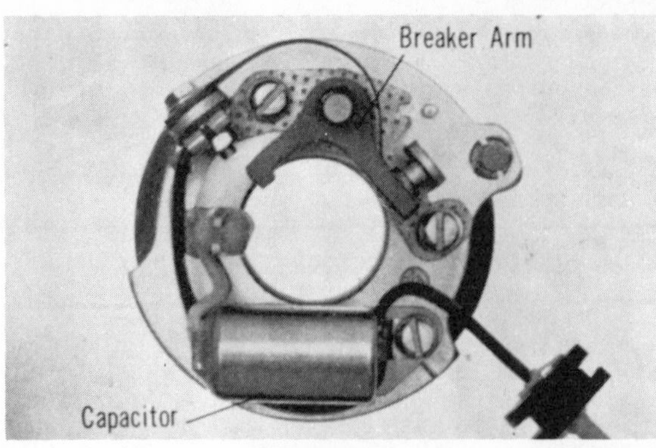

Fig. 4.3. Contact breaker points, baseplate and condenser (capacitor)

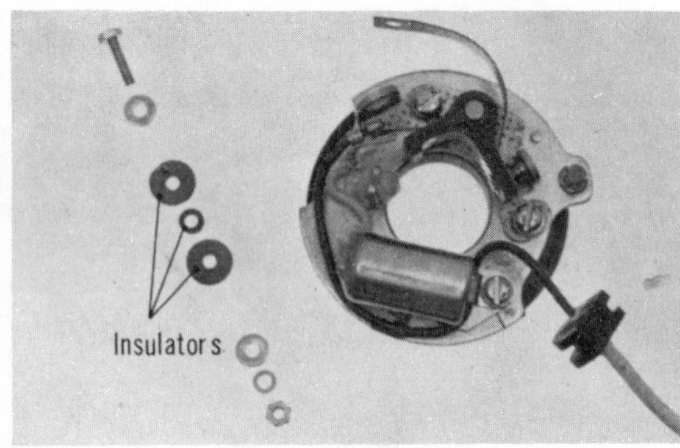

Fig. 4.4. Exploded view of the contact breaker LT terminal

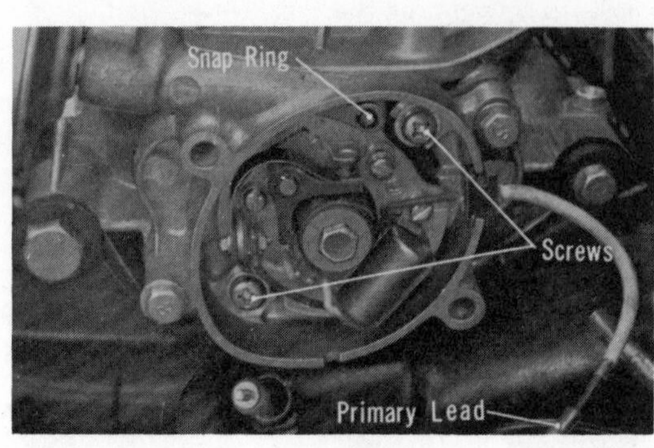

Fig. 4.5. Location of baseplate securing screws and vacuum capsule operating rod snap ring

Fig. 4.6. Removing the cam securing bolt

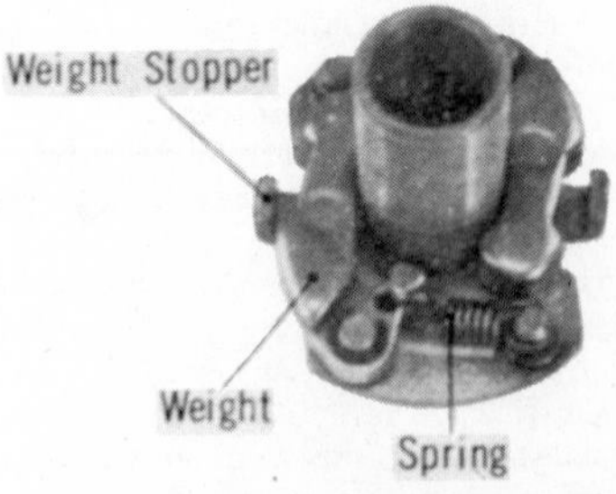

Fig. 4.7. The mechanical advance mechanism

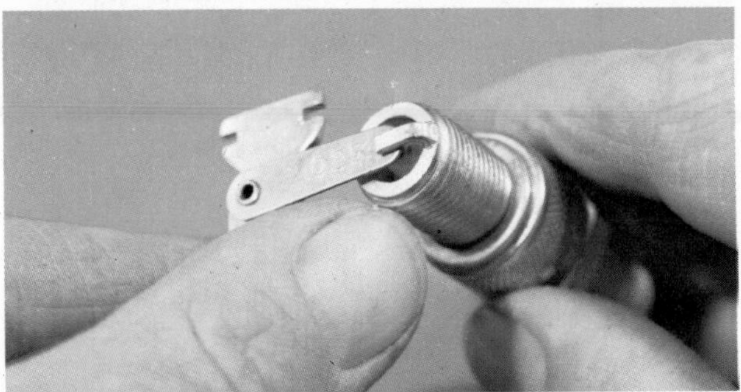

Measuring plug gap. A feeler gauge of the correct size (see ignition system specifications) should have a slight 'drag' when slid between the electrodes. Adjust gap if necessary

Adjusting plug gap. The plug gap is adjusted by bending the earth electrode inwards, or outwards, as necessary until the correct clearance is obtained. Note the use of the correct tool

Normal. Grey-brown deposits lightly coated core nose. Gap increasing by around 0.001 in (0.025 mm) per 1000 miles (1600 km). Plugs ideally suited to engine and engine in good condition

Carbon fouling. Dry, black, sooty deposits. Will cause weak spark and eventually misfire. Fault: over-rich fuel mixture. Check: carburettor mixture settings, float level and jet sizes; choke operation and cleanliness of air filter. Plugs can be re-used after cleaning

Oil fouling. Wet, oily deposits. Will cause weak spark and eventually misfire. Fault: worn bores/piston rings or valve guides; sometimes occurs (temporarily) during running-in period. Plugs can be re-used after thorough cleaning

Overheating. Electrodes have glazed appearance, core nose very white - few deposits. Fault: plug overheating. Check: plug value, ignition timing, fuel octane rating (too low) and fuel mixture (too weak). Discard plugs and cure fault immediately

Electrode damage. Electrodes burned away; core nose has burned, glazed appearance. Fault: initial pre-ignition. Check: as for 'Overheating' but may be more severe. Discard plugs and remedy fault before piston or valve damage occurs

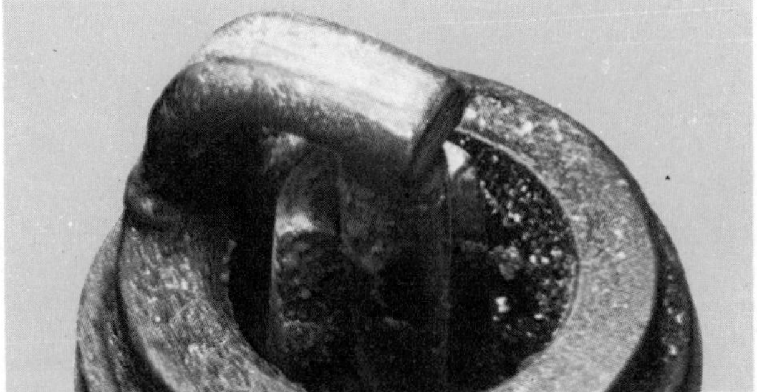

Split core nose (may appear initially as a crack). Damage is self-evident, but cracks will only show after cleaning. Fault: pre-ignition or wrong gap-setting technique. Check: ignition timing, cooling system, fuel octane rating (too low) and fuel mixture (too weak). Discard plugs, rectify fault immediately

2 Detach the snap ring which secures the vacuum capsule operating rod to the baseplate.
3 Unscrew and remove the two screws which secure the baseplate assembly and lift the assembly from the camshaft holder housing.
4 Unscrew and remove the bolt from the end of the camshaft and withdraw the cam and centrifugal advance mechanism. Unbolt and remove the vacuum advance capsule.
5 Examine the components for wear or lack of tension in the restraining springs and renew as necessary.
6 If there is evidence of oil within the housing, the camshaft holder must be removed and the oil seal renewed as described in Chapter 1. A faulty non-return valve in the camshaft chain hydraulic tensioner can also cause oil saturation within the contact breaker unit.
7 Refitting is a reversal of removal but ensure that the groove in the mechanical advance mechanism engages with the dowel pin on the camshaft.
8 Adjust the points gap (see Section 2).
9 Adjust the timing after refitting the vacuum capsule. (Section 6).

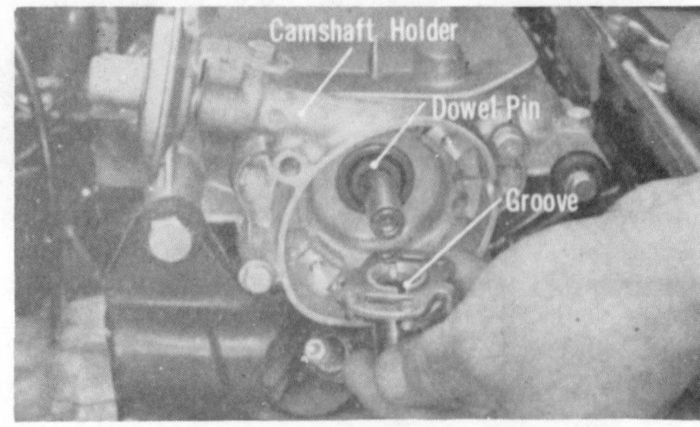

Fig. 4.8. Refitting the mechanical advance mechanism

Fig. 4.9. Ignition timing marks (600cc 135.5 cu in)

Fig. 4.10. Ignition timing marks (360cc 121.5 cu in)

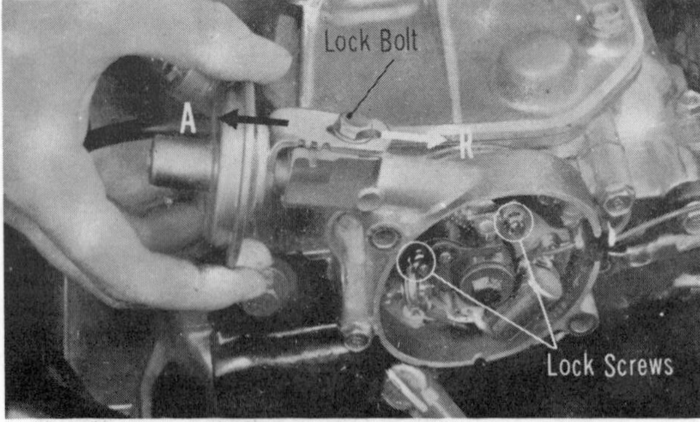

Fig. 4.11. Location of vacuum capsule lock bolt

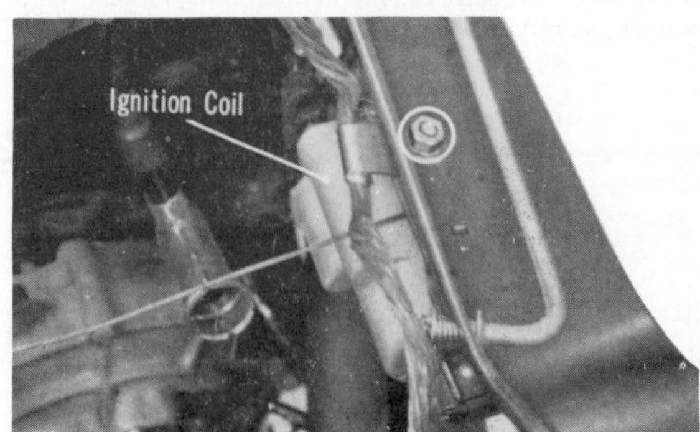

Fig. 4.12. Location of ignition coil

6 Ignition timing

1 Remove the sparking plugs and with a spanner applied to the crankshaft pulley bolt, turn the engine until the notch and "F" marks on the pulley wheel and the flywheel housing (600cc 135.5 cu in) or generator cover (360cc 21.5 cu in) are in alignment. The "T" mark is for setting the camshaft (Chapter 1).
2 Connect a 12-volt bulb between the LT terminal on the baseplate and earth. Switch on the ignition.
3 Loosen the vacum capsule clamp bolt and move the capsule in or out until the bulb *just* extinguishes. Tighten the capsule clamp bolt. This will set the static ignition timing.
4 If a stroboscope and tachometer are available, remove the vacuum tube from the capsule and with the engine running check the timing which should be 10^{0} (before-top-dead-centre) at 1600 rev/min and 30^{0} (before-top-dead-centre) at 4000 rev/min. This advance is solely due to the mechanical advance mechanism. If the serviceability of the vacuum capsule is to be (simply) checked it can either be carried out with a stroboscope, or if one is not available, suck the end of the vacuum tube and observe the movement of the baseplate within the camshaft holder housing.

7 Ignition system - fault finding

Failure of the ignition system will either be due to faults in the HT or LT circuits. Initial checks should be made by observing the security of spark plug terminals, snap connectors, coil and battery connection. More detailed investigation and the explanation and remedial action in respect of symptoms of ignition malfunction are described in the next section.

8 Ignition system - fault disgnosis and rectification

1 **Engine Fails to Start:** If the engine fails to start and the car was running normally when it was last used, first check there is fuel in the petrol tank. If the engine turns over normally on the starter motor and the battery is evidently well charged, then the fault may be in either the high or low tension circuits. First check the HT circuit. Note: If the battery is known to be fully charged; the ignition light comes on, and the starter motor fails to turn the engine **check the tightness of the leads on the battery terminals** and also the secureness of the earth lead to its **connection to the body.** It is quite common for the leads to have worked loose, even if they look and feel secure. If one of the battery terminal posts gets very hot when trying to work the starter motor this is a sure indication of a faulty cone connection to that terminal.
2 Remove each plug lead in turn and hold the end of the (suitably insulated) near to the cylinder block. Spin the engine on the starter and check that a fat spark jumps the lead to the block.
3 Remove each plug in turn and lay it on the top of the camshaft cover. Again spin the engine on the starter and check for a healthy spark between the electrodes. These tests, if positive, prove the coil to be O.K.
4 Prise open the contact breaker points with the fingers and with the ignition switched on observe if there is a large flash at the points. This indicates failure of the condenser which must be renewed.

5 **Engine starts readily but the performance is sluggish, so misfiring**
Check the contact breaker points gap.
Check the plugs.
Check the static ignition timing.
Check the fuel octane rating.

6 **Engine misfires, runs unevenly, cuts out at low revolutions only**
Check the contact breaker gap (too large).
Check the plugs.
Check the fuel system (carburettor).

7 **Engine misfires at high revolutions**
Check the plugs.
Check the contact breaker gap (too small).
Check the fuel system (carburettor).

9 Spark plugs and HT leads

1 The correct functioning of the spark plugs is vital for the correct running and efficiency of the engine. The plugs fitted as standard are listed in the specification page.
2 At intervals of 6000 miles (10.000 km) the plugs should be removed, examined, cleaned and, if worn excessively, renewed. The condition of the spark plug will also tell much about the oveall condition of the engine.
3 If the insulator nose of the spark plug is clean and white, with no deposits, this is indicative of a weak mixture, or too hot a plug. (A hot plug transfers heat away from the electrode slowly - a cold plug transfers it away quickly).
4 If the top and insulator nose is covered with hard black looking deposits, then this is indicative that the mixiture is too rich. Should the plug be black and oily, then it is likely that the engine is fairly worn, as well as the mixture being too rich.
5 If the insulator nose is covered with light tan to greyish brown deposits, then the mixture is correct and it is likely that the engine is in good condition.
6 If there are any traces of long brown tapering stains on the outside of the white portion of the plug, then the plug will have to be renewed, as this shows that there is a faulty joint between the plug body and the insulator, and compression is being allowed to leak away.
7 Plugs should be cleaned by a sand blasting maching, which will free them from carbon more thoroughtly than cleaning by hand. The machine will also test the condition of the plugs under compression. Any plug that fails to spark at the recommended pressure should be renewed.
8 The sparking plug gap is of considerable importance, as, if it is too large or too small the size of the spark and its efficiency will be seriously impaired. The spark plug gap should be set to between 0.028 and 0.032 in. (0.7 to 0.8 mm) for the best results.
9 To set it, measure the gap with a feeler gauge, and then bend open, or close, the outer plug electrode until the correct gap is achieved.
The centre electrode should never be bent as this may crack the insulation and cause plug failure, if nothing worse.

Chapter 5 Clutch

Contents

Specifications

Type	Single dry plate with diaphragm spring
Pressure:	
600 cc/35.5 cu in.	772 to 838 lb (350 to 380 kg)
360 cc/21.5 cu in.	706 to 816 lb (320 to 370 kg)
Friction disc:	
Lining diameter	6.50 in. (165 mm)
Lining area	18.4 in^2 (118 cm^2)
Lining thickness	0.28 in. (7.0 mm) minimum 0.23 in. (5.75 mm)
Number of torsion rubber inserts	4
Release bearing	Sealed ball
Pedal free movement	0.118 in. (3.0 mm)
Clutch actuation	Cable

Torque wrench settings:	**lb/ft**	**kg/m**
Clutch drum bolts	8	1.106
Clutch pressure plate to drum bolts	8	1.106
Clutch housing bolts	8	1.106

1 General description

The clutch is of dry single plate type. It incorporates a diaphragm spring and is cable operated.The power from the engine is transmitted through the primary chains to the driven sprocket on which are bolted the clutch drum and pressure plate assembly, all freely rotating round the transmission mainshaft.

The clutch friction disc is engaged on the splines of the transmission mainshaft and as the clutch pedal is depressed, the release bearing is pushed forward to bear against the diaphragm spring fingers. This action causes the outer edge of the diaphragm spring to deflect and to move the pressure plate rearwards thus disengaging the pressure plate from the friction disc. In this 'clutch disengaged' mode, the clutch pressure plate assembly is rotating freely (with the engine running) but the friction disc and mainshaft are at rest.

When the clutch pedal is released, the diaphragm spring forces the pressure plate into contact with the friction disc and at the same time pushes the disc forward on its splines and squeezes it against the surface of the clutch drum which is bolted to, and revolving with, the driven sprocket. As the friction disc is progressively sandwiched between the pressure plate and the clutch drum so the drive is taken up. The clutch is accessible with the engine in position in the car.

2 Clutch - adjustment

1 Check the setting of the clutch pedal. This should be at the same level as the foot brake pedal. If necessary, loosen the lock-nut on the adjusting bolt and turn the bolt until the correct clutch pedal setting is obtained,(photo).

2 Now check the clutch pedal free movement. Do this by gently pushing and pulling the end of the clutch release lever. The tip of the lever should move through a distance of 0.118 in (3mm) before the resistance of the clutch diaphragm spring can be felt.

3 Adjust the free movement by loosening the locknut on the release arm adjusting bolt and screwing it in or out as appropriate.

3 Clutch pedal - removal and refitting

1 The clutch pedal pivots on a cross-shaft jointly with the brake pedal.

2 Remove the circlip and thrust washer from the end of the cross-shaft and withdraw the clutch pedal.

3 Now disconnect the clutch operating cable clevis from the pedal arm by removing the split pin and clevis pin.

4 Refitting is a reversal of removal but grease the cross-shaft, use a new split pin and check the pedal height and free movement as described in the preceding Section (2).

4 Clutch operating cable - renewal

4 Clutch operating cable - renewal

1 Unscrew the release arm (free movement) adjusting bolt as far as possible.

2 The slackness now created will enable the clutch cable to be withdrawn from its release lever slot after the rubber cushion has been removed. (photo).

3 Now push the clutch outer cable towards the engine and release it from the clutch housing.

4 Withdraw the clutch cable through to the right handside of the engine.

5 Disconnect the cable clevis at the clutch pedal and withdraw the cable assembly (complete with rubber grommet) through the engine rear bulkhead.

6 Refitting is a reversal of removal but check and adjust the free movement (section 2) and seal the bulkhead grommet to prevent entry of water or fumes.

5 Clutch - removal and dismantling

1 Disconnect the clutch inner and outer cables from the clutch housing and release lever as described in the preceding Section (4).

2 Remove the clutch housing cover. (photo).

3 Remove the clutch pressure plate assembly. (photo).

4 Withdraw the friction disc from the splines of the transmission mainshaft. (photo).

5 Unbolt and withdraw the clutch drum taking care not to damage the oil seal as it passes over the mainshaft splines. (photo).

6 Pull out the spring retaining clip from the hole in the release bearing shaft where it projects from the clutch housing. Extract the washer, spring and release bearing.

7 Detach the circlip from inside the clutch housing and push out the bushing.

2.1 Adjusting clutch release arm to give specified free movement

4.2 Clutch cable connection to release lever and clutch housing stop

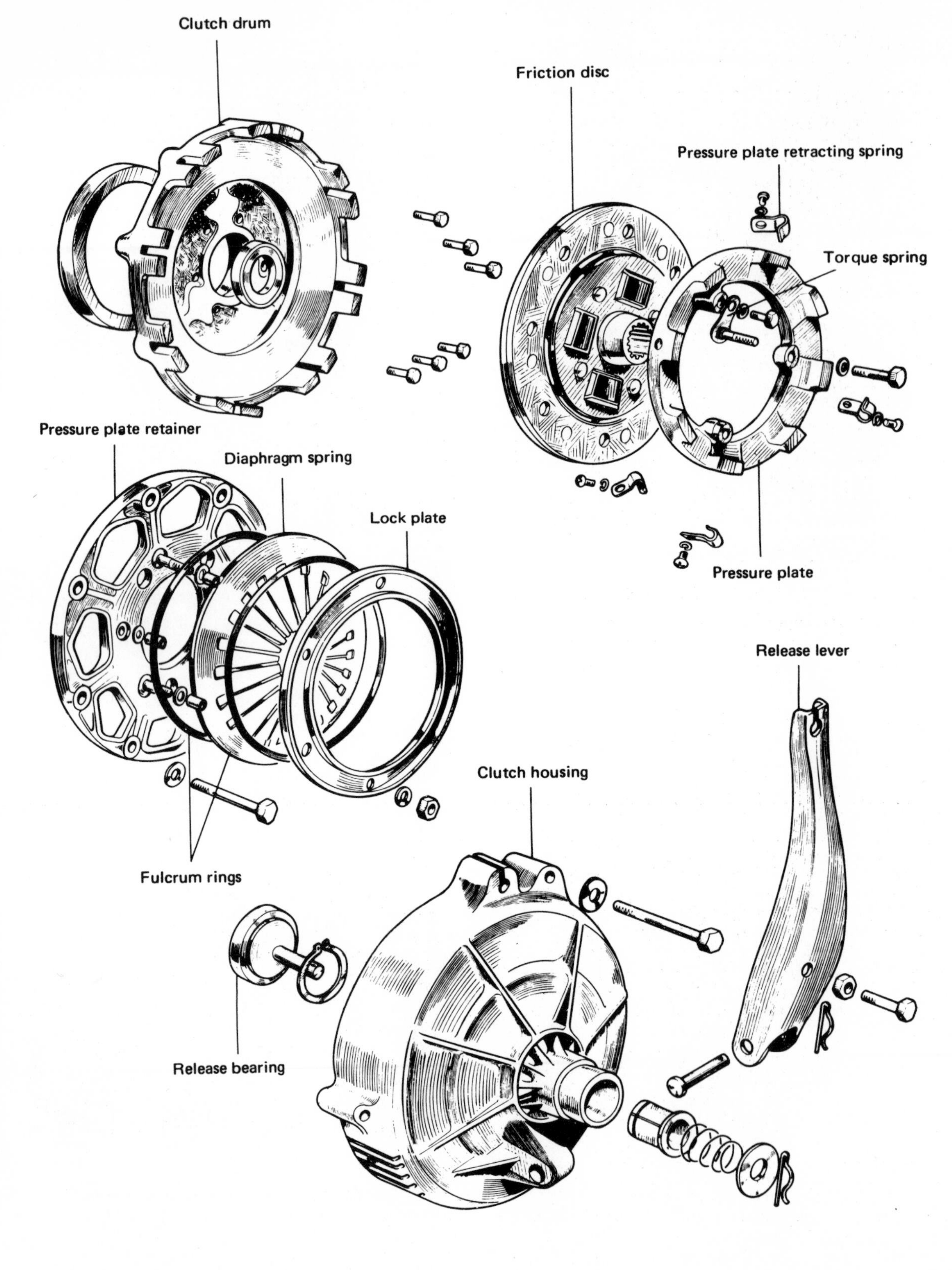

Fig. 5.1. Components of the clutch

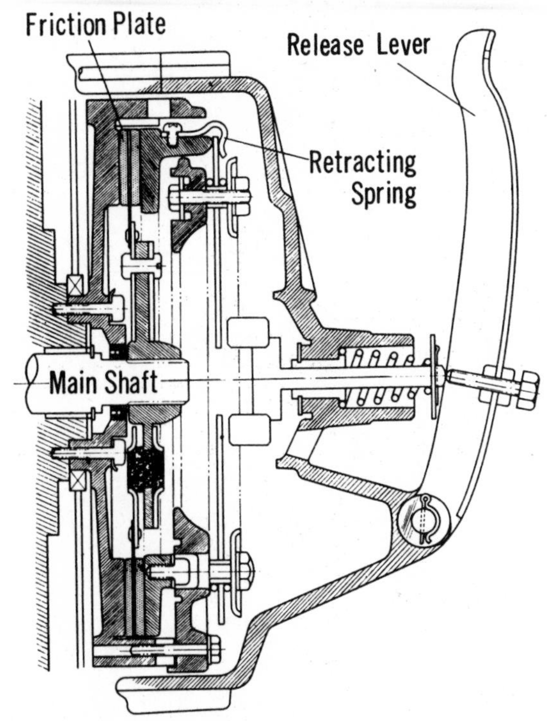

Fig. 5.2. Sectional view of clutch engaged (pedal released)

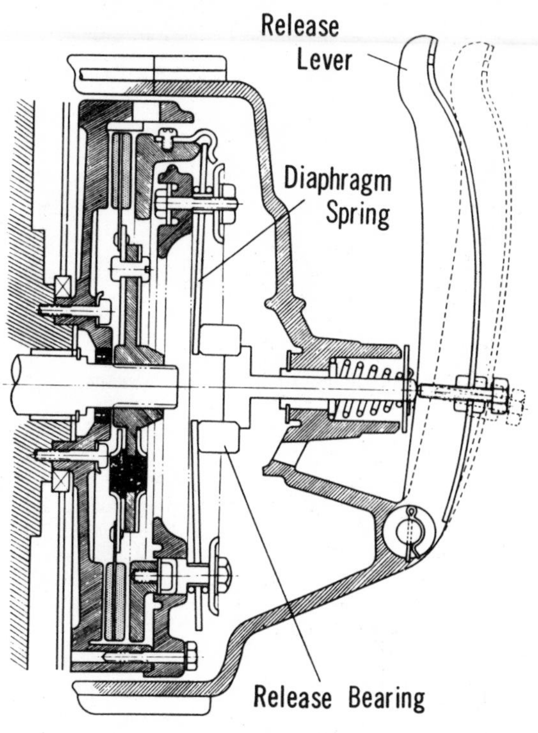

Fig. 5.3. Sectional view of clutch disengaged (pedal depressed)

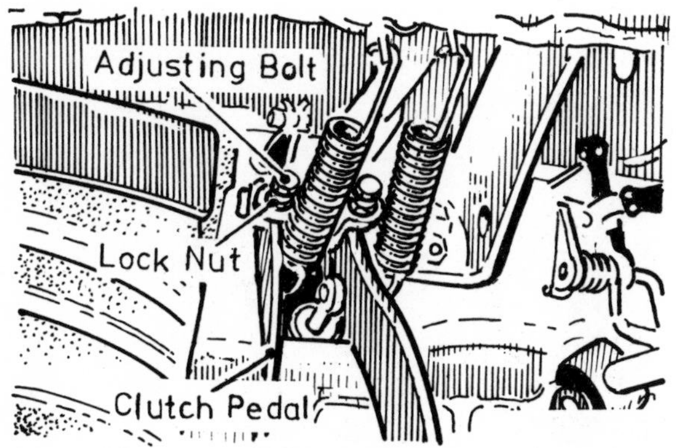

Fig. 5.4. Clutch pedal height adjustment

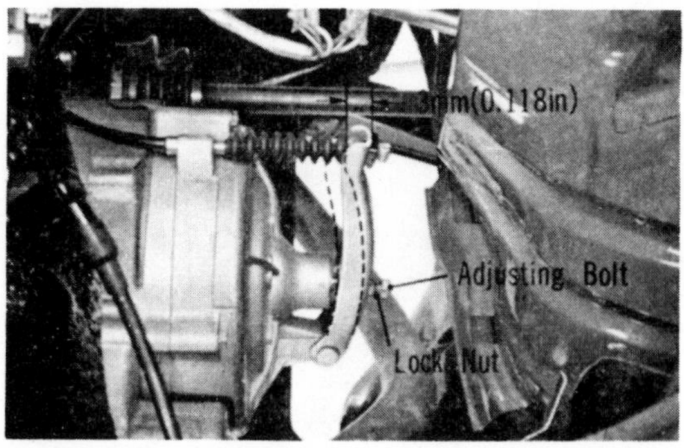

Fig. 5.5. Clutch pedal free movement diagram

Fig. 5.6. Attachment of clutch cable to pedal

Fig. 5.9. Removing spring clip from release bearing shaft

5.2 Removing clutch cover

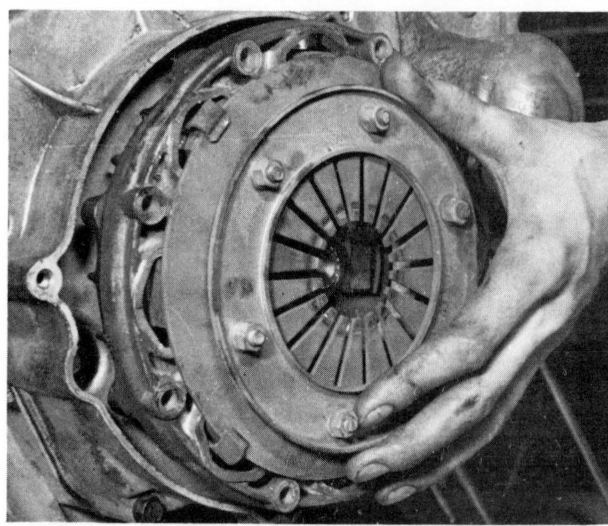

5.3 Removing the pressure plate assembly

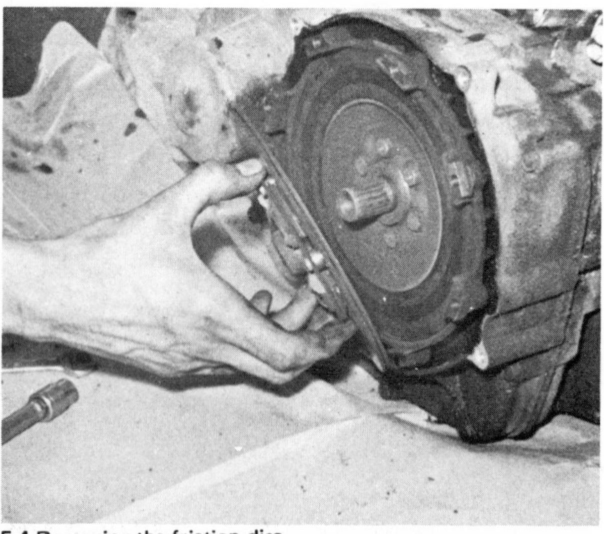

5.4 Removing the friction disc

5.5 Removing the clutch drum

6 Clutch components - inspection and servicing

1 Examine the faces of the pressure plate and clutch drum. If there is heavy scoring or grooves, renew the components.
2 Examine the segments of the diaphragm spring for cracks or distortion. Dismantling of the pressure plate assembly is not recommended and in the event of a fault or wear occurring - renew it on an exchange basis.
3 Examine the friction disc linings for wear, loose rivets, cracks, worn hub splines and perished torsion rubbers.
4 If the linings are nearly worn down to the rivets, renew the disc to avoid later major dismantling.
5 The surface of the friction material may be highly glazed but provided the pattern of the friction material can be clearly seen, the disc is suitable for further use. If the linings are stained or saturated with oil, rectify the cause (almost certainly failed clutch drum oil seal) and renew the linings.
6 Extract the larger seal from the crankcase left-hand side cover and drift in a new one, keeping it perfectly square and with the lip towards the engine.
7 Renew the oil seal in the centre of the clutch drum using a suitable drift.
8 Check the condition of the clutch release bearing. If it is worn or noisy renew it. This is carried out by supporting the bearing so that it rests on two blocks (shaft downwards) and then tapping the larger endface of the shaft, to drive the shaft from the bearing.
9 Check the release lever pivot pin for excessive wear. The hole may be drilled out and an oversize pin inserted if necessary.
10 Check the release bearing shaft bushing in the projecting boss of the clutch housing and renew if there is visible wear.

Fig. 5.10. Release bearing shaft bushing and retaining circlip

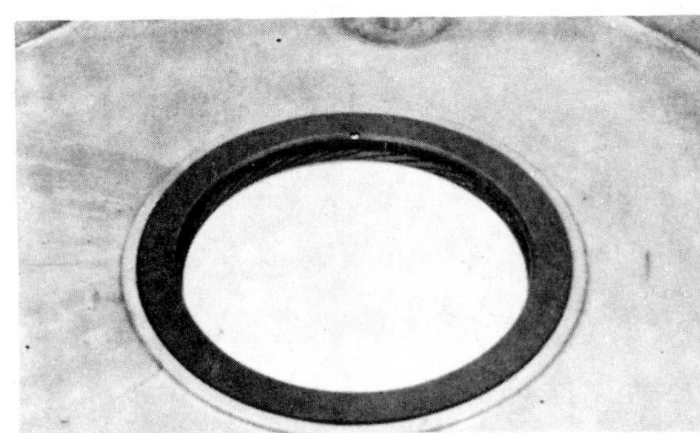

Fig. 5.11. Crankcase left-hand cover oil seal

7 Clutch - reassembly

1 Reassembly is a reversal of dismantling but check the following points. The longer boss of the friction disc splined hub must face towards the clutch housing cover, (photo).
2 Ensure that the release bearing is installed on the shaft so that the seal side is towards the shaft spring clip hole.
3 Grease the inside of the release shaft bushing with high melting point grease.
4 When bolting the pressure plate assembly to the clutch drum, ensure that the mating marks are in alignment Fig. 5.17 in order to maintain rotational balance and to eliminate vibration.

8 Clutch - faults

There are four main faults to which the clutch and release mechanism are prone. They may occur by themselves or in conjunction with any of the other faults. They are; clutch squeal, slip, spin and judder.

9 Clutch squeal - diagnosis and cure

1 If on taking up the drive or when changing gear, the clutch squeals, this is a sure indication of a badly worn clutch release bearing.
2 As well as regular wear due to normal use, wear of the clutch release bearing is much accentuated if the clutch is ridden, or held down for long periods in gear, with the engine running. To minimize wear of this component the car should always be taken out of gear at traffic lights and for similar hold-ups.
3 The clutch release bearing is not an expensive item but difficult to get at.

7.1 Correct installation of clutch friction disc

Fig. 5.12. Renewing the central oil seal of the clutch drum

Fig. 5.13. Removing the release bearing from its shaft

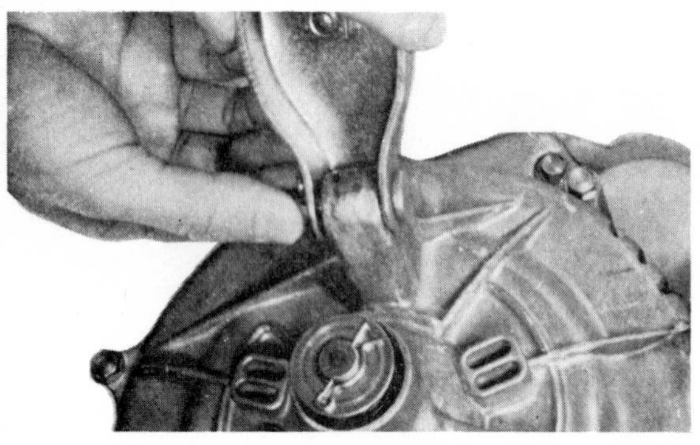

Fig. 5.14. Checking release lever pivot for wear

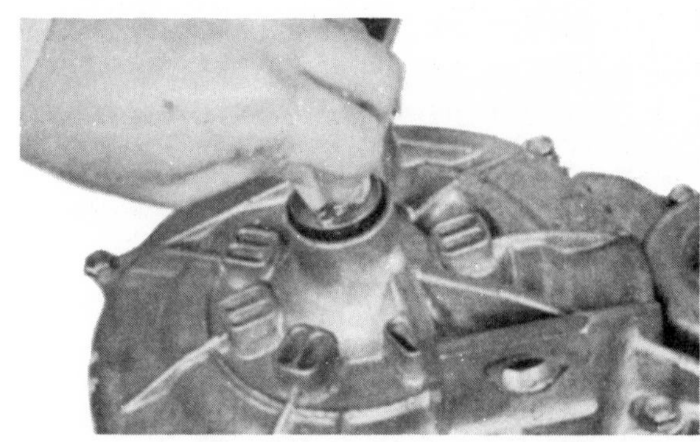

Fig. 5.15. Checking release bearing shaft bushing for wear

Fig. 5.16. Correct orientation of clutch release bearing on its shaft

Fig. 5.17. Clutch pressure plate to drum alignment marks

10 Clutch slip - diagnosis and cure

1 Clutch slip is a self-evident condition which occurs when the clutch friction plate is badly worn; the release arm free travel is insufficient; oil or grease have got onto the drum or pressure plate faces; or the pressure plate itself is faulty.
2 The reason for clutch slip is that, due to one of the faults listed above, there is either insufficient pressure from the pressure plate, or insufficient friction from the friction plate, to ensure solid drive.
3 If small amounts of oil get onto the clutch, they will be burnt off under the heat of clutch engagement, and in the process, gradually darken the linings. Excessive oil on the clutch will burn off leaving a carbon deposit which can cause quite bad slip, or fierceness, spin and judder.
4 If clutch slip is suspected, and confirmation of this condition is required, there are several tests which can be made:
5 With the engine in second or third gear and pulling lightly up a moderate incline, sudden depression of the accelerator pedal may cause the engine to increase its speed without any increase in road speed. Easing off on the accelerator will then give a definite drop in engine speed without the car slowing.
6 In extreme cases of clutch slip the engine will race under normal acceleration conditions.
7 If slip is due to oil or grease on the linings a temporary cure can sometimes be effected by squirting carbon tetrachloride into the clutch. The permanent cure is, of course, to renew the clutch driven plate and trace and rectify the oil leak.

11 Clutch spin - diagnosis and cure

1 Clutch spin is a condition which occurs when the release arm free travel is excessive; there is an obstruction in the clutch either on the primary gear splines, or in the operating lever itself; or oil may have partially burnt off the clutch linings and have left a resinous deposit which is causing the clutch disc to stick to the pressure plate or drum.
2 The reason for clutch spin is that due to any or a combination of, the faults just listed, the clutch pressure plate is not completely freeing from the friction disc even with the clutch pedal fully depressed.
3 If clutch spin is suspected, the condition can be confirmed by extreme difficulty in changing gear, and very sudden take-up of the clutch drive at the fully depressed end of the clutch pedal travel as the clutch is released.

If these points are checked and found to be in order then the fault lies internally in the clutch, and it will be necessary to remove the clutch for examination.

12 Clutch judder - diagnosis and cure

1 Clutch judder is a self-evident condition which occurs when the gearbox or engine mountings are loose or too flexible; when the gearbox or engine mountings are loose or too flexible; when there is oil on the faces of the clutch friction disc or when the clutch pressure plate has been incorrectly adjusted.
2 The reason for clutch judder is that due to one of the faults just listed, the clutch pressure plate is not freeing smoothly from the friction disc, and is snatching.
3 Clutch judder normally occurs when the clutch pedal is released in first or reverse gears, and the whole car shudders as it moves backwards or forwards.

Chapter 6 Manual gearbox, final drive and automatic transmission

Contents

Specifications

Part 1: Manual gearbox

Type	Constant mesh, four forward speeds and reverse
Ratios:	
1st	2.529 : 1
2nd	1.565 : 1
3rd	1.000 : 1
4th	0.714 : 1 (Estate Wagon 360 cc/21.5 cu in.) 0.649 : 1
Reverse	2.437 : 1

Part 2: Final drive (differential unit)

Reduction gear type	Helical
Reduction ratio:	
360 cc/21.5 cu in. (manual)	3.192 : 1
360 cc/21.5 cu in. (Estate Wagon)	3.954 : 1
360 cc/21.5 cu in. (automatic)	3.542 : 1
600 cc/35.5 cu in. (manual)	3.037 : 1
600 cc/35.5 cu in. (automatic)	3.542 : 1

Part 3: Automatic transmission

Torque convertor	3 element, single stage, two phase
Primary drive	Single chain

Reduction ratio (crankshaft to transmission):

360 cc/21.5 cu in.	2.118
600 cc/35.5 cu in.	1.526

Primary clutch	Multi-plate wet type
Transmission	Constant mesh, 3 forward speeds and reverse

Gear ratios:

360 cc/21.5 cu in.	1st	2.556 : 1	600 cc/35.5 cu in.	2.421 : 1
	2nd	1.357 : 1		1.357 : 1
	3rd	0.861 : 1		0.838 : 1
	Reverse	3.857 : 1		3.857 : 1

Capacity	5½ pints (3.2 litres)

Torque wrench settings:	**lb/ft**	**kg/m**
Manual gearbox		
Lock ball spring cap bolts	28	3.871
Final drive (differential unit)		
Driven gear securing bolts	20	2.765
Automatic transmission		
Main valve body securing screws	5	0.691
Torque convertor case bolts	9	1.244
Torque convertor case cover bolts	7	0.967
Crankcase right-hand cover bolts	9	1.200
Crankcase half section bolts (small)	8	1.106
Crankcase half section bolts (large)	20	2.765

Part 1 : Manual gearbox

1 General description of manual gearbox

The gearbox is of constant mesh four-spreed type with reverse gear. The power train includes the drive from the crankshaft drive sprocket through the primary chains to the driven sprocket and clutch mechanism. The gearbox mainshaft then transmits the power through the selected gears to the integral final drive (differential unit and through the driveshafts to the front road wheels.

Lubrication of the gearbox and differential components is by a common oil supply, contained within the crankcase.

The gear selector mechanism comprises the necessary shift plates, forks and shafts with adequate interlock devices to prevent the selection of more than one gear at a time. The gear selector hand control may be steering column or floor mounted.

2 Gearbox - removal and refitting

1 As the gearbox forms part of a unit which includes the engine and differential, access to it can only be attained by removing the engine/transmission from the car as described in Chapter 1.
2 Installation is again as described for the complete unit in Chapter 1.

3 Gearbox - removal and refitting of major assemblies

1 With the engine/transmission assembly removed from the car, invert it and then remove the right-hand side cover from the crankcase, discard the gasket and obtain a new one.
2 Bend back the lockwasher and remove the bolt which secure the reverse gearshift fork.
3 Remove the reverse gearshift fork and reverse gear from thı selector shaft.
4 Remove the crankcase half housing after withdrawal of the securing bolts and right-hand main bearing retainer bolts as described in Section 16, of Chapter 1.
5 Lift out the mainshaft assembly from the upper half of the crankcase followed by the countershaft assembly (photo).
6 Refitting of the two assemblies is a reversal of removal but align carefully the oil holes and pegs of the main bearings.

4 Mainshaft and countershaft - checking for wear before dismantling

1 Temporarily, lay the mainshaft and countershaft assemblies into the half housing.
2 Measure the clearance between the needle roller bearing and the mainshaft top gear and then between the countershaft needle roller bearing and low gear using a feeler gauge. If the endfloat in either case is greater than 0.0158 in (0.4 mm) renew the thrust washer ("C" mainshaft; "A" countershaft), selecting them from the three thicknesses which are available (0.05906 in 1.5 mm, 0.06888 in 1.75 mm 0.07874 in 2.0 mm), and dismantling and reassembling the shafts as described in the following two Sections.
3 Measure the endfloat of the mainshaft third gear by measuring the clearance of the cotters within their mainshaft groove with a feeler gauge. If it is more than 0.0197 in (0.5 mm) renew the cotters.

5 Mainshaft - dismantling, examination, reassembly

1 Remove the circlip from the groove just in front of the reverse gear.
2 Withdraw the reverse gear from the mainshaft, detach the snap ring from the groove in the needle bearing retainer and remove the retainer.
3 Remove the thrust washer "C", fourth gear and thrust washer "B".
4 Withdraw the 3rd/4th shift gear, detach the snap ring and

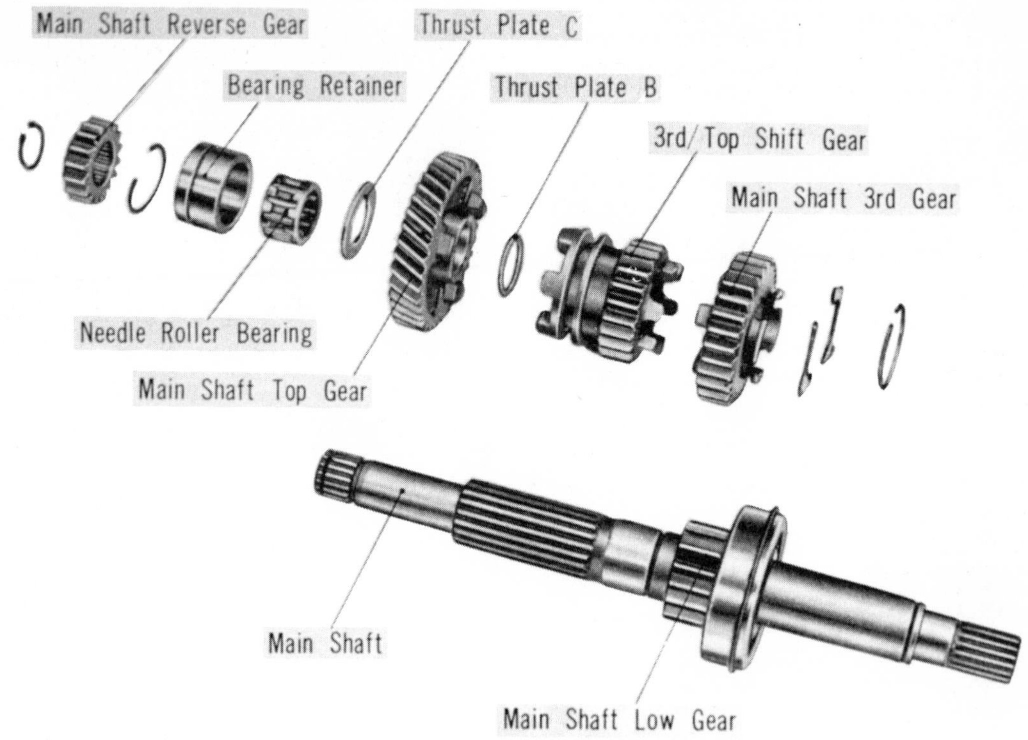

Fig. 6.1. Components of the mainshaft

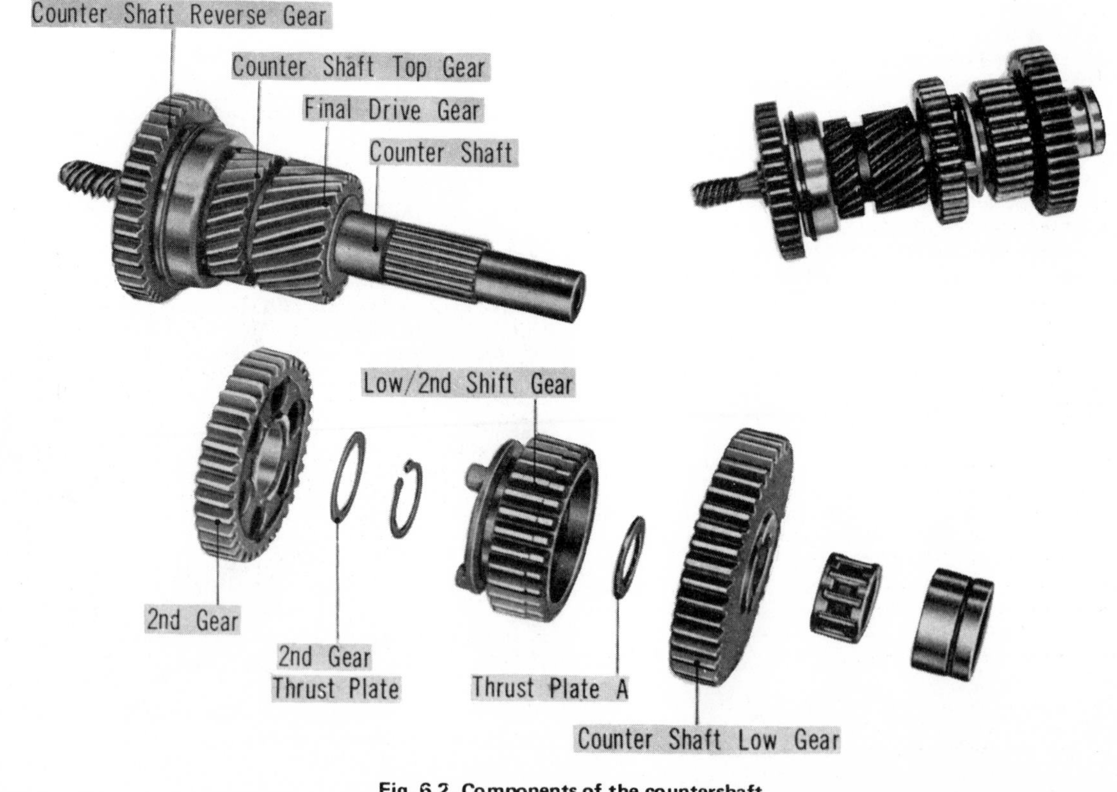

Fig. 6.2. Components of the countershaft

remove the third gear.

5 Measure the diameter of the mainshaft with a micrometer at several different points to test for out of roundness. Now compare the outside diameters of the shaft with the internal bore dimensions of the gears. If there is a running clearance of more than 0.0039 in (0.1 mm) the components must be renewed.

6 Test for shaft spline wear by turning the shift gears as shown in Fig. 6.10.

7 Measure the gear dogs on the 3rd/4th shift gear with a vernier gauge. If the measurement shown in Fig. 6.11 is less than 0.3780 in (9.6 mm) on the 3rd gear side, or 0.3701 in (9.4 mm) on the fourth gear side, the gear must be renewed.

8 Measure the clearance of the bearing snap rings in their grooves using a feeler gauge. If the clearance is more than 0.0028 in (0.07 mm) renew the rings.

9 Measure the wear of the 3rd/fourth shift fork finger as shown in Fig. 6.13. If the measurement is below 0.1811 in (4.6 mm) the fork must be renewed. Reassembly is a reversal of dismantling but check the backlash of the gears (locked) which should not exceed 0.0079 in (0.2 mm). Locate the thrust washers with chamfered faces leading.

Fig. 6.3. Measuring clearance between mainshaft roller bearing and top gear

6 Countershaft - dismantling, examination, reassembly

1 Remove the needle bearing circlip and withdraw the needle bearing retainer and then the needle bearing.

2 Withdraw the 1st gear and thrust washer "A".

3 From the splined end of the countershaft remove the 1st/2nd shift gear, the circlip and thrust washer followed by the 2nd gear.

4 Do not attempt to remove the reverse gear from the countershaft. If either component is worn renew the assembly.

5 Measure the diameter of the countershaft with a micrometer at several different points to test for out of roundness. Now compare the outside diameters of the shaft with the internal bore dimensions of the gears. If there is a running clearance of more than 0.0039 in (0.1 mm), the components must be renewed.

6 Test for spline wear in a manner similar to that described for the mainshaft in paragraph 5 of the preceding Section.

7 Measure the width of the 1st/2nd shift gear dogs and if less than 0.3701 in (9.2 mm) renew the gear.

8 Measure the clearance of the bearing snap rings as described in paragraph 7 of the preceding Section.

9 Measure the wear of the 1 st/2nd shift fork as described in paragraph 8 of the preceding Section.

10 Reassembly of the countershaft is a reversal of dismantling but check gear backlash as for mainshaft and locate thrust washers with chamfered faces leading.

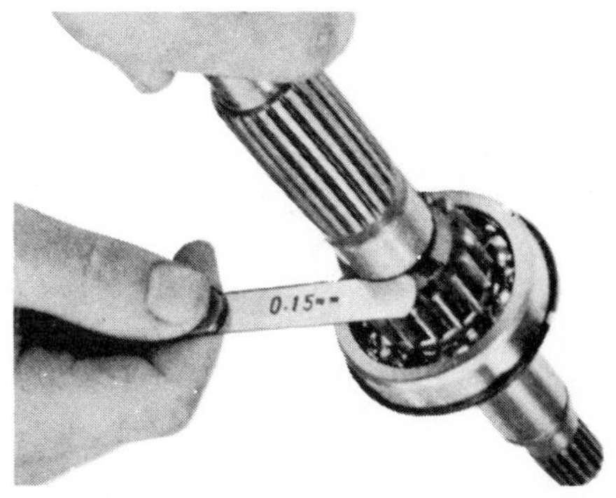

Fig. 6.4. Measuring mainshaft third gear endfloat

7 Gearshift mechanism - dismantling and reassembly

1 Bend back the tabs from the shaft lock bolts and unscrew them. (photo)

2 Unscrew the securing bolts and remove the interlock guide plate, then remove the interlock pin and balls (photo).

3 Withdraw the shafts and detach the shift forks.

4 Loosen the lock ball spring cap bolts and withdraw the washers springs and balls from the gear shift rod and reverse pin (photo).

5 Remove the reverse spring seat and withdraw the restrictor pin and spring. (photos)

6 Bend back the tab washer and remove the gearshift arm setscrew (photo). Pull out the arm and oil seal assembly. (photo).

7 Unscrew and remove the gearshift guide plate setscrews and withdraw the guide plate assembly from the crankcase housing. (photo).

3.5 Removing mainshaft assembly

6.10 Location of countershaft thrust washer

7.1 Removing a selector shaft lock bolt

7.2a Unbolting the interlock guide plate

7.2b Removing the interlock pin

7.2c Location of the interlock balls

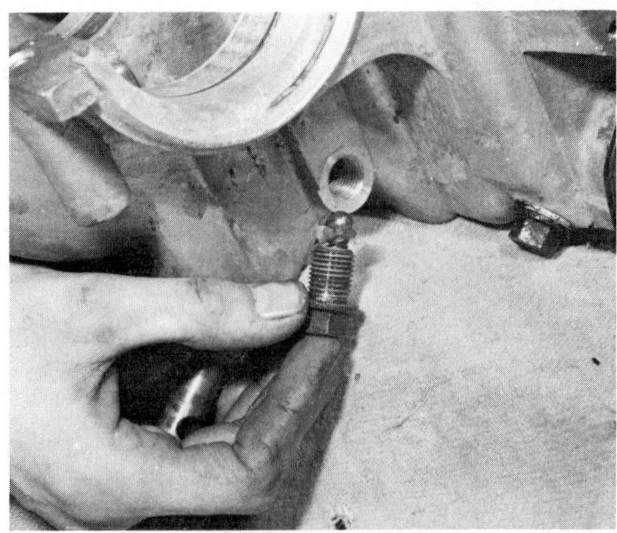
7.4a Gearshift rod cap bolt and ball

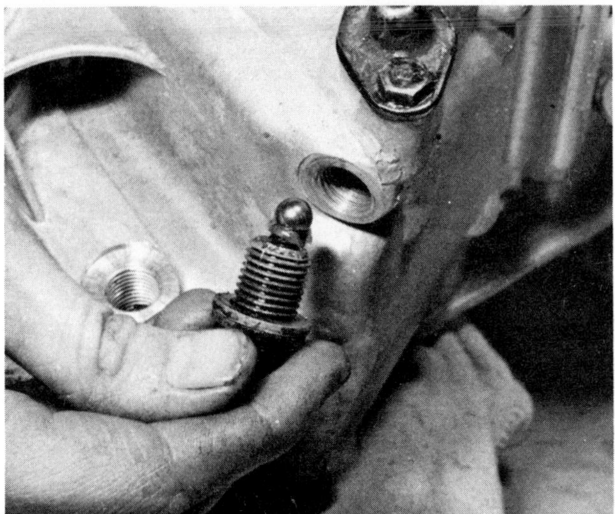
7.4b Reverse restrictor pin cap bolt and ball

7.5a Removing the reverse spring seat

7.5b Reverse restrictor pin and spring

7.6a Gearshift arm setscrew and locking tab

7.6b Withdrawing the gearshift arm and oil seal assembly

7.7 Removing the guide plate assembly from the crankcase

Fig. 6.5. Removing circlip from face of mainshaft reverse gear

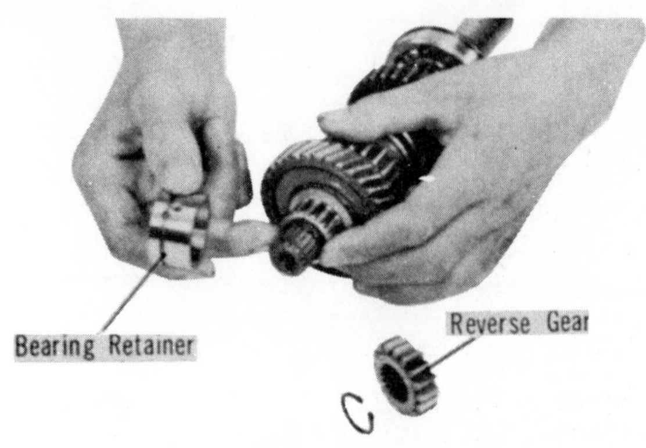

Fig. 6.6. Withdrawing reverse gear and bearing retainer from mainshaft

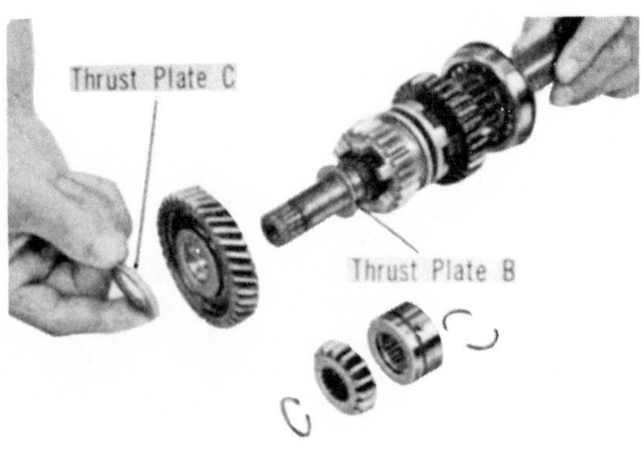

Fig. 6.7. Removing thrust washers and fourth gear from mainshaft

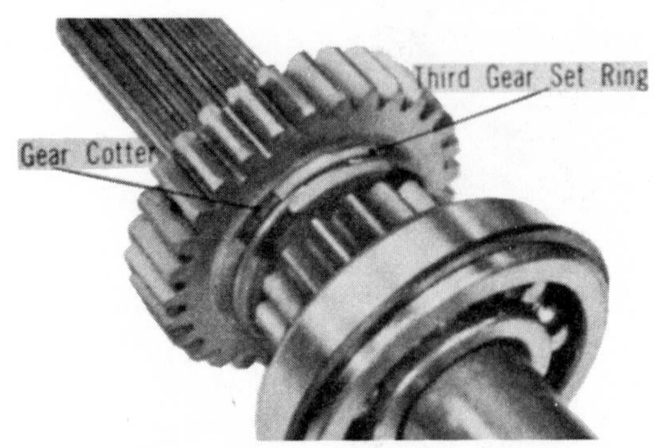

Fig. 6.8. Removing third gear from mainshaft

Fig. 6.9. Measuring bore of gear wheel

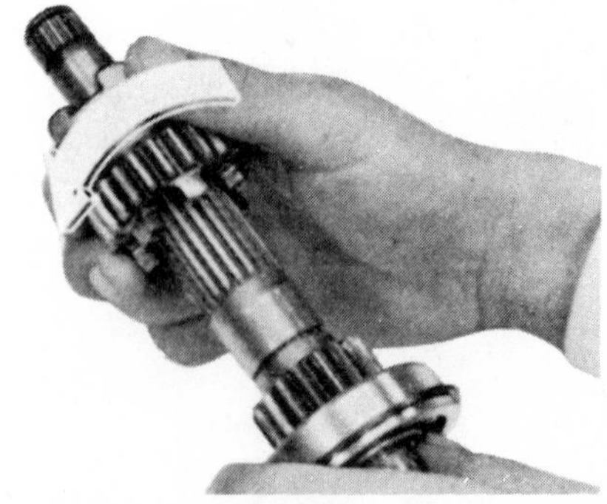

Fig. 6.10. Testing for spline wear

Fig. 6.11. Shift gear dog wear measurement diagram

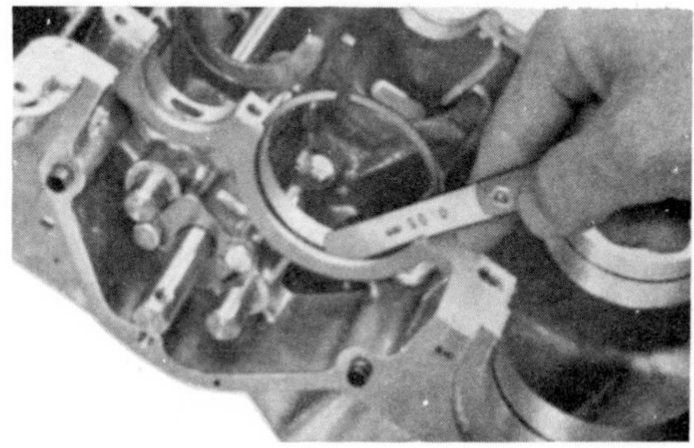

Fig. 6.12. Measuring bearing snap ring clearance in groove

Fig. 6.13. Measuring wear of shift fork finger

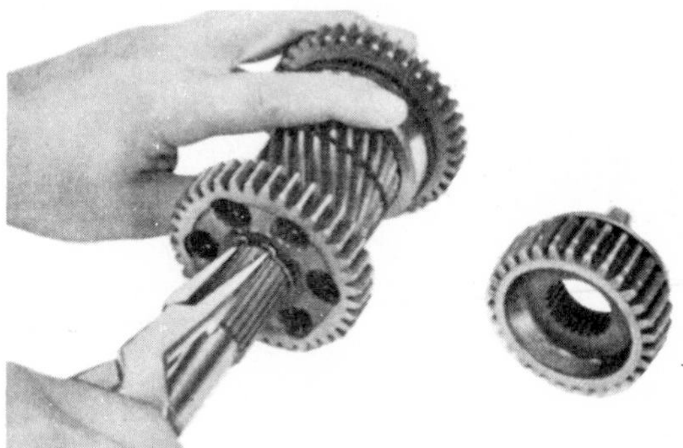

Fig. 6.14. Removing 2nd gear retaining circlip from countershaft

Fig. 6.15. Fitting thrust washer to shaft with chamfered face leading

Fig. 6.16. Location of shift forks and shafts

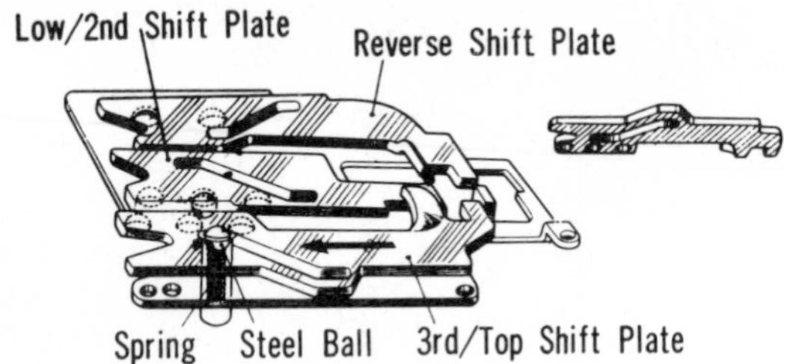

Fig. 6.17. Identification of shift plates

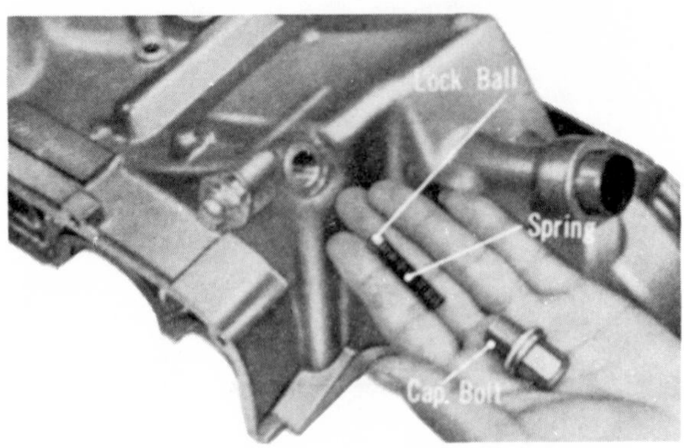

Fig. 6.21. Components of a lock ball assembly

Fig. 6.22. Location of reverse gear restrictor pin and lock ball holes

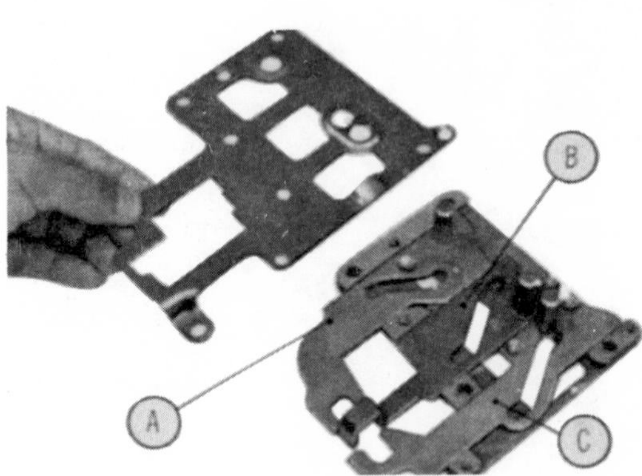

Fig. 6.24. Identification of gearshift guide plates

A Reverse
B 1st/2nd
C 3rd/4th

8 The gearshift guide plate is held together by countersunk screws and a reverse selector lever pivot bolt, which may be removed to renew a worn component.

9 Examine all components for wear, particularly the shaft detents, balls and springs and renew as appropriate.

10 Assembly is a reversal of dismantling but ensure that the lock ball spring cap bolts are tightened to a torque of 28 lb/ft (3.871 kg/m). Always renew the gearshift arm oilseal.

8 Gearshift hand controls and linkage - adjustment

1 Two types of gearshift control may be encountered, the floor mounted type or fascia mounted. The disconnection of both types is described in Chapter 1, Section 4 for the purpose of engine/transmission removal.

2 Both types of control are supported by brackets which have elongated bolt holes to permit minor adjustment to suit the individual drivers' reach.

3 Wear in the universal joint of the fascia mounted type control can be kept to a minimum by peeling back the upper bellows and applying multi-purpose grease periodically.

4 With the gearshift control in neutral, its arc of travel when moved gently to the left, should not exceed 2.4 in (60 mm). If it does, the gear control lever and joint assembly are worn and must be renewed - no adjustment being possible.

Fig. 6.25. Fascia mounted gearshift lever support bracket

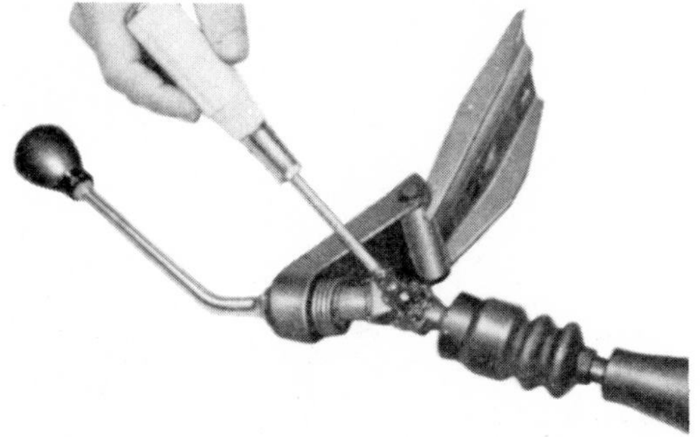

Fig. 6.26. Greasing fascia mounted type lever joint

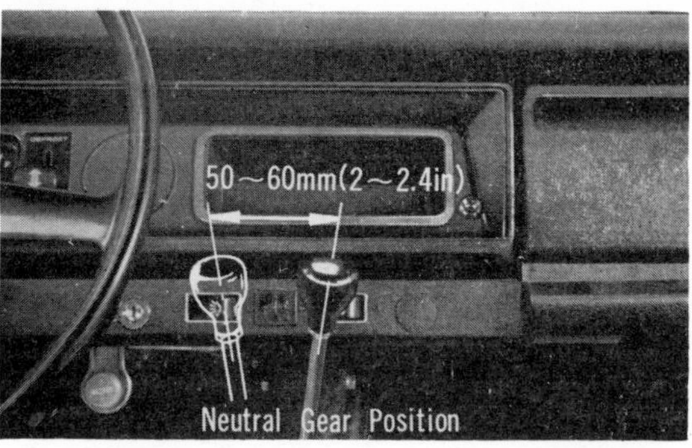

Fig. 6.27. Movement diagram (fascia mounted gearshift control)

9 Manual gearbox - fault diagnosis

Symptom	Cause	Remedy
Noisy operation	Clutch not releasing fully	Adjust free movement.
	Primary drive chains tight	Check tensioner spring.
	Worn primary drive sprocket bearing	Renew.
	Worn mainshaft bearings	Renew.
	Worn countershaft bearings	Renew.
	Worn gearwheels	Renew.
	Sticky clutch friction disc	Clean or renew.
Slips out of gear	Weak detent springs	Renew.
	Worn detent grooves in selector shafts	Renew.
	Worn shift gears	Renew.
	Worn or damaged interlock mechanism	Renew.
Tendency to catch reverse gear when selecting 2nd gear	Weak reverse interlock ball spring	Renew spring or fit shim.

Part 2 : Final drive (differential unit)

10 Final drive (differential) unit - general description

The differential is driven directly by the final drive gear which is an integral part of the countershaft. The differential unit is enclosed within the crankcase together with the transmission gears and relies upon the engine oil supply for lubrication as does the transmission (manual only). The final drive is identical for manual and automatic transmission. The principle gears are helically cut for quiet operation.

11 Final drive unit - inspection and adjustment

1 The final drive is accessible after removal of the engine/transmission and removal of the crankcase lower half housing as described in Chapter 1.

2 Remove the final drive unit from the crankcase. Using a dial gauge and holding the final driven gear and one driveshaft joint flange quite still, check the backlash by moving the opposite joint flange in both directions as shown in Fig. 6.29. If the backlash is greater than 0.0158 in (0.4 mm) check for wear in the differential side gear splines and renew if necessary. Check the movement of the pinion gear teeth with the side gear teeth using a feeler gauge, Fig. 6.30. If the movement is greater than between 0.0039 and 0.0079 in (0.1 and 0.2 mm) fit shims to correct.

3 Measure the diameter of the pinion shaft and the bore of the pinion gears at several different points. If any subtraction, the running clearance is greater than 0.0059 in (0.15 mm) renew the components.

4 Finally check the concentricity of the differential driven gear on the carrier. To do this, support the bearings on 'V' blocks and measure the gear at several different points. If eccentricity is greater than 0.0039 in (0.1 mm) bend back the tabs of the lock plates and loosen the securing bolts. Now tap the periphery of the gear until on re-test it comes within the specified tolerance.

12 Final drive unit - dismantling and reassembly

12 Final drive unit - dismantling and reassembly

1 Refer to Fig. 6.28 and detach the circlips (15). Withdraw the joint flanges (2), oil seals (10) and thrust washers (17).

2 Bend back the tabs on the lockplates (8) unscrew the securing bolts (12) and remove the driven gear (3).

3 Bend back the tabs on the lockplates (9) unscrew and remove the bolts (14) and remove the differential carrier cap (5) from the carrier (4).

4 Dismantle the differential gears and pinion shaft, noting the location of the 'O' ring adjacent to the splines on each of the differential side gears.

5 Examine the bearings for wear and if they must be renewed, draw them off the differential and carrier and press on new ones.

6 Before reassembling renew the 'O' rings, oil seals and lock-

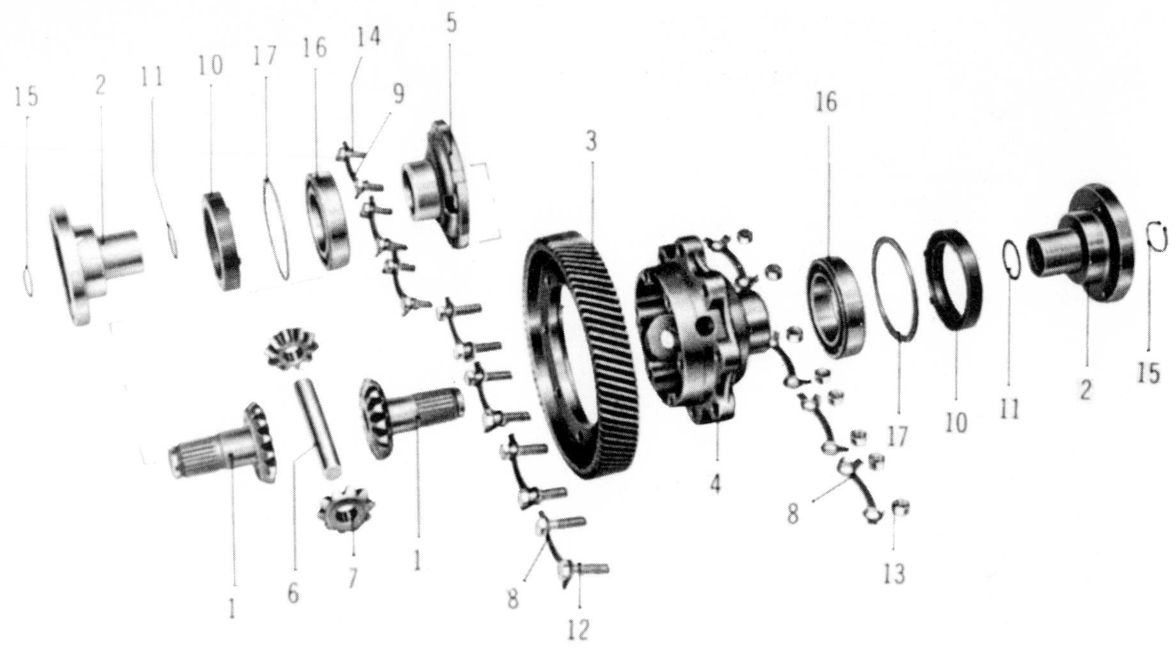

Fig. 6.28. Exploded view of differential unit

1 *Differential side gear*
2 *Drive joint flange*
3 *Driven gear*
4 *Differential carrier*
5 *Carrier cap*
6 *Pinion shaft*
7 *Pinion gear*
8 *Lock plates*
9 *Lock plates*
10 *Oil seal*
11 *'O' ring*
12 *Bolt*
13 *Nut*
14 *Bolt*
15 *Circlip*
16 *Ball race*
17 *Thrust washer*

Fig. 6.29. Checking differential back lash

Fig. 6.30. Checking mesh of pinion and side gear teeth

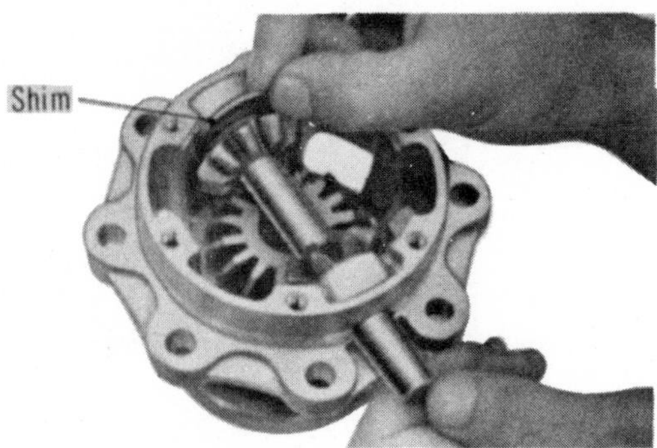

Fig. 6.31. Fitting shims to adjust mesh of gear teeth

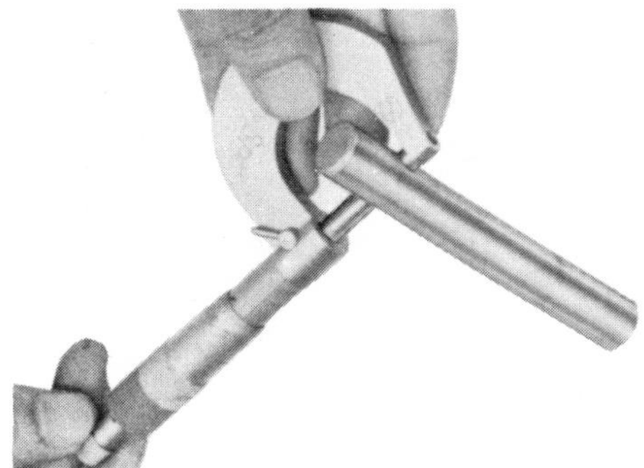

Fig. 6.32. Checking pinion shaft for wear

Fig. 6.33. Checking that driven gear is mounted concentrically on differential carrier

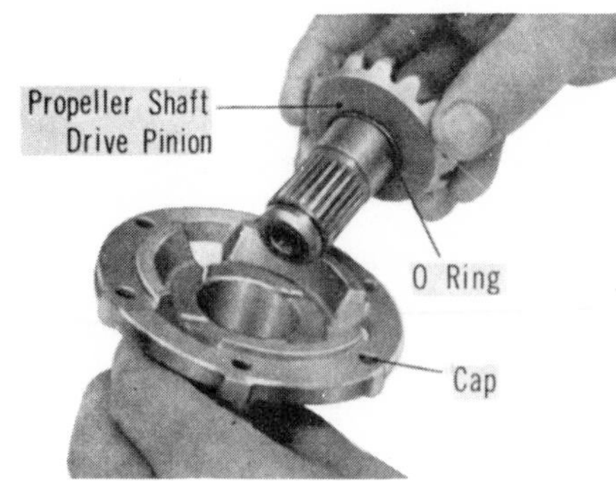

Fig. 6.34. Location of 'O' ring on differential side gear

Fig. 6.35. Prising oil seals against bearings prior to fitting crankcase lower half section

plates.

7 Reassembly is a reverseal of dismantling but tighten the driven gear securing bolts to a torque of 20 lb/ft (2.765 kg/m) and check for concentric mounting as described in the preceding Section. Bend up the tabs of the lockplates.

8 When installing the differential unit into the crankcase prise the oil seals against the ball bearing races and note that the differential carrier is on the same side as the speedometer gear (photo).

13 Differential oil seals - renewal with unit in vehicle

1 Leakage of oil from the rear of the driveshaft joint flanges is due to failure of the oil seal, or 'O' ring seal, or both. Observe absolute cleanliness during the following operations.

2 Jack up the front of the car and drain the engine oil.

3 Disconnect the driveshaft from the differential flange as described in Chapter 7.

4 Remove the circlip and withdraw the joint flange, catching any oil which may be ejected.

5 Extract the oil seal with a suitable two-legged puller using the endface of the side gear splined shaft as the fulcrum point.

6 Check to see that none of the lip sealing spring rings have

been left inside the casing after removal of the old seal.
7 Pick out the 'O' ring from its location adjacent to the splined section of the side gear and fit a new one.
8 Select the correct oil seal which is marked "L" or "R" according to the side of the car and with a directional arrow which will align with the normal rotation of the driveshaft when the car is moving in a forward direction.
9 Grease the inner and outer edges of the seal and drive it into position with a tubular drift. Keep the seal perfectly square during this operation and as the inner lip has to engage over the projecting boss of the differential carrier cap or carrier, the seal must not be driven in too far until it can be manipulated over the rim of the boss with the fingers. Finally dirve the seal into contact with the bearing race.
10 Refit the joint flange, circlip and driveshaft.
11 Refill the engine with oil.

12.8 Correct installation of final drive

Part 3 : Automatic transmission

14 Automatic transmission - general description

The 'Hondamatic' automatic transmission may be optionally specified on all models in the range. It provides three forward speeds and reverse.

The gear-train is located within the crankcase housing as for manually operated transmission but to facilitate access for servicing, the automatic content of the mechanism and hydraulic assemblies can be serviced from the left or right-hand sides without the necessity of splitting the crankcase or removing the engine head or block.

On the left-hand side of the engine are located the torque convertor, hydraulic controls, primary reduction and clutch mechanism, the regulator valve and fluid pressure pump.

On the right-hand side of the engine are located the reverse gear, starter and generator.

The torque convertor is located at the left-hand end of the crankshaft and transmits engine power through the primary drive sprocket and chain to the primary driven sprocket and primary clutch assembly. The primary clutch is actuated automatically by fluid pressure which increases with the engine speed.

Changes of speed are carried out within pre-determined ranges by the internal clutches, pressure and servo valves of the hydraulic system and depend upon engine and vehicle speeds and the relationship of the throttle secondary cable to the transmission throttle valves. With the speed selector lever in 'D' the transmission is completedly automatic and will adjust itself to all road requirements and also provide a 'kick-down' facility which will give an immediate change to a lower gear for overtaking purposes.

Manual selection of the three forward speeds is provided for, and when '1','2' or '3' is selected, the transmission remains locked in that particular speed range.

The selection of 'P' ensures a mechanical lock-up with a pawl engaging with second gear. When the handbrake is applied at the same time, this provides locking of all four road wheels.

It is not recommended that individual assemblies of the automatic transmission are stripped and serviced by the home mechanic but operations limited to those described in this Chapter for the purpose of gaining access to the engine components.

Fig. 6.36. Extracting oil seal (differential in position in car)

15 Automatic transmission - removal and refitting

1 As the automatic transmission forces part of a unit which includes the engine and differential, access to it can only be attained by removing the engine/automatic transmission unit as described in Chapter 1.
2 Installation is again as described for the complete unit in Chapter 1.

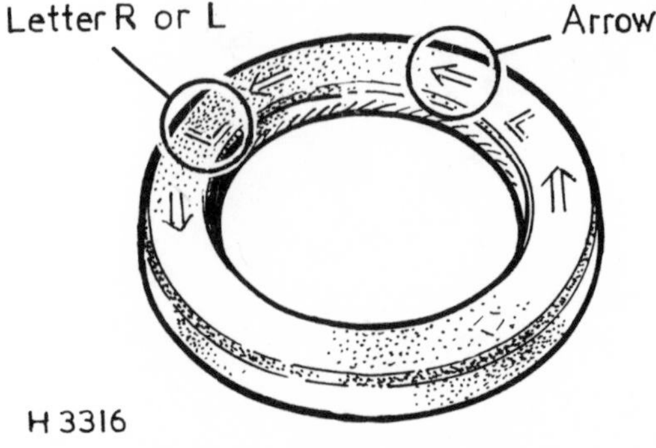

Fig. 6.37. Identification marks on a differential unit oil seal

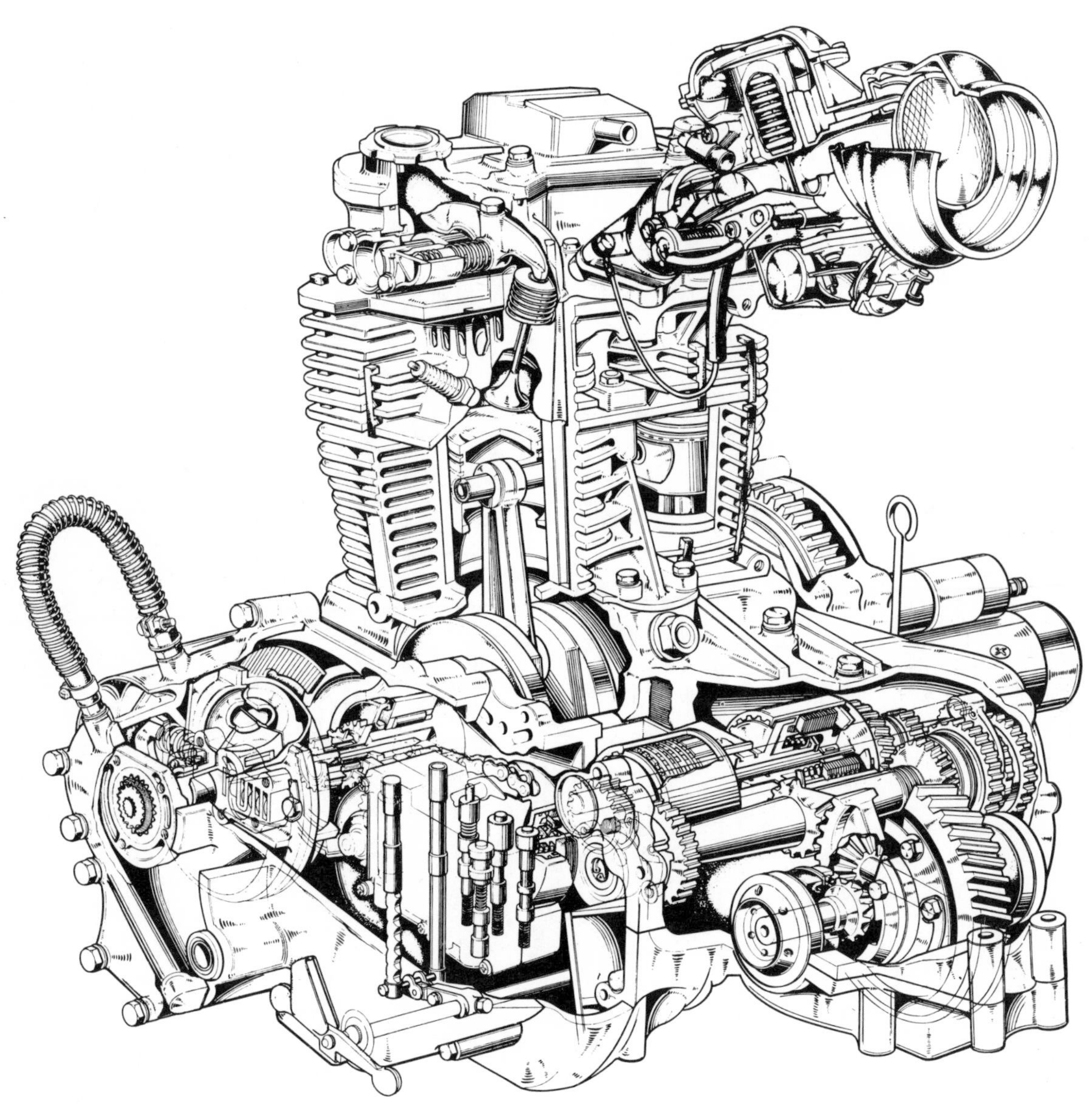

Fig. 6.38. Cutaway view of automatic transmission

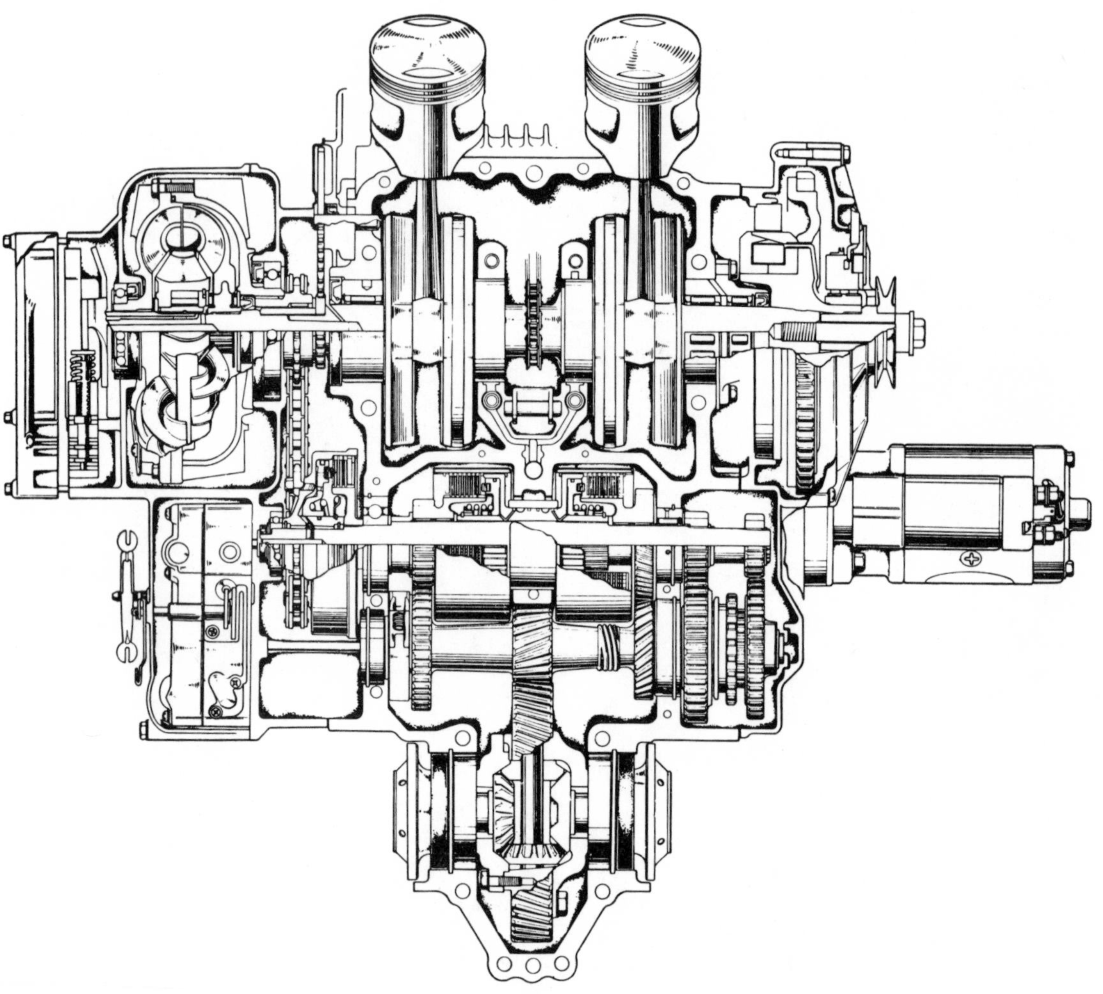

Fig. 6.39. Sectional view of engine/automatic transmission/final drive unit

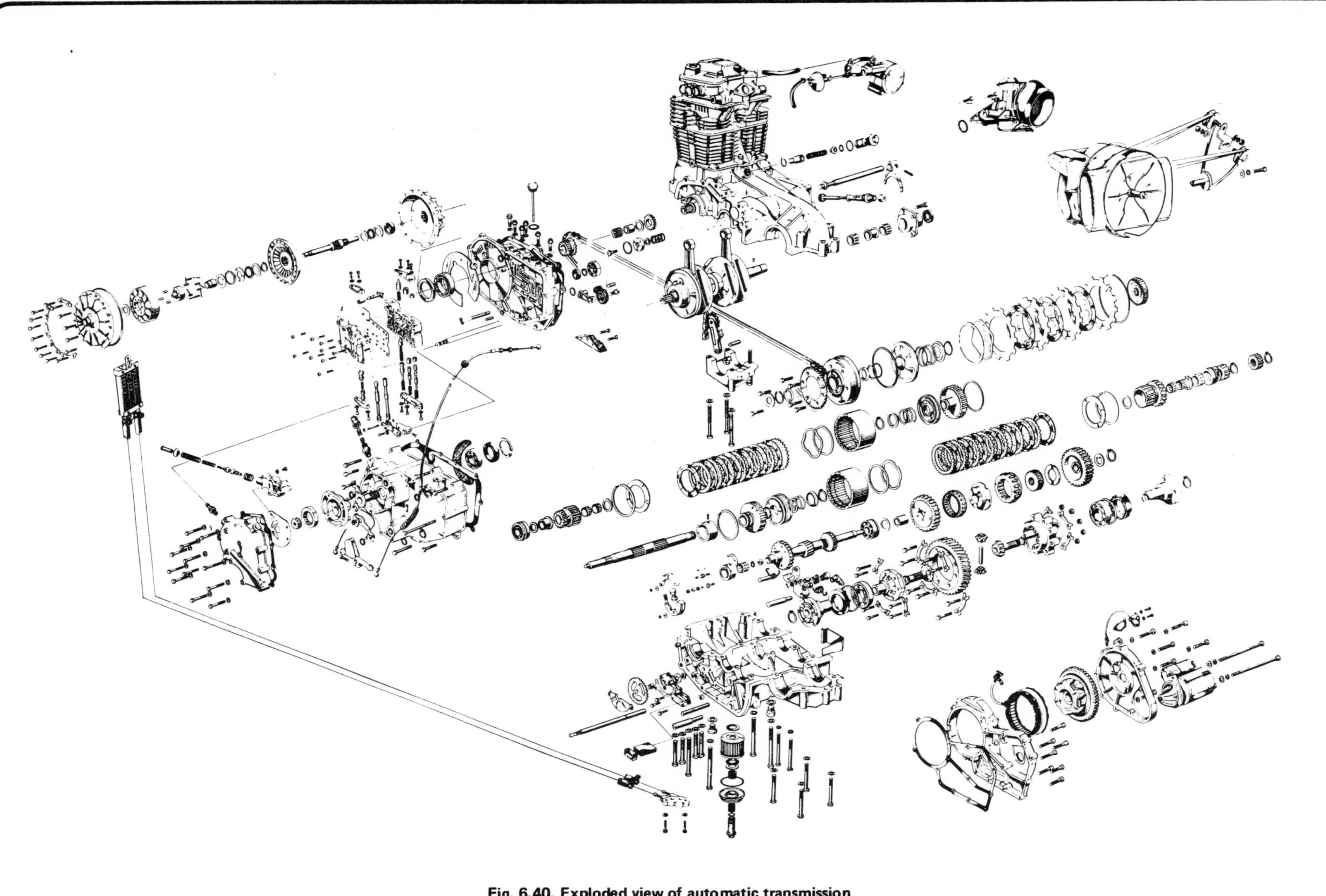

Fig. 6.40. Exploded view of automatic transmission

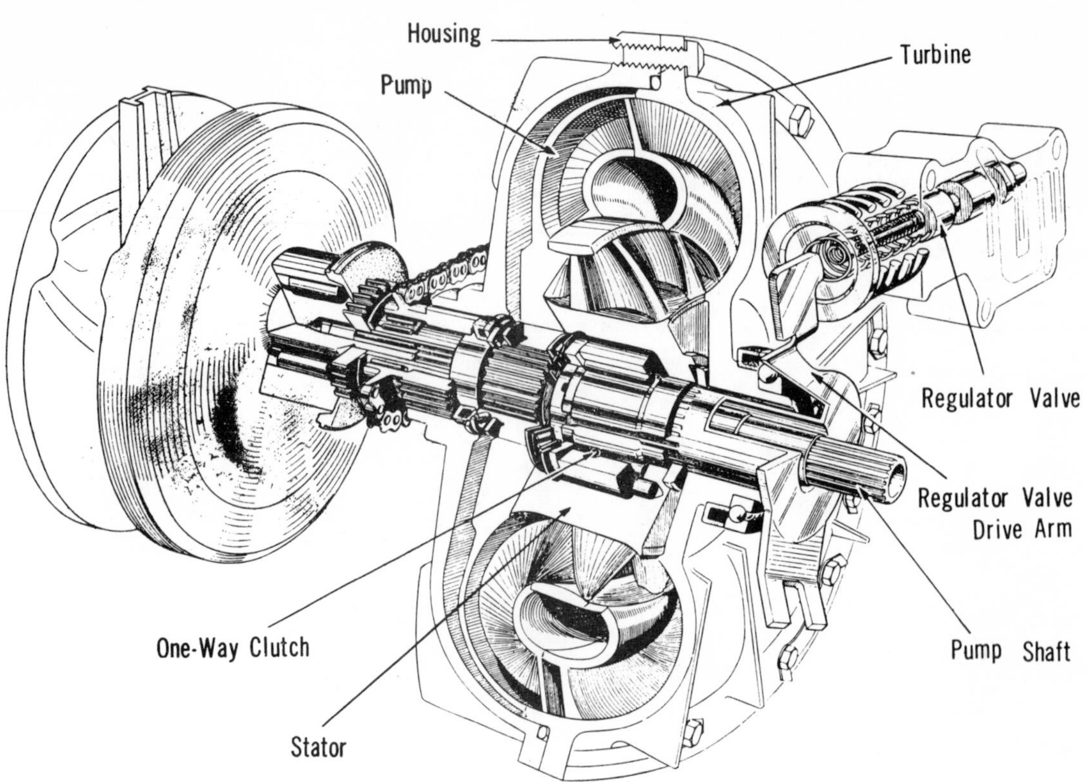

Fig. 6.41. Cutaway view of torque convertor

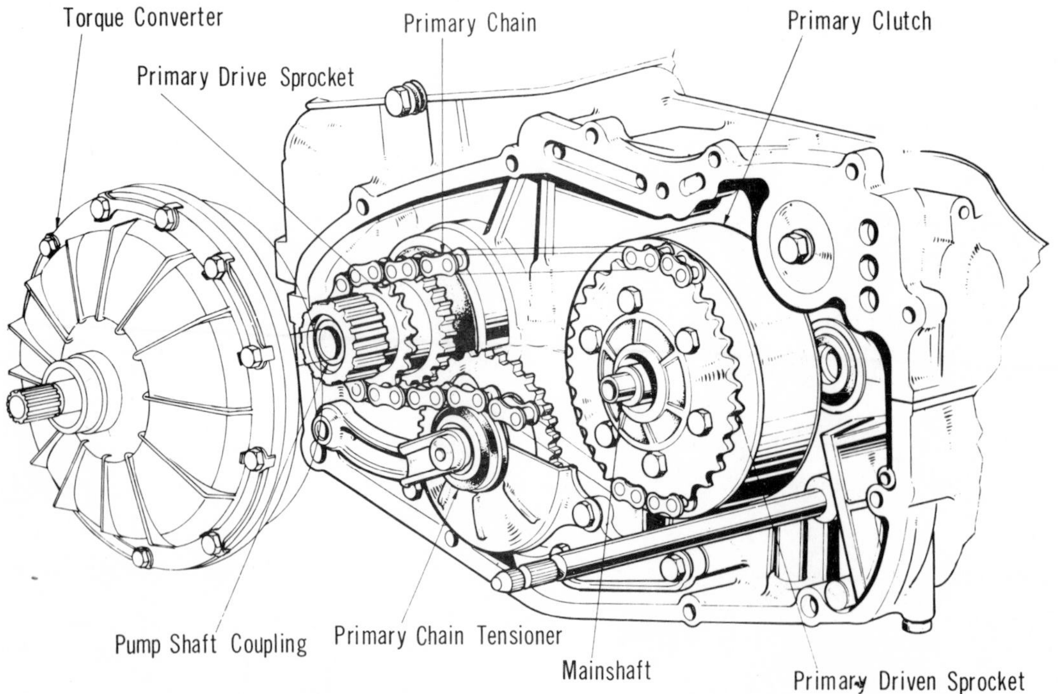

Fig. 6.42. Automatic transmission primary drive mechanism

16 Removal of automatic transmission components from engine (left-hand side)

1 Remove the non-return valve hose from the torque convertor case.

2 Remove the securing bolts and withdraw the torque convertor casing cover, complete with regulator valve.

3 Remove the pressure pump housing and gears as a unit from the pump shaft and then detach the regulator valve drive arm.

4 Detach the throttle valve drive arm and the manual valve control lever from the front of the torque convertor case, remove the securing bolts and withdraw the torque convertor case.

5 Pull the torque convertor from the crankshaft. Considerable force will be needed to achieve this. Use the hands only and do not resort to levers or the convertor will be damaged.

6 Remove the manual shift valve lock bolt (Fig. 6.50) and the nine bolts which secure the valve body to the crankcase cover. Withdraw the valve body.

7 The bolts which secure the crankcase left side cover may now be removed and the cover and fluid strainer removed.

8 Dismantling of the primary drive mechanism is described in Chapter 1, Section 13.

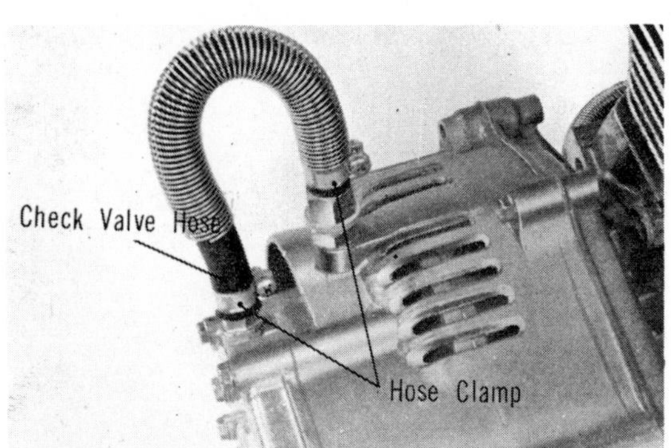

Fig. 6.43. Automatic transmission non-return valve hose

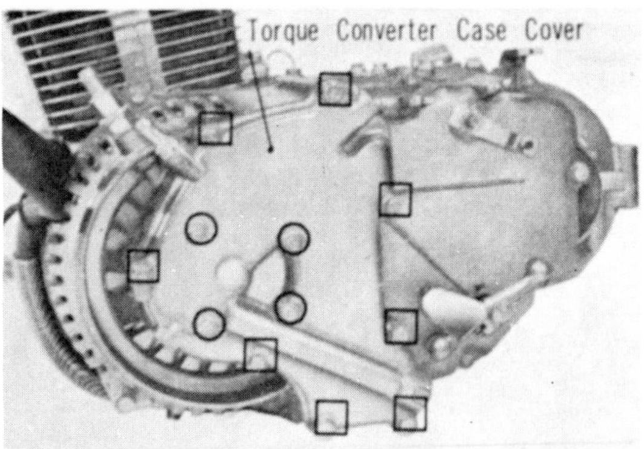

Fig. 6.44. Torque convertor cover securing bolts

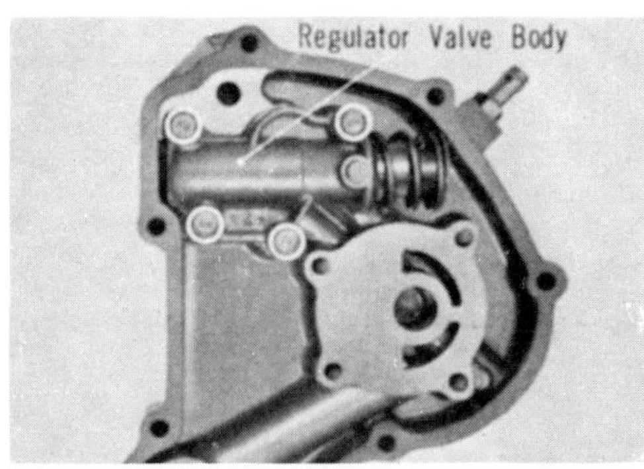

Fig. 6.45. Location of regulator valve within torque convertor case cover

Fig. 6.46. Removing pressure pump assembly from pump shaft

Fig. 6.47. Location of regulator valve drive arm on pump shaft

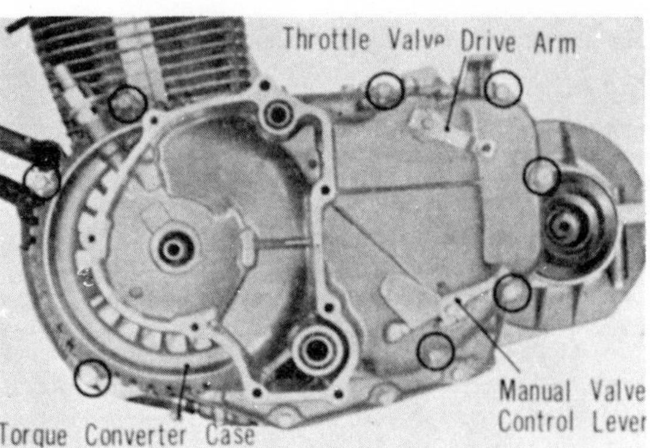

Fig. 6.48. Location of throttle valve drive arm and manual valve control lever

Fig. 6.49. Removing torque convertor

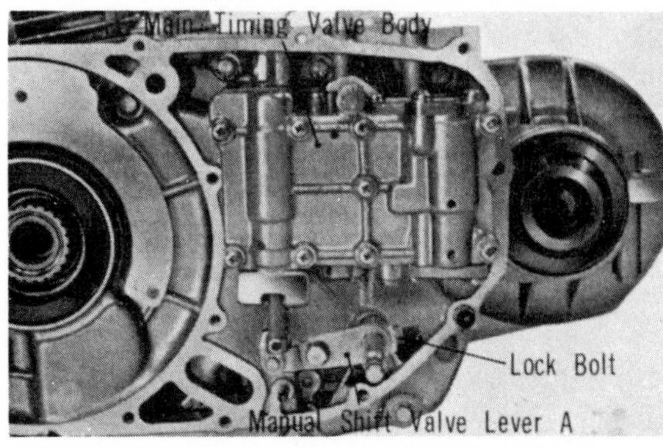

Fig. 6.50. Location of manual shift valve lever and main valve body

Fig. 6.51. Location of crankcase left-hand cover bolts

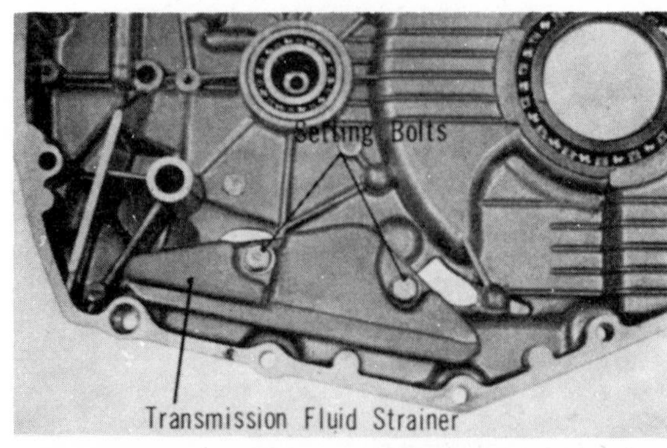

Fig. 6.52. Location of transmission fluid strainer on reverse side of crankcase left-hand side cover

17 Removal of automatic transmission components from engine (right-hand side)

1 Remove the combined starter/dynamo (360 cc 21.5 cu in) or the starter and alternator (600 cc /35.5 cu in) as described in Chapter 11.
2 Unscrew and remove the crankcase right-hand cover securing bolts and remove the cover.
3 Remove the reverse idler shaft and gear.
4 Remove the circlip and reverse gear from the end of the mainshaft.
5 Remove the circlip thrust washer, reverse gear, gear hub and cotters from the end of the countershaft.
6 Partly withdraw the shift fork shaft and drift out the tension pin and then remove the shift forks and reverse selection gear from the countershaft.
7 Remove the circlip and withdraw the low gearwheel from the mainshaft. Remove the clutch hub, one-way clutch, 1st gear, spacer and thrust washer from the countershaft (Fig. 6.56).
8 Unscrew and remove the speedometer drive gear.

18 Crankcase lower section - removal

1 Remove the bolts which hold the lower crankcase half section to the upper crankcase
2 Withdraw the section and then either detach the oil cooler hose clips or remove the bolts from the oil bridge if the crankcase half section is to be removed completely.
3 The mainshaft and countershaft assemblies will now be lying together with the differential unit in the upper crankcase. All three assemblies may be removed but it is not recommended that either the mainshaft or countershaft are dismantled. Servicing of the differential is identical to the procedure described in Part 1, Sections 11 - 13 of this Chapter.

19 Reassembly of left-hand components

1 This is a reversal of removal but the following points must be observed. Use new gaskets and 'O' rings.
2 Ensure that the thrust washer is fitted to the face of the primary driven sprocket.
3 Check the adjustment of the parking lock-up as described in Section 22.
4 Tighten the main valve body screws to a torque of 5 lb/ft (0.691 kg/m).
5 Tighten the torque convertor case bolts to a torque of 9 lb/ft (1.244 kg/m) in diagonal sequence.
6 Tighten the torque convertor case cover bolts to a torque of 7 lb/ft (0.967 kg/m).

20 Reassembly of right- hand and crankcase components

1 This is a reversal of removal but observe the following and renew all sealing gaskets and 'O' rings.
2 Remember to install new 'O' rings at the crankcase oil bridge and apply gasket cement to the crankcase mating faces.
3 Tighten the crankcase bolts to a torque of 9lb/ft (1.2 kg/m) for the smaller ones, and 18 lb/ft (2.5 kg/m) for the larger ones. Tighten in diagonal sequence.
4 Tighten the crankcase right-hand cover bolts to a torque of 9lb/ft (1.2 kg/m)
5 Re-fit the starter and generator assemblies as described in Chapter 11.

21 Parking lock-up - adjustment

1 In the event of the car not being held when 'P' is selected, the

Fig. 6.53. Location of crankcase right-hand cover bolts

Fig. 6.54. Reverse gears

Fig. 6.55. Location of reverse shift fork on countershaft

Fig. 6.56. Location of low gearwheels

Fig. 6.57. Location of speedometer drive gear

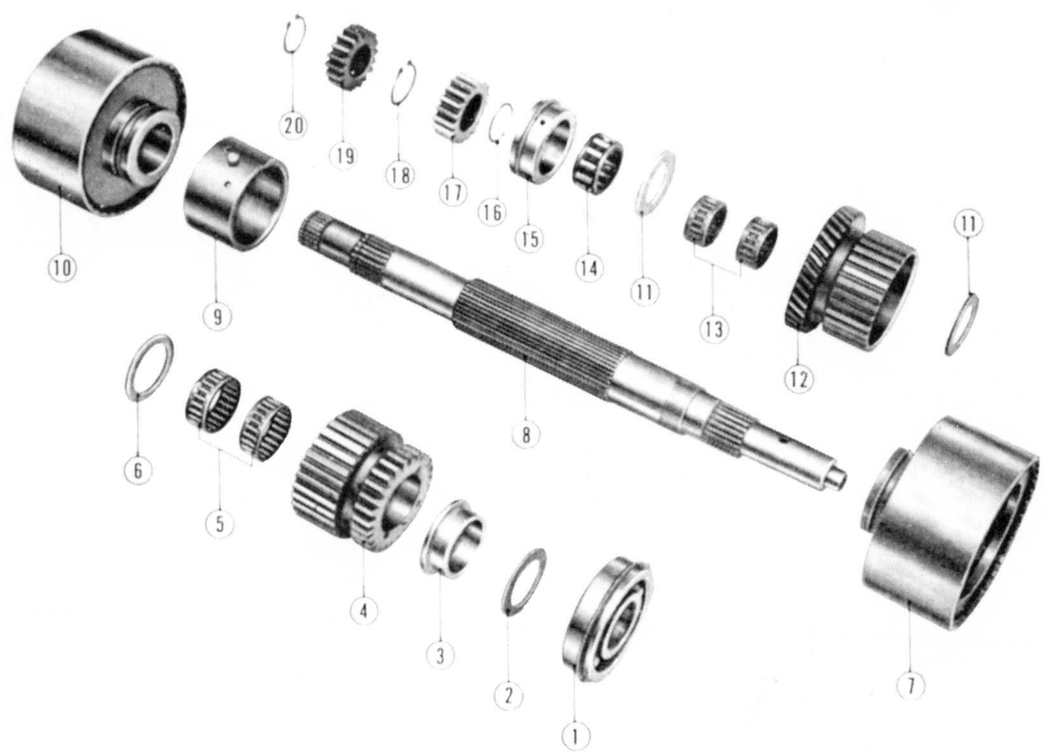

Fig. 6.58. Exploded view of automatic transmission mainshaft

1 *Ball race*
2 *Thrust washer*
3 *Spacer*
4 *2nd gear*
5 *2nd gear needle bearing*
6 *Thrust washer*
7 *Second clutch*
8 *Mainshaft*
9 *Sealing ring guide*
10 *Third clutch*
11 *Thrust washer*
12 *3rd gear*
13 *3rd gear needle bearing*
14 *Needle bearing*
15 *Bearing holder*
16 *Circlip*
17 *Low gearwheel*
18 *Circlip*
19 *Reverse gearwheel*
20 *Circlip*

cause will be lack of engagement between the pawl and the teeth of the second gearwheel of the mainshaft.

2 Remove automatic transmission components including the torque convertor case as described in Section 16.

3 Temporarily fit the manual value control lever to the drive arm shaft and then rotate the control lever until the joint link of the drive arm contacts the manual valve stopper pin. At this point tighten the adjusting nut (Fig. 6.62).

4 Re-fit the transmission components to the left-hand side of the engine as described in Section 19.

22 Automatic transmission - adjustments

1 Apart from topping-up and changing the automatic transmission fluid as recommended in the 'Routine Maintenance' section of this manual, cable adjustment is the only likely operation required at infrequent intervals.

2 With the speed selector lever in 'N' adjust the idling speed to 1200 rev/min. Switch off the engine.

3 Check for play at the throttle cam lever mounting on the torque convertor casing. The cam lever should be in balance between the long and short throttle valves without the secondary cable exerting any force upon it. Adjust the nut at the carburettor end of the cable to attain this situation.

4 Set the mating marks on the drive arm shaft and the control lever in alignment with the 'N' mark on the transmission casing. Adjust the cables by rotating the nuts at the bracket until all slack has been removed from them and yet the control lever is not undertension in either direction.

5 Check the correct selection of all speed positions by moving the hand control without the engine running. Start the engine and repeat the test. Each engagement should occur when the appropriate speed or position, number or letter is 1/3 rd of the way into the index window.

6 Road test the car and check the speed shift positions. These should be as follows:

	360cc/21.5 cu in	600 cc/35.5 cu in
1st to 2nd gear	22 mph (35 km/h)	26 mph (42 km/h)
2nd to 3rd gear	40 mph (65 km/h)	50 mph (80 km/h)

Shift point adjustment can be carried out by altering the position of the adjuster nut on the throttle secondary cable. Shortening the inner cable delays the point of speed shift and lengthening expedites it.

Fig. 6.59. Exploded view of automatic transmission countershaft

1 *Circlip*
2 *Thrust washer*
3 *Reverse gear*
4 *Thrust washer*
5 *Reverse gear hub*
6 *Cotters*
7 *Reverse selector gear*
8 *One way clutch hub*
9 *One way clutch hub*
10 *Low gear*
11 *Spacer*
12 *Thrust washer*
13 *Snap ring*
14 *Ball race*
15 *Countershaft with governor*
16 *Needle bearing*
17 *Bearing holder*

Fig. 6.60. Tightening sequence of main valve screws

Fig. 6.61. Sealing 'O' rings at crankcase oil bridge

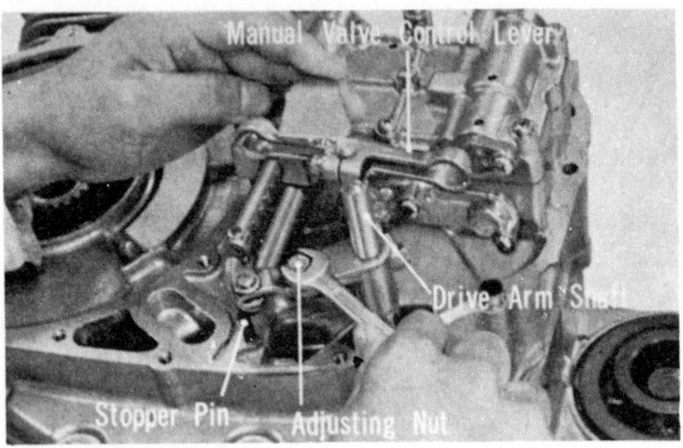

Fig. 6.62. Adjusting parking pawl lock-up

Fig. 6.63. Secondary throttle cable adjuster nuts

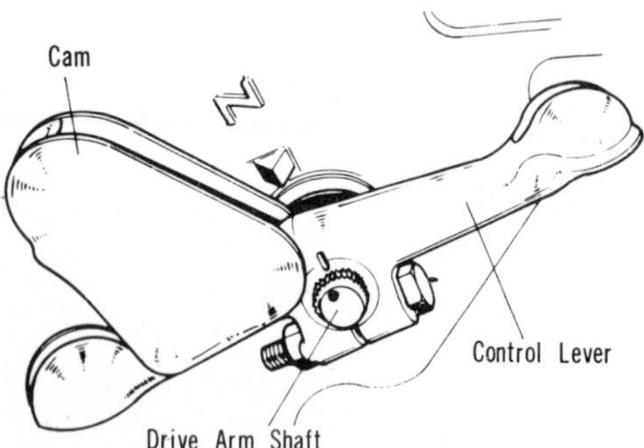

Fig. 6.64. Control lever and drive arm shaft alignment marks

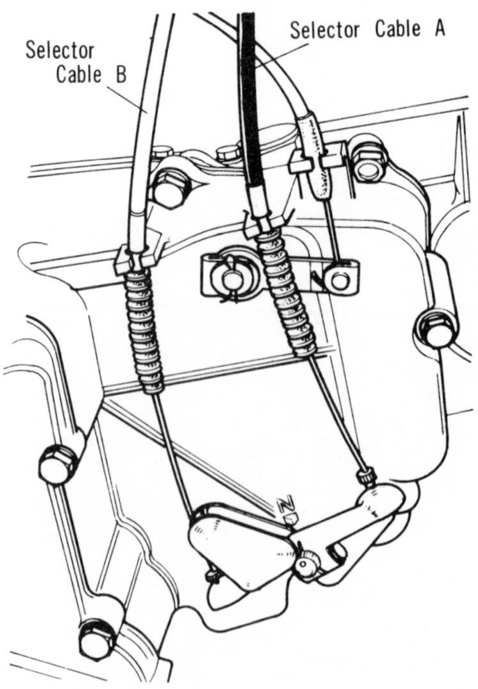

Fig. 6.65. Selector cable connections at transmission housing

23 Speed selector lever and linkage - removal and refitting

1 Loosen the selector cable locknuts and detach the cable from the selector strap arm.
2 Disconnect the electrical wiring.
3 Disconnect the steering column clamp-bolt and the four bolts which retain the column to the instrument panel, remove the crash pad from the centre of the steering wheel and remove the steering wheel-all as described in Chapter 8.
4 Dismantle the direction indicator switch and slide out the steering column assembly from the pinion gear splines.
5 The shrouds at the top of the steering column can now be removed and the speed selector mechanism dismantled.
6 Refitting is a reversal of dismantling and removal and when installation is complete, adjust the selector cables as described in the preceding Section.

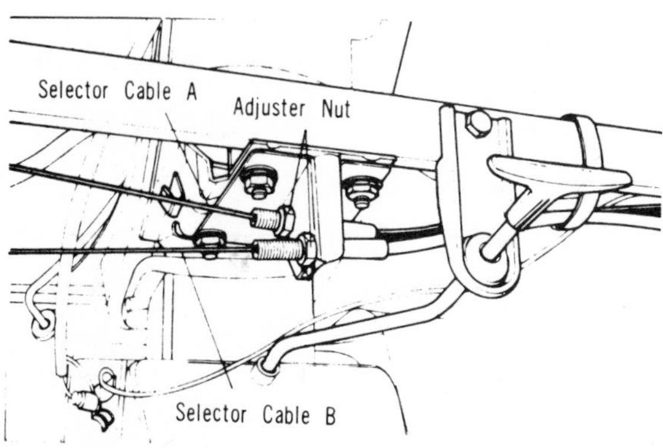

Fig. 6.66. Location of speed selector cable adjuster nuts

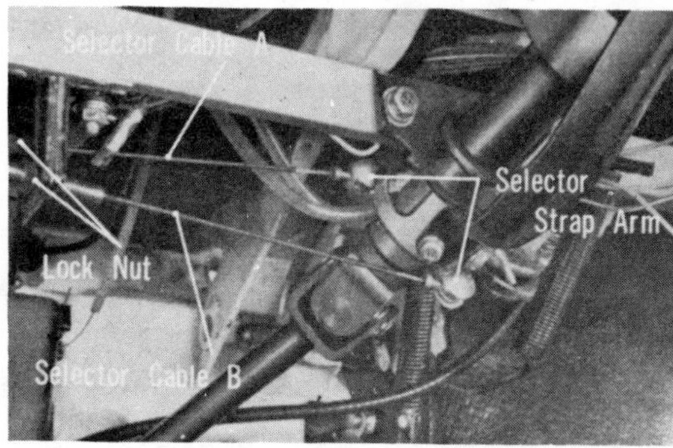

Fig. 6.67. Attachment of selector cables to steering column strap arms

Fig. 6.68. Electrical wiring harness at base of fascia panel

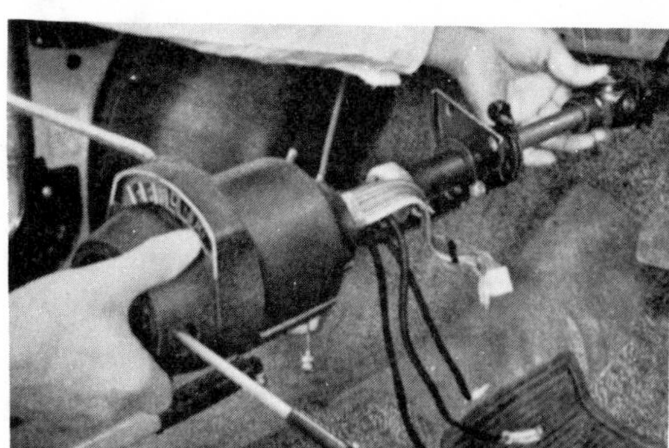

Fig. 6.69. Withdrawing steering column complete with speed selector hand control mechanism

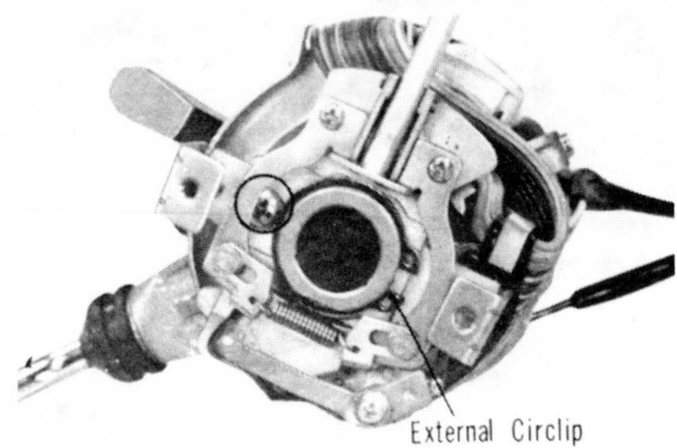

Fig. 6.70. Selector mechanism retaining circlip

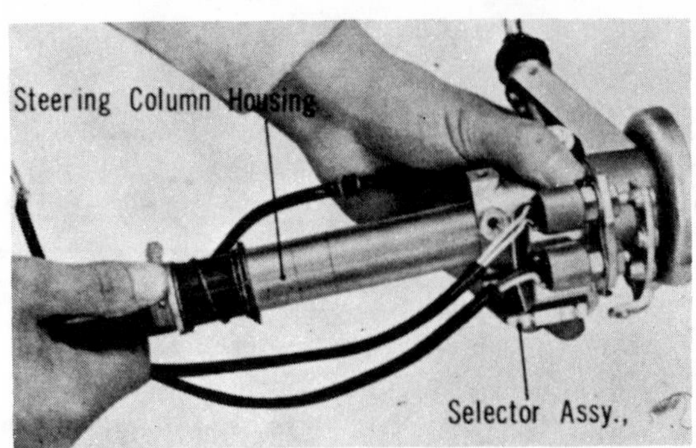

Fig. 6.71. Removing selector hand control mechanism from steering column

24 Automatic transmission - fault diagnosis

This Section does not specify the nature of the internal faults as their rectification is considered beyond the scope of the home mechanic and should be left to a Honda dealer.

Symptom	Cause	Remedy
Harsh speed selector movements	Incorrect engine idling Internal fault	Adjust. Consult dealer.
Slow speed shift after control moved	Incorrect fluid level Incorrect engine Idling Incorrect engine oil level Engine out of tune Internal fault	Correct. Adjust. Top-up. Rectify (ignition timing, carburettor, valves etc). Consult dealer.
No drive with selector in any position	Incorrect fluid level Broken primary drive chain Clogged automatic fluid filter screen Seized mainshaft, countershaft or differential bearings Internal fault	Correct. Renew (Chapter 1). Clean (Section 16). Renew bearings. Consult dealer.
Incorrect speed up-shift points	Incorrect adjustment of throttle secondary cable Internal fault	Adjust (Section 22). Consult dealer.
Parking lock-up does not hold	Selector cables incorrectly adjusted Pawl engagement incorrect	Adjust (Section 22). Adjust (Section 21).

Chapter 7 Front suspension and driveshafts

Contents

Specifications

Suspension:

Type ...	Independant 'MacPherson strut' with anti-roll bar (on North American models only)

Driveshafts:

Type ...	Solid with two universal joints
600 cc/35.5 cu in. models ...	Two constant velocity ball type joints
360 cc/21.5 cu in. models ...	Inner joint - constant velocity ball type joint Outer joint - double universal joint - needle bearing type

Torque wrench settings:	**lb/ft**	**kg/m**
Suspension lower arm to subframe bolt ...	35	4.8
Radius-rod to subframe bolt ...	35	4.8
Suspension lower arm balljoint nut ...	30	4.1
Suspension strut clamp bolt (small) ...	25	3.5
Suspension strut clamp bolt (large) ...	40	5.5
Suspension strut rod lower nut ...	20	2.8
Suspension strut rod locknut ...	35	4.8
Suspension strut upper flange mounting nuts ...	12	1.7
Anti-roll bar end bolts ...	35	4.8
Anti-roll bar subframe bracket bolts ...	16	2.2
Driveshaft flange to differential bolts ...	22	3.0
Driveshaft (stub axle) castellated nut ...	100/145	13.8/20.0

1 General description

The front suspension is of 'MacPherson strut' type. Each strut incorporates a hydraulic damper and coil road spring and is connected to the bodyframe at its upper end and at the lower end to the stub axle carrier by means of a clamp ring and pinch bolt.

Positive location of the strut is provided by a daduis rod and lower arm. Vehicle destined for operation in North America have a modified front suspension layout.

The driveshafts are of solid section with constant-velocity ball joints at their inner ends. The same type of joint is fitted to the outer ends of the driveshaft on 600 cc 35.5 cu in models, but on 36o cc 21.5 cu in models the outer joint is of double universal type.

The front hub disc and driveshaft are supported in double bearings separated by a spacer and installed in the stub axle carrier.

2 Inspection and maintanance

1 Periodically inspect the condition of the rubber bellows and renew them if they are cut, or have deteriorated.

2 Jack-up the front road wheels and check the driveshaft for

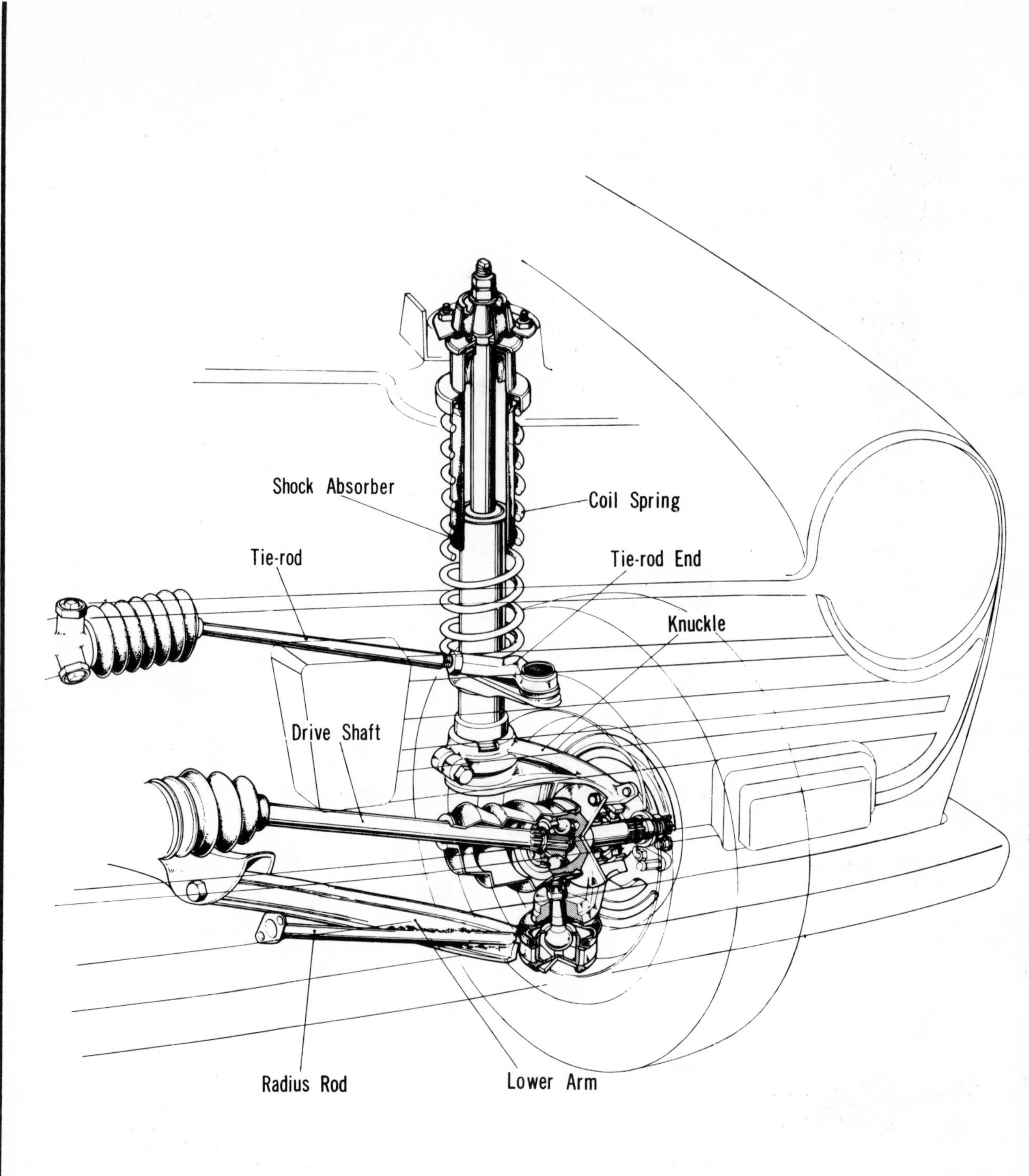

Fig. 7.1. Layout of the front suspension

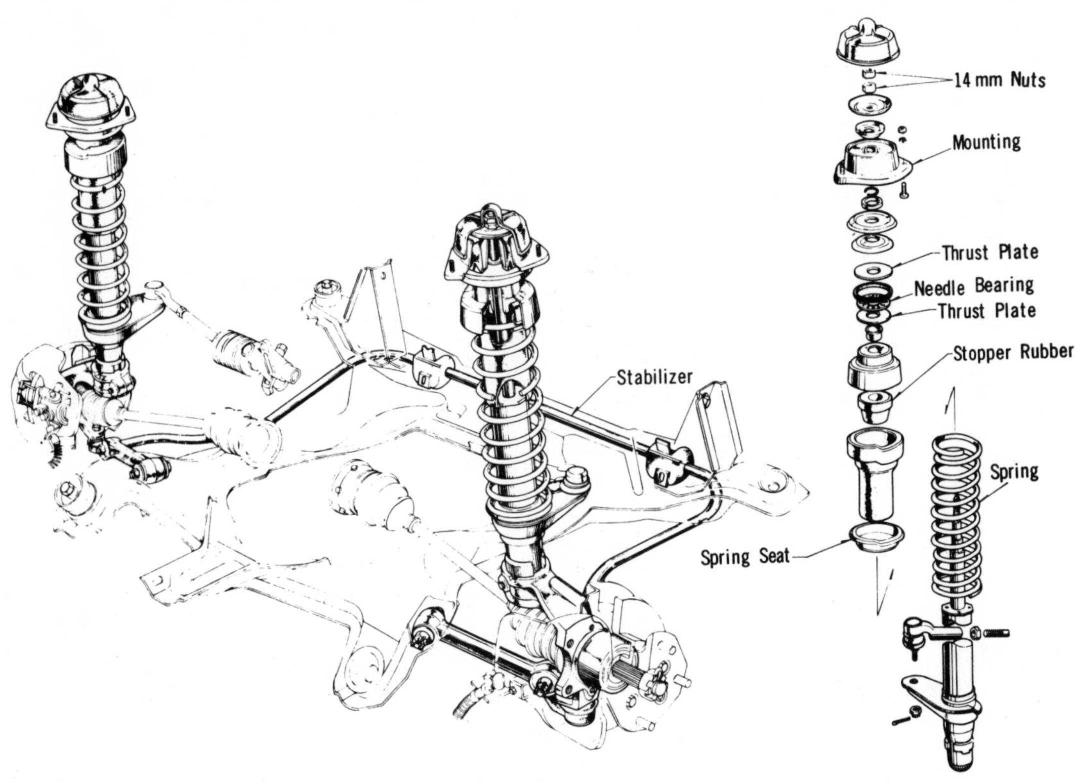

Fig. 7.2. Modified suspension fitted to North American vehicles

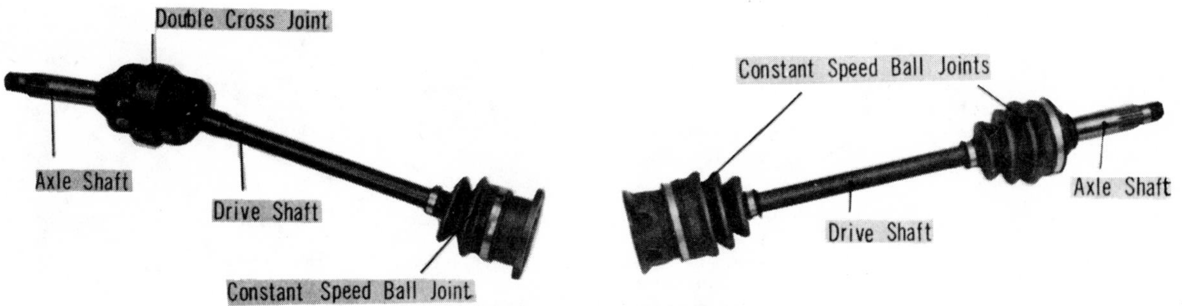

Fig. 7.3. The two types of driveshaft

excessive play in both rotational and axial directions. If play is evident, check the outer joint for wear.

Wear in this joint may be suspected if a rattling noise can be heard when the car is being driven.

3 Remove the split pin from the stub axle castellated nut split pin from the stub axle castellated nut and check that the nuts are tightened to a torque of between 100 and 145 lb/ft (13.8/20kg/m). If the split pin hole and the slots in the nut do not line up, always increase the torque, never loosen the nut.

4 Finally check the security of the driveshaft mounting bolts at the differential unit and check the splines at the ends of the driveshafts for wear.

Fig. 7.4. Testing for wear in the driveshaft joints

3 Anti-roll bar (North American models) - removal and refitting

1 Raise the front of the car so that the lower suspension arms hang free.

2 Withdraw the split pins and unscrew the two castellated nuts which secure the ends of the bar and then remove the bolts from the mountings on the subframe.

3 Refitting is a reversal of removal but the longer mounting bracket is located on the left and the shorter one on the right. Tighten the endbolts to a torque of 35lb/ft (4.8kg/m) and the subframe mounting bracket bolts to 16lb/ft(2.2 kg/m).

Fig. 7.5. Checking the torque of the front stub axle nuts

4 Suspension strut - removal and refitting

1 Raise the front of the car and disconnect the track rod to steering arm ball joint. Use either a special track-rod end extractor or wedges for this operation.

2 Unscrew and remove the pinch bolt from the clamp at the lower end of the strut and tap the steering arm downwards off the strut. The pinch bolt locates as a cotter pin in a groove at the base of the strut and must be completely withdrawn before the steering arm and strut can be separated.

3 If the strut is to be dismantled, now is the time to loosen the central damper rod nuts at the top of the unit before removing it from the car.

4 Unscrew and remove the three nuts which secure the top mounting flange of the strut to the bodywork and withdraw the complete strut assembly.

5 Refitting is a reversal of removal but tighten the nuts to the correct tightening torques listed in 'Specifications'.

5 Suspension strut - diamantling and reassembly

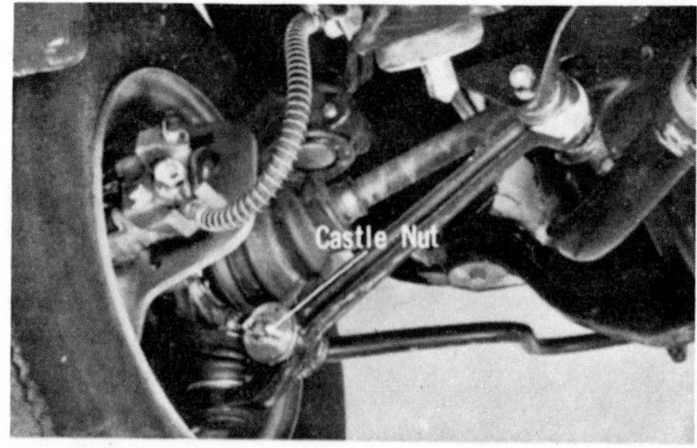

Fig. 7.6. Anti-roll bar end bolts

5 Suspension strut - dismantling and reassembly

1 Refer to Fig. 7.9 and remove the nuts (1) spacer (2) washer (3) and mounting flange (4).

2 Using a suitable coil spring compressor, compress the road spring until the jump ring is visible in its groove in the damper rod.

3 Detach the jump ring and carefully release the spring compressor. Remove the washer (6), thrust plate (7), 'O' ring (8) thrust washer (9), bush (10), spring seat (11), bumper (12), dust cover (13) and coil road spring (14).

4 Examine the hydraulic strut components for corrosion or oil leaks and test the movement of the damper rod in both directions for resistance. If the unit is faulty in any of these respects, it must be renewed as an assembly as it cannot be dismantled.

5 Reassembly is a reversal of dismantling but always use a new jump ring.

Fig. 7.7. Anti-roll bar front bracket mounting bolts

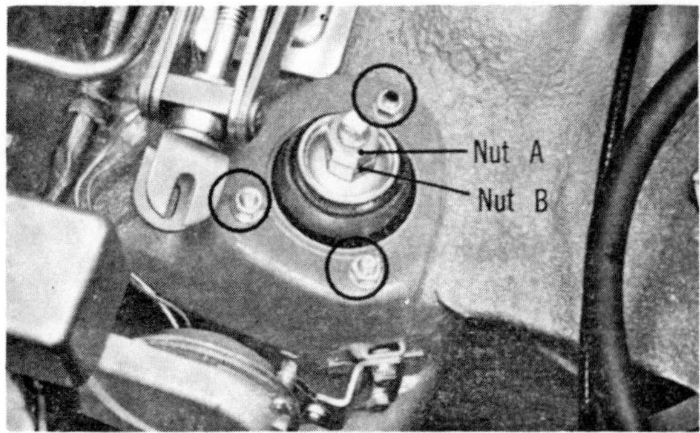

Fig. 7.8. Suspension strut damper rod locknut (A) and srcuring nut (B)

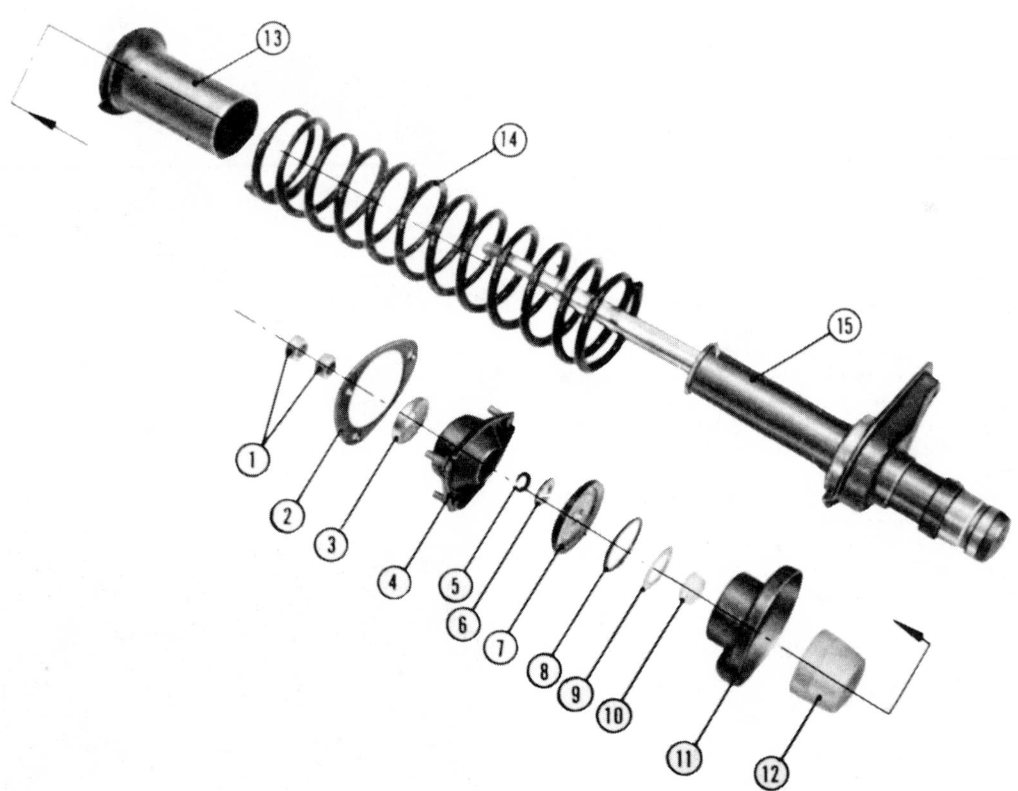

Fig. 7.9. Exploded view of front suspension leg

1 Rod securing nuts
2 Spacer
3 Washer
4 Mounting flange
5 Jump ring
6 Washer
7 Thrust plate
8 'O' ring
9 Thrust bearing
10 Bush
11 Spring pan
12 Rebound stop
13 Dust excluder
14 Spring
15 Strut

6 Stub axle carrier and suspension lower arm - removal and refitting

1 Where drum type front brakes are fitted, jack-up the front of the car, and remove the road wheel.

2 Withdraw the split pin from the castellated nut and unscrew and remove the nut.

3 With a suitable two or three legged puller, remove the brake drum.

4 Where disc type front brakes are fitted, unscrew and remove the two bolts which secure the caliper unit to the stub axle carrier. The location of these bolts is shown in Fig. 7.14. The

7 Hub bearings - renewal

1 Remove the stub axle carrier as described in the preceding Section. Remove the bearing cover.

2 Two bearings are used, an inner and an outer, separated by a tubular spacer. Tap each bearing out of its recess by using a screwdriver **against the outer bearing track.** The dust seal located against the fact of the outer bearing will be ejected at the same time.

3 Refit the bearings, which are of grease sealed type, using a tubular drift located against the bearing outer track and finally drive in a new dust seal.

bolts are accessible from below the hub and a socket with universal joint should be used to remove them. Retain the adjusting shims which are fitted between the caliper and the stub axle carrier.

5 Pull out the split pin and remove the castellated nut. Withdraw the hub and disc assembly using a suitable extractor.

6 Now unbolt and remove the brake back plate (drum type) or splash shield (disc type). The hydraulic brake hoses need not be disconnected for this operation.

7 Preferably using the official tool, extract the splined end of the driveshaft from the stub axle carrier. The end of the centre bolt of the extractor should be struck with a club hammer to start the disconnection - but ensure that the shock is not transmitted through the driveshaft to the differential unit. When the splined section of the driveshaft has been withdrawn, about two thirds of its length, disconnect the stub axle carrier from the base of the suspension strut as described in Section 4 before finally removing the carrier from the driveshaft.

8 Withdraw the split pin from the lower ball joint, remove the nut and disconnect the lower suspension arm from the axle carrier using a suitable extractor or wedges.

9 Disconnect the lower suspension arm and the radius rod from the subframe. (photo). Connect the driveshaft to the stub axle carrier as described in Section 8.

10 Refitting is a reversal of removal but tighten all nuts to the specified torque and check the wheel alignment as described in Chapter 8.

6.9 Removing a radius rod to subframe bolt

Fig. 7.10. Removing a front brake drum

8 Driveshafts - removal and refitting

1 Jack up the front of the car, remove the roadwheels.

2 Remove the drum or disc brake components as described in Section 6.

3 Unscrew and remove the securing bolts from the differential joint flange.

4 Disconnect the splined section of the driveshaft from the stub axle carrier as described in Section 6.

5 Refitting should commence by fitting the driveshaft flange to the differential unit, then driving on the stub axle carrier complete with bearings onto the splined end of the driveshaft. Use a tubular drift located against the outer track of the bearing and check that the outer bearing has not become displaced during the operation. If it has, drive it fully into its recess.

6 Finally install a new dust seal.

Fig. 7.11. Location of front caliper mounting bolts

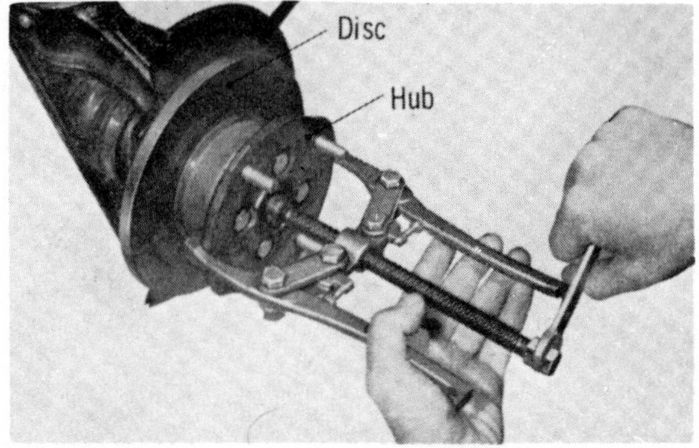

Fig. 7.12. Removing a front hub/disc assembly

Fig. 7.13. Back plate securing bolts (drum type)

Fig. 7.14. Splash shield securing bolts (disc type)

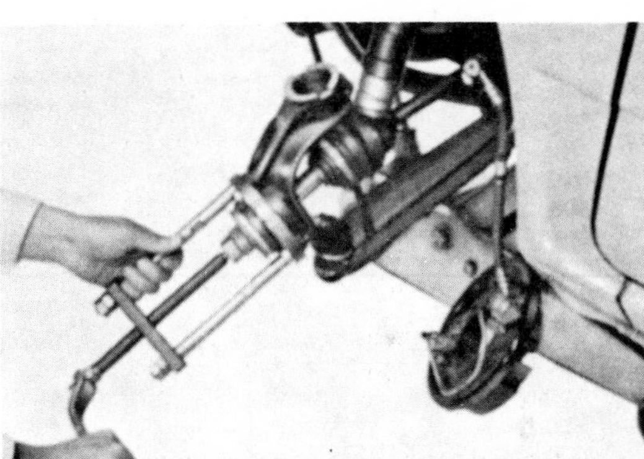

Fig. 7.15. Disconnecting the splined shorter section of the driveshaft from the stub axle carrier

Fig. 7.16. Pulling split pin from lower balljoint

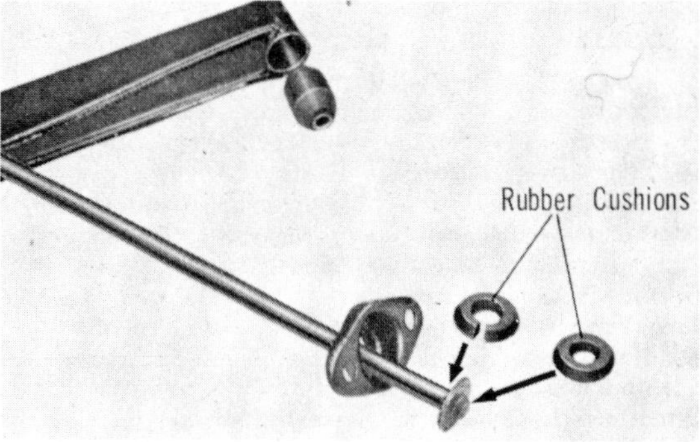

Fig. 7.17. Attachment of radius rod to sub-frame

Fig. 7.18. Driving out a front hub bearing

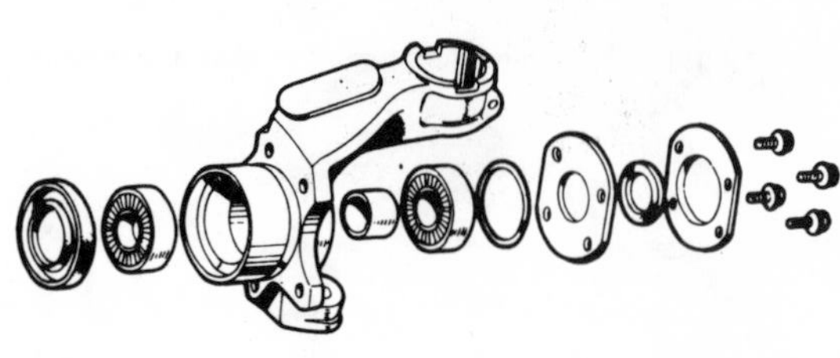

Fig. 7.19. Exploded view of stub axle carrier and bearings

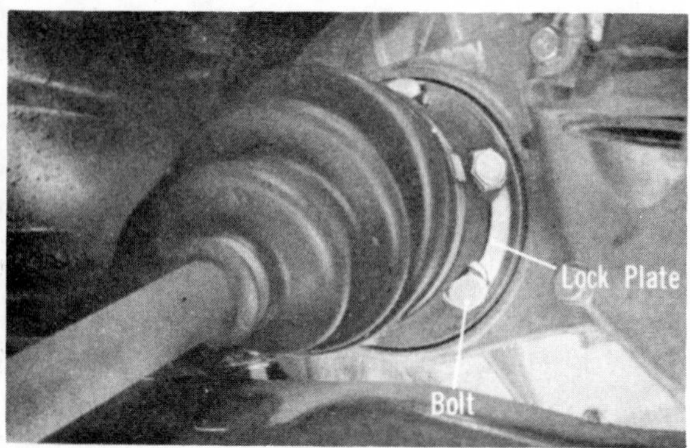

Fig. 7.20. Driveshaft to differential flange mounting bolts and lockplate

Fig. 7.21. Driving the stub axle carrier/bearing assembly onto the driveshaft

9 Constant-velocity ball joints - servicing

1 This type of joint is fitted to the inner and outer ends of the driveshafts on 600cc 35.5 cu in cars and to the inner ends only on 360cc 21.5 cu in cars. Renewal of damaged or perished bellows and grease re-packing should be carried out in the following manner. Dismantling (paragraphs 10 and 11) applies only to the inner constant velocity joints, the 60cc 35.5 cu in outer joints cannot be dismantled.
2 Remove the driveshaft as described in the preceding Section.
3 Remove the bellows securing band.
4 Peel back the bellows and detach the circlip to separate the flange from the driveshaft.
5 Extract the inner circlip, remove the steel balls in their retainer from the driveshaft.
6 Clean all components, in paraffin until free from grease.
7 Obtain replacements for worn components and a pack of specified grease.
8 On the driveshaft locate the two bellows securing bands and the bellows.
9 Fill the cavity within the flange with approximately 2/3rd's of the grease supplied.
10 If new balls are being fitted, they should be installed in the retainer using a copper mallet.
11 Insert the retainer onto the driveshaft and secure with the internal circlip.
12 Insert the driveshaft into the joint flange to compress the grease already there and then pack the remaining grease into the flange cavity. Connect the driveshaft to the joint flange by engaging the peripheral circlip.
13 Position the bellows on the flange by aligning it with the flange groove and then fit the securing band and tighten and lock it securely.
14 Carefully insert a thin screwdriver at the narrower neck of the bellows to permit any trapped air to escape and allow the bellows to take up their normal set. Tighten the securing band.
15 With the constant velocity joint now fully assembled, press the driveshaft in and check that no grease emerges from the joint between the sealing plate and the flange. Should there be a leakage, attempt to spread the sealing plate (similar to a convex core plug) by hammering a screwdriver positioned at six points about 2 mm from the plate edge, as shown in Fig. 7.25.

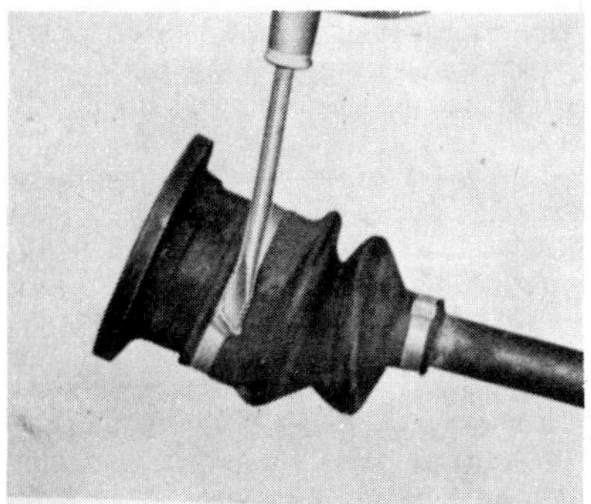

Fig. 7.22. Removing the bellows securing band from a constant velocity joint

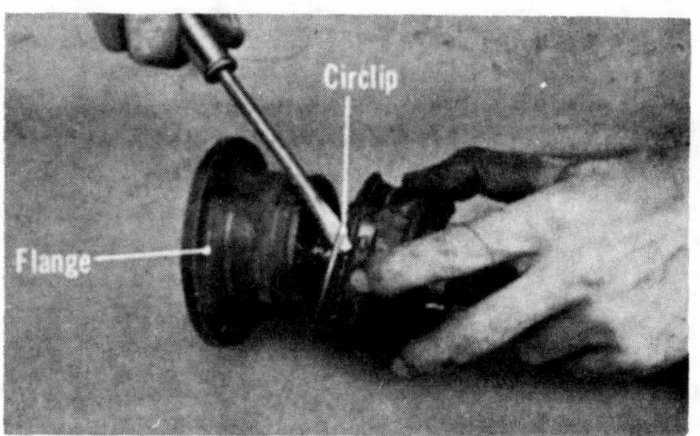

Fig. 7.23. Separating flange from driveshaft (constant velocity joint)

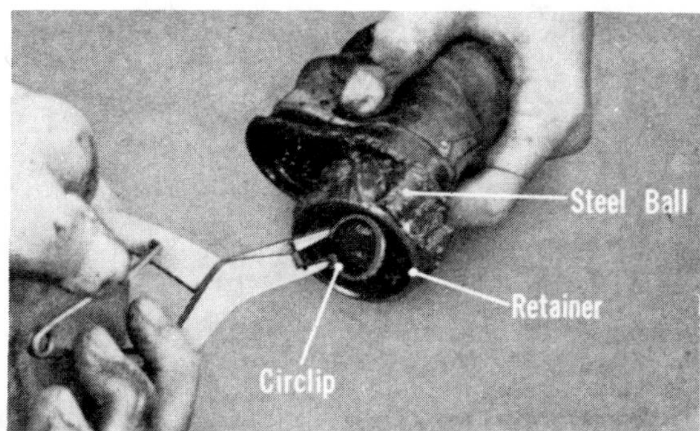

Fig. 7.24. Extracting inner circlip from driveshaft constant velocity joint

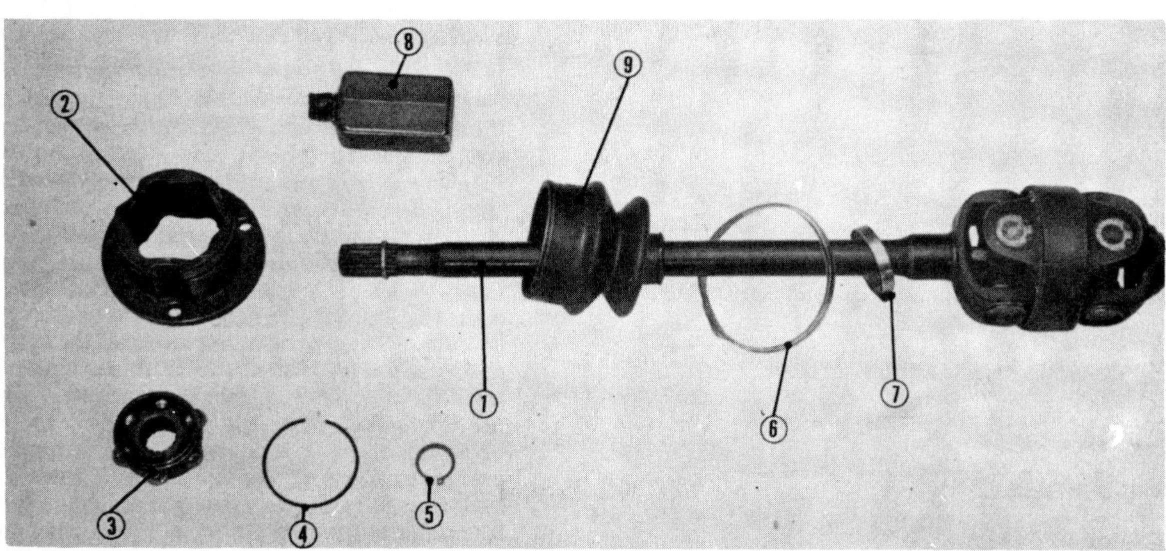

Fig. 7.25. Exploded view of driveshaft constant velocity joint (sealing plate removed)

1 Driveshaft
2 Flange
3 Steel ball retainer
4 External circlip
5 Internal circlip
6 Bellows securing band
7 Bellows securing band
8 Grease pack (supplied as service item)
9 Bellows

10 Double universal joint - servicing

1 This type of joint is fitted to the driveshaft outer ends of the 360cc 21.5 cu in models.

2 Servicing will be required if wear is evident after carrying out one or more of the following checks.

3 Drive the car forward in 1st gear (or 1st speed-auto transmission) and turn the steering from one lock to another and listen for knocking noises.

4 Using a long screwdriver inserted through the outer joint yoke, hold it quite still while attempting to move the inner joint in all directions - rotational, and up and down.

5 Dismantle the joints by first removing the circlips from their recesses. If they are tight in their grooves, tap them on their end faces using a suitable drift.

6 Tap each of the yoke ears in turn with a soft-faced mallet until the bearing cup emerges from its housing. If they are very tight they should be pressed out in the jaws of a vice using two socket spanners. Once the bearing cups project sufficiently, they should be gripped in a self-locking wrench and twisted out.

7 When the bearing sups have been removed, depress the spiders and withdraw the outer sections from the centre yoke.

8 Remove the centring ball as shown in Fig. 7.30.

9 The dismantling of the spider attached to the driveshaft yoke cab only be carried out after the centre shaft has been withdrawn. To do this it must be gripped in an extractor and pressure applied to the endface of the spider not the yoke. Measure the projection of the centre shaft before removing it.

10 Locate the spiders in the yokes and ensure that the needles are stuck round the inside of the bearing cups with heavy grease. Press the cups onto two opposing spider trunnions using the jaws of a vice. Take care that the needles do not become displaced during the operation. Use distance pieces or socket spanners to press the cups in sufficiently far to enable the circlips to be located in their grooves, Fig. 7.30.

11 A new centre shaft must now be tapped into position through the driveshaft joint spider (Fig. 7.30 and finally pressed in so that it projects the same amount as originally measured. The new shaft must be an interference fit, and for this reason one of oversize dimensions must be obtained which will have a yellow paint mark as identification.

12 Fit the ball into the yoke of the shorter section of the driveshaft and pack it with specified grease.

13 Pack the dust seal with grease as shown in Fig. 7.32 and fit it with its retaining clip to the yoke.

14 Assemble the two driveshaft joint spiders to the centre connection yoke and press in the needle bearing cups and fit the remaining circlips.

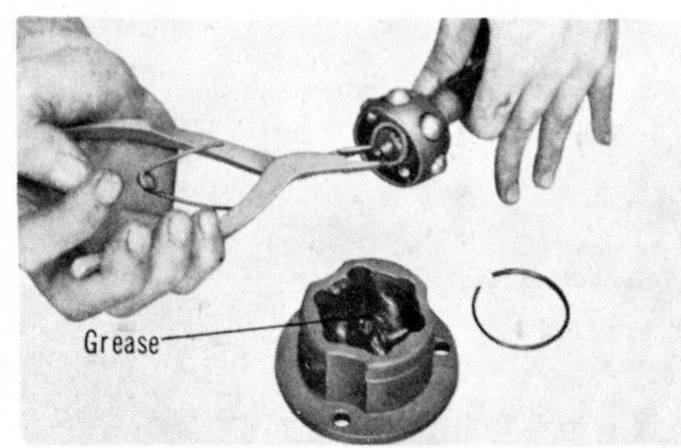

Fig. 7.26. Securing the constant velocity joint ball retainer

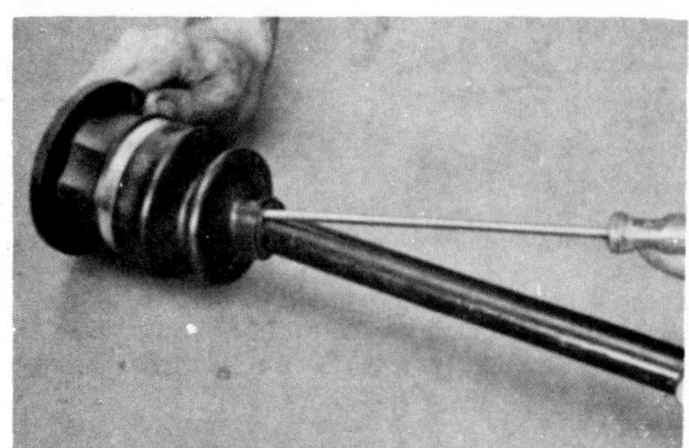

Fig. 7.27. Releasing trapped air from joint bellows

Fig. 7.28. Striking points to spread a joint flange sealing plate

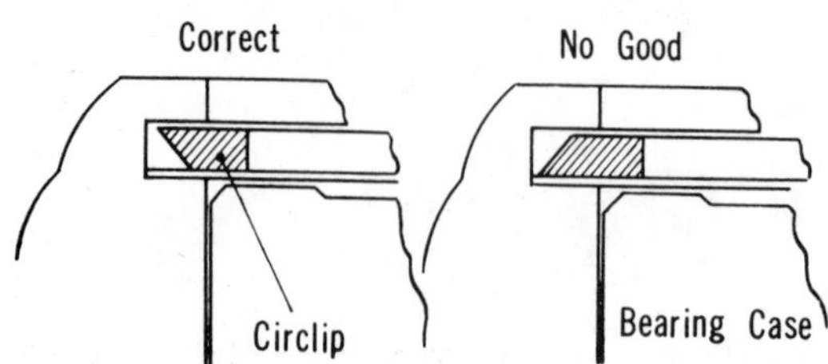

Fig. 7.29. Correct orientation of bearing cup circlips

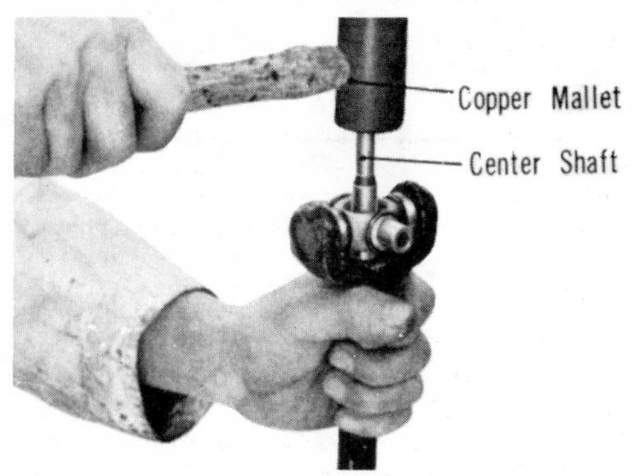

Fig. 7.30. Driving in a new centre shaft

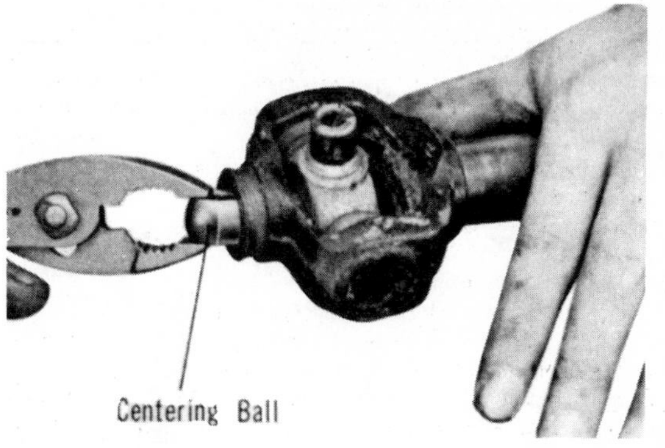

Fig. 7.30A. Withdrawing the driveshaft centring ball

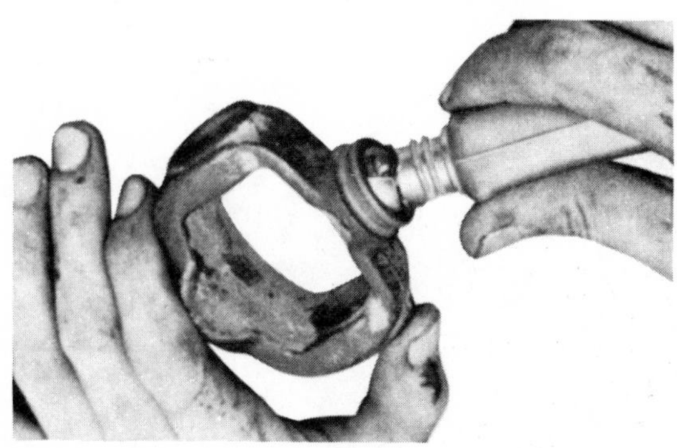

Fig. 7.31. Packing the driveshaft joint centring ball recess with grease

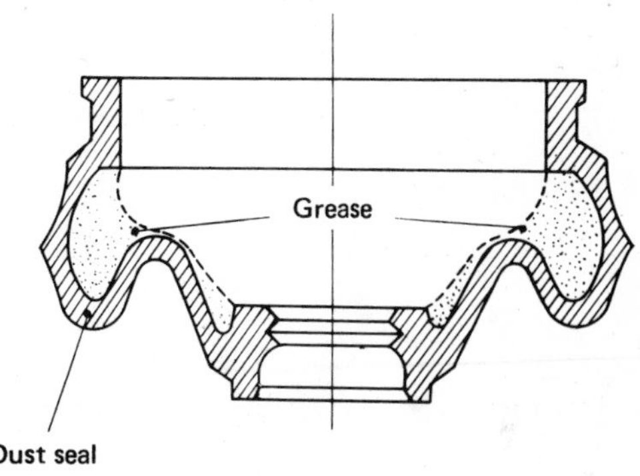

Fig. 7.32. Joint dust seal grease packing diagram

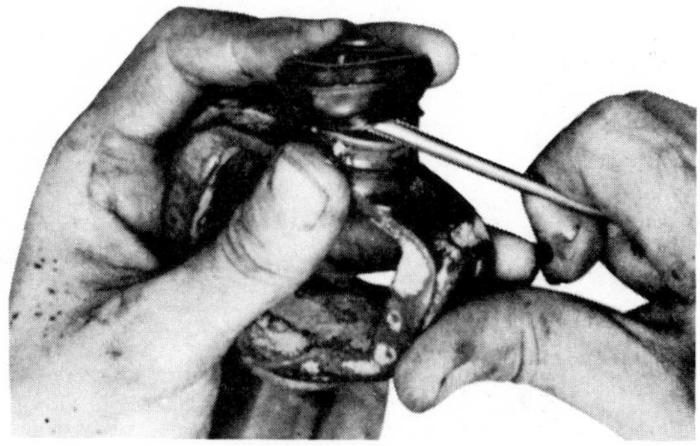

Fig. 7.33. Fitting dust seals to driveshaft joint yoke

Fig. 7.34. Connecting the driveshaft joint spiders to the centre yoke

11 Front suspension and driveshafts - fault diagnosis

Symptom	Cause	Remedy
Wander	Hub bearings worn	Renew.
	Balljoints worn or loose	Renew or tighten.
Wheel wobble and vibration or knocking	Defective hydraulic damping action of suspension strut	Renew strut.
	Broken coil spring	Renew.
	Loose top mounting on suspension strut	Tighten.
	Loose mountings on radius rod or lower suspension arm	Tighten.
	Worn driveshaft joints	Renew.
	Worn driveshaft splines	Renew shafts.
Excessive pitching when braking or rolling on corners	Weak damping action of suspension strut	Renew strut.
	Loose or broken anti-roll bar (North American vehicles)	Renew.

Chapter 8 Steering

Contents

Specifications

Steering:

Type ...	Rack and pinion with double jointed column
Number of turns (lock-to-lock) ...	3.1 Ratio 17.4 : 1
Steering wheel diameter ...	15 in. (38 cm)
Column universal joint lockplate availability ...	0.067 in. (1.7 mm) 0.075 in. (1.9 mm) 0.051 in. (1.3 mm) 0.059 in. (1.5 mm)
Camber ...	0.5°
Caster ...	1.0°
Steering axis inclination ...	14.5°
Toe-out ...	0.08 in. (2 mm)
Turning circle:	
360 cc/21.5 cu in. ...	30.8 ft (9.4 m)
600 cc/35.5 cu in. ...	31.2 ft (9.5 m)
600 cc/35.5 cu in. (Z) Coupe ...	31.5 ft (9.6 m)

Wheels and tyres:

Tyre size ...	5.20 x 10	
Tyre pressures *:	**Front**	**Rear**
Saloon (manual gearbox) ...	24 lb/in^2	22 lb/in^2
Saloon (automatic transmission) ...	26 lb/in^2	22 lb/in^2
Estate/Wagon (unloaded) ...	24 lb/in^2	22 lb/in^2
(loaded) ...	29 lb/in^2	34 lb/in^2
600 (Z) Coupe ...	24 lb/in^2	24 lb/in^2

** Pressures quoted are for those tyres fitted as standard. If other tyres are fitted follow their manufacturer's instructions with regard to tyre pressures.*

Torque wrench settings:

	lb/ft	kg/m
Steering box mounting bolts ...	17	2.3
Rack end to rack gear ...	35	4.8
Track rod end locknuts ...	35	4.8
Track rod balljoint taper pin nut ...	28	3.9
Steering wheel nut ...	25	3.5
Pinion mounting bolt ...	18	2.5

1 General description

The steering gear is of rack and pinion type. The steering column is in three sections, cranked with two universal joints. Provision is made for adjustment of the backlash between the pinion gear and the rack.

2 Steering gear - adjustment

1 To rectify lost movement at the steering wheel due to an increase in the backlash between the pinion teeth and the rack which is caused by wear, the rack guides must be adjusted.
2 Loosen the rack guide locknut "B" (Fig 8.4) and tighten the adjusting bolt with the fingers. Now unscrew the bolt about 20 degrees (use a small protractor for this) and tighten the locknut.
3 Loosen the rack guide locknut "A" (nearest the pinion) and repeat the adjustment as for bolt "B".

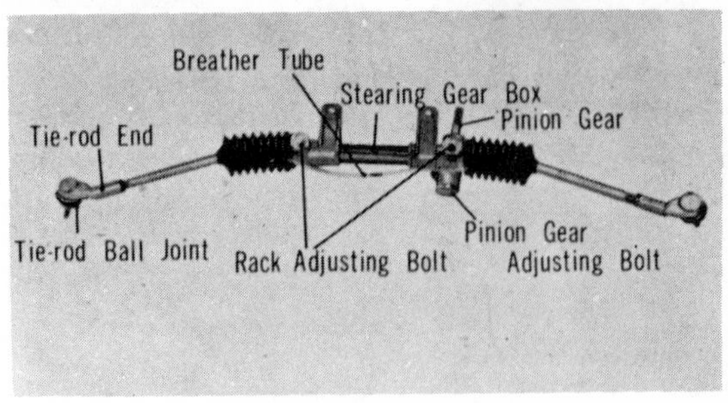

Fig. 8.1. The steering gear

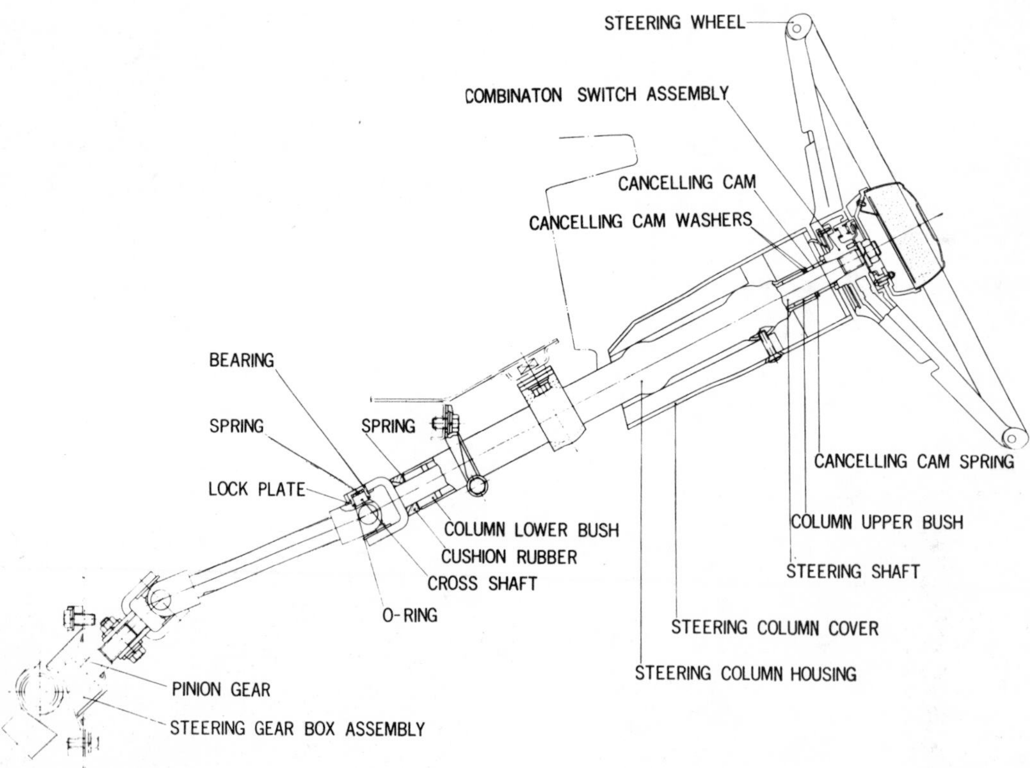

Fig. 8.2. Sectional view of steering column

3 Steering wheel and column - removal and refitting

1 Remove the three screws which retain the safety crash pad at the centre of the steering wheel.
2 Disconnect the terminal screw from the horn positive (+) lead within the steering wheel boss.
3 Holding the steering wheel quite still, unscrew the central securing nut.
4 Remove the two horn contact plate screws and extract the plate.
5 Using a suitable puller, remove the wheel from the column.
6 Loosen the clamp pinch bolt at the connection of the steering shaft to the pinion gear which is located below the fascia panel.
7 Disconnect the electrical wiring connector plug below the choke control knob and unscrew the four bolts which retain the steering column to the fascia panel. Withdraw the steering column.
8 On vehicles fitted with automatic transmission, the speed selector mechanism is interconnected with the steering column and reference should be made to Chapter 6, Section 23 for details of selector cable and linkage disconnection.
9 Installation of the steering column is a reversal of removal but following points must be observed.

Before fitting the steering wheel to the shaft splines, set the road wheels in the straight-ahead position and check that the direction indicator cancelling cam is in the neutral position, Fig 8.11.

Tighten the steering wheel nut to a torque of 25 lb/ft (3.5 kg/m).

Before tightening the steering column mounting bolts position the steering column housing so that any play between the shaft and housing is elimated and finally check that the clearance between the column upper shroud and the steering wheel boss lower edge is between 0.04 and 0.16 in (1.0 to 4.0 mm).

4 Steering column - testing for wear, dismantling and re-assembly

1 Grip the steering wheel (road wheels in straight-ahead position) and check for lost motion. This is the movement of the wheel without any corresponding movement of the roadwheels occurring.
2 Where this free movement is excessive, check that the steering column mounting bolts are tight, that the steering wheel is tight on its splines and that the cushion rubber is not worn or compressed, Fig 8.14.
3 If these factors are correct and the rack adjustment (Section 2) is correct then the steering column must be dismantled for renewal of worn components.
4 Remove the column and wheel as described in the preceding Section.
5 From the top of the column pull off the direction indicator cancelling cam and spring washers.
6 Remove the shroud from the upper end of the column (one screw).
7 Loosen the single retaining screw and tap the combination switch from the top of the steering column. (on cars fitted with steering lock, set the ignition key to the 'O' position).
8 Check the steering shaft universal joints for play by twisting the yokes in opposite directions. Two types of joints may be encountered, one which can be dismantled by prising off the lockplates with a screwdriver (Fig 8.20) and another which is factory sealed. Wear in the former type can probably be rectified by fitting new lockplates or trunnion caps. Wear in the factory sealed type may be eliminated by additional staking at the points indicated in Fig 8.18. If this cannot be achieved, the whole steering shaft assembly will have to be renewed.
9 Check the bush at the top of the steering column, wear here

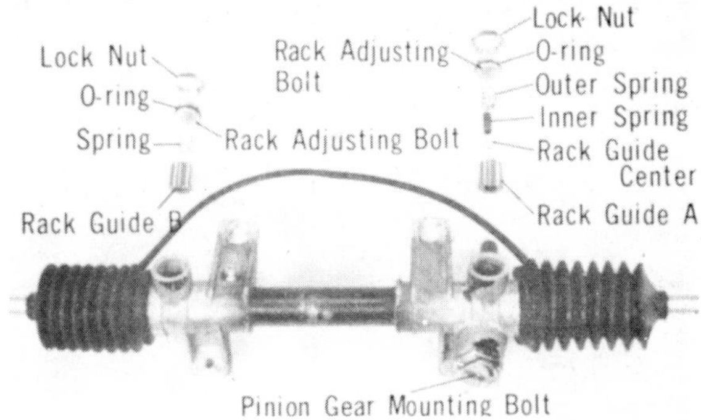

Fig. 8.3. Steering rack guide adjuster components

Fig. 8.4. Loosening a rack guide adjuster locknut

Fig. 8.5. Steering wheel crash pad retaining screws

Fig. 8.6. Steering wheel horn lead terminal

Fig. 8.7. Horn contact plate and securing screws

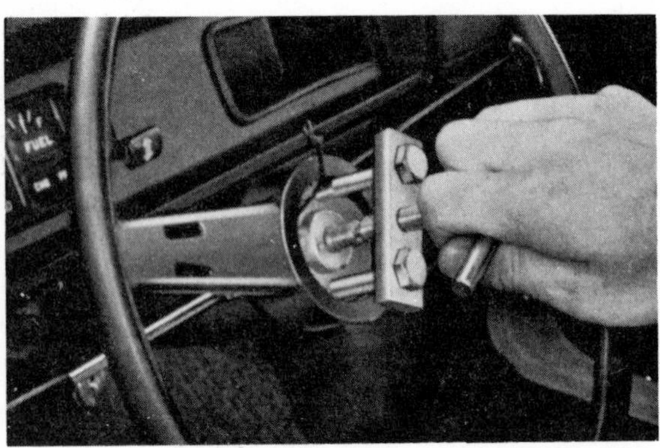

Fig. 8.8. Removing the steering wheel

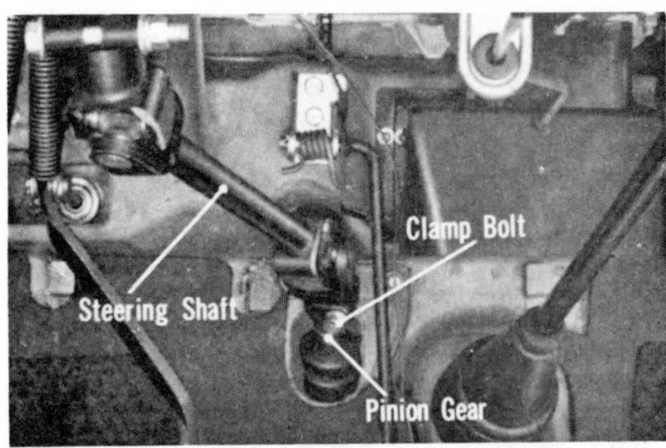

Fig. 8.9. Location of steering shaft to pinion clamp

Fig. 8.10. Location of wiring harness connector and column bracket bolts

Fig. 8.11. Neutral position of direction indicator switch cancelling cam

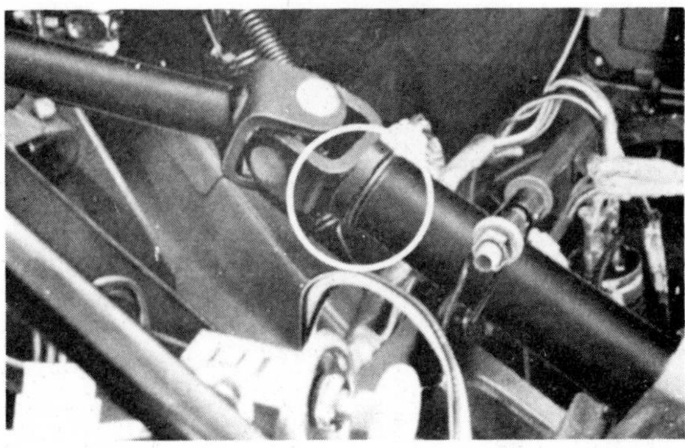

Fig. 8.12. Position where column and shaft end play must be eliminated

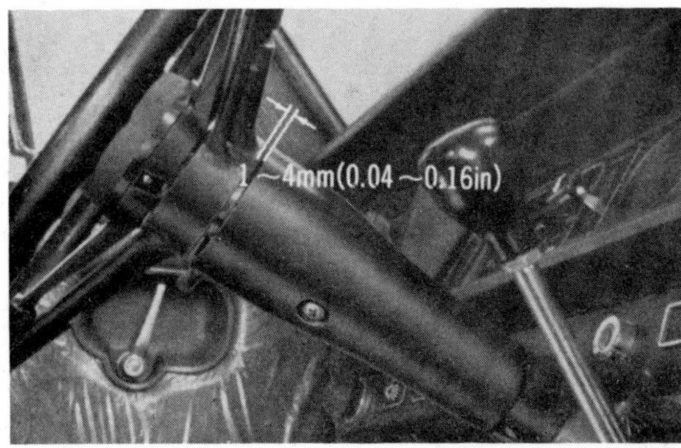

Fig. 8.13. Correct clearance between shroud and steering wheel boss

will often cause a rattle in the steering wheel.

10 Resssembly is a reversal of dismantling but should the lock-plate type universal joints become tight after fitting lockplates (see specifications for availability) then they may be eased by tapping the yokes lightly with a plastic face hammer.

11 Connect the steering shaft so that the longer splined section of the universal joint mates with the steering pinion.

12 On cars equipped with a steering column lock, check that the shaft lock positioning key is installed in its groove and that the lock sleeve is secured with a circlip at the top and a circlip and wave washer at the bottom.

13 Check that the rubber cushion (flat side upwards) and wave (spring) washer are correctly positioned as shown in Fig 8.22.

14 On vehicles equipped with a steering lock, the shaft must be finally assembled and installed so that with the road wheels in the straight ahead position and ignition key in the 'O' position, the grooves in the combination switch and steering housing will be in exact alignment. To obtain this situation, vary the engagement of the shaft to pinion splines..

15 Fit the tapered locking piece (concave side to column and tapered side to switch to secure the combination switch to the steering column and insert and tighten the securing screw.

Fig. 8.14. Steering column shaft cushion rubber and wave washer

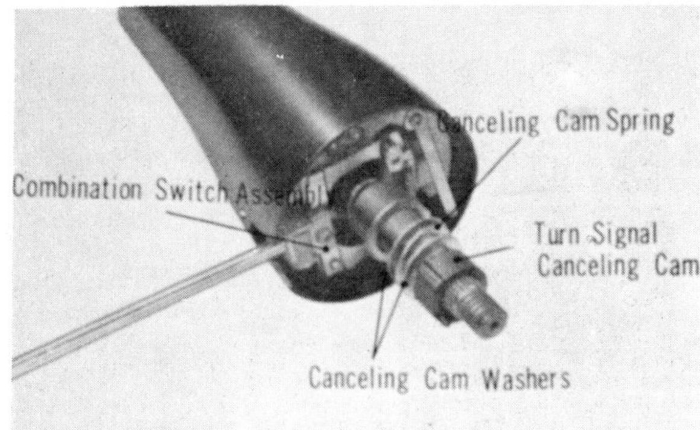

Fig. 8.15. Location of direction indicator switch actuating components

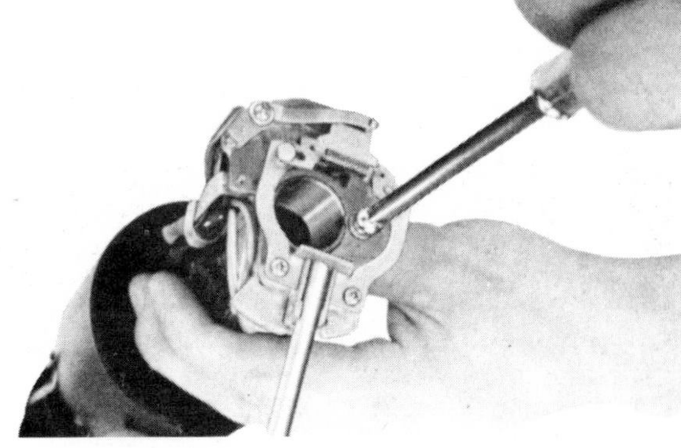

Fig. 8.16. Removing combination switch from top of steering column

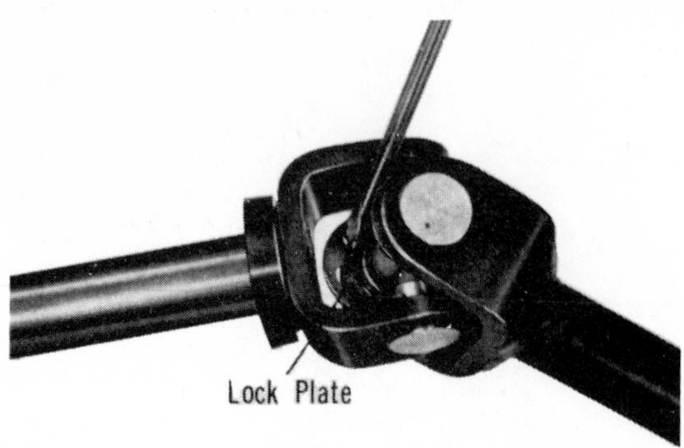

Fig. 8.17. Dismantling a lockplate type steering shaft joint

Fig. 8.18. Staking points to eliminate wear on factory sealed joint

Fig. 8.19. Steering column top bushing

Fig. 8.20. Easing lockplate universal joints

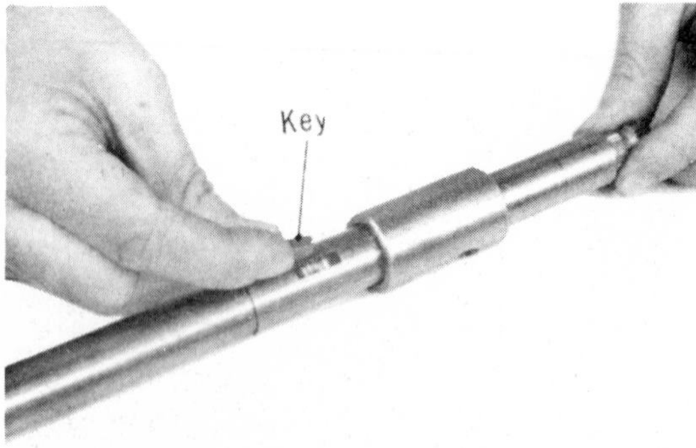

Fig. 8.21. Fitting steering lock tongue to shaft groove

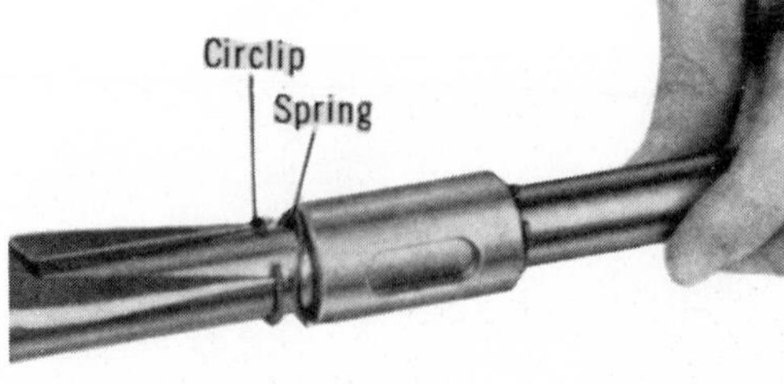

Fig. 8.22. Correct location of steering lock sleeve circlips and wave washer

5 Steering rack and pinion gear - removal and refitting

1 Disconnect the track-rod end ball joints from the steering arms of the stub axle carrier using either an extractor or wedges.
2 Remove the pinch bolt from the clamp which connects the steering column shaft to the pinion.

Mark the relative position of the shaft to the pinion for ease of refitting.
3 Remove the four bolts which secure the steering gearbox to the rear bulkhead of the engine compartment. Two of the bolts are accessible from within the engine compartment and the other two from inside the car.
4 Installation of the steering gear is a reversal of removal but remember to connect the steering column shaft to the pinion splines so that the marks made on dismantling are in alignment. If new components have been fitted then the rack must be set in the central position and the steering wheel with the spokes horizontal before connecting the shaft to pinion clamp.
5 Tighten the gearbox mounting bolts to a torque of 17 lb/ft (2.3 kg/m). Connect the track-rod end ball joints.
6 Check the adjustment as described in Section 2 and check the front wheel alignment as described in Section 8.

6 Steering gear - dismantling and reassembly

1 Peel back the rubber bellows from the pinion end of the gearbox. Prise up the tab of the lockwasher and release the locknut.
2 Unscrew the right-hand track-rod from the rack.
3 Unscrew and remove the two adjusting bolts and their locknuts.
4 Withdraw the rack from the gearbox housing.
5 Loosen the pinion mounting bolt locknut and unscrew the mounting bolt, Fig 8.27.
6 Detach the 'U' shaped thrust plate and tap the pinion from the steering box.
7 The track-rod ends may be removed from the track rods after first loosening the locknuts.
8 Inspect all dismantled components for wear, scoring or damage after they have been thoroughly cleaned in paraffin.
9 Check the gear housing for cracks, particularly round the mounting bolt holes.

Fig. 8.23. Combination switch to steering column alignment grooves

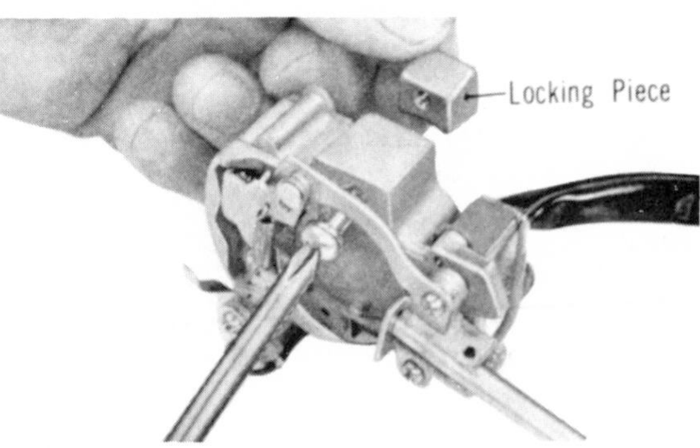

Fig. 8.24. Combination switch tapered locking piece

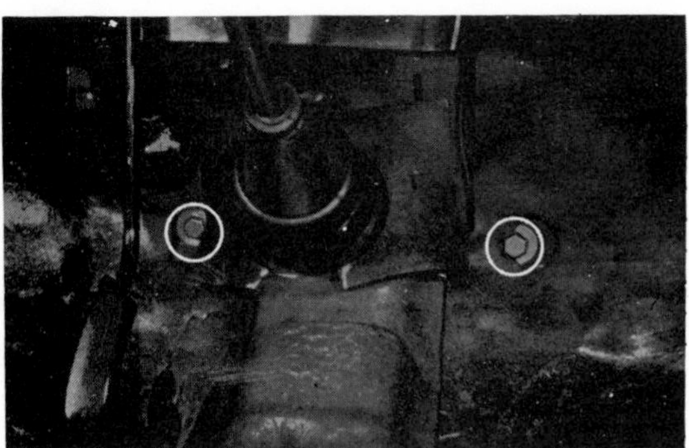

Fig. 8.25. Location of steering box retaining bolts

Fig. 8.26. Loosening the track-rod to rack locknut

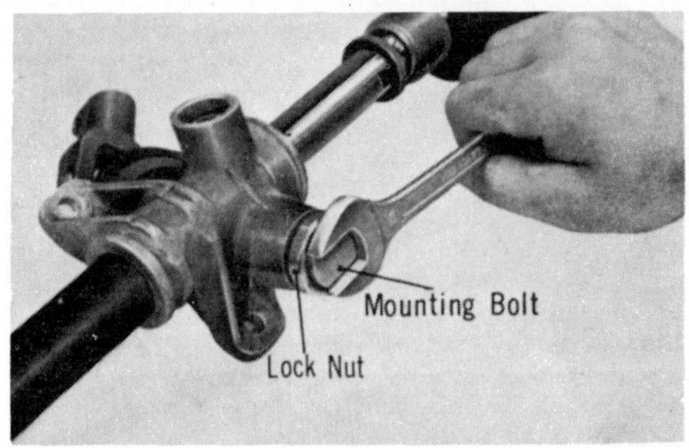

Fig. 8.27. Removing the pinion mounting bolt and locknut

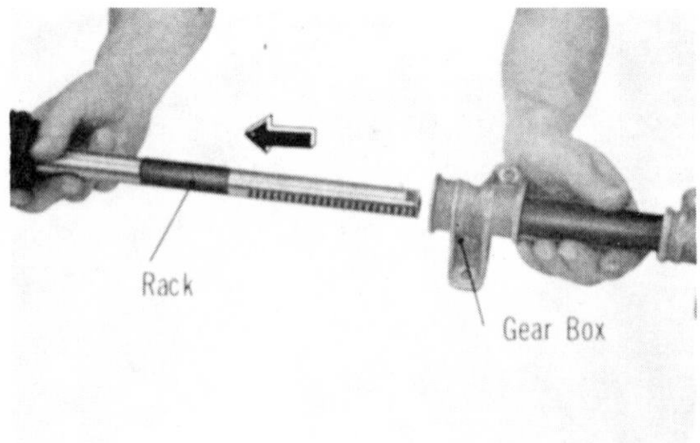

Fig. 8.28. Withdrawing the rack from steering box

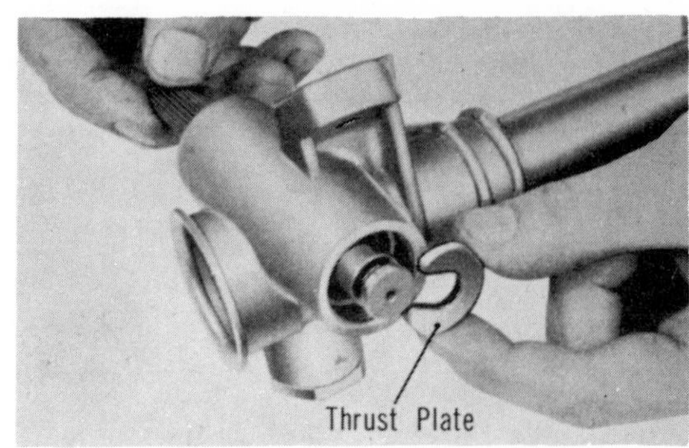

Fig. 8.29. Removing pinion thrust plate

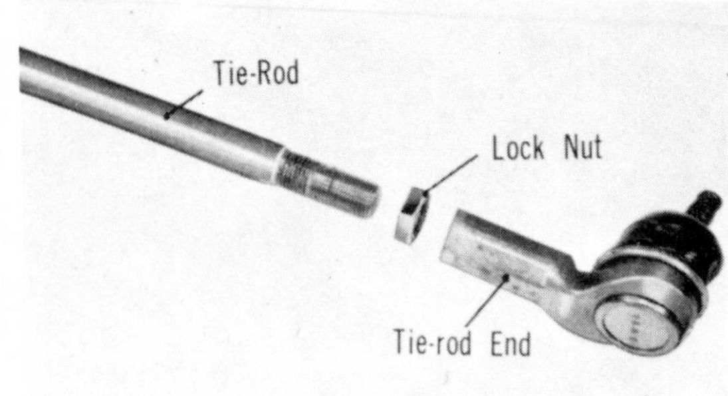

Fig. 8.30. Track-rod components

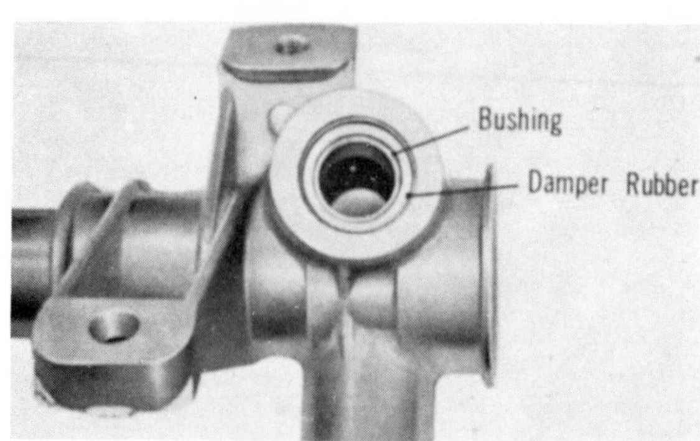

Fig. 8.31. Pinion bush and rubber damper

10 Check the pinion bushing and damper (Fig 8.31). If renewal is required due to wear or deterioration of the rubber component, drift the old one out and drive the new one in, fitting an oversize cap to ensure that the new components are securely held in position.
11 Check the ball joints at the rack ends for play. If evident, renew the track-rods.
12 Insert the rack into the gearbox housing and test for wear in the housing bushes. Where this is apparent, renew the housing.
13 Commence reassembly by liberally coating the pinion, thrust plate and mounting bolt with graphite grease and installing them in the steering box. Note that the rounded edge of the 'U' shaped thrust plate faces inwards.
14 Tighten the pinion mounting bolt and the locknut to a torque of 18 lb/ft (2.5 kg/m).
15 Grease the rack liberally with graphite grease and insert it into the steering housing.
16 Assemble the rack end/track-rod assemblies to the ends of the rack gear. Fit the thrust plate and a new lockwasher making sure to engage its tongue in the slot in the rack. Screw the rack ends in tightly and bend over the lockwashers.
17 Refit the rack guides and adjustment bolts to their original locations having well greased the components and renewed the 'O' rings if necessary.
18 Adjust the steering gear as described in Section 2.
19 Refit the rubber bellows and pressure equalising tube.
20 Early type steering boxes are fitted with grease nipples and six strokes of the grease gun should be given to each nipple every 12000 miles (20000 km).
21 On later models, greasing can only be carried out by removing the adjusting bolts and screwing in an adapter. Provided the steering gear is adequately greased on assembly, it is unlikely that the latter operation will be required unless the bellows have split or the rack becomes noisy in operation.

Fig. 8.32. Greasing and inserting the steering rack into the housing

7 Suspension and steering ball joints - inspection and renewal

1 Periodically inspect the condition of the rubber dust excluders on the ball joints. If they are split or have perished, they must be renewed immediately.
2 Check the ball joint for wear by moving the connected components in all directions. Play or shake cannot be corrected and the ball joint must be renewed.
3 Ball joint taper pins are usually separated from their eyes by one of three methods. (a) the use of an extractor, (b) using two forked wedges, (c) using two club hammers and striking the eye on both side simultaneously when the taper pin will be released.
4 The ball joints are all of sealed type and do not require lubrication.

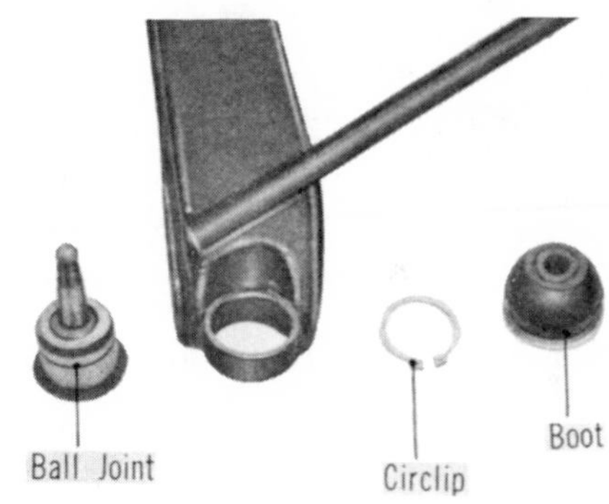

Fig. 8.33A. Lower suspension arm balljoint

8 Front wheel alignment and steering angles

1 Accurate front wheel alignment is essential for good steering and tyre wear. Before considering the steering angles, check that the tyres are correctly inflated, that the front wheels are not buckled, the hub bearings are not worn or incorrectly adjusted and that the steering linkage is in good order, without slackness or wear at the joints.
2 Wheel alignment consists of four factors:
Camber, which is the angle at which the front wheels are set from the vertical when viewed from the front of the car. Positive camber is the amount (in degrees) that the wheels are tilted outwards at the top from the vertical.
Castor is the angle between the steering axis and a vertical line when viewed from each side of the car. Positive castor is when the steering axis is inclined rearwards.
Steering axis inclination is the angle, when viewed from the front of the car, between the vertical and an imaginary line drawn between the upper and lower suspension leg pivots.
lower suspension leg pivots.

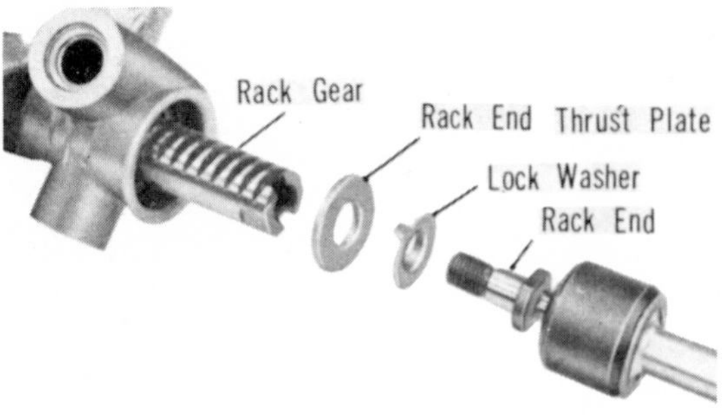

Fig. 8.33. Fitting a rackend assembly to the rack gear

Toe-in or toe-out is the difference between the measurements of the inside edges of the road wheel rims at the front and rear of the wheels measured at hub height. Honda front wheels are toed-out.

3 Front wheel alignment checks are best carried out with modern setting equipment but the toe-out can be checked in the following manner.

4 Position the car on level ground with the wheels in the straight ahead position.

5 Obtain a propreitary tracking gauge or make one from a length of tubing, cranked to clear the crankcase and differential unit and having an adjustable nut and setscrew at one end.

6 With the gauge, measure the distance between the inner wheel rims at hub height at the rear of the roadwheel.

7 Rotate the road wheel through 180° (half a turn) by pushing the car backwards or forwards. Insert the track gauge (with the previous measurement still set on it) between the inner wheel rims, at hub height, at the front of the roadwheel. The gauge should show this dimension to be more than the one at the rear by 0.08 in (2 mm) which is the correct toe-out of the front wheels.

8 If the toe-out is incorrect, loosen the locknuts on the track-rod ends and rotate each track-rod equally.

For ease of turing, the rubber bellows can be pushed back and a spanner applied to the rack end flats as shown in Fig 8.xx. Rotating the right-hand track-rod in the direction of roadwheel forward motion and the left-hand one in the opposite direction will increase the toe-out. If the track-rods have previously been maladjusted, set the roadwheels in the straight ahead position and rotate each track-rod until the distance between the centre points of the track-rod ends and the end faces of the rack gear are equal. Commence adjustment rotating each track-rod an equivalent amount.

Fig. 8.34. Adjusting the front wheel track

9 When adjustment is correct, tighten the track-rod end lock-nuts without moving the track-rod and ensuring that the track-rod ball joint is correctly set at the centre of its arc of travel.

10 Finally re-set the rubber bellows, seeing that they are not twisted or with their convolutions pressed in.

9 Steering - fault diagnosis

Before beginning to diagnose faults from the list below first make quite sure that any irregularities are not caused by:-

1 Incorrect tyre pressures
2 Incorrect mix of radial and crossply tyres
3 Misalignment of bodyframe or rear axle
4 Binding brakes

Symptom	Cause	Remedy
Steering wheel can be rotated more than 30° before the road wheels react	Wear in linkage or steering gear	Check and renew.
	Steering box mounting bolts loose	Tighten.
Steering stiff and heavy	Seized track rod end balljoints	Renew.
	Lack of grease in steering gearbox	Lubricate (Section 6).
Wheel wobble, vibration or 'wander'	Road wheels require balancing	Balance professionally.
	Incorrect front end alignment	Check and adjust.
	Wear in steering balljoints	Renew.
	Rack guides require adjustment	Adjust (Section 2).

Chapter 9 Rear suspension, axle hubs

Contents

Specifications

Suspension:

Type	Semi-elliptic leaf springs with double acting hydraulic shock-absorbers
Shock-absorbers	Double acting, telescopic incorporating nitrogen gas

Rear axle:

Type	Tubular steel

Torque wrench settings:	**lb/ft**	**kg/m**
'U' bolts	34	4.7
Spring shackle bolts	35	4.8
Rear shock-absorber upper mounting nuts	10	1.4
Rear shock-absorber lower mounting bolt	32	4.4
Axle spindle nuts	72/78	10/11

1 General description

The new suspension is of semi-elliptical, leaf spring type with double acting, nitrogen gas type shock absorbers. The rear axle is a tubular fabrication terminating in spindles on which the drums run on bearings pressed into their centres.

2 Maintenance

1 The only maintenance required is to keep the shackle bolts and 'U' bolt nuts tightened to the specified torque.
2 Periodically jack-up the rear road wheels; grip the top and bottom of the tyre and test for bearing shake.
3 Check the torque of the axle nuts after removing the end cap and split pin. They should be tightened to between 72 and 78lb/ft (10 and 11kg/m.)

3 Hubs and bearings - removal and refitting

1 Jack-up the road wheel and remove it.
2 Remove the three securing bolts from the end cap and detach it.
3 Pull out the split pin from the castellated nut and unscrew and remove the nut.
4 Withdraw the brake drum, the spacer and the 'O' ring from its groove in the axle spindle.
5 The bearings and oil seal are pressed into the brake drum and if renewal is required they should be tapped out with a brass drift.
6 Refitting of bearings and seal is a reversal of dismantling. Always locate a new 'O' ring in the axle spindle groove before fitting the spacer against the axle end flange.
7 Tighten the axle nut to a torque of between 72 and 78 lb/ft (10 and 11 kg/m) and fit a new split pin.
8 Fit the end cup and road wheel and lower the jack.

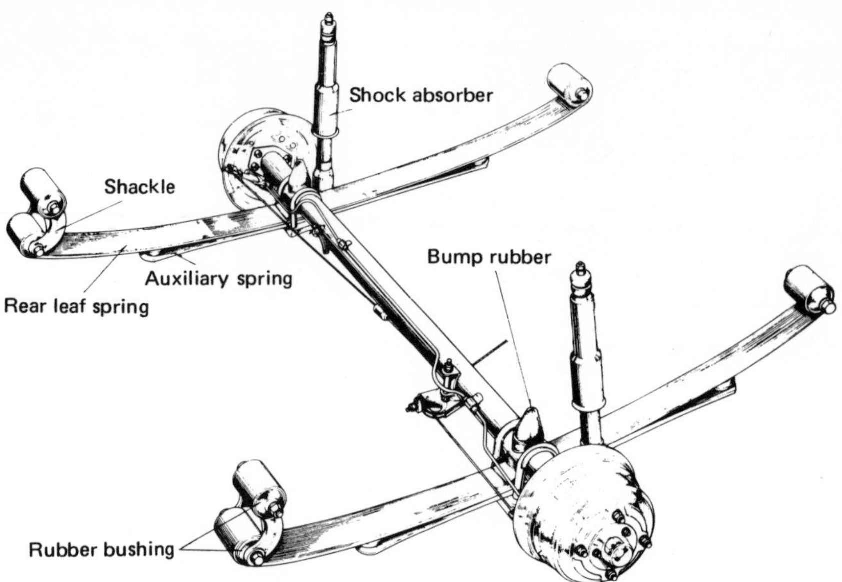

Fig. 9.1. Layout of rear axle and suspension

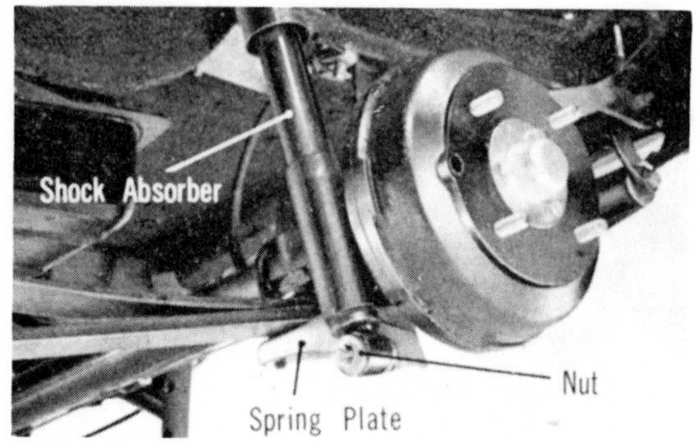

Fig. 9.2. Rear brake drum and end cap

Fig. 9.3. Location of rear wheel bearings and oil seal

4 Shock absorbers - removal, testing and refitting

1 Remove the shock absorber lower mounting bolt from the leaf spring plate.
2 Unscrew and remove the nut and locknut at the upper mounting within the luggage boot.
3 Note the fitting sequence of the upper mounting rubber cushions and plates.
4 A simple test for shock absorber serviceabilty can be carried out by gripping the bottom mounting eye in a vice and extending and compressing the unit to the full extent of its travel about ten times. Any loss of resistance in either direction will indicate a fault or wear in the internal components and the unit must be renewed.
5 Refitting is a reversal of removal but check the lower rubber mountings for deterioration and renew them if necessary.
6 Make sure that the protectiove shield on the shock absorber lower body faces the front of the car.
7 Tighten the upper and lower shock absorber mounting bolts and nuts to the specified torque settings.

5 Road springs - removal, inspection and refitting

1 It will usually be more realistic to remove the rear axle and leaf springs together, but where a single spring is to be renewed and the hydraulic braking circuit is not to be disconnected, carry out the following operations.
2 Jack up the rear of the car and support the body frame on axle stands.
3 Remove the road wheels and then support the axle tube on jacks or blocks.
4 Remove the shackle bolt which attaches the shackle to the bodyframe.
5 Unscrew and remove the 'U''bolt nuts and pull down the spring plate complete with shock absorber still attached.
6 Lower the road spring so that it rests on the ground and then remove the bolt from the front spring eye. The spring can now be removed from the car.

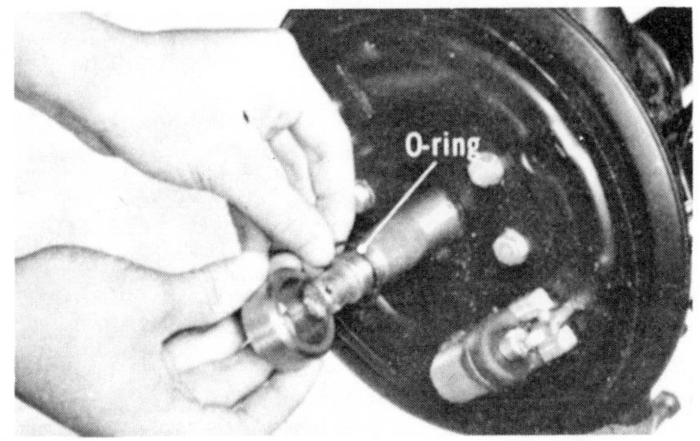

Fig. 9.4. Rear axle spindle 'O' ring and spacer

Fig. 9.5. Shock absorber upper mounting

Fig. 9.6. Bodyframe supported under rear crossmember

Fig. 9.7. Rear road spring shackle

Fig. 9.8. Road spring front attachment bolt

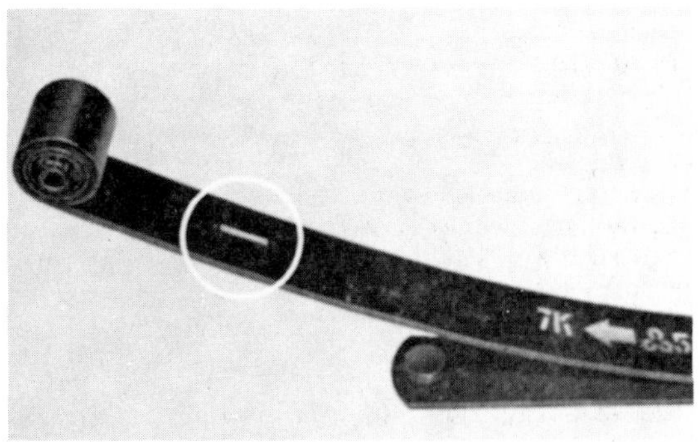

Fig. 9.9. Road spring forward facing mark

7 Inspect the spring leaves for cracks or lack of set. Also the rubber bushes in the rear spring eyes and shackles and if they are worn or have deteriorated have the components re-bushed at your Honda dealer. Check the anti-friction buttons which are located between the spring leaves and renew them if necessary.
8 Refitting is a reversal of removal but if one spring only is being renewed, ensure that the spring rating number matches that of the one being replaced. If this number is not visible the two rear road springs should be renewed as a set. The mark on the top leaf (Fig. 9.9) should be towards the front of the car.
9 Tighten the 'U' bolt nuts to a torque of 34lb/ft (4.7 kg/m), and all shackle bolts to 35lb/ft (4.8 kg/m).

6 Rear axle - removal and refitting

1 Jack-up the rear of the car and support the bodyframe on axle stands. Support the axle on jacks.
2 Remove the road wheels.
3 Disconnect the handbrake cable from the equaliser on the axle.
4 Disconnect the flexible brake hose from the rigid pipe and plug both to prevent loss of fluid.
5 Disconnect the shock absorber lower mountings.
6 Unscrew and remove the 'U' bolt nuts and the rear shackle (to body frame) bolts and lower the rear ends of the road springs to the ground.
7 Draw the axle out sideways from beneath the car after lowering the jacks.
8 Refitting is a reversal of removal but tighten all nuts and bolts to the specified torques. Reconnect the handbrake cable and hydraulic brake line and bleed the brakes as describedin the next Chapter.

7 Rear wheel alignment

1 The rear wheel alignment is set during manufacture and cannot be altered. It is essential however to ensure that the axle spindle nuts are correctly tightened and after removal of either the road springs or the rear axle, the locating leaf spring to axle tube dowels are in engagement.
2 A simple method of checking the rear wheel alignment is to wet the tyre treads and then to drive onto a dry concrete surface (steering in straight ahead position) when the tyre tracks of both front and rear wheels should be parallel with the rear ones slightly inboard of the front ones. Any deviation or 'crabbing' could be caused by distortion of the bodyframe or a bent axle tube if the attachment of the rear axle and springs has previously been checked as being correct.

8 Rear suspension, axle and hubs - fault diagnosis

Symptom	Cause	Remedy
Car pulls to one side	Incorrect tyre pressures	Correct.
Severe wear on tyre edge	Worn bearings	Renew.
Vehicle down on one side	Sagging (weak) leaf spring	Renew.
	Incorrectly tightened 'U' bolt nuts	Loosen and tighten to specified torque.
	Overtightened spring rear shackle bolts	Loosen and tighten to specification.

Chapter 10 Braking system

Contents

Specifications

System type:	Four wheel hydraulic, mechanically operated handbrake on rear wheels only. Rear drum, front disc or drum
Master cylinder:	
360 cc/21.5 cu in. and early 600 cc/35.5 cu in. vehicles	Single type master cylinder of 0.748 in. (19 mm) diameter bore
600 cc/35.5 cu in. vehicles from chassis number 1000001 to 1010298	Parallel type master cylinder of 0.551 in. (14 mm) diameter bore
600 cc/35.5 cu in. vehicles from chassis number 1010299 onwards and with addition of vacuum servo unit (chassis number 1013096 onwards)	Tandem type master cylinder of 0.750 in. (19.05 mm) diameter bore
Disc brakes:	
Disc outside diameter	7.17 in. (182 mm)
Thickness (standard)	0.374 in. (9.5 mm)
Thickness (reground minimum)	0.299 in. (7.6 mm)
Caliper bore diameter	1.688 in. (42.85 mm)
Friction pad thickness (standard)	0.406 in. (10.3 mm)
Friction pad thickness (minimum)	0.079 in. (2.0 mm)
Friction pad area	4 x 2.89 in^2 (18.7 cm^2)
Drum brakes:	
Type:	
360 cc/21.5 cu in.	Leading/trailing (front and rear)
600 cc/35.5 cu in.	Two leading (front) leading/trailing (rear)
Drum inside diameter	7.087 in. (180.0 mm)

Friction lining dimensions:	
Each shoe	5.56 x 1.38 x 0.20 in. thick (141.5 x 35.0 x 5.0 mm thick)
Total area	31.54 in.^{2} (198 cm^2) per shoe

Wheel cylinders:

Bore diameter:	
Front	1.0 in. (25.40 mm)
Rear	0.5626 in. (14.29 mm)
Rear (North America)	0.6248 in. (15.87 mm)

Vacuum servo unit:

Type	DHM 4500/1Z
Diaphragm unit diameter	4.5 in. (114.3 mm)
Stroke	0.6 in. (14.3 mm)
Hydraulic cylinder:	
Blue identification	0.6 in. (14.3 mm)
Red identification	0.68 in. (17.5 mm)
Relay valve piston diameter	½ in. (12.7 mm)

Torque wrench settings:	**lb ft**	**kg m**
Caliper to stub axle carrier bolts	40	5.5
Rigid pipe unions	14	1.9
Flexible hose unions	18	2.5
Wheel cylinder to backplate nuts	16	2.2

1 General description

The four wheel brakes are hydraulically operated with a mechanically operated handbrake working on the rear wheels only.

A number of different braking layouts may be encountered according to the vehicle model, date of manufacture and the territory in which it is destined to operate. Drum or disc brakes may be fitted to the front wheels but the rear wheels are always of drum type.

The master cylinder may be of single type or with a dual hydraulic circut, tandem or parallel (600 cc/35.5 cu in models only).

A pressure regulating valve is fitted to all models to balance the pressure between the more heavily loaded front wheels and the rear wheels during brake retardation. 600 cc/35.5 cu in models with dual circuit and a parallel master cylinder are also fitted with a by-pass valve to equalise the pressures within the two circuits. Vehicles supplied to the North American market have a brake failure warning lamp fitted to the instrument panel and vacuum servo assistance as standard features.

2 Maintenance and adjustment

1 Carry out the routine maintenance tasks as described in the Chapter in the front of this manual.

2 Inspect the condition of all pipes and hoses and renew as necessary (see Section 6).

3 Examine the caliper and wheel cylinder units for leaks (also indented by a drop in the fluid reservoir level) and rectify immediately.

4 Disc brakes require no adjustment but adjust drum type brakes in the following manner.

5 Depress the foot brake pedal several times to centralise the shoes in the drums. Jack-up each wheel in turn and turn the adjuster clockwise (or downwards in the case of star type adjuster wheels) until the shoes are locked to the drum and it will not rotate. Now turn the adjuster anticlockwise the lease amount to permit the drum to turn without dragging or scraping.

6 Adjustment of the handbrake is quite automatic whenever the brake shoes are adjusted but from time-to-time the cable stretches or wear occurs in the mechanical linkage and additional adjustment will be required as described in Section 5.

3 Disc brakes pads - inspection, removal and refitting

1 Jack up the front of the car and remove the roadwheel.

2 Inspect the thickness of the friction pads. The minimum thickness is 0.8 in (2.0 mm) at which time they must be renewed.

3 To do this, pull out the retaining clip from the holes in the pad retaining pins.

4 Withdraw the pins with a pair of pliers and detach the pad retaining springs.

5 Pull each friction pad straight out with a pair of pliers. Anti-squeak shims are fitted at the back of each pad and will come out with the pad. **Do not depress the brake pedal.**

6 If the thickness of the friction material differs appreciably between the two pads check the operation of the caliper unit.

7 Installation of the new thicker pads will necessitate pushing the caliper inner piston into its bore and the outer piston back against the retaining ring by applying pressure to the yoke. This action will rasie the level of the fluid in the reservoir and it is a good plan to syphon some of the fluid out beforehand. Alternatively, open the caliper bleed screw before depressing the pistons to allow displaced fluid to be ejected.

8 Refit the pads and anti-squeak shims, pins, spring and clips. Note that the coil spring is located on the lower pin.

9 With the new pads installed, depress the footbrake two or three times and then check the top-up the fluid level in the reservoir.

4 Drum brake shoes - inspection, removal and refitting

1 The drum brakes fitted to front wheels may be either of leading/trailing type or two leading shoe type. Rear brakes are of leading/trailing type.

2 Jack-up the car and remove the brake drum as described in either Chapter 7 or 9.

3 Examine the thickness of the bonded friction linings. If they have worn down to 0.055 in (1.4 mm) or less than the shoes must be renewed on an exchange basis. Examine the linings for oil or grease and if evident rectify the cause which will probably be due to a leaking wheel cylinder or failed grease seal or 'O' ring in the axle stub or spindle components.

4 Before removing the brake shoes, unscrew the adjusters completely and note (sketch if in doubt) the shoe web holes in which the return springs engage and also the relative positions of

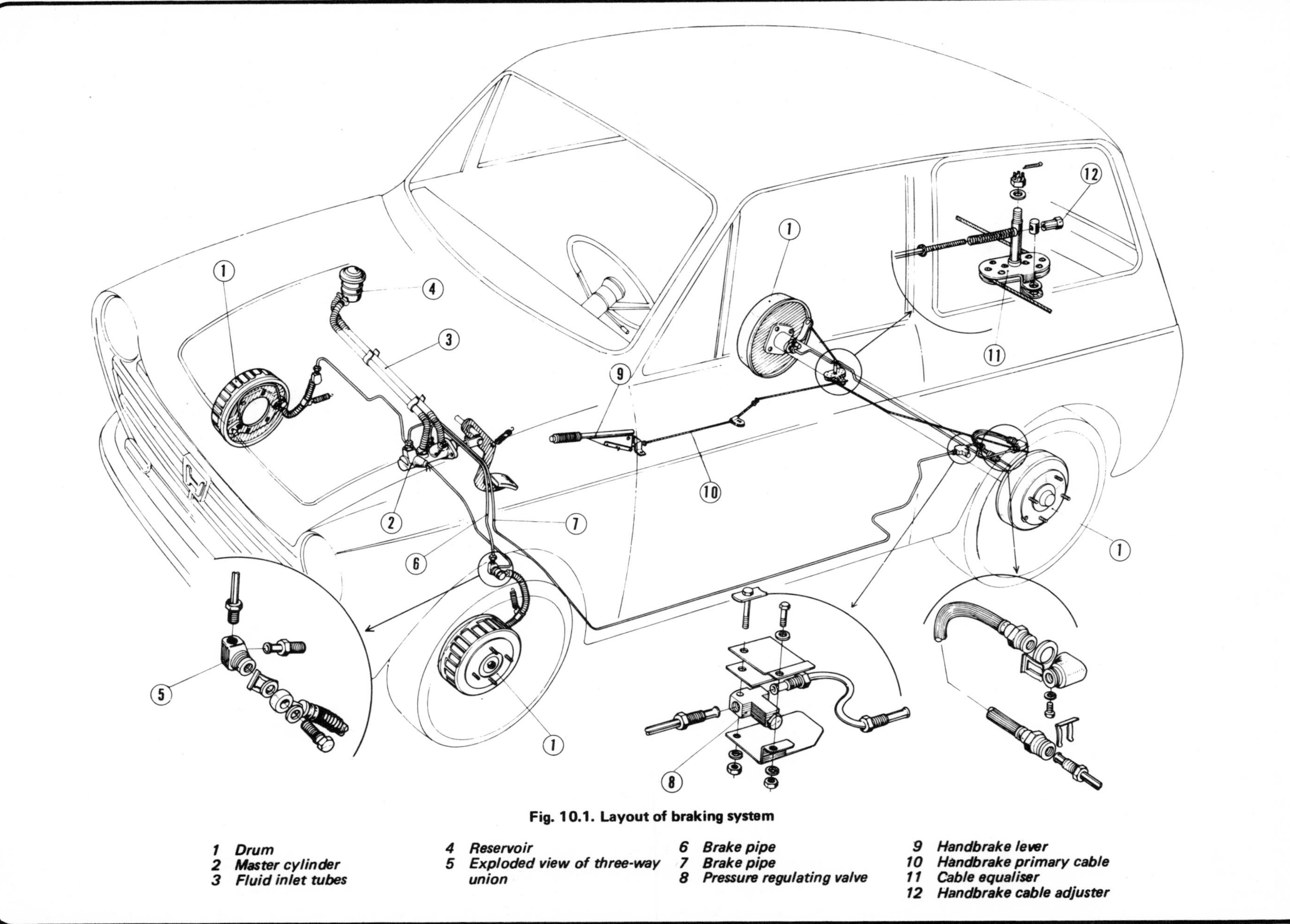

Fig. 10.1. Layout of braking system

1 *Drum*
2 *Master cylinder*
3 *Fluid inlet tubes*
4 *Reservoir*
5 *Exploded view of three-way union*
6 *Brake pipe*
7 *Brake pipe*
8 *Pressure regulating valve*
9 *Handbrake lever*
10 *Handbrake primary cable*
11 *Cable equaliser*
12 *Handbrake cable adjuster*

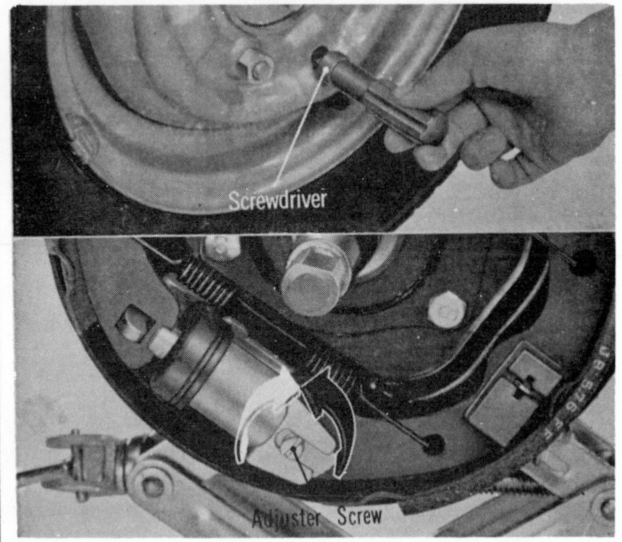

Fig. 10.2. Screw type adjuster (accessible through roadwheel)

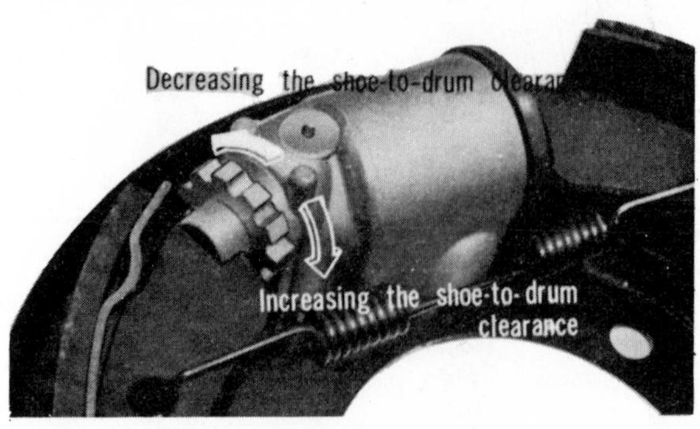

Fig. 10.3. Star wheel type brake shoe adjuster (one of two fitted with 2 leading shoe type drum brakes)

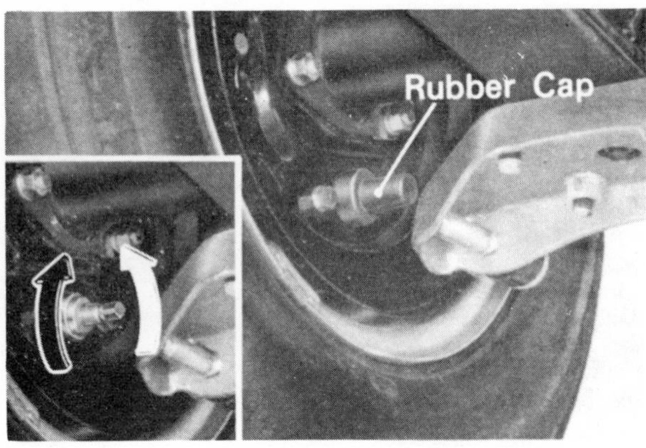

Fig. 10.4. Backplate located square type shoe adjuster fitted to 600 (Z) Coupe models

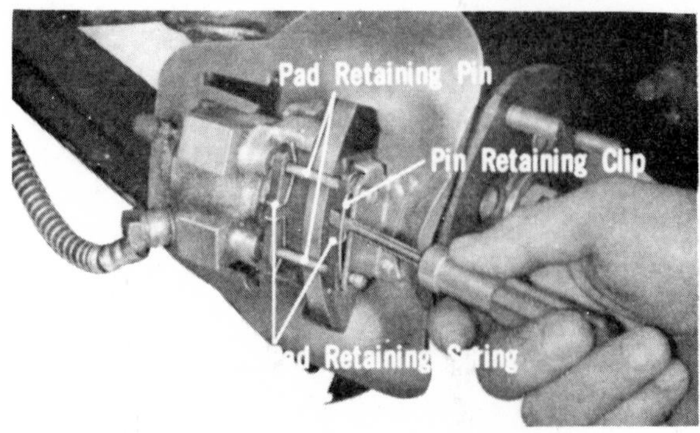

Fig. 10.5. Removing disc pad retaining pin clip

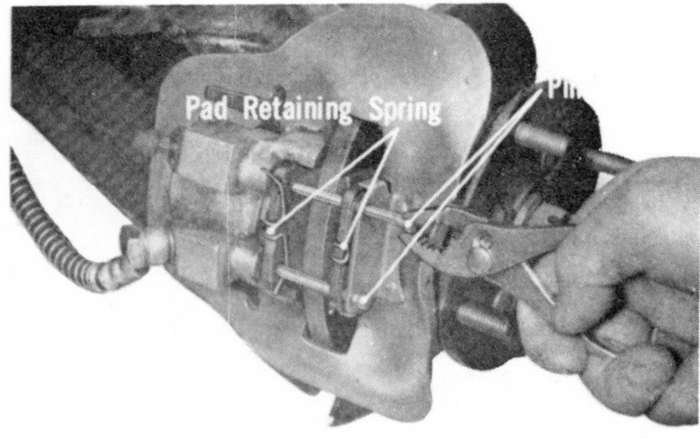

Fig. 10.6. Withdrawing disc pad retaining pin

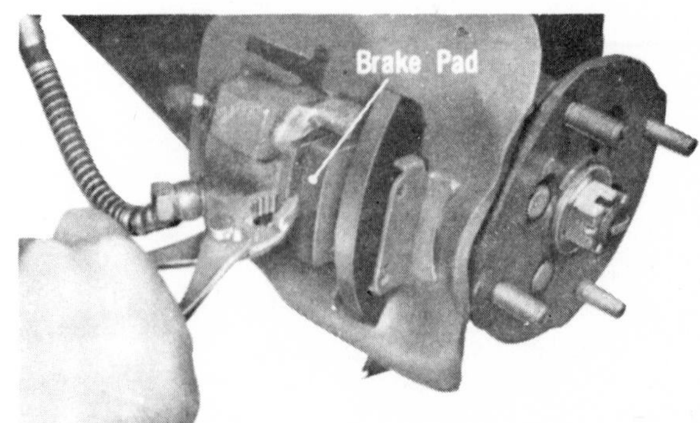

Fig. 10.7. Withdrawing a disc pad with a pair of pliers

the leading and trailing ends of the shoes.
5 Release the shoe posts from the springs by turning them through 90° with a pair of pliers.
6 Prise one shoe away from contact with the wheel cylinders (or wheel cylinder and fixed pivot - leading/trailing type)ease it towards the centre of the hub and disconnect the opposite shoe still with the return springs engaged.
7 **Do not depress the brake pedal while the shoes are removed.**
8 Lay the new shoes on the bench correctly positioned with regard to leading and trailing ends and engage the shoe return springs in the web holes.
9 Refitting is a reversal of removal but before doing so, apply a smear of heavy grease to the high points, (rubbing surfaces) of the backplate.
10 Fit the brake drum and adjust the shoes as described in Section 22.

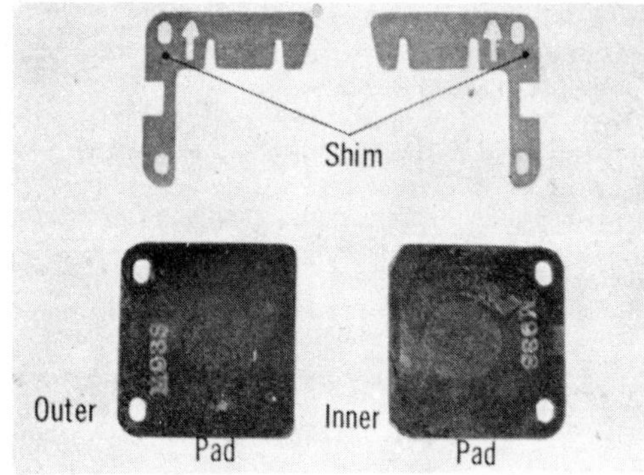

Fig. 10.8. Correct alignment of disc pads and anti-squeak shims

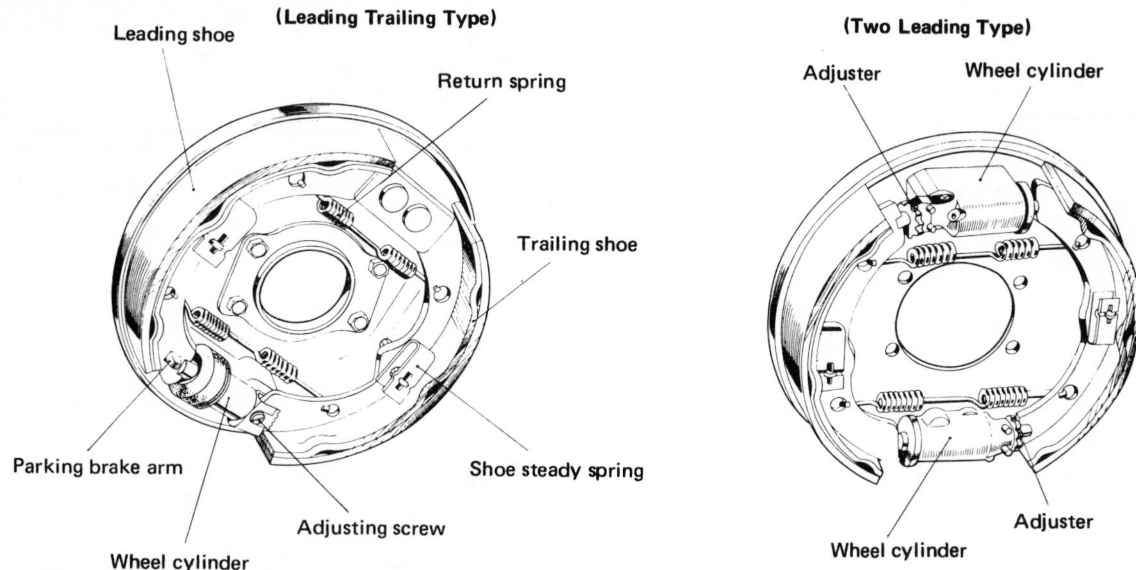

Fig. 10.9. The two types of brake drum

5 Handbrake - adjustment and cable renewal

1 If with the rear drum brakes properly adjusted, the handbrake lever travels more than 3 notches of the ratchet to lock the wheels, then rotate the adjuster nut on the equaliser (Fig 10.10) until the movement is correct.
2 To renew a cable, unscrew and remove the adjuster nut from the threaded portion of the cable at the equaliser.
3 Release the handbrake lever completely and disconnect the operating cable from it after removal of the split pin and clevis pin.
4 Pull off the handbrake warning lamp switch lead connector.
5 Detach the cable guides from the front and side of the fuel tank. The front guide is secured by one bolt. Remove the primary cable.
6 The secondary cable can be removed by detaching both ends from the rear wheel cylinder levers and then disconnecting it from the equaliser.
7 Refitting is a reversal of removal but grease the cable guides.
8 Should the handbrake lever ratchet be worn or the warning lamp switch not operate, the lever can be removed by unscrewing the two mounting bolts from the car floor.

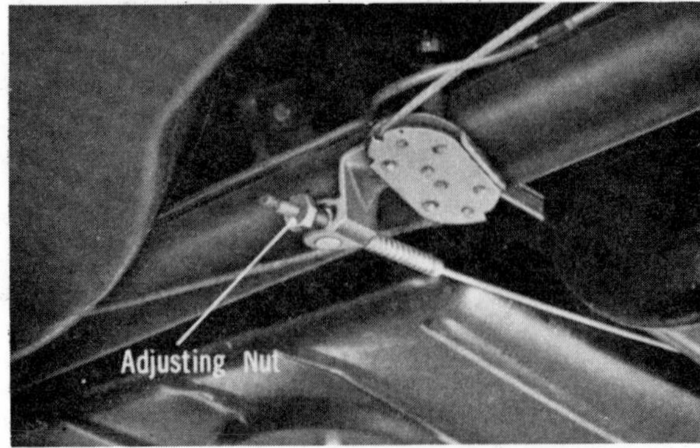

Fig. 10.10. Location of handbrake cable adjusting nut

6 Hydraulic pipes and hoses - inspection, removal and refitting

1 Periodically carefully examine all brake pipes, both rigid and flexible, for rusting, chafing and deterioration. Check the security of unions and connections.
2 First examine for signs of leakage where the pipe unions occur. Then examine the flexible hoses for signs of chafing and fraying and, of course, leakage. This is only a preliminary part of the flexible hose inspection, as exterior condition does not necessarily indicate their interior condition which will be considered later in the Chapter.
3 The steel pipes must be examined equally carefully. They must be cleaned off and examined for any signs of dents or other precussive damaged and rust and corrosion. Rust and corrosion should be scraped off and if the depth of pitting in the pipes is significant, they will need replacement. This is particularly likely in those areas underneath the car body and along the rear axle where the pipes are exposed to the full force of road and weather conditons.
4 If any section of pipe is to be taken off, first of all remove the fluid reservoir cap and line it with a piece of polythene film to make it air tight and replace it. This will minimise the amount of fluid dripping out of the system, when pipes are removed, by preventing the replacement of fluid by air in the reservoir.
5 Rigid pipe removal is usually quite straightforward. The unions at each end are undone and the pipe and union pulled out and the centre sections of the pipe removed from the body clips where necessary. Underneath the car, exposed unions can sometimes be very tight. As one can use only an open ended spanner and the unions are not large, burring of the flats is not uncommon when attemption to undo them. For this reason a self-locking grip wrench (mole) is often the only way to remove a stubborn union.
6 Rear flexible hoses are always mounted at both ends in a rigid bracket attached to the body or a sub-assembly. To remove them it is necessary first of all to unscrew the pipe unions of the rigid pipes which go into them. Then, with a spanner on the hexagonal end of the flexible pipe union, the locknut and washer on the other side of the mounting bracket need to be removed. Here again exposure to the elements often tends to seize the locknut and in this case the use of penetrating oil or Plus-gas is necessary. The mounting brackets, particularly on the body-frame, are not very heavy gauge and care muts be taken not to wrench them off. A self-grip wrench is often of use here as well. Use it on the pipe union in this instance as one is able to get a ring spanner on the locknut. Detach the pipe support and tension spring (photo) from the front pipes. These have banjo

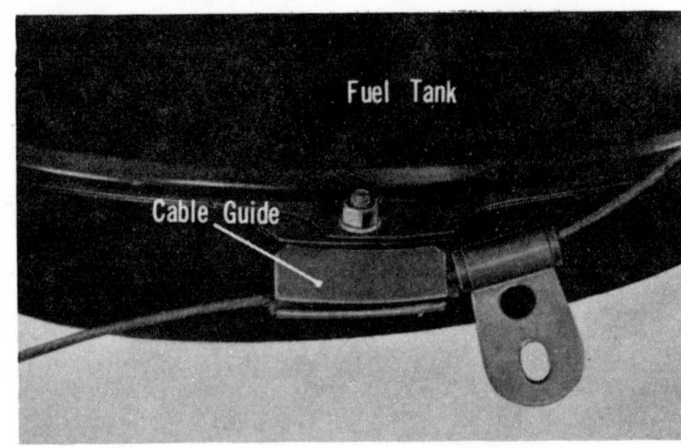

Fig. 10.11. Fuel tank cable guide

6.6A Front flexible brake hose tension spring

type unions at the front ends (photo).

7 With the flexible hose removed, examine the internal bore. If it is blown through first, it should be possible to see through it. Any specks of rubber which come out, or signs of restriction in the bore, mean that the inner lining is breaking up and the pipe must be replaced.

8 Rigid pipes which need replacement can usually be purchased at any local garage where they have the pipe, unions and special tools to make them up. All they need to know is the total length of the pipe and the type of flare used at each end with the union. This is very important as one can have a flare and a mushroom on the same pipe.

9 Replacement of pipes is a straightforward reversal of the removal procedure. If the rigid pipes have been made up it is best to get all the sets (or bends) in them before trying to install them. Also if there are any acute bends, ask your supplier to put these in for you on a tube bender. Otherwise you may kink the pipe and thereby restrict the bore area and fluid flow.

10 With the pipes replaced, remove the polythene film from the reservoir cap (paragraph 4) and bleed the system as described in Section 20. It is not necessary always to bleed at all four wheels. It depends which pipe has been removed. Obviously if the main one from the master cylinder is removed, air could have reached any line from the later distribution of pipes. If, however, a flexible hose at a front wheel is replaced, only that wheel needs to be bled.

6.6B Front flexible brake hose banjo union

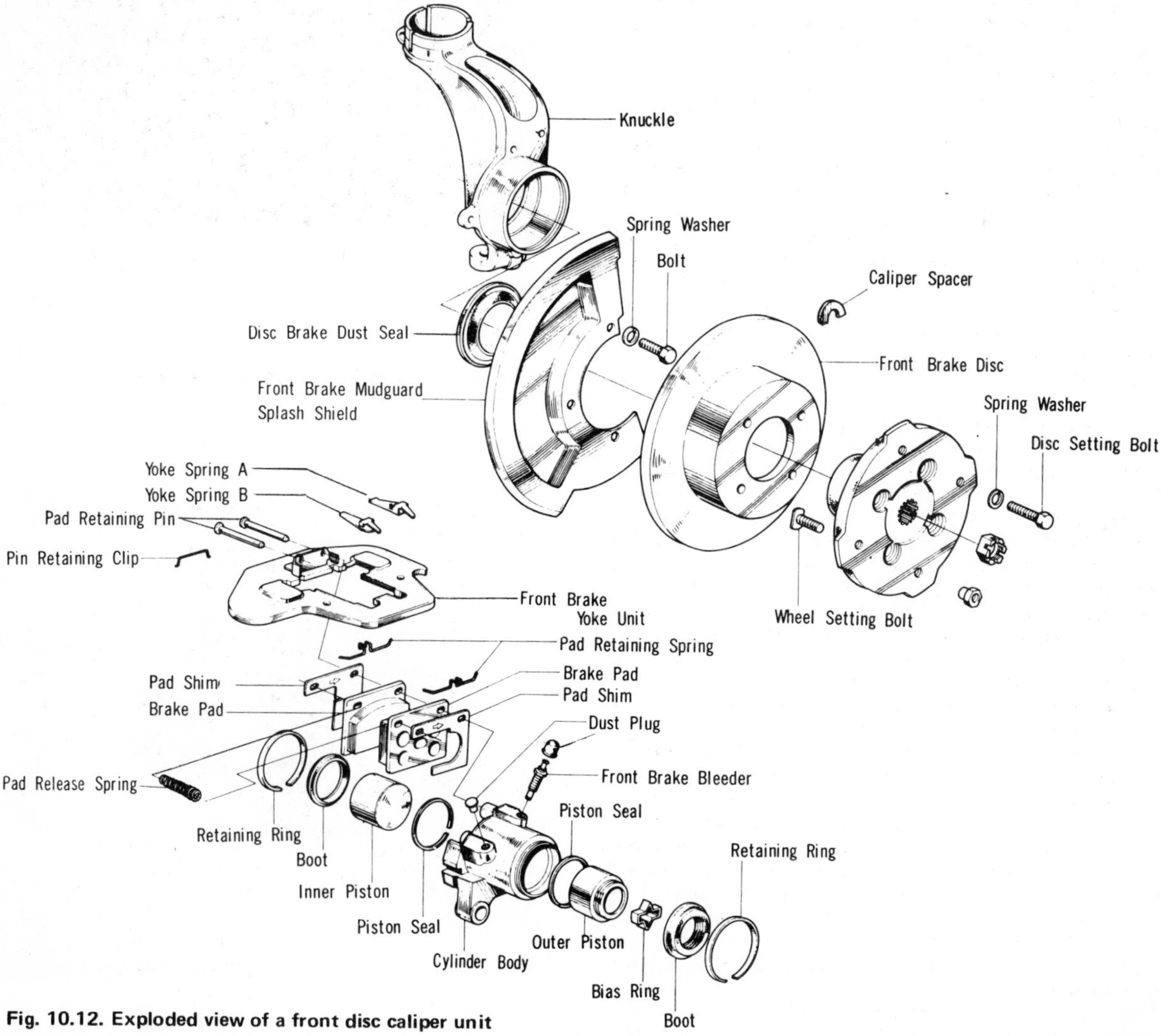

Knuckle
Spring Washer
Bolt
Caliper Spacer
Disc Brake Dust Seal
Front Brake Disc
Front Brake Mudguard
Splash Shield
Spring Washer
Disc Setting Bolt
Yoke Spring A
Yoke Spring B
Pad Retaining Pin
Pin Retaining Clip
Front Brake
Yoke Unit
Wheel Setting Bolt
Pad Retaining Spring
Pad Shim
Brake Pad
Brake Pad
Pad Shim
Dust Plug
Front Brake Bleeder
Pad Release Spring
Piston Seal
Retaining Ring
Boot
Retaining Ring
Inner Piston
Piston Seal
Outer Piston
Cylinder Body
Bias Ring
Boot

Fig. 10.12. Exploded view of a front disc caliper unit

7 Caliper - removal, servicing and refitting

1 Jack-up the front of the car and remove the road wheel.
2 Disconnect the flexible brake pipe at its junction with the rigid line and plug both the open pipe ends.
3 Unscrew the caliper securing bolts and withdraw the caliper from the stub axle carrier. Retain the shims which are fitted between the caliper and the stub axle carrier at the bolt holes.
4 Remove the disc pads from the caliper as described in Section 3.
5 Now tap the caliper body with a plastic faced mallet at the points indicated in Fig 10.13 and separate the cylinder body from the yoke assembly.
6 From the outer piston, remove the bias ring and from the yoke the two springs.
7 Remove the rubber dust excluder retaining rings from both ends of the cylinder body and detach the dust excluders.
8 Remove both pistons by pushing them out with a wooden dowel rod. Note their locations as they are not interchangeable.
9 Remove the piston seals from their grooves inside the cylinder using a screwdriver but take great care not to scratch the surface of the cylinder walls.
10 Discard all rubber components and the bias ring and obtain new ones supplied in repair kit form. Examine the surfaces of the pistons and cylinder walls for scoring or 'bright' wear areas. If these are evident, renew the complete caliper unit.
11 Wash all components in methylated spirit or clean brake fluid.
12 Commence reassembly by applying brake grease to the grooves and sliding surfaces of the yoke and then installing the yoke springs with the tongue positioned as shown in Fig. 10.17.
13 Dip the new piston seals in clean brake fluid and insert them into their grooves in the cylinder. Use only the fingers to manipulate them and ensure that the rounded corner is toward the end of the cylinder as shown in Fig 10.18.
14 Dip each piston into clean brake fluid and enter it into its respective cylinder end using a twisting motion to avoid turning up the lip of the seal.
15 Insert a new bias ring into the outer piston ensuring that tis rounded rim is towards the bottom of the piston and it is inserted to full depth.
16 Install two new dust excluding covers and fit their retaining rings.
17 Apply a smear of grease to the sliding surfaces of the yoke assembly and the cylinder body, align the bias ring so that the slot will engage with the tongue of the yoke and fit the two components together ensuring that the rubber dust excluder does not become damaged or pinched.
18 Refit the caliper into the the stub axle carrier, inserting the original alignment shims, tighten the securing bolts to a torque of 40 lb/ft (5.5 kg/m).
19 Insert the disc pads as described in Section 3, connect the brake hose and bleed the brakes (Section 20).

8 Discs and drums - inspection and servicing

1 The disc is bolted to the hub and can be removed as described in Chapter 7.
2 Under normal conditions of usage, the disc will appear lightly scored. If after a considerable mileage, deep grooves are evident, then the disc should be professionally reground. Note the minimum regrinding tolerance in Specifications' Section.
3 If the disc is suspected to be out of true due to accidental damage it must be immediately checked for run-out using a dial gauge. The maximum permissible run-out is 0.004 in (0.10 mm) otherwise renew the disc.
4 If deeply scored or worn oval, the drums must be reground but if the regrinding cause the inside diameter to exceed 7.126 in (181 mm) they must be renewed.

9 Wheel cylinders (drum brakes) - removal, servicing and refitting

1 Remove the brake drum as described in Chapter 7 or 9 according to whether a front or rear brake is involved.
2 Remove the brake shoes as described in Section 4 of this Chapter.
3 Disconnect the flexible brake hose from the rigid hydraulic pipe and plug the pipe. Unscrew the flexible hose from the wheel cylinder.

Rear brakes (Leading/Trailing - single cylinder)

4 Disconnect the handbrake cable from the lever on the wheel cylinder, remove the brake backplate from the axle flange.
5 Remove the dust seal and clip plate followed by the pressure spring. Detach the wheel cylinder from the backplate and disconnect the handbrake lever.

Front brakes (Two - leading - two cylinders)

6 Carry out the operations described in paragraphs 1 to 3 of this Section.
7 Disconnect and remove the bridge pipe between the two wheel cylinders, unscrew and remove the wheel cylinder retaining nuts and remove the cylinders from the backplate.
8 Some early model front brakes were of single cylinder leading/trailing type and are removed in a similar manner to the double cylinder.
9 Dismantling and reassembly of the wheel cylinder fitted with a star type adjuster is described in this Section but cylinders fitted to brakes having screw or square type adjusters are handled in a similar way and only differ in detail design.
10 Loosen the adjuster lock spring screw and remove the adjuster and its slotted screw.
11 Detach the rubber boot and apply air pressure from a tyre pump to the fluid inlet and eject the piston assembly.
12 Discard the rubber seal and boot and obtain the appropriate repair kit. Clean all components in brake fluid or methylated spirit. Examine the piston and cylinder bore surfaces for scoring or 'bright' wear areas and if evident, renew the complete wheel cylinder.
13 Dip the new piston seal in clean fluid and manipulate it into its groove using the fingers only. Note the direction of the chamber, Fig. 10.25.
14 Insert the piston into the cylinder using a twisting motion to avoid cutting the seal lip.
15 Installation of the wheel cylinder is a reversal of removal but with the rear wheel cylinders, lightly grease the sliding contact surfaces of the cylinder and backplate.
16 When the shoes and drums have been refitted, adjust the brakes and bleed the system as described in Section 20.

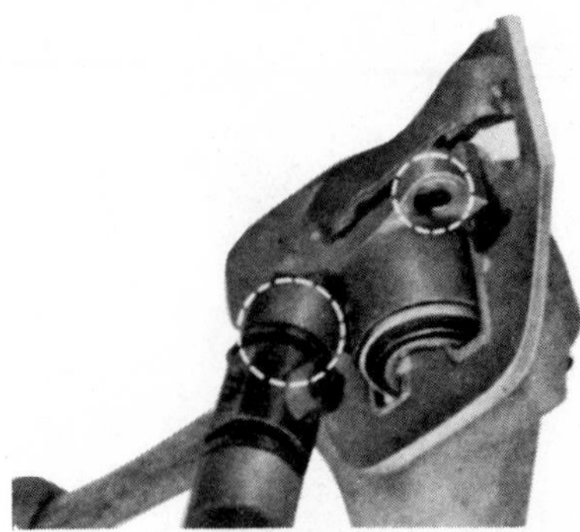

Fig. 10.13. Removing caliper body from yoke

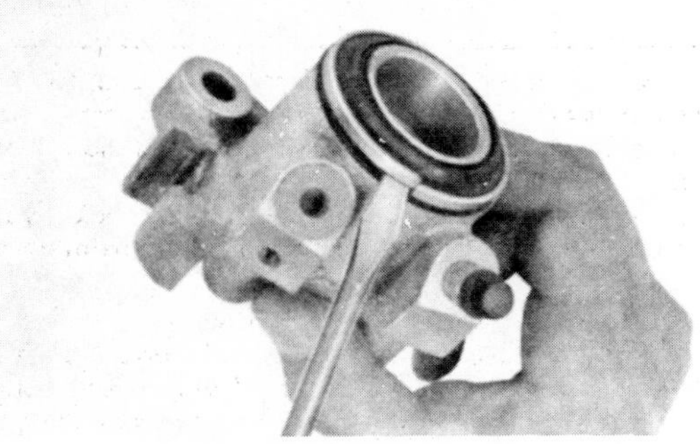
Fig. 10.14. Removing caliper dust excluder retaining ring

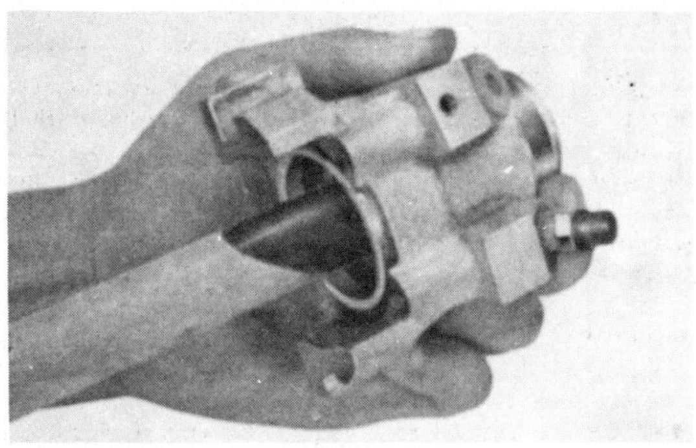
Fig. 10.15. Removing pistons from caliper body

Fig. 10.16. Removing seals from caliper cylinder grooves

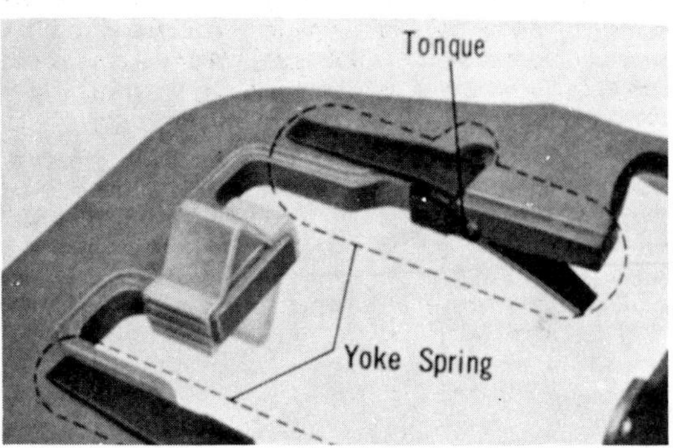

Fig. 10.17. Correct installation of yoke springs

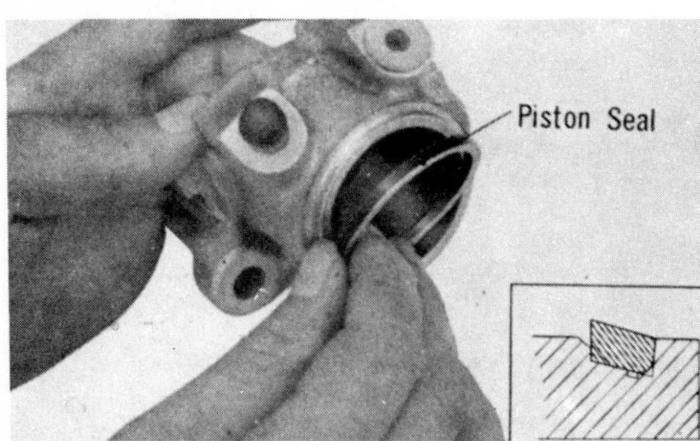

Fig. 10.18. Correct installation of piston seals

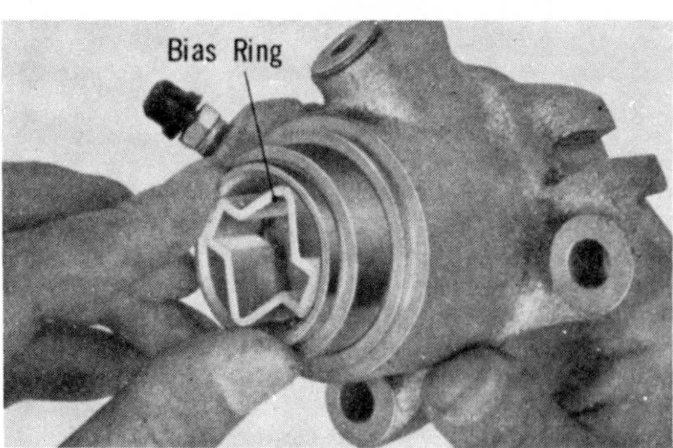

Fig. 10.19. Inserting bias ring into caliper outer piston

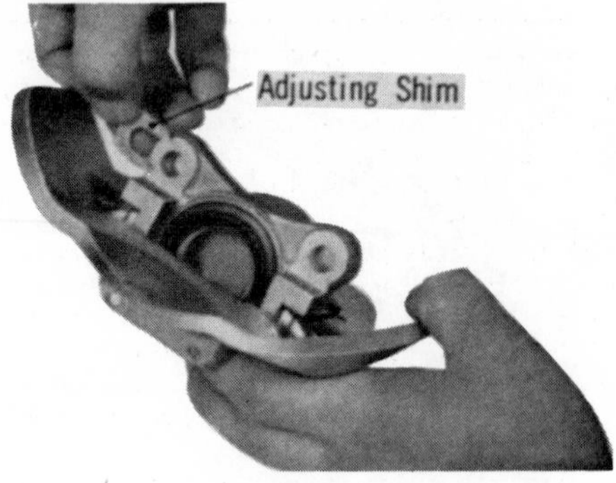

Fig. 10.20. Location of shim between caliper and stub axle carrier

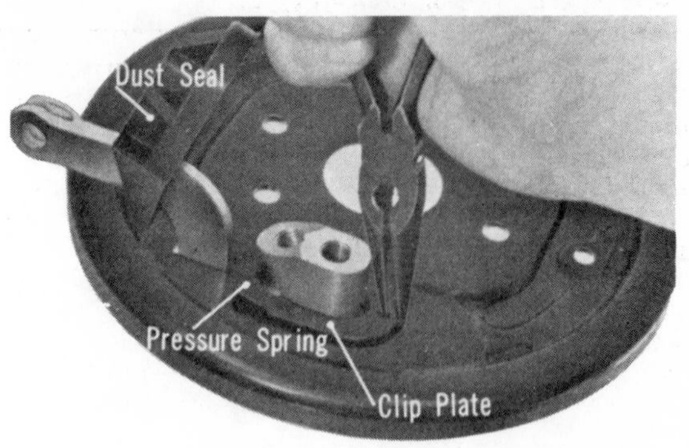

Fig. 10.21. Removing rear wheel cylinder clip plate

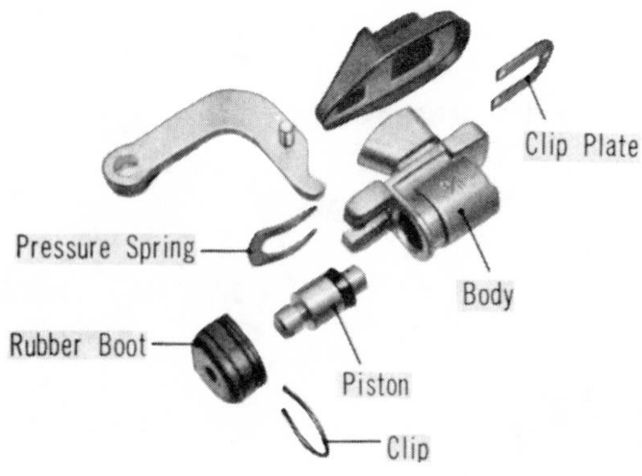

Fig. 10.22. Components of a rear wheel cylinder

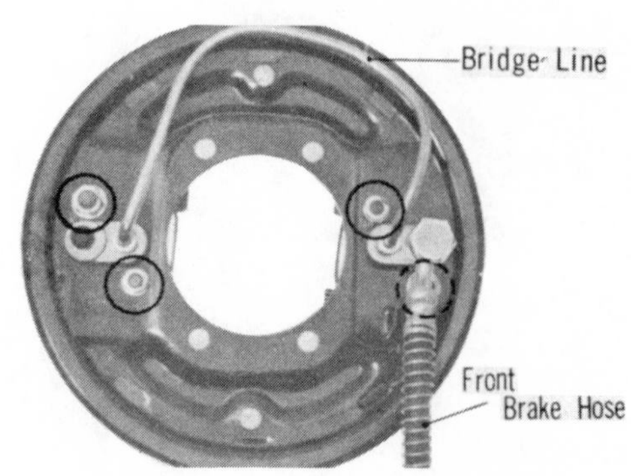

Fig. 10.23. Front drum brake bridging pipe

Fig. 10.24. Two leading shoe type adjusters

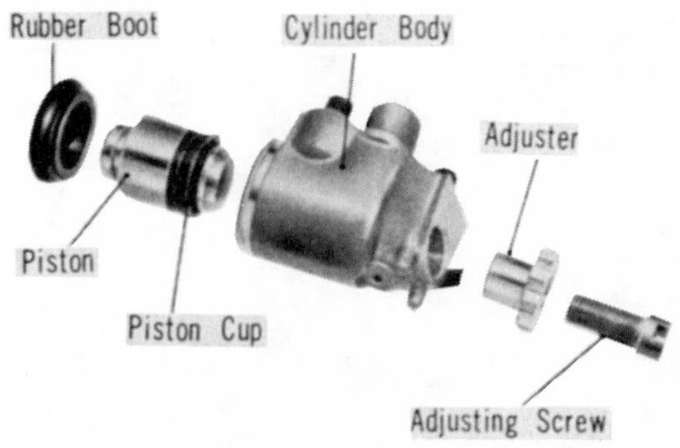

Fig. 10.25. Exploded view of two leading shoe type wheel cylinders

10 Master cylinders - description of types

The type of master cylinder fitted varies according to the vehicle model, date of manufacture and operating territory and reference should be made to the specifications Section for precise identification.

Generally a single type master cylinder is fitted with single circuit layouts and a tandem or parallel master cylinder is installed with dual circuit systems.

The pendant type foot pedal actuates the master cylinder through a pushrod.

On vehicles manufactured for the North American market and certain other territories, a vacuum servo system is employed and the booster unit is connected to a specially designed master cylinder.

On 600 cc/35.5 cu in vehicles equipped with a dual braking circuit and a parallel master cylinder, a bypass valve is located adjacent to the master cylinder to equalise the braking pressures within the two hydraulic circuits. On all models, a regulator valve is fitted at the rear of the car to adjust the pressures between the front and rear wheels to compensate for the heavier front axle loading.

11 Master cylinder - removal and installation

1 The removal of all types of master cylinder is similar although the number of connecting unions, pipe and stop lamp switchs will depend upon whether it is a single or double unit.

2 From below the instrument panel, remove the split pin and clevis pin and disconnect the master cylinder pushrod from the arm of the brake pedal.

3 Pull off the electrical connectors from the stop lamp switches at the front of the master cylinder.

4 On units having a remotely mounted fluid reservoir, disconnect the flexible pipes which connect it to the master cylinder and drain the fluid into a clean container. Do not allow fluto come into contact with the body paintwork or it will act as a very efficient paint stripper!

5 Disconnect the rigid pipe unions from the master cylinder body and plug them to prevent ingress of dirt.

6 Unbolt the master cylinder from the engine rear bulkhead.

7 Installation is a reversal of removal but when it has been refitted, bleed the system (Section 20).

Note that on parallel type master cylinders there is an equaliser link between the two brake pedal arms.

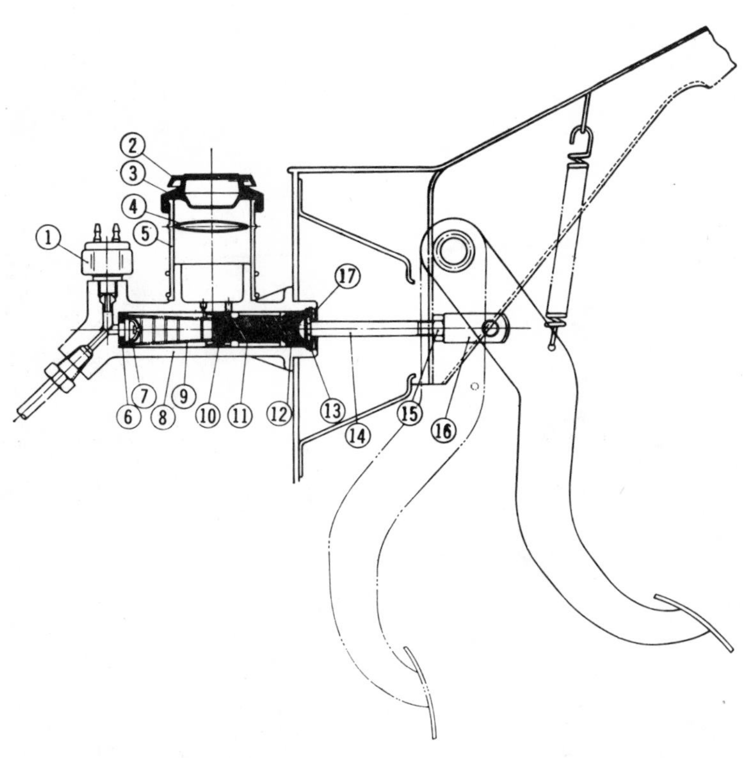

Fig. 10.26. Sectional view of single type master cylinder

1 Stop lamp switch
2 Reservoir cap
3 Baffle
4 Float
5 Reservoir
6 Non-return valve seat
7 Non-return valve
8 Cylinder body
9 Return spring
10 Primary cup seal
11 Piston
12 Secondary cup seal
13 Circlip
14 Push-rod
15 Locknut
16 Clevis fork
17 Dust excluder

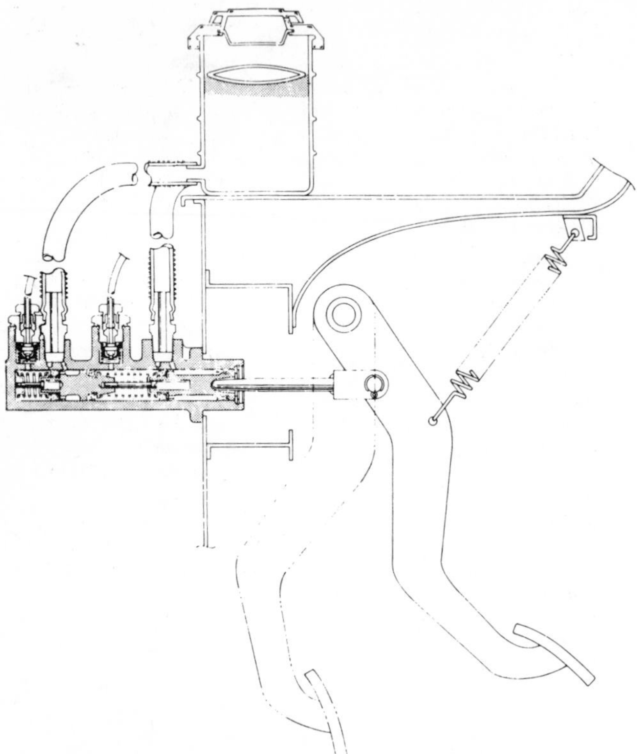

Fig. 10.27. Sectional view of tandem type master cylinder

Fig. 10.28. Tandem master cylinder with remote reservoir

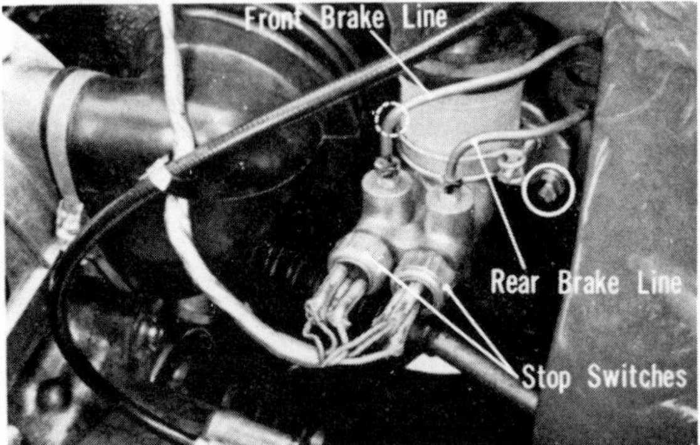

Fig. 10.29. Parallel type master cylinder with integral reservoir

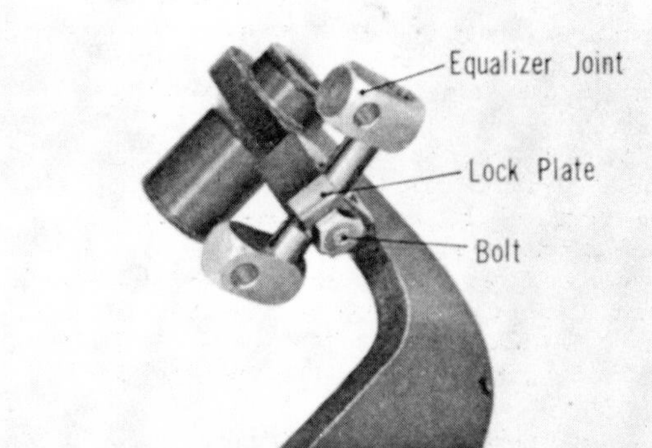

Fig. 10.30. Pedal equaliser fitted with parallel type master cylinders

12 Single type master cylinder - servicing

1 During all operations, observe strict cleanliness and use the fingers only to manipulate the seals in and out of their locations. Obtain the appropriate repair kit which will contain all the necessary seals and renewable items.
2 Refer to Fig. 10.26 and remove the dust seal (17), and push-rod (14) from the end of the master cylinder body.
3 Remove the circlip (13) and extract the piston assembly (11) return spring (9) and non-return valve. Use air from a tyre pump if necessary applied at the fluid inlet, to eject them.
4 Wash all components in methylated spirit or clean hydraulic fluid and discard the seals.
5 Examine the surface of the piston and the internal bore of the cylinder body. If there are 'bright' wear areas or score marks, renew the complete master cylinder.
6 Reassembly is a reversal of dismantling but dip each component in clean hydraulic fluid before assembling and ensure that the piston cups and seals have their lips located in the correct direction.

13 Tandem master cylinder - servicing

1 Pull off the dust cover and extract the pushrod from the end of the cylinder body.
2 Extract the circlip from the end of the master cylinder body.
3 Remove the piston stop, the primary and secondary piston assemblies and their springs after reference to Fig 10.37. Use air pressure from a tyre pump applied at the fluid inlet to eject them.
4 Remove the non-return valves and stop lamp switches if necessary. Discard all seals and wash components in methylated spirit or clean brake fluid.
5 Examine the surfaces of the pistons and cylinder bores for scoring or 'bright' wear areas and if evident, renew the master cylinder assembly complete.
6 Manipulate the new seals into position using the fingers only and ensuring that the lips and contours are correctly located.
7 Reassembly is a reversal of dismantling but dip each component in clean hydraulic fluid before entering it into the master cylinder bore

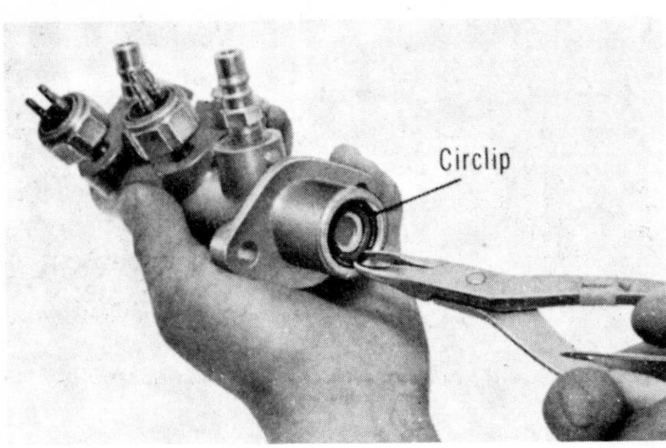

Fig. 10.31. Extracting circlip from tandem type master cylinder

14 Parallel type master cylinder - servicing

1 Invert the master cylinder and drain the hydraulic fluid from the reservoir.
2 Extract each of the two circlips and remove the two pushrods and stop plates.
3 Refer to Fig 10.32 and extract the secondary and primary piston assemblies and their springs. If necessary, apply air pressure at the fluid inlet to eject the interval components. The non-return valve seat can be extracted using a piece of hooked wire.
4 Wash all components in methylated spirit or clean brake fluid and discard the seals. Obtain the appropriate repair kit which will contain all the necessary renewable items.
5 Examine the surfaces of the pistons and the cylinder bores. If they are scored or have 'bright' wear areas, then renew the master cylinder unit complete.
6 Fit the piston seals using the fingers only to manipulate them into their grooves and ensuring that their lips face the correct way.
7 Reassemble the unit, dipping the components in clean hydraulic fluid before inserting them into the cylinder bores.

15 Pressure regulating by-pass valve - servicing

1 This valve operates on the floating piston (in balance) principle to equalise the hydraulic pressure in front and rear circuits to prevent any two road wheels locking.
2 The valve is located adjacent to the master cylinder and servicing should be restricted to the fitting of new seals.
3 Unscrew and remove the blanking plug and its sealing washer from the end of the valve body. Extract the spring.
4 Disconnect the forward fluid inlet pipe from the valve body and then have an assistant depress the brake foot pedal gently. This will cause the valve piston to be ejected. Catch any displaced fluid from the valve body or open end of the fluid inlet pipe.
5 Fit new seals to the piston ensuring that their lips face the correct way and reassemble the valve in the reverse order to dismantling.
6 Reconnect the fluid inlet pipe and bleed the system (Section 20).

16 Pressure regulating valve - removal and refitting

1 The valve is located under the floor of the rear compartment.
2 The valve cannot be serviced and in the event of its malfunction, it must be renewed as an assembly.
3 Remove the valve securing bolts and protective cover.
4 Unscrew the inlet and outlet fluid pipes from the valve ports.
5 Refitting is a reversal of removal but bleed the brakes on completion.

17 Pedals and stop lamp switch - servicing and adjustment

1 The brake and clutch pedals pivot on a common shaft.
2 The removal of either pedal is carried out by first detaching the return spring, removing the split pin and clevis pin and then removing the circlip from the end of the shaft. The pedal can now be withdrawn from the shaft.
3 The bush in the pedal arm can be renewed by drifting it out with a screwdriver or similar tool.
4 Refitting is a reversal of removal but grease the pivot bush and shaft and adjust the pedal height by means of the stop lamp switch adjuster bolts, Fig 10.42. This adjustment must be carried out with the system bled of air if the hydraulic system has been disconnected during the overhaul operations.
5 Adjust the height of the clutch pedal to match that of the brake pedal as described in Chapter 5.

18 Vacuum servo unit - description

The servo unit is designed to assist at the brakes the effort applied by the driver's foot to the brake pedal. The unit is an independent mechanism so that in the event of its failure the normal braking effort of the master cylinder is retained. A vacuum is created in the servo unit by its connection to the engine inlet manifold and with this condition applying on one side of a diaphragm atmospheric pressure applied on the other side of the diaphragm is harnessed to assist the foot pressure on the master cylinder.

Refer to Fig. 10.43. With the brake pedal released the diaphragm (1) is fully recuperated and is held against the rear shell by the return spring (5). The valve rod assembly (8) is also fully recuperated by the return spring (10). With the valve rod in this position, the vacuum port is fully open and there is a vacuum each side of the diaphragm.

With the brake applied, the valve rod assembly moves forward until the control valve closes the vacuum port. Atmospheric pressure then enters behind the diaphragm and is assisted by the valve rod to push the diaphragm plate (2) forward and enables the pushrod (4) to actuate the master cylinder plunger.

With the pressure on the brake pedal released the vacuum port is opened and the atmospheric pressure in the rear chamber is extracted to the front chamber and thence to the inlet manifold via the non-return valve (14). The atmospheric pressure port remains closed whilst the valve rod assembly returns to its original position, assisted by the diaphragm return spring. The diaphragm then remains suspended in vauum until the next occasion on which the brake pedal is depressed when the operating cycle is repeated.

19 Brake servo unit - removal and refitting

1 The servo unit is fitted to the engine rear bulkhead, adjacent to the air cleaner body.
2 Disconnect the vacuum tube at the servo unit.
3 Disconnect the two hydraulic pipes at the master cylinder unions.

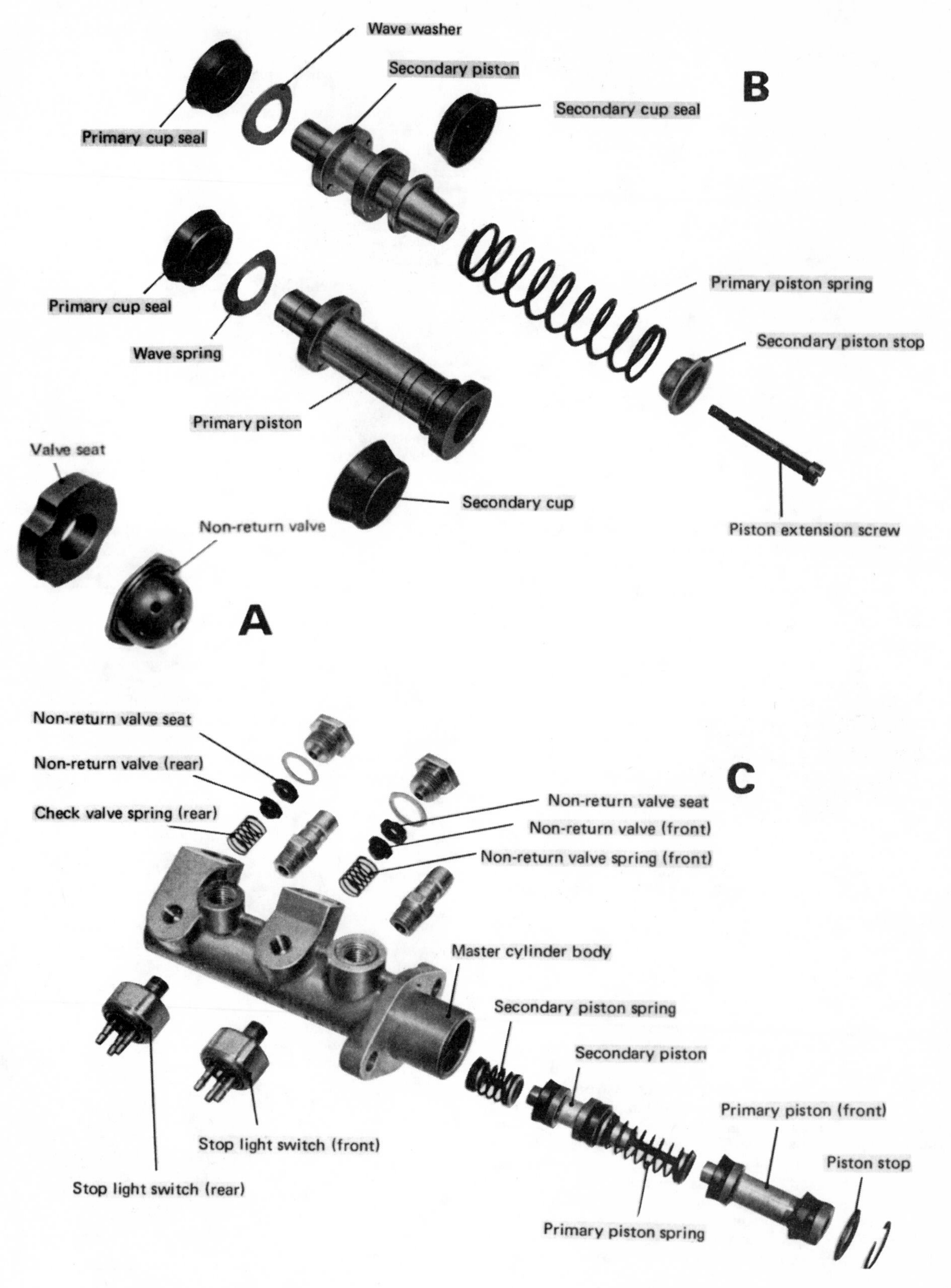

Fig. 10.32. Exploded view of tandem type master cylinder

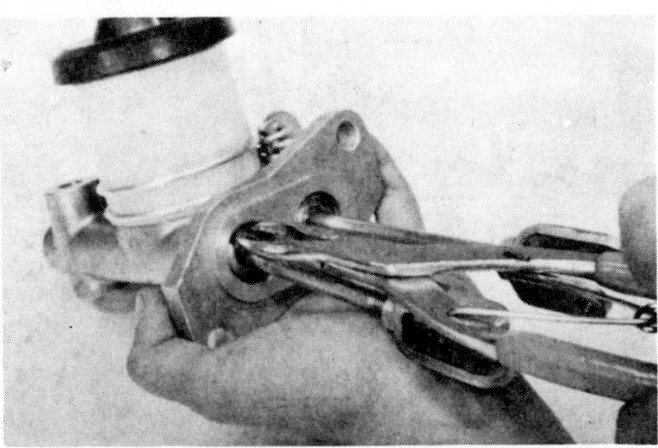

Fig. 10.33. Extracting circlips from parallel type master cylinder

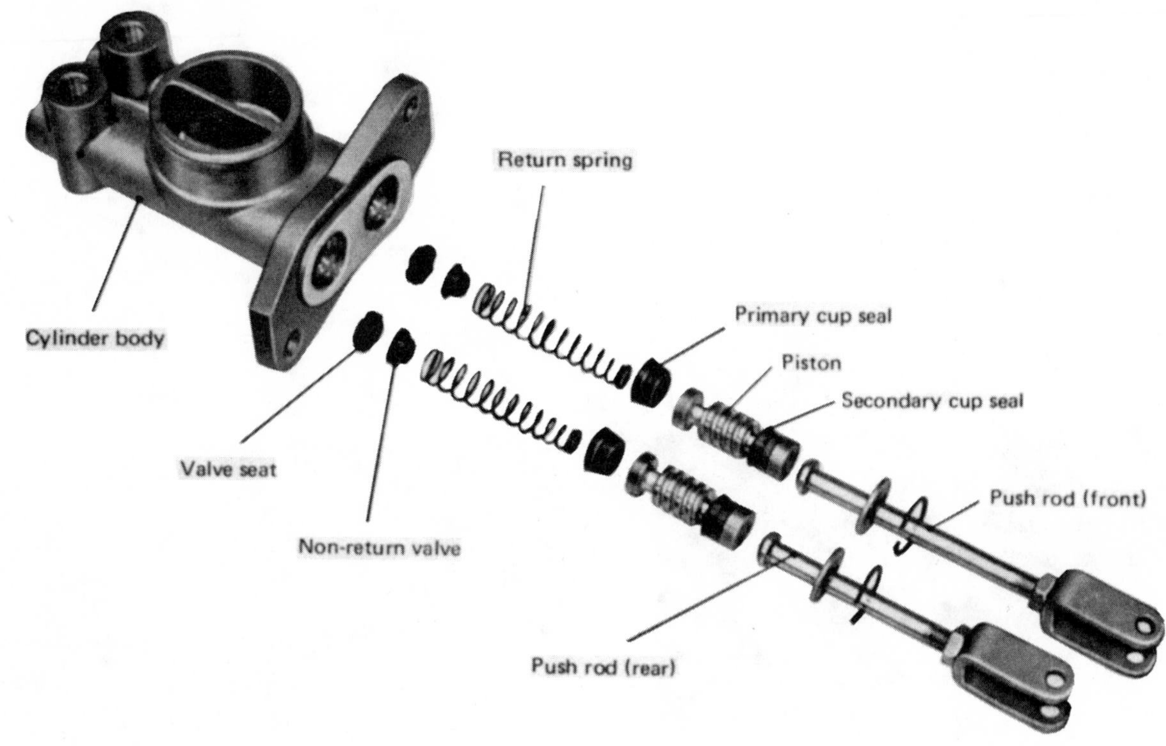

Fig. 10.34. Exploded view of parallel type master cylinder

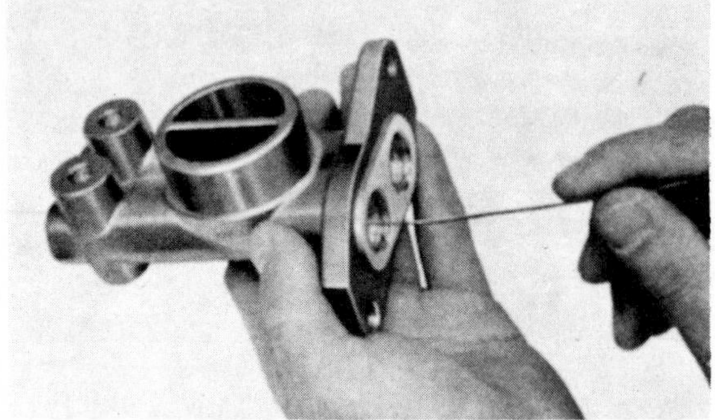

Fig. 10.35. Extracting a non-return valve seat using a piece of wire

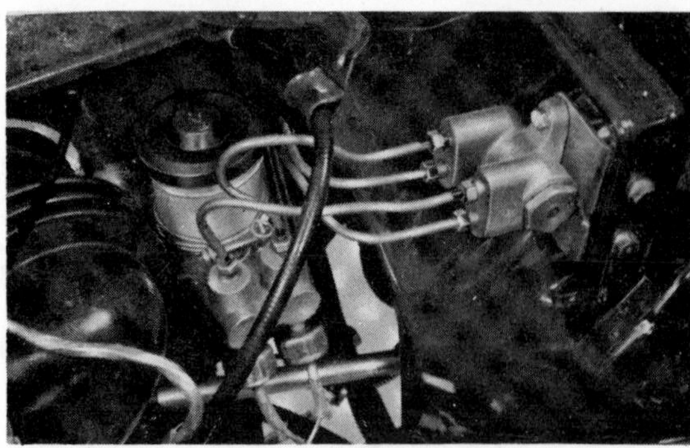

Fig. 10.36. Location of bypass valve (600 cc/35.5 cu in. parallel master cylinder)

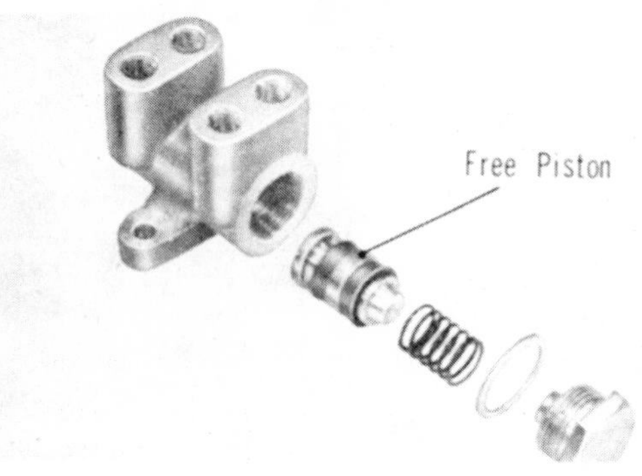

Fig. 10.37. Exploded view of by-pass valve

Fig. 10.38. Securing bolts of pressure regulating valve

Fig. 10.39. Pressure regulating valve pipeline connections

Fig. 10.40. Brake pedal removal

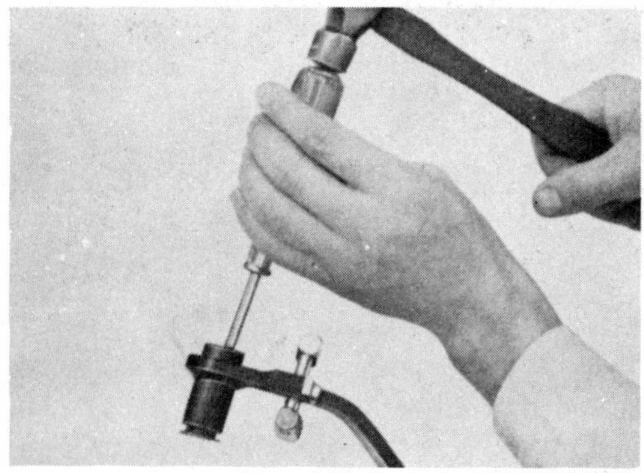

Fig. 10.41. Drifting out a pedal arm bush

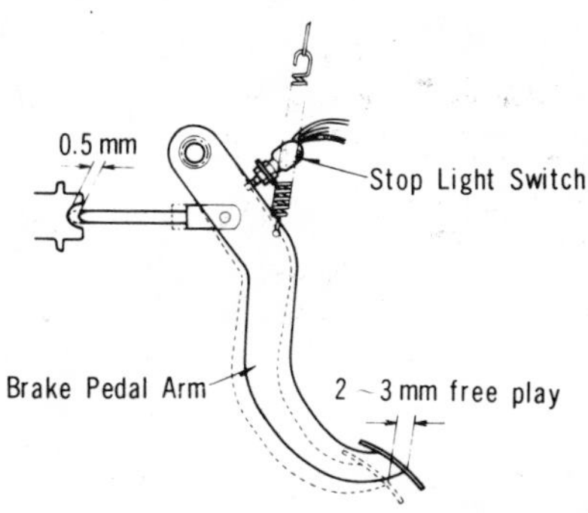

Fig. 10.42. Brake pedal height adjustment diagram

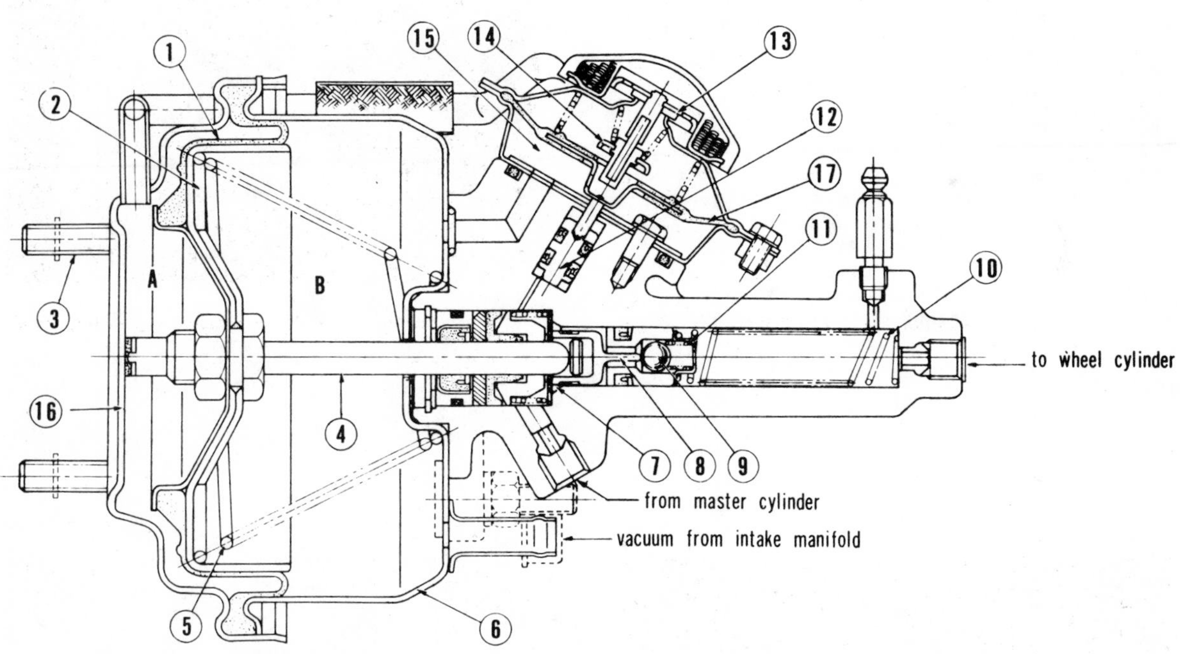

Fig. 10.43. Sectional view of vacuum servo unit (pedal released)

1 Diaphragm
2 Diaphragm plate
3 Mounting stud
4 Pushrod
5 Diaphragm return spring
6 Front shell
7 Piston stop washer
8 Yoke
9 Non-return valve
10 Return spring
11 Master cylinder piston
12 Relay valve piston
13 Air valve
14 Vacuum valve
15 Relay valve
16 Rear shell
17 Relay valve diaphragm

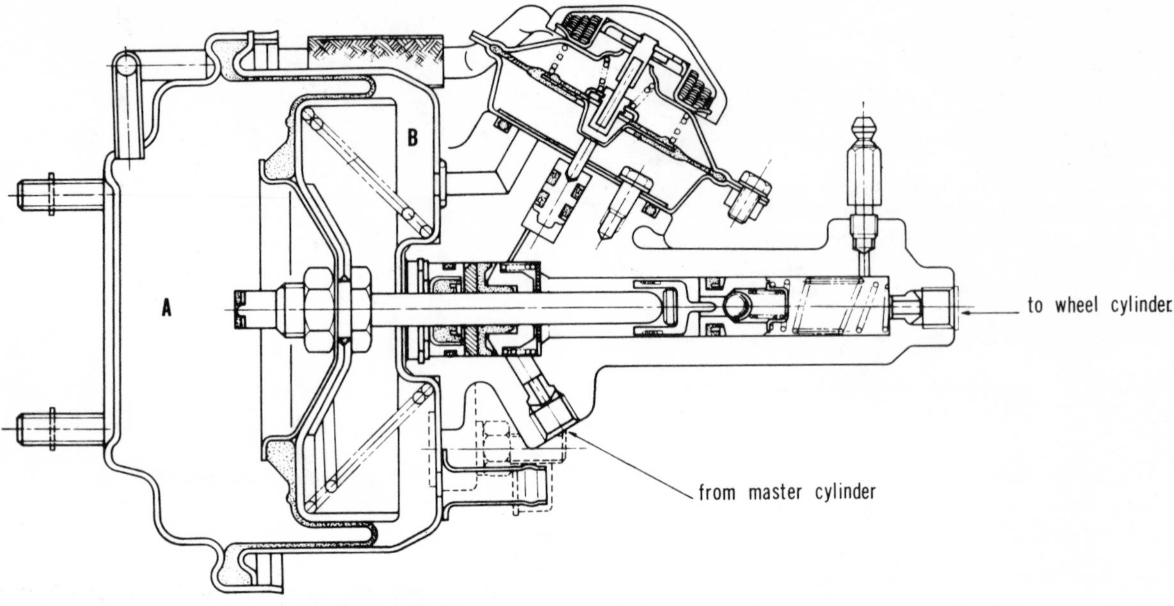

Fig. 10.44. Sectional view of vacuum servo unit (pedal depressed)

4 Unscrew the three mounting bolts and remove the unit. The foot pedal pushrod will disconnect automatically as the unit is withdrawn.
5 Servicing should be limited to cleaning the air filter at specified intervals (see 'Routine Maintenance' Section). Overhaul of the hydraulic master cylinder may be carried out in a similar manner to that described for single types (Section 12) but the servo unit itself, if faulty should be renewed on an exchange basis due to the need for special tools and skills.
6 Refit the unit by engaging the brake pedal pushrod and bolting it to the bulkhead. Reconnect the fluid pipes, the vacuum hose and bleed the brakes as described in the next Section.

Fig. 10.45. Location of brake vacuum servo unit

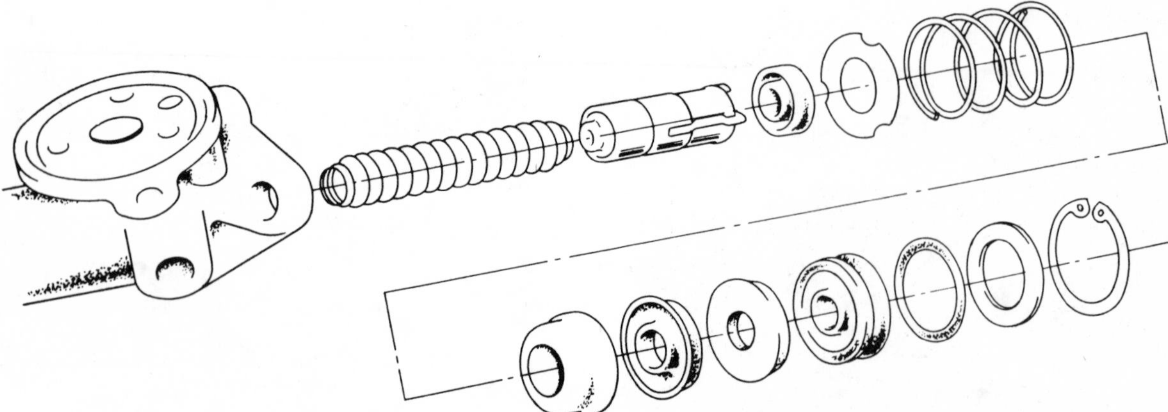

Fig. 10.46. Exploded view of servo unit hydraulic master cylinder

20 Bleeding the brakes

1 Check that the hydraulic reservoir is filled to the correct level.
2 Pour an inch or two of clean fluid into a jar and then fit a rubber or plastic bleed tube to one of the rear wheel cylinder bleed nipples (left rear for right-hand drive or right rear for left-hand drive).
3 Immerse the open end of the tube in the fluid in the jar and keep it under the fluid surface throughout the operation (photo).
4 Unscrew the bleed nipple half a turn and have an assistant depress the brake pedal fully. Give long slow and quick depressions (alternating) of the pedal until air bubbles no longer emerge from the end of the bleed tube. With the pedal held down at the end of a stroke, tighten the nipple and remove the tube.
5 Top-up the reservoir with clean fluid which has been stored in an airtight container and has remained unshaken for at least 24 hours.
6 Repeat the operation on the other rear wheel cylinder and then the front left (rhd) or front right (lhd).
7 Always keep the reservoir filled throughout the operation otherwise air will be drawn into the system and the bleeding sequence will have to be started all over again.
8 **Discard all fluid expelled during bleeding** and do not be tempted to use it for replenishing the system.
9 Where a vacuum servo unit is fitted, dissipate the vacuum by repeated applications of the brake pedal before commencing bleeding operations.

21 Brake failure warning lamps (North American Models)

1 An indicator lamp is fitted to the instrument panel which will illuminate if there is loss of pressure within the front or rear hydraulic circuits. The switches, adjacent to the fluid reservoir also provide a warning of low fluid level with the reservoir.
2 Obviously, a system in good condition will not provide a check that the saftey circuit is operational and therefore every 24000 miles (38000 kmcarry out carry out the following tests.
3 Depress the indicator lamp on the instrument panel when if it is good condition it should illuminate.
4 Check the level and top-up the fluid reservoir if necessary.
5 Open a rear wheel cylinder bleed nipple and have an assistant depress the foot pedal. Due to loss of fluid the warning light should come on. Keep the pedal depressedand tighten the bleed nipple.
6 If these tests prove negative, check the low fluid level and stop lamp switches for security of connections and operation and renew the switches if defective.

20.3 Bleeding a front brake

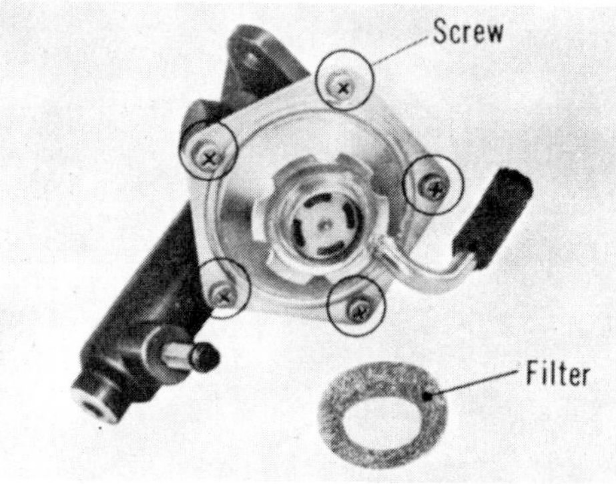

Fig. 10.47. Vacuum servo unit steel wool air filter

Fig. 10.49. Brake hydraulic system warning lamp (North America)

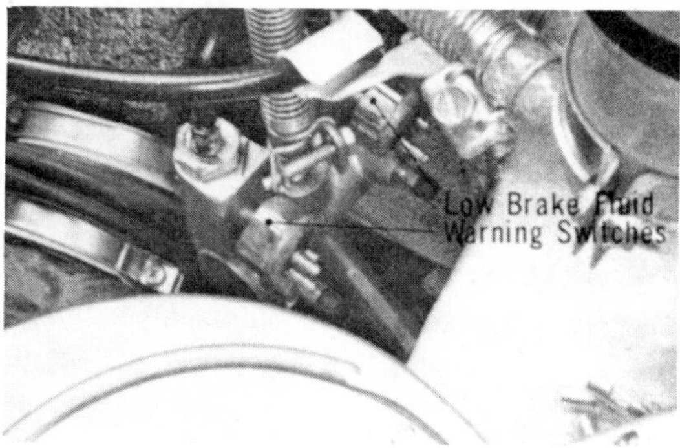

Fig. 10.50. Location of brake fluid low level warning switches (North America)

22 Braking system - fault diagnosis

Symptom	Reason/s	Remedy
Pedal travels a long way before the brakes operate	Rear brakes require adjusting	Check and adjust rear brake shoes.
	Disc pads or linings excessively worn	Inspect and renew as necessary.
Stopping ability poor, even though pedal pressure is firm	Linings, pads, discs or drums badly worn or scored	Dismantle, inspect, and renew as required.
	One or more caliper pistons or rear wheel cylinders seized, resulting in some pads/ shoes not pressing against discs/drums	Dismantle and inspect cylinders and repair or renew as necessary.
	Brake pads or linings contaminated with oil	Renew pads or linings and repair source of oil contamination.
	Wrong type of pads or linings fitted (too hard)	Verify type of material which is correct for the car and fit it.
	Brake pads or shoes incorrectly assembled	Check for correct assembly.
	Servo unit (where fitted) not functioning	Check and renew as necessary.
Car veers to one side when brakes are applied	Brake pads on one side are contaminated with oil	Renew pads and repair source of oil contamination.
	Hydraulic pistons in calipers are partially or wholly seized on one side	Inspect caliper pistons for correct movement and repair as necessary.
	A mixture of pad materials used between sides	Standardize on types of pads fitted.
	Unequal wear between sides caused by partially seized hydraulic pistons in brake calipers	Check pistons and renew pads and discs as required.
Pedal feels spongy when the brakes are applied	Air is present in the hydraulic system	Bleed the hydraulic system and check for any signs of leakage.
Pedal feels springy when the brakes are applied	Rear brake linings not bedded into the drums (after fitting new ones)	Allow time for new linings to bed in.
	Master cylinder, brake caliper or drum backplate mounting bolts loose	Tighten mounting bolts as necessary.
	Severe wear in rear drums causing distortion when brakes are applied.	Renew drums and linings.
Pedal travels right down with little or no resistance and brakes are virtually non-operative	Leak in hydraulic system resulting in lack of pressure for operation of wheel cylinders.	Examine the whole of the hydraulic system and locate and repair the source of the leak(s). Test after repairing each and every leak source.
	If no signs of leakage are apparent the master cylinder internal seals are failing to sustain pressure	Overhaul the master cylinder. If indications are that seals have failed for reasons other than wear, all the wheel cylinder seals should be checked also and the system replenished with the correct fluid.
Binding, juddering, overheating	One, or a combination of causes given in the foregoing sections	Complete and systematic inspection of the whole braking system.

Chapter 11 Electrical system

Contents

Specifications

System type: ... 12 volt negative earth

Battery: ... 40 amp/hr

Starter/generator (360 cc/21.5 cu in.):

Rated output (starter)	350 W	
Rated output (generator)	250 W	
Brush length	1.02 in. (26.0 mm)	
Regulator voltage	14.8 to 15.8 volts	) For gap specifications
Cut-in voltage	12.5 to 13.5 volts	) see 600 cc type
Reverse current	4 to 12 amps	) regulator
Starter relay operating voltage	Less than 8 volts	
Starter relay operating current	2.5 amps at 8 volts	
Starter relay contact resistance	0.2 volts	

Starter motor (600 cc/35.5 cu in.):

Type	Pre-engaged with solenoid switch
Output	0.8 KW
No-load current	60 amps
No-load speed	700 rev/min.

Alternator (600 cc /35.5 cu in.):

Type	Hitachi, AC continuous rating
Operating speed	1200 to 7500 rev/min.
Output	12 volts 30 amp (North America 12 volts 35 amp)
Rectifier output	12 volts 35 amp (North America 12 volts 40 amp)

Brush length:	
Standard	0.57 in. (14.5 mm)
Minimum	0.28 in. (7.0 mm)

Regulator:	
Yoke gap	0.035 to 0.039 in. (0.9 to 1.0 mm)
Core gap	0.032 to 0.047 in. (0.8 to 1.2 mm)
Points gap	0.016 to 0.020 in. (0.4 to 0.5 mm)
Cut-out:	
Yoke gap	0.008 in. (0.2 mm)
Core gap	0.020 to 0.024 in. (0.5 to 0.6 mm)
Points gap	0.016 to 0.020 in. (0.4 to 0.5 mm)

Horn:	
Operating voltage	9 to 15 volts
Current	Less than 3.5 amps
Accoustic rating	98 - 108 db
Frequency	440 HZ (model UH - 2D) 520 (model UL - 2D)

Wiper motor:	
No-load speed	60 rev/min.
No-load current	Less than 1.5 amps
Current under load	Less than 17 amps

Bulbs (12V):	
Headlamps (sealed beam)	50/40 W
Headlamps (bulb type)	36/45 W - 35/35 W - 36/36 W according to operating territory
Front direction indicators	21 W (UK) 18 W (France/Germany)
Front parking lights	6 W (UK) 4 W (France/Germany)
Combined front direction/parking	25/8 W
Gauges and warning lamps	3 W
Interior light	5 W
Rear combined stop/tail	18/5 W (UK and Australia)
Rear combined stop/tail/direction indicator	25/8 W (UK), 18/5 W (France), 21/5 W (Germany)
Rear direction indicator	21 W (UK and Australia)
Reversing lamps	10 W or 6 W (UK and Australia)
Rear index plate	8 W, 6 W or 5 W depending on territory

Fuses:	
Rating	20 amp or 10 amp (see Section 16)

Torque wrench settings:	**lb ft**	**kg m**
Starter motor (600 cc/35.5 cu in.) bolts	30	4.1
Crankshaft pulley bolt	35	4.8

1 General description

The electrical system is of 12 volt, negative earth, type. On 360cc 21.5 cu in vehicle, a combined starter generator is fitted to the end of the crankshaft, whilst on 600cc 35.5 cu in models, an alternator is installed on the end of the crankshaft and a separate pre-engaged type starter motor is fitted which meshes with the ring-gear on the edge of the alternator rotor.

The battery supplies a steady amount of current for the ignition, lighting, and other electrical circuits and provides a reserve of electricity when the current consumed by the electrical equipment exceeds that being produced by the alternator or dynamo. The alternator has its own integral regulator which ensures a high output if the battery is in a low state of charge or the demand from the electrical equipment is high, and a low output if the battery is fully charged and there is little demand from the electrical equi ment.

When fitting electrical accessories to cars with a negative earth system it is important, if they contain Silicone Diode or Transistors, that they are connected correctly, otherwise serious damage may result to the components concerned. Items such as radios, tape recorders, electronic ignition systems, electronic tachometer, automatic dipping etc., should all be checked for correct polarity.

It is important that the battery positive lead is always disconnected if the battery is to be boost charged when an alternator is fitted. Also if body repairs are to be carried out using electronic arc welding equipment the alternator must be disconnected otherwise serious damage can be caused to the more delicate instruments. When the battery has to be disconnected it must always be reconnected **with the negative terminal earthed.**

2 Battery - removal and installation

1 The battery is on a carrier fitted to the right-hand wing valance of the engine compartment. It should be removed once every three months for cleaning and testing. Disconnect the positive and then the negative leads from the battery terminals by undoing and removing the plated nuts and bolts.

2 Unscrew and remove the bolt, and plain washer that secures the battery clamp plate to the carrier. Lift away the clamp plate. Carefully lift the battery from its carrier and hold it vertically to ensure that none of the electrolyte is spilled.

3 Replacement is a direct reversal of this procedure. **NOTE: Replace the negative lead before the positive** lead and smear the terminals with vaseline to prevent corrosion: **Never** use an ordinary grease.

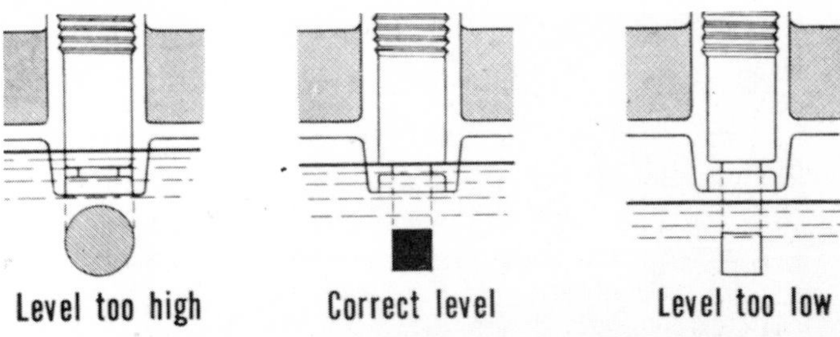

Fig. 11.1. Battery location and electrolyte level diagram

3 Battery - maintenance and inspection

1 Normal weekly battery maintenance consists of checking the electrolyte level of each cell to ensure that the separators are covered by ¼ inch (6.35 mm) of electrolyte. If the level has fallen top up the battery using distilled water only. Do not overfill. If a battery is overfilled or any electrolyte spilled, immediately wipe away the excess as electrolyte attacks and corrodes any metal it comes into contact with very rapidly.
2 As well as keeping the terminals clean and covered with petroleum jelly, the top of the battery, and especially the top of the cells, should be kept clean and dry. This helps prevent corrosion and ensures that the battery does not become partially discharged by leakage through dampness and dirt.
3 Once every three months remove the battery and inspect the battery securing bolts, the battery clamp plate, tray and battery leads for corrosion (white fluffy deposits on the metal) which are brittle to touch). If any corrosion is found clean off the deposit with ammonia and paint over the clean metal with an anti-rust-acid paint.
4 At the same time inspect the battery case for cracks. If a crack is found, clean and plug it with one of the proprietary compounds marketed by such firms as Holts for this purpose. If leakage through the crack has been excessive then it will be necessary to refill the appropriate cell with fresh electrolyte as detailed later. Cracks are frequently caused to the top of the battery cases by pouring in distilled water in the middle of winter **AFTER** instead of **BEFORE** a run.This gives the water no chance to mix with the electrolyte and so the former freezes and splits the battery case.
5 If topping up the battery becomes excessive and the case has been inspected for cracks that could cause leakage, but none are found, the battery is being overcharged and the voltage regulator will have to be checked and reset.
6 With the battery on the bench at the three monthly interval check, measure the specific gravity with a hydrometer to determine the state of charge and condition of the electrolyte. There should be very little variation between the different cells and, if a variation in excess of 0.025 is present it will be due to either:

a) Loss of electrolyte from the battery at sometime caused by spillage or a leak, resulting in a drop in the specific gravity of the electrolyte when the deficiency was replaced with distilled water instead of fresh electrolyte.
b) An internal short circuit caused by buckling of the plates or similar malady pointing to the likelihood of total battery failure in the near future.

7 The correct readings for the electrolyte specific gravity at various states of charge and conditions are:

	Temperate	Tropical
Fully charged	1.285	1.23
Half charged	1.20	1.14
Discharged	1.12	1.08

4 Electrolyte replenishment

1 If the battery is in a fully charged state and one of the cells maintains a specific gravity reading which is 0.025 or more lower than the others, and a check of each cell has been made with a voltage meter to check for short circuits (a four to seven second test should give a steady reading of between 1.2 to 1.8 volts), then it is likely that electrolyte has been lost from the cell with the low reading at some time.
2 Top the cell up with a solution of 1 part sulphuric acid to 2.5 parts of water. If the cell is already fully topped up draw some electrolyte out of it with a pipette.
3 When mixing the sulphuric acid and water never add water to sulphuric acid - always pour the acid slowly onto the water in a glass container. If water is added to sulphuric acid it will explode.

4 Continue to top up the cell with the freshly made electrolyte and then recharge the battery and check the hydrometer readings.

5 Battery - charging

1 In winter time when heavy demand is placed upon the battery, such as when starting from cold, and much electrical equipment is continually in use, it is a good idea occasionally to have the battery fully charged from an external source at the rate of 3.5 to 4 amps.
2 Continue to charge the battery at this rate until no further rise in specific gravity is noted over a four hour period.
3 Alternatively, a trickle charger, charging at the rate of 1.5 amps, can be safely used overnight.
4 Specially rapid 'boost' charges which are claimed to restore the power of the battery in 1 to 2 hours are most dangerous as they can cause serious damage to the battery plates through over-heating.
5 While charging the battery note that the temperature of the electrolyte should never exceed 10°F.
6 Make sure that your charging set and battery are set to the same voltage.
7 On 600cc 35.5 cu in vehicles (alternator) always disconnect the battery positive lead before connecting a mains charger.

6 Starter/generator (360cc 21.5 cu in) - inspection and testing

1 Lack of charge and a discharged battery are most likely due to worn brushes or dirty commutator.
2 With one spanner holding the crankshaft pulley flats, unscrew and remove the crankshaft pulley bolts. Withdraw the pulley and slip the driving belt from it.
3 Remove the generator cover bolts and withdraw the cover.
4 With the brushes exposed, check their length. If this is less than 0.4in (12 mm) they should be renewed.
5 Clean the surface of the commutator with a fuel soaked non-fluffy rag and check that the mica insulators are below the surface of the copper segments otherwise they will have to be undercut as described in Section 7.
6 Using two wonder leads, a test bulb and battery, check the continuity of the wiring and insulation of the rotor by placing one probe on each commutator segment in turn and earthing the other.
7 Refit the generator cover, the crankshaft pulley and the driving belt, start the engine.
8 Disconnect the lead connector (Fig 11.5) and earth the "F" terminal (white/red cable). Set the engine speed to approximately 2000 rev/min and check the voltage at the "D" terminal using a voltmeter. If it is in excess of 15 volts then the generator is performing satisfactorily.
9 Where the foregoing operations do not prove succussful then the unit must be removed from the crankshaft (next Section) or the regulator tested as described in Section 8.

7 Starter/generator - removal, servicing and refitting

1 Remove the crankshaft pulley, generator cover and brush gear as described in the preceeding Section. Remove the stator bolts and the stator.
2 The rotor is a taper fit on the end of the crankshaft and the hollow end of the crankshaft is tapped to take a special removal tool. An alternative is to obtain a bolt with a matching thread and screw it tightly in and then give the end of the tool or bolt a blow with a mallet to release the rotor from its taper.
3 Measure the outer diameter of the commutator, if it is worn below 1.93 in (49.0mm) then the rotor must be renewed.
4 Examine the mica insulators. These should be undercut to a depth of between 0.020 and 0.032 in (0.5 to 0.8 mm) using an

Fig. 11.2. Removing crankshaft pulley bolt (360 cc/21.5 cu in.)

Fig. 11.3. Removing starter/generator cover (360 cc/21.5 cu in.)

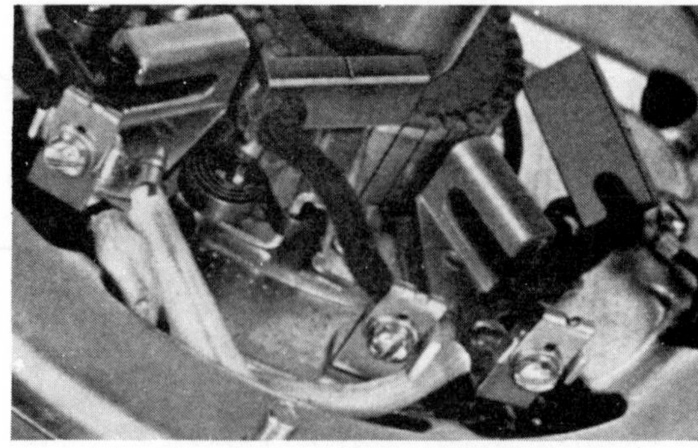

Fig. 11.4. Location of starter/generator brushes (360 cc/21.5 cu in.)

Fig. 11.5. Starter/generator wiring connector (360 cc/21.5 cu in.)

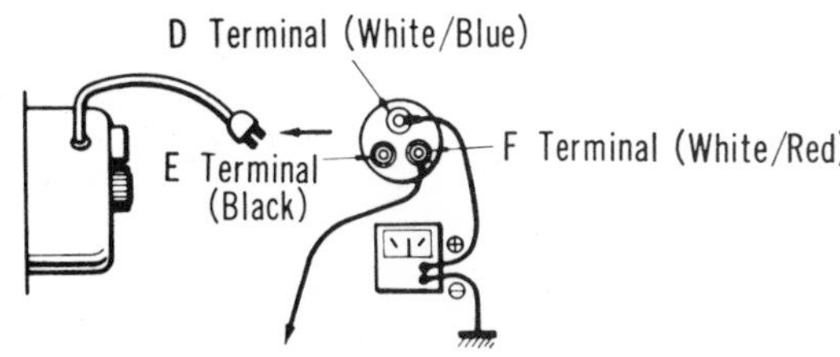

Fig. 11.6. Voltage test diagram (360 cc/21.5 cu in. starter/generator)

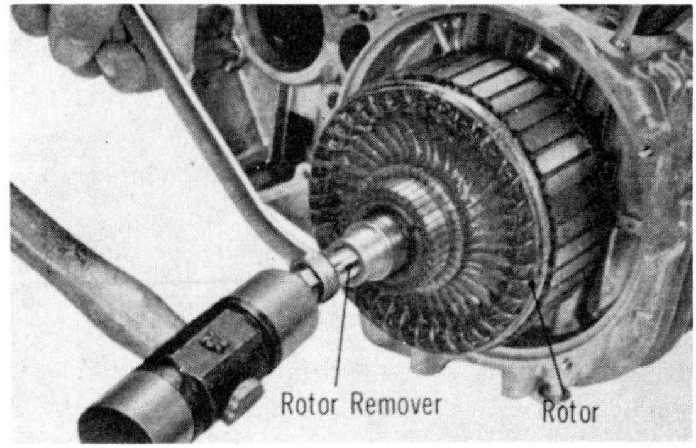

Fig. 11.7. Removing the rotor from a 360 cc/21.5 cu in. crankshaft

Fig. 11.8. Measuring the outside diameter of the commutator (360 cc/21.5 cu in. starter/generator)

Fig. 11.9. Rotor installation guide pin (360 cc/21.5 cu in. starter/generator)

Fig. 11.10. Brush gear connections (360 cc/21.5 cu in. starter/generator)

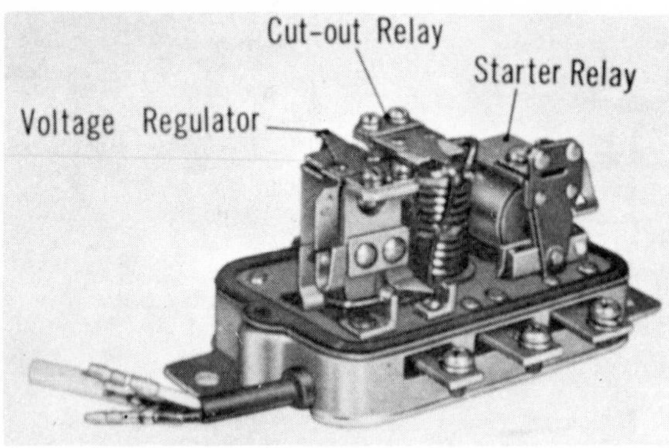

Fig. 11.11. Voltage regulator (360 cc/21.5 cu in. starter/generator)

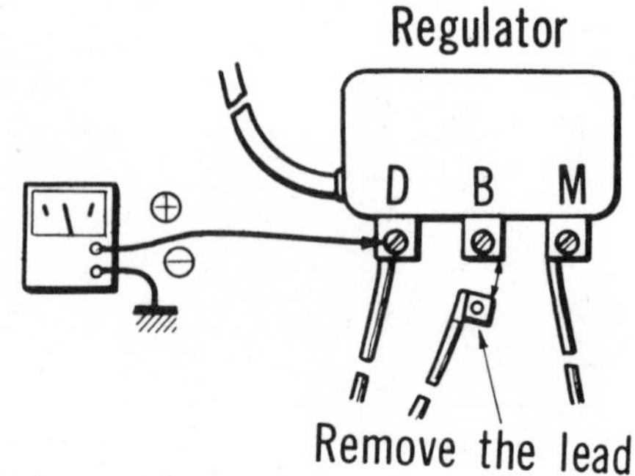

Fig. 11.12. Testing regulator voltage (360 cc/21.5 cu in. starter/generator)

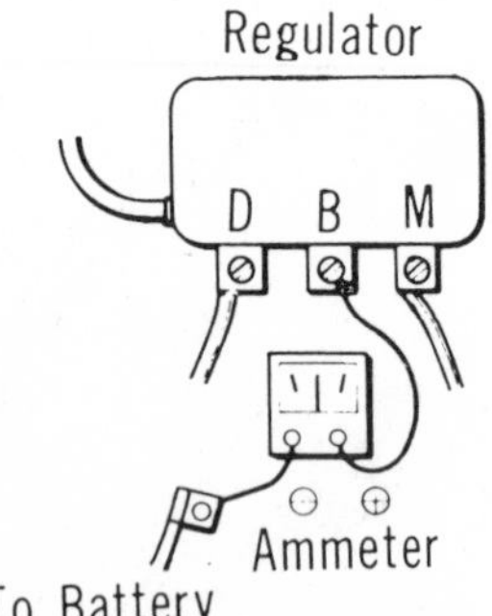

Fig. 11.13. Checking output current (360 cc/21.5 cu in. starter/generator)

old hacksaw blade suitably ground to the correct width.

5 If the segments of the commutator are burnt or pitted they should be rubbed lightly with a strip of glass paper (not emery) wrapped round it.

6 Refitting is a reversal of removal but check that the crankshaft guide pin and the rotor spot engage correctly and ensure that the brush terminals are correctly connected. Tap the rotor into position using a tubular drift.

8 Voltage regulator (36occ) - testing and adjustment

1 The voltage regulator unit fitted in conjunction with the starter/generator incorporates the cut-out and starter relay and is located adjacent to the battery.

2 When the tests and adjustments described in the preceding Sections have not proved successful, carry out the following electrical checks to the regulator.

3 Refer to Fig 11.13 and connect a voltmeter to the "D" terminal. Disconnect the "B" terminal, start the engine and increase the engine speed from 2000 to 4000 rev/min.. The indicated voltage should be between 14.8 and 15.8 volts.

4 Refer to Fig 11.13 and connect an ammeter between the battery lead and the "B" terminal. Run the engine at between 2000 and 3000 rev/min with the headlamps and other electrical accessories switched on and check the charging current, if it is 10amps or more the unit is serviceable. Where the readings are incorrect, the regulator should be adjusted in a manner similar to that described for the 600 cc/ 35.5 cu in voltage regulator in Section 11, of this Chapter.

9 Alternator (600cc) 35.5 cu in - inspection and testing

1 Lack of charging current from the unit may be due to worn brushes, disconnected lead terminals or breakdown ot insulation. Page 5

2 First check the security of the lead snap connectors.

3 Remove the brush gear cover plate and withdraw the brush holder (photo). If the brushes are worn to 0.276 in (7.0mm) or less, renew them. Check that the brushes slide easily in their holder. If the alternator still does not charge, carry out the following operations.

4 Disconnect the battery negative terminal and the four white leads from the rectifier.

5 Separate the white (red striped) lead from the black lead adjacent to the rectifier.

6 Detach the starter motor cables and remove the starter motor (2 bolts). Remove the driving belt from the pulleys.

7 Remove the crankshaft pulley bolt by holding the flats on the end of the crankshaft with another spanner. (photos).

8 Remove the brush holder assembly, the cover setscrews and withdraw the cover. (photo).

9 Using a set of wander leads, a test bulb and battery test the slip rings for continuity. There should be continuity between the two slip rings but not between either slip ring and earth (shaft or crankcase). Renew faulty components as necessary.

10 Using the same testing equipment, check for continuity between the lead terminals of the stator.

11 Where these tests are not successful, remove the rotor and stator as described in the next Section and check the regulator (Section 11).

10 Alternator (600cc) 35.5 cu in removal, servicing and refitting

1 Remove the crankshaft pulley, starter motor, brushgear and flywheel cover as described in the preceding Section.

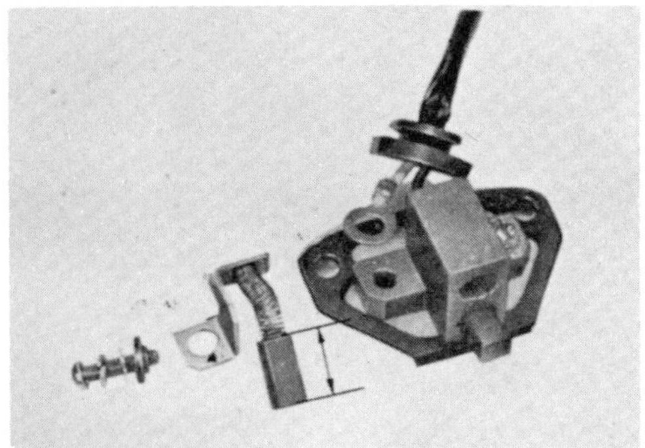

Fig. 11.14. Alternator brush gear 600 cc/35.5 cu in.

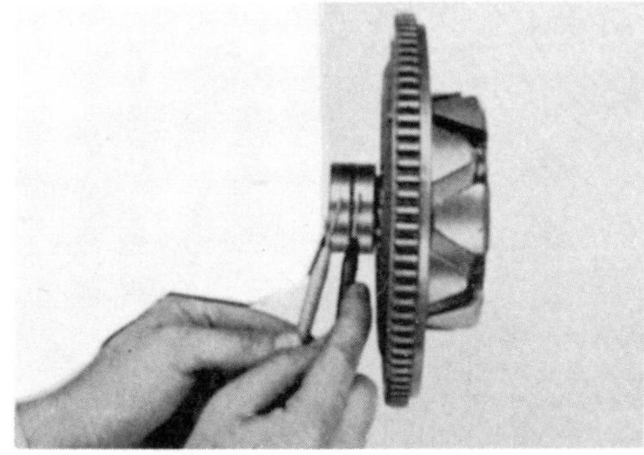

Fig. 11.16. Testing slip rings for continuity (600 cc/35.5 cu in. alternator)

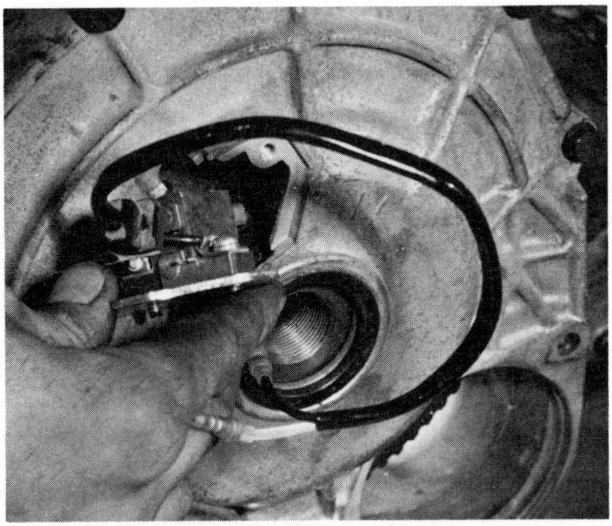

9.3 Removing brushes and holder from generator

9.7A Loosening crankshaft pulley bolt

9.7B Withdrawing crankshaft pulley

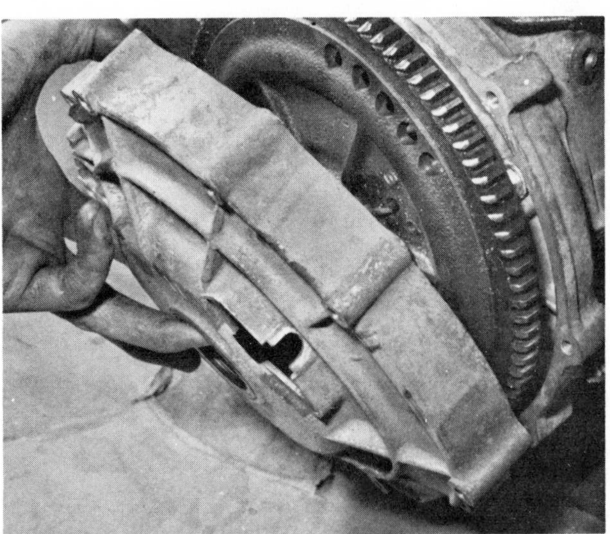

9.8 Removing flywheel cover

2 The flywheel/rotor assembly is taper fitted to the end of the crankshaft and it should be removed using a special tool or suitable bolt in a similar manner to that described for the 360cc 21.5 cu in model starter generator in Section 7. (Photo).
3 Unbolt the flywheel housing (four bolts) and then unbolt the stator from the housing. (Photo).
4 Examine the starter ring gear on the flywheel/rotor assembly and renew the unit if the tteeth are worn or damaged.
5 Renew the starter and rotor if electrical tests have proved them to be defective.
6 If the slip rings are discoloured or marked, polish them with fine emery cloth. Renew the flywheel cover oil seal.
7 Refitting is a reversal of removal but ensure that the flywheel housing engages correctly with the positioning dowels and that the crankshaft pulley engages with the two cutouts in the end of the crankshaft. (Photo). Tap the flywheel rotor into position using a tubular drift.
8 Tighten the crankshaft pulley bolt to a torque of 35lb/ft (4.8 kg/m) (Photo)

Fig. 11.17. Removing flywheel/rotor from the crankshaft (600 cc/35.5 cu in.)

Fig. 11.19. Crankshaft pulley locating cut-outs (600 cc/35.5 cu in.)

10.2 Flywheel/rotor removed from crankshaft

10.3 Withdrawing the stator complete with stator

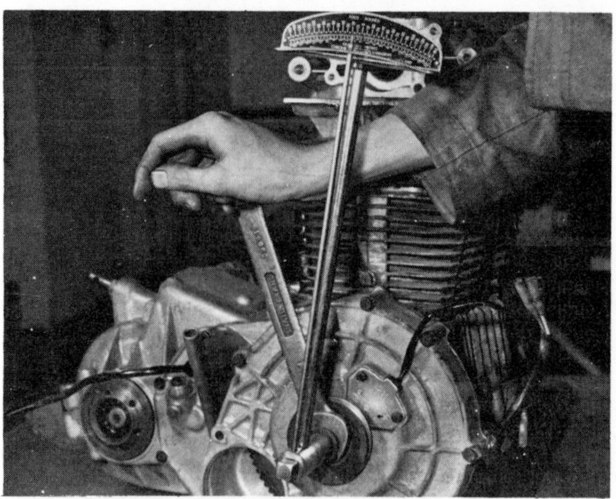

10.8 Tightening the crankshaft pulley bolt

11 Voltage regulator (600cc) 35.5 cu in - testing and adjustment

1 The regulator unit is fitted on the right-hand side of the engine compartment, adjacent to the battery.
2 Remove the cap from the regulator unit and check all the points gaps with feeler gauges in accordance with Fig. 11.21. Check that the contact points are clean and not pitted, otherwise dress them with fine emery cloth. A special tool is needed to turn the adjusting screws. Always carry out the checking and adjusting in this order, yoke gap, core gap and points gap.
3 Assemble a voltmeter and ammeter and incorporate them in the charging circuit as shown in Fig. 11.22.
4 With the engine idling, close the switch (SW1), raise the engine speed to 800 rev/min and open the switch (SW1).
5 Increase the engine speed to 5000 rev/min and check to no-load voltage. If it is lower than 13.5 volts, turn the adjuster upwards or if higher, turn the adjuster downwards.
6 To check the cutout voltage, increase the engine speed as previously described and check that the voltage is between 8 and 10 volts, if higher bend the hanger upwards, if lower bend it downwards.
7 If the foregoing tests and adjustments do not prove satisfactory then the unit must be renewed.

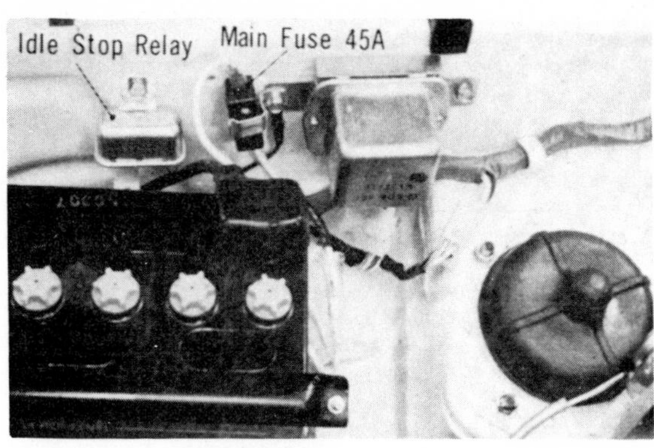

Fig. 11.20. Location of voltage regulator (600 cc/35.5 cu in.)

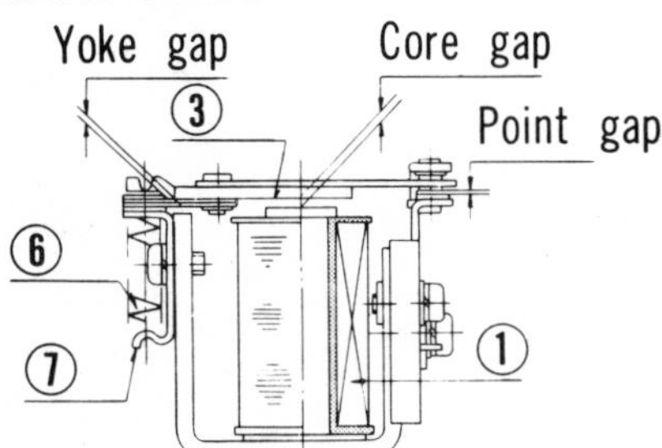

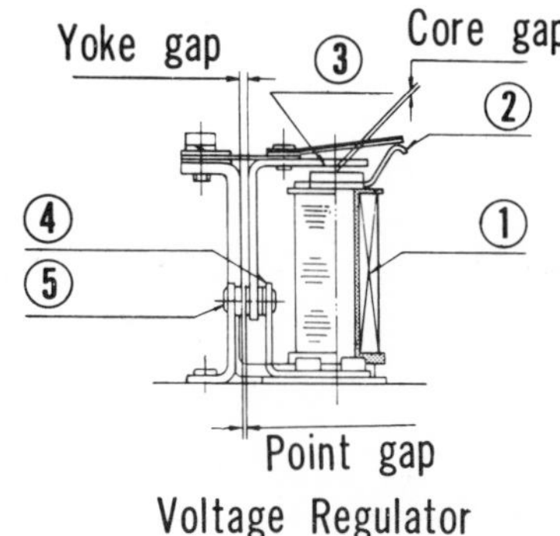

Fig. 11.21. 600 cc/35.5 cu in. regulator points adjustment diagram (for gaps see Specifications

1 Shunt coil
2 Adjuster tab
3 Armature
4 Lower contact
5 Upper contact
6 Spring
7 Hanger

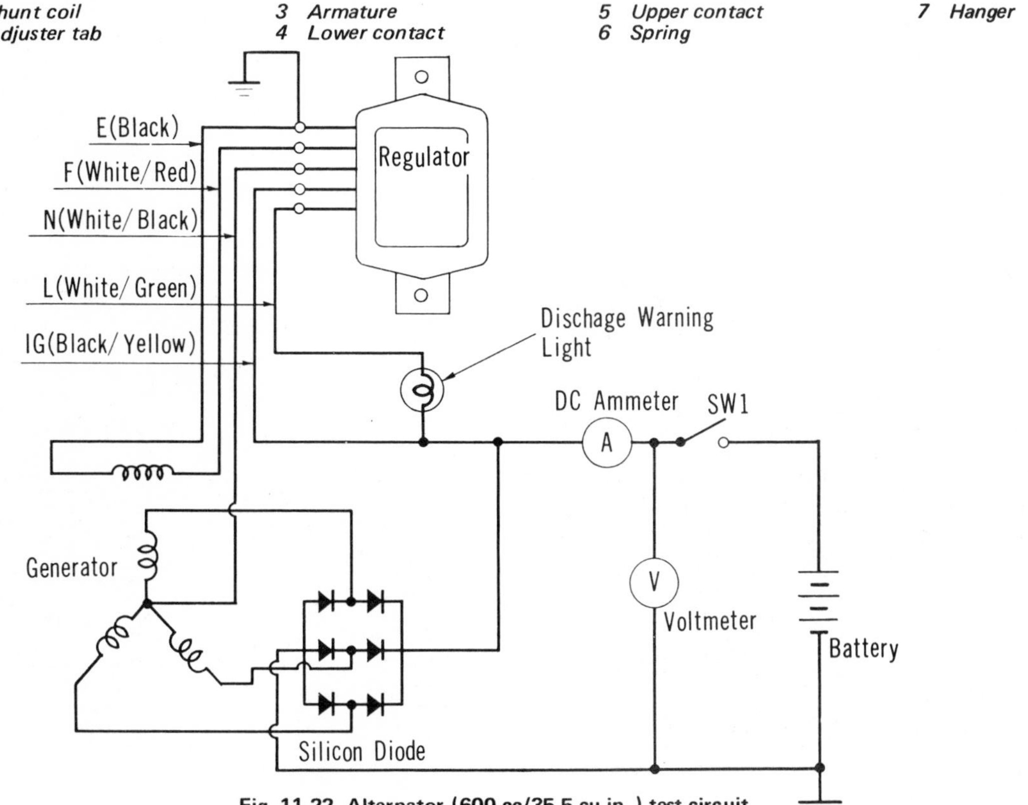

Fig. 11.22. Alternator (600 cc/35.5 cu in.) test circuit

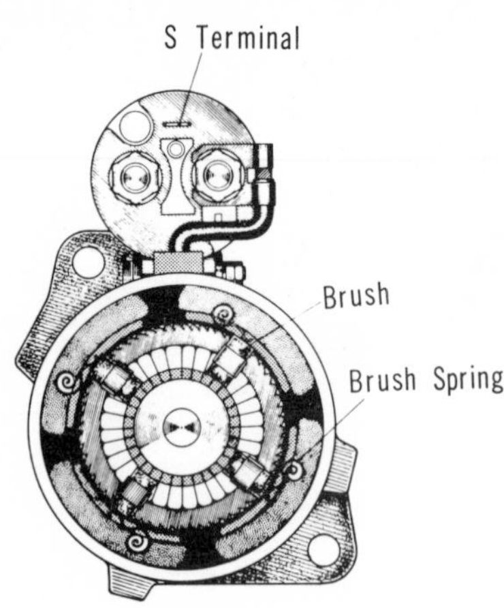

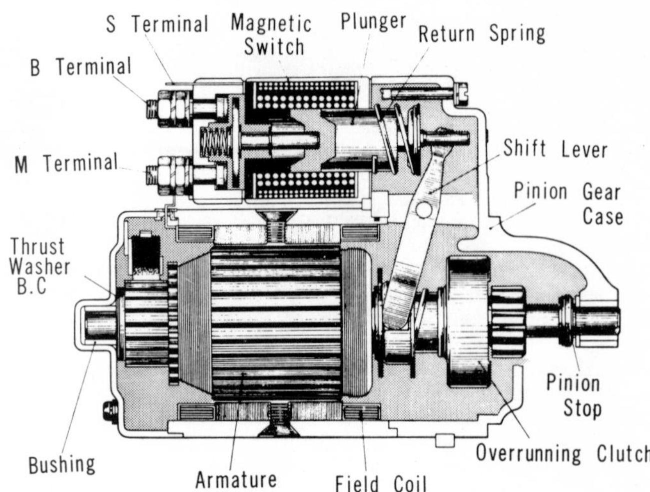

12 Starter motor (600cc) 35.5 cu in - description and maintenance

The starter motor is of pre-engaged type and incorporates a solenoid switch and drive gear. When the ignition switch is operated, the solenoid actuates the shiftlever and engages the pinion gear with the flywheel ring gear. At the moment of engagement the main contacts close and the starter motor rotates the engine. As soon as the engine fires, as in-built overrunning clutch disconnects the drive from the faster running ring gear. This type of starter helps to reduce wear on the ring gear. No maintenance is required other than keeping the securing bolts tight; also the solenoid terminal nuts. Occasionally, check the adjustment of the pinion protrusion as described in Section 15.

13 Starter motor (600cc) 35.5 cu in - testing on engine

1 If the starter motor fails to operate then check the condition of the battery by turning on the headlamps. If they glow brightly for several seconds and then gradually dim the battery is in an uncharged condition.

2 If the headlights continue to glow brightly and it is obvious that the battery is in good condition, then check the tightness of the battery wiring connections (and in particular the earth lead from the battery terminal to its connection on the body frame). If the positive terminal on the battery becomes hot when an attempt is made to work the starter this is a sure sign of a poor connection on the battery terminal. To rectify remove the terminal, clean the mating faces thoroughly and reconnect. Check the connections on the rear of the starter solenoid. Check the wiring with a voltmeter or test lamp for breaks or shorts.

3 Test the continuity of the solenoid windings by connecting a test lamp circuit comprising a 12 volt battery and low wattage bulb between the "S" terminal and the solenoid body and between the "S" and "M" terminals. If the two windings are in order the lamp will light. Next connect the test lamp (fitted with a high wattage bulb) between the solenoid main terminals. Energise the solenoid by applying a 12 volt supply between the small "S" terminal and the solenoid body. The solenoid should be heard to operate and the test bulb light. This indicates full closure of the solenoid contacts.

4 If the battery is fully charged, the wiring in order, the starter/ignition switch working and the starter motor still fails to operate then it will have to be removed from the car for examination.

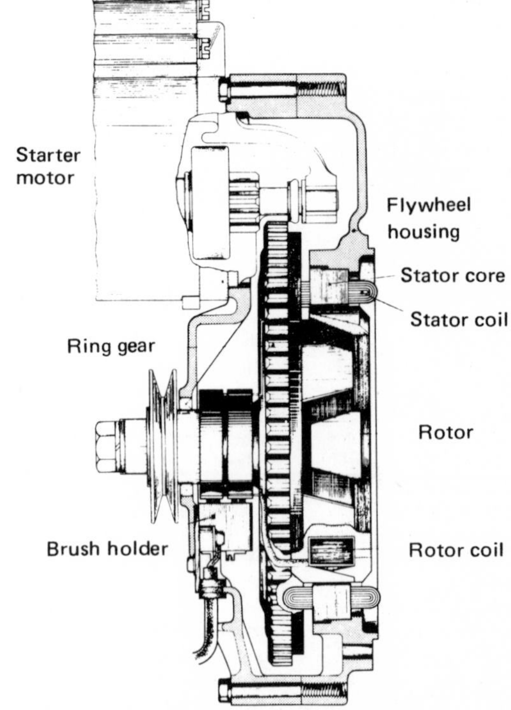

Fig. 11.23. Sectional view of 600 cc/35.5 cu in. starter motor and flywheel ring gear

14 Starter motor (600cc) 35.5 cu in - removal and installation

1 Remove the splash guard from below the engine.
2 Disconnect the battery negative terminal.
3 Disconnect the black and white leads (in that order) from the starter "B" and "S" terminals.
4 Unscrew and remove the starter motor securing bolts (two) and withdraw the starter. (photo).
5 Installation is a reversal of removal.

15 Starter motor (600cc) 135.5 cu in - dismantling, servicing and reassembly

1 Remove the nut from the "M" terminal and detach the cable.
2 Unscrew and remove the three tie bolts from the front of the solenoid switch and detach the switch from the starter motor.(Photo).
3 Unscrew and remove the two rear cover securing bolts from the starter motor and withdraw the cover after the two screws retaining the brush gear to the inside of the cover have also been removed. (Photo).
4 Extract the four brushes from the brush holder and remove the brush holder.
5 Separate the yoke from the gearcase after withdrawal of the positioning tension pin.
6 Remove the shiftlever pin and plunger from the shiftlever then withdraw the armature and detach the shiftlever.
7 To dismantle the armature, remove the thrust washer from the end of the armature shaft and then prise off the pinion stop washer using a screwdriver. (photo).
8 Slide the pinion stop towards the armature and detach the pinion stop clip using a pair of pliers.
9 Remove the pinion sleeve slip and dismantle the pinion assembly.
10 Inspect all components of the pinion drive for wear or damage. The pinion/overrunning clutch mechanism is a sealed unit and wear on the pinion teeth will necessitate renewing the complete unit.
11 Using two wander leads, a battery and a test bulb, check the armature for continuity between the commutator and the shaft and the commutator and the core. If there is continuity (bulb lights) then renew the armature.
12 Inspect the surface of the commutator. If it is burned or discoloured, clean it by wrapping a piece of fine emery cloth round it and polishing it. Check that the mica insulators are undercut, if not use an old hacksaw blade, ground to the required thickness and undercut them to between 0.020 and 0.032 in (0.5 and 0.8 mm).
13 Again, using the test bulb and battery method, check for continuity between the terminals of the field coils. If the test bulb fails to light up then the field coils must be renewed which is a job for your Honda dealer.
14 Check the brushes for wear and if they are less than 0.492 in (12.5mm) in length, renew them. Ensure that the brushes slide freely in their holders and that the brush springs have not lost their tension.
15 Reassembly of the starter motor is a reversal of dismantling but the following points must be observed.
16 Apply grease to the front and rear bearings, the pinion sliding section of the armature shaft and the sliding or pivot surfaces of the solenoid plunger, shift lever and splines before reassembly.
17 Ensure that the locating tab connects with its notch when fitting the yoke to the gearcase. (Photo).
18 When the starter motor is assembled, attach two leads to the battery terminals and connect the negative one to the solenoid switch body and the positive one to the "S" terminal. This will cause the solenoid switch to actuate. Check that the pinion is fully extended by pushing it out with the finger to eliminate any end-play and then check the gap between the end of the pinion and the face of the pinion stop on the gearcase using a feeler gauge. This gap should be between 0.012 and 0.059 in (0.3 and

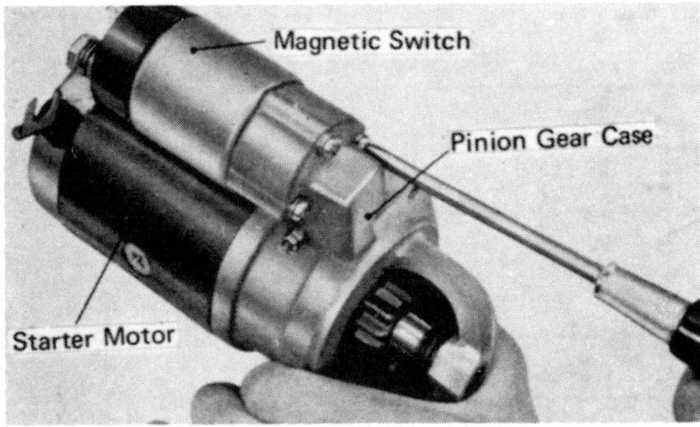

Fig. 11.24. Starter solenoid 600 cc/35.5 cu in. tie bolts

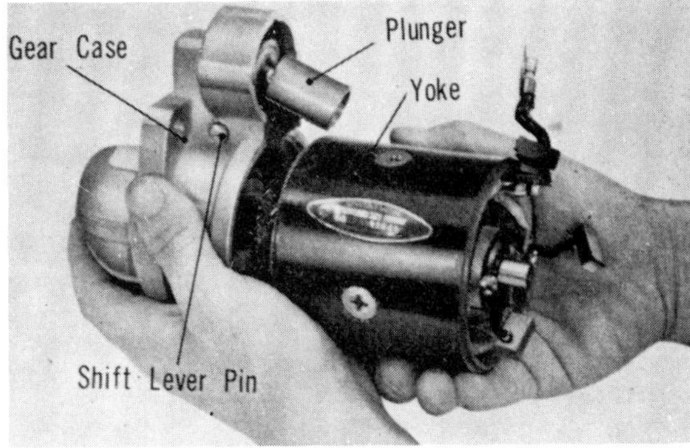

Fig. 11.25. Separating yoke from gearcase (600 cc/35.5 cu in. starter)

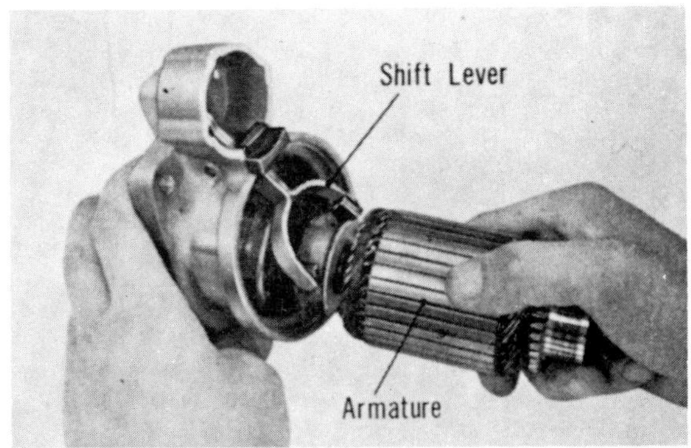

Fig. 11.26. Withdrawing armature from gearcase (600 cc/35.5 cu in. starter)

1.5 mm). Where the gap is found to be incorrect, change the adjusting plate after withdrawing the solenoid switch.

16 Fuses

1 Three types of fuse box may be encountered according to the vehicle operating territory and model number. It will either have four, eight or twelve positions.

2 The location of the fuse box is either on the rear bulkhead of the engine compartment or just above,and to the right, of the front wheel arch within the car inerior. A 45 amp fusible link is located next to the battery.

3 When an accessory fails to operate, always check the appropriate circuit fuse and renew it with one of the same rating, never substitute a piece of wire or foil as a temporary measure and always find the cause of the blown fuse and rectify it.

14.4 Removing the starter

15.2 Withdrawing the starter solenoid

15.3 Detaching the starter motor end cover

15.7 Driving off the pinion stop from the starter motor shaft

15.17 Starter motor (yoke to gearcase) alignment tab

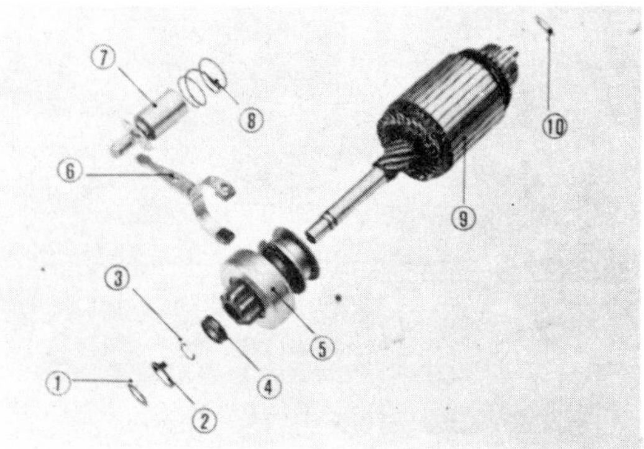

Fig. 11.27. Exploded view of armature assembly (600 cc/35.5 cu in. starter)

1 Thrust washer
2 Pinion stop washer
3 Pinion stop clip
4 Pinion stop
5 Pinion/clutch assembly
6 Shift lever
7 Solenoid plunger
8 Return spring
9 Armature
10 Thrust washer

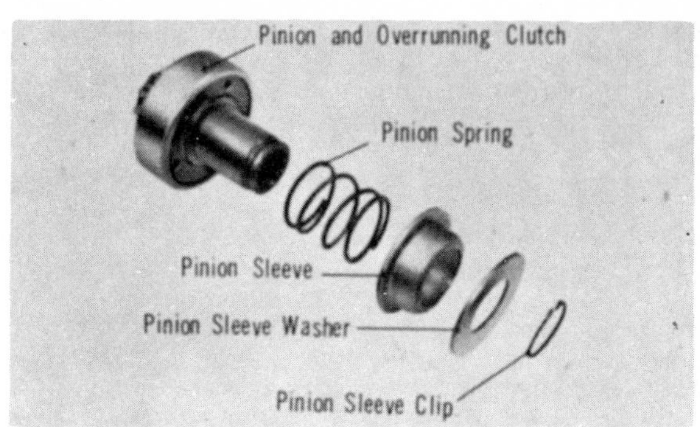

Fig. 11.28. Exploded view of the pinion assembly (600 cc/ 35.5 cu in. starter)

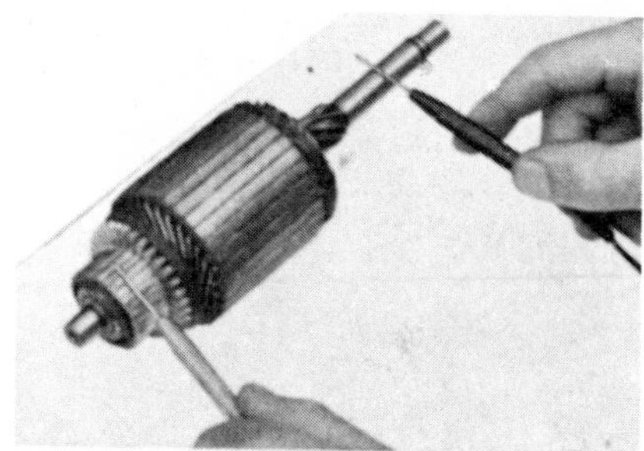

Fig. 11.29. Testing the armature for insulation breakdown (600 cc/35.5 cu in. starter)

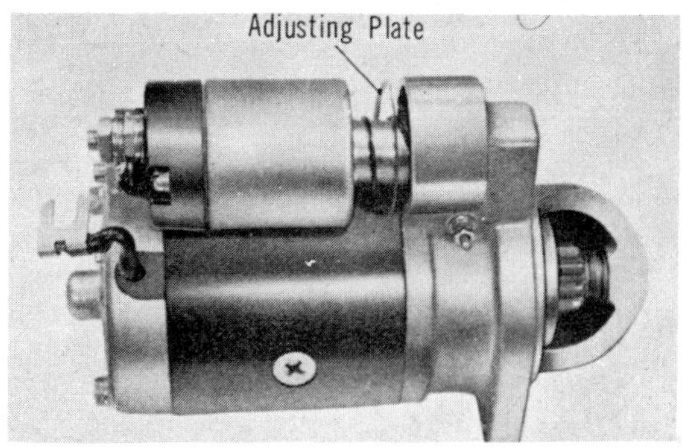

Fig. 11.30. Location of starter pinion protrusion adjusting plate

17 Flasher circuit - fault diagnosis and rectification

1 The direction indicator flasher is a sealed/component located below the instrument panel. It gives both a visual and audible warning when the direction indicator switch is actuated.

2 If the flashers fail to operate or work very slowly, first examine the front and rear bulbs also the fascia warning lamp for broken filaments and renew as required.

3 Check the security of the circuit connections to the flasher unit and also to the front and rear bulb holders.

4 Check the fuse in the fuse box or check that other accessories on the same circuit are functioning.

5 Switch on the ingintion and check that current is reaching the flasher unit by connection a voltmeter between the unit "B" terminal and earth. If the meter does not register, check for broken wiring or a faulty direction indicator switch.

6 If it is established that current is reaching the flasher unit, bridge the unit terminals (BL) and operate the flasher switch. If the flasher bulbs go on (on the appropriate side) and stay on, then the unit is faulty and must be renewed.

18 Horns - fault diagnosis and rectification

1 Should the horn fail to work check that current is reaching the horn terminals. Connect a 12 volt test lamp to the feed wire and depress the horn button with the ignition switched on. If the test bulb lights up then the fault must lie in the horn or the horn switch-assuming that all terminals are secure, and that the horn circuit fuse has not blown.

2 To adjust the horn note, turn the screw which is located on the top casing. Turning the screw clockwise increases the horn volume; anticlockwise reduces it.

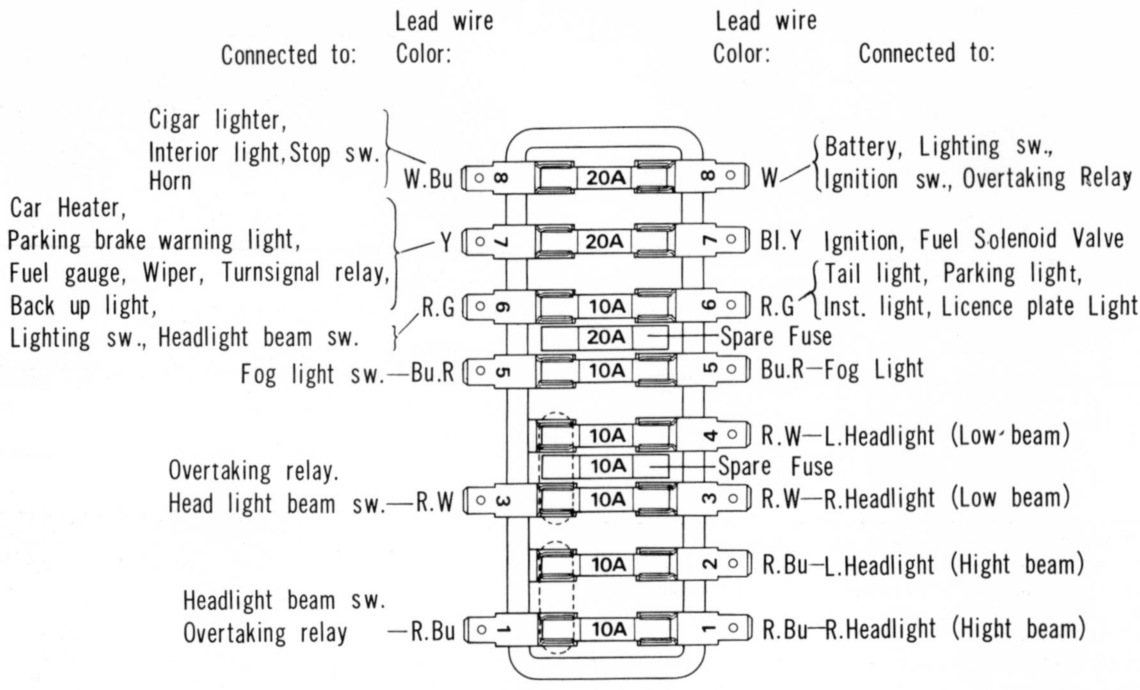

Fig. 11.31. Fuse circuits from body No. 1253433 (N 360)
1014822 (LN 360)
1085151 (N 600)

Wiring code:

RW	Red/white	Bl.Y	Black/yellow	R.G	Red/green	Bl.R	Black/red
W.Bu	White/blue	Y	Yellow	Bu.R	Blue/red	R	Red
W	White	R.Bu	Red/blue				

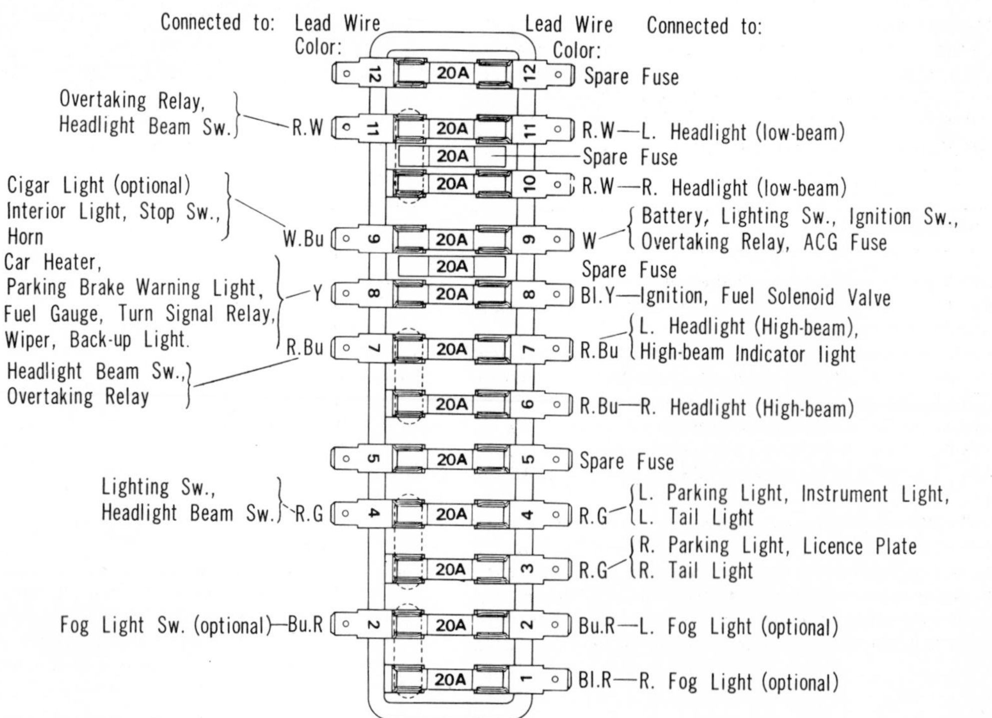

Fig. 11.32. Fuse circuits (Europe)

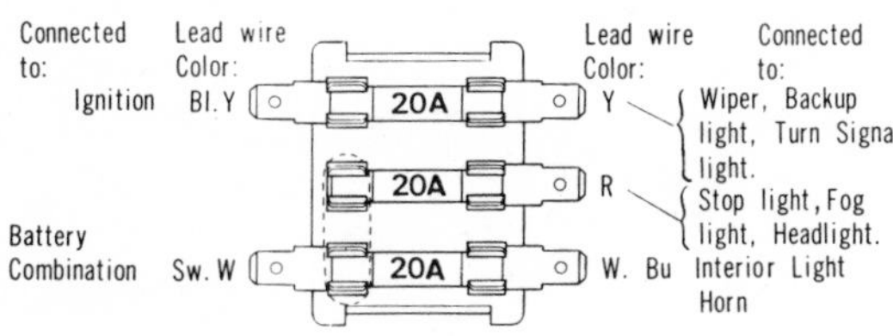

Fig. 11.33. Fuse circuits (North America)

19 Headlamps - renewal of bulbs or sealed beam units

1 Raise the bonnet and press in and turn the lamp unit clockwise to withdraw it sufficiently far to disconnect the connection plug or bulb holder.

2 This method of removal applies to the various types of headlamp unit encountered whether they have sealed beams or separate bulbs. One type of headlamp incorporates a festoon type parking lamp bulb instead of parking lamps being installed as independent units.

3 Cars operating in North America cannot have their sealed beam type headlamps removed simply by depressing and turning them but require the withdrawal of two rim securing screws.

4 Renew the sealed beam unit with the "TOP" mark correctly located. If it is a bulb which is being renewed, ensure that the staggered pins engage correctly with their respective grooves. reaseon, the healdamp housing is to be removed, detach the connector plug from the leads and remove the three retaining

5 If for any reason, the headlamp housing is to be removed, detach the connector plug from the leads and remove the three retaining screws which are visible after withdrawal of the headlamp unit screws and tension spring.

20 Headlamps - alignments

1 Although it is preferable to have the headlamps correctly set on modern beam setting equipment, the following procedure will provide a good alternative.

2 Set the car on a level surface with the fuel tank less than half full and the weight of one person in the front passenger compartment. Check that the tyre pressures are as specified.

3 Position the car 25ft. (7.62 mm) from, and at right-angles to, a wall or door. Mark the wall to correspond with the centre point of each headlamp at a height of 25½ in (647.7 mm) from the ground.

4 Mask each headlamp in turn and switch to main beam. Adjust the upper (vertical adjustment) or the two lower (horizontal adjustment) screws located on the headlamp rim until the centre of the light pattern is on the mark made on the wall. Repeat the procedure with the other headlamp. When correctly adjusted on main beam setting, the low or dipped position will automatically be correct.

21 Windscreen wiper - description and maintenance

1 The wiper assembly comprises an electric motor driving a crank and wiper arm linkage through a worm reduction gear.

2 Some vehicles are fitted with two speed wipers and this

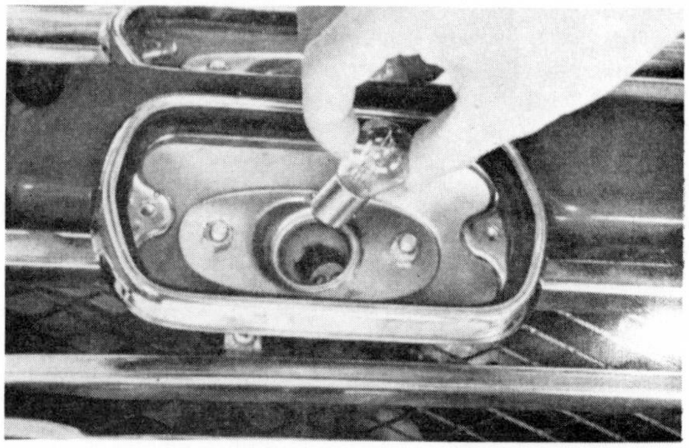

Fig. 11.34. Checking a front direction indicator flasher bulb

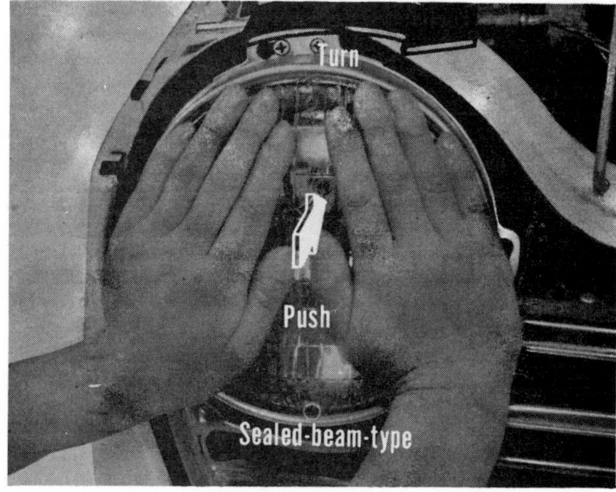

Fig. 11.35. Removing a sealed-beam type headlamp unit

facility is obtained by the addition of a third brush and the appropriate switching mechanism.

3 The wiper is self-parking by the incorporation of an autostop relay.

4 Maintenance is confined to renewal of the wiper blade inserts every two years or whenever they fail to wipe clearly.

5 To remove a blade, depress the spring link at the arm to blade connection socket and pull the blade from the arm.

6 The wiper arms should always park parallel to the base of the windscreen. Where they require adjustment, unscrew the lock bolt which secures the arm to the driving spindle and move the arm to the desired position. Retighten the lockbolt.

22 Windscreen wiper assembly - testing, removal and refitting

1 If the wipers will not operate, check the security of the electrical connections both at the motor and the switch. Check that the circuit fuse has not blown.

2 Withdraw the split pin at the connection of the crank, and link, and disconnect them. Connect leads directly from the battery to the motor. It it runs at normal speed then the fault must lie in the wiring or switch.

3 It is not recommended that the wiper motor is dismantled if faulty but rather exchange it for a factory reconditioned unit.

4 To remove the wiper motor from its engine rear bulkhead mounting, remove the four bolts and their rubber insulators. Note the earth tag located below one of the bolts.
5 If the operating linkage is worn or distorted it can be removed by detaching the wiper arms and then the spindle support plates.
6 Refitting is a reversal of removal but remember to align the wiper arms in their correct positions with the wiper mechanism self-parked.

23 Standard type instrument panel - removal and refitting.

1 The standard type fascia panel comprises an instrument console, in which the instrument assembly is inset and a glove compartment.
2 From behind the fascia panel disconnect the wiring harness plug and the speedometer drive cable, also the heater control cable at the valve end.
3 Remove the three console mounting screws. On some models the left-hand screw cannot be withdrawn unless the windscreen wiper switch is first removed.
4 Pull the console forward, and to the left, until there is sufficient clearance to release the sliding rail track, then disconnect the instrument console from the fascia panel.
5 The instrument assembly can be removed from the instrument console after the removal of the five retaining screws. Refitting is a reversal of removal.
6 Individual pilot lamps can be removed and replaced from behind the instrument casing without first removing the instrument console.

24 De-luxe type instruments - removal and refitting

1 The circular type speedometer and combination instrument cluster are retained in position by tension springs.
2 To remove eitherinstrument , first detach the tension springs and pull each instrument far enough forward to enable either the speedometer cable to be disconnected or the instrument electrical lead connections to be detached.
3 Refitting is a reversal of removal.
4 If for any reason the complete De-luxe type instrument panel is to be removed then all electrical leads must be disconnected from the rear of the panel, also the windscreen washer pipes and the choke cable. Disconnect the steering column bracket and lower the column to rest on the driver's seat. Remove the six panel mounting screws.

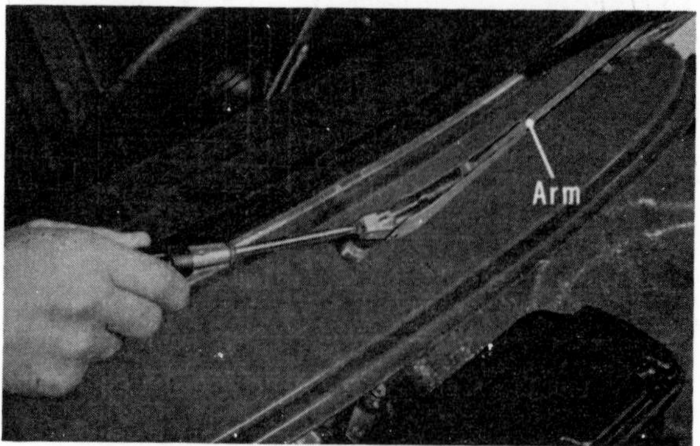

Fig. 11.36. Tightening a wiper arm locking bolt

Fig. 11.37. Wiper motor mounting

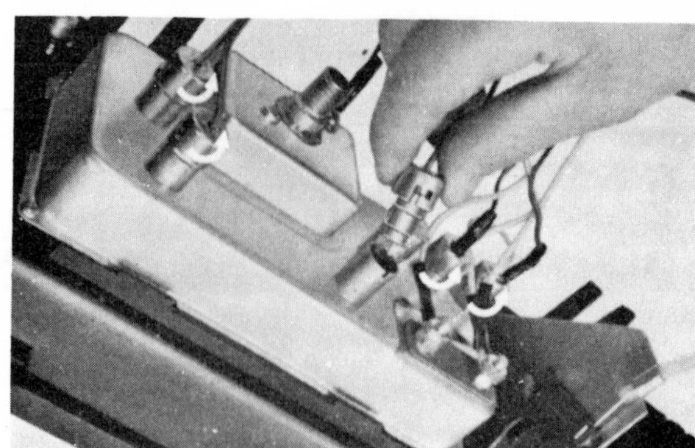

Fig. 11.38. Changing an instrument panel warning lamp bulb

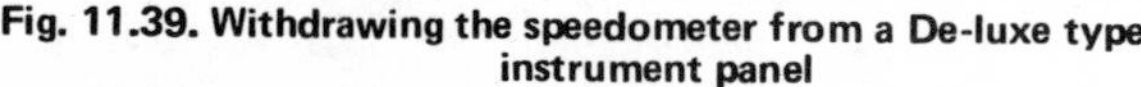
Fig. 11.39. Withdrawing the speedometer from a De-luxe type instrument panel

Fig. 11.40. Instrument retaining springs (De-luxe type panel)

25 Electrical system - fault diagnosis

Symptom	Reason/s	Remedy
Starter motor fails to turn engine	Battery discharged	Charge battery.
	Battery defective internally	Fit new battery.
	Battery terminal leads loose or earth lead not securely attached to body	Check and tighten leads.
	Loose or broken connections in starter motor circuit	Check all connections and tighten any that are loose.
	Starter motor switch or solenoid faulty	Test and replace faulty components with new.
	Starter brushes badly worn, sticking, or brush wires loose	Examine brushes, replace as necessary, tighten down brush wires.
	Commutator dirty, worn or burnt	Clean commutator, recut if badly burnt.
	Starter motor armature faulty (600 cc/ 35.5 cu in.)	Overhaul starter motor, fit new armature.
	Field coils earthed (600 cc/35.5 cu in.)	Overhaul starter motor.
	Rotor or stator earthed (360 cc/21.5 cu in.)	Overhaul starter/generator
Starter turns engine very slowly	Battery in discharged condition	Charge battery.
	Starter brushes badly worn, sticking, or brush wires loose (600 cc/35.5 cu in.)	Examine brushes, replace as necessary, tighten down brush wires.
	Loose wires in starter motor circuit	Check wiring and tighten as necessary.
Starter motor operates without turning engine (600 cc/35.5 cu in. only)	Starter motor pinion sticking on the screwed sleeve	Remove starter motor, clean starter motor drive.
	Pinion or flywheel gear teeth broken or worn	Fit new gear ring to flywheel, and new pinion to starter motor drive.
Starter motor noisy or excessively rough engagement (600 cc/35.5 cu in. only)	Pinion or flywheel gear teeth broken or worn	Fit new gear teeth to flywheel, or new pinion to starter motor drive.
	Starter motor retaining bolts loose	Tighten starter motor securing bolts. Fit new spring washer if necessary.
Battery will not hold charge for more than a few days	Battery defective internally	Remove and fit new battery.
	Electrolyte level too low or electrolyte too weak due to leakage	Top up electrolyte level to just above plates.
	Plate separators no longer fully effective	Remove and fit new battery.
	Battery plates severely sulphated	Remove and fit new battery.
	Fan belt slipping	Check belt for wear, replace if necessary, and tighten.
	Battery terminal connections loose or corroded	Check terminals for tightness and remove all corrosion.
	Dynamo or alternator not charging	Remove and overhaul.
	Short in lighting circuit causing continual battery drain	Trace and rectify.
	Regulator unit not working correctly	Check setting, clean and replace if defective.
Ignition light fails to extinguish, battery runs flat in a few days	Brushes worn, sticking, broken or dirty	Examine, clean or replace brushes as necessary.

Symptom	Reason/s	Remedy
	Brush springs weak or broken	Examine and test. Replace as necessary.
	Commutator dirty, greasy, worn or burnt	Clean commutator and undercut segment separators.
	Dynamo or alternator field coils burnt, open, or shorted	Remove and fit rebuilt unit.
	Commutator worn	Turn down on lathe or renew.
	Pole pieces very loose	Strip and overhaul unit. Tighten pole pieces.
	Regulator incorrectly set	Adjust regulator correctly.
	Cut-out incorrectly set	Adjust cut-out correctly.
	Open circuit in wiring of cut-out and regulator unit	Remove, examine, and renew as necessary.
	HORN	
Horn operates all the time	Horn push either earthed or stuck down	Disconnect battery earth. Check and rectify source of trouble.
	Horn cable to horn push earthed	Disconnect battery earth. Check and rectify source of trouble.
Horn fails to operate	Blown fuse	Check and renew if broken. Ascertain cause.
	Cable or cable connection loose, broken or disconnected	Check all connections for tightness and cables for breaks.
	Horn has an internal fault	Remove and overhaul horn.
Horn emits intermittent or unsatisfactory noise	Cable connections loose	Check and tighten all connections.
	Horn incorrectly adjusted	Adjust horn until best note obtained.
	LIGHTS	
Lights do not come on	If engine not running, battery discharged	Push-start car, charge battery.
	Light bulb filament burnt out or bulbs broken	Test bulbs in live bulb holders.
	Wire connections loose, disconnected or broken	Check all connections for tightness and wire cable for breaks.
	Light switch shorting or otherwise faulty	By-pass light switch to ascertain if fault is in switch and fit new switch as appropriate.
Lights come on but fade out	If engine not running battery discharged	Push-start car, and charge battery.
	Light bulb filament burnt out or bulbs or sealed beam units broken	Test bulbs in live bulb holder, renew sealed beam units.
	Wire connections loose, disconnected or broken	Check all connections for tightness and wire cable for breaks.
	Light switch shorting or otherwise faulty	By-pass light switch to ascertain if fault is in switch and fit new switch as appropriate.
Lights give very poor illumination	Lamp glasses dirty	Clean glasses.
	Lamps badly out of adjustment	Adjust lamps correctly.
	Incorrect bulb with too low wattage fitted	Remove bulb and replace with correct grade.
	Existing bulbs old and badly discoloured	Renew bulb units.
Lights work erratically - flashing on and off, especially over bumps	Battery terminals or earth connection loose	Tighten battery terminals and earth connection.
	Lights not earthing properly	Examine and rectify.
	Contacts in light switch faulty	By-pass light switch to ascertain if fault is in switch and fit new switch as appropriate.
	WIPERS	
Wiper motor fails to work	Blown fuse	Check and replace fuse if necessary.
	Wire connections loose, disconnected, or broken	Check wiper wiring. Tighten loose connections.
	Brushes badly worn	)
	Armature worn or faulty	)
	Field coils faulty	)
Wiper motor works very slowly and takes excessive current	Commutator dirty, greasy or burnt	)
	Armature bearings dirty or unaligned	) Fit replacement unit
	Armature badly worn or faulty	)
Wiper motor works slowly and takes little current	Brushes badly worn	)
	Commutator dirty, greasy or burnt	)
	Armature badly worn or faulty	)
Wiper motor works but wiper blades remain static	Wiper motor gearbox parts badly worn	)

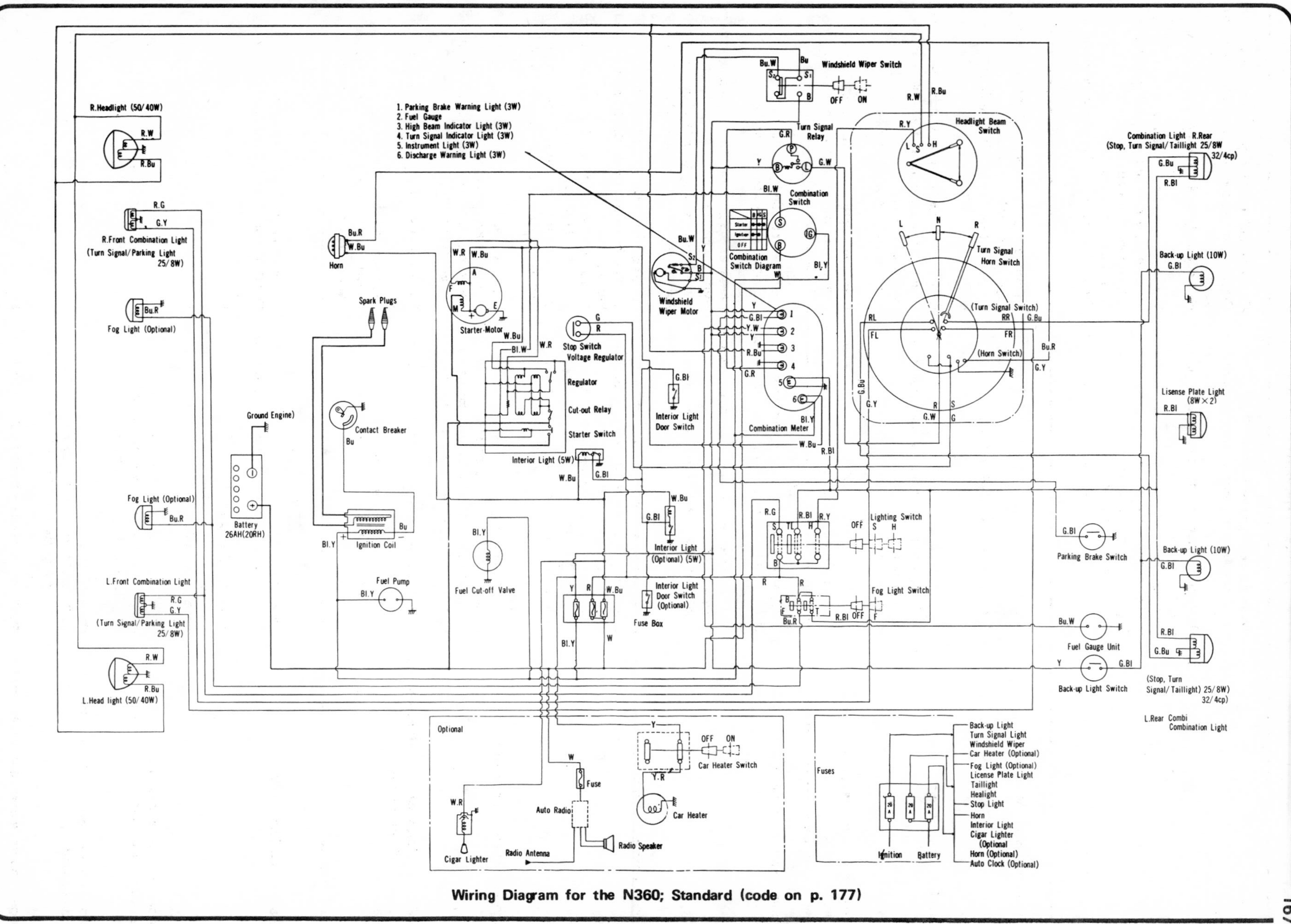

Wiring Diagram for the N360; Standard (code on p. 177)

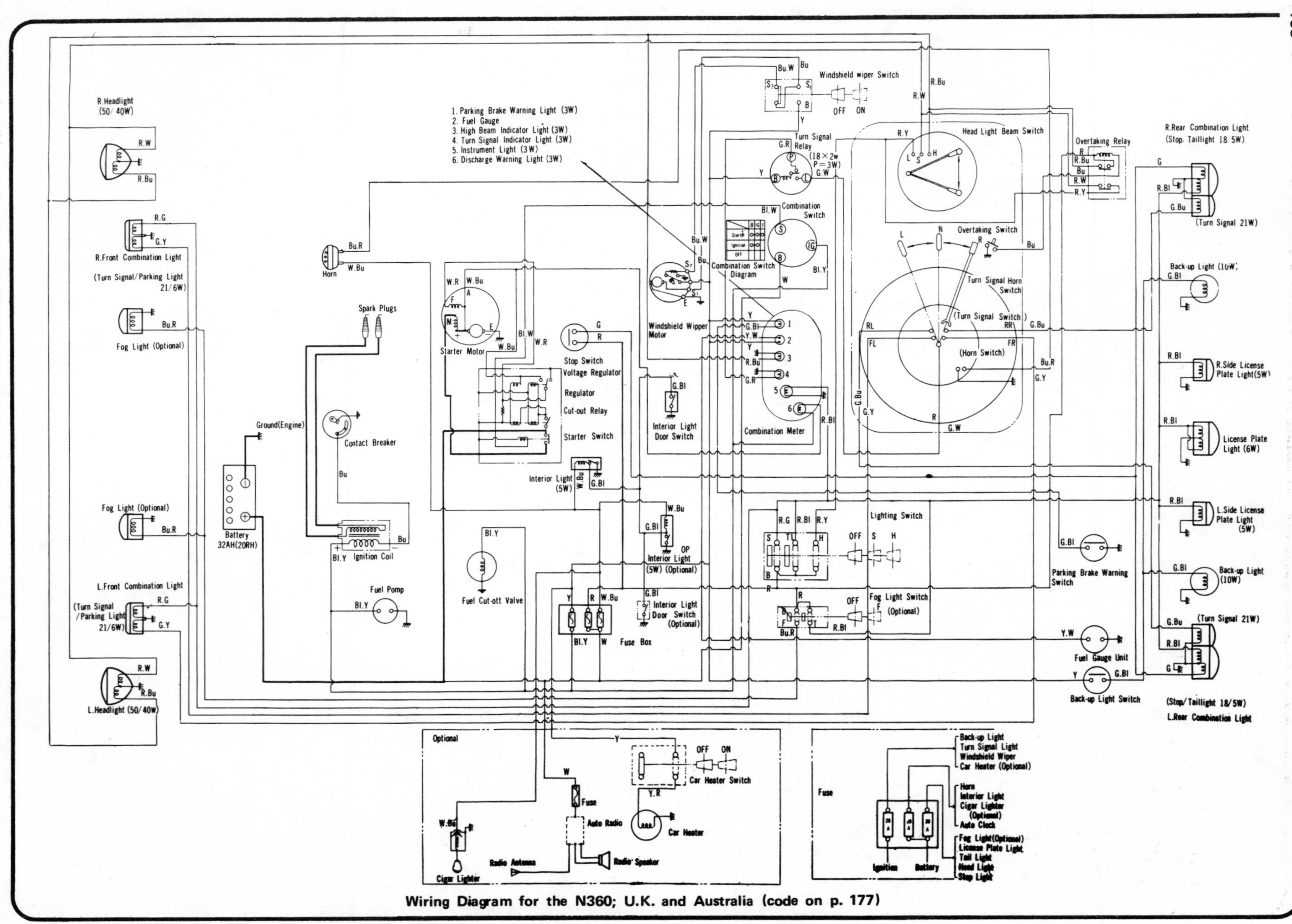

Wiring Diagram for the N360; U.K. and Australia (code on p. 177)

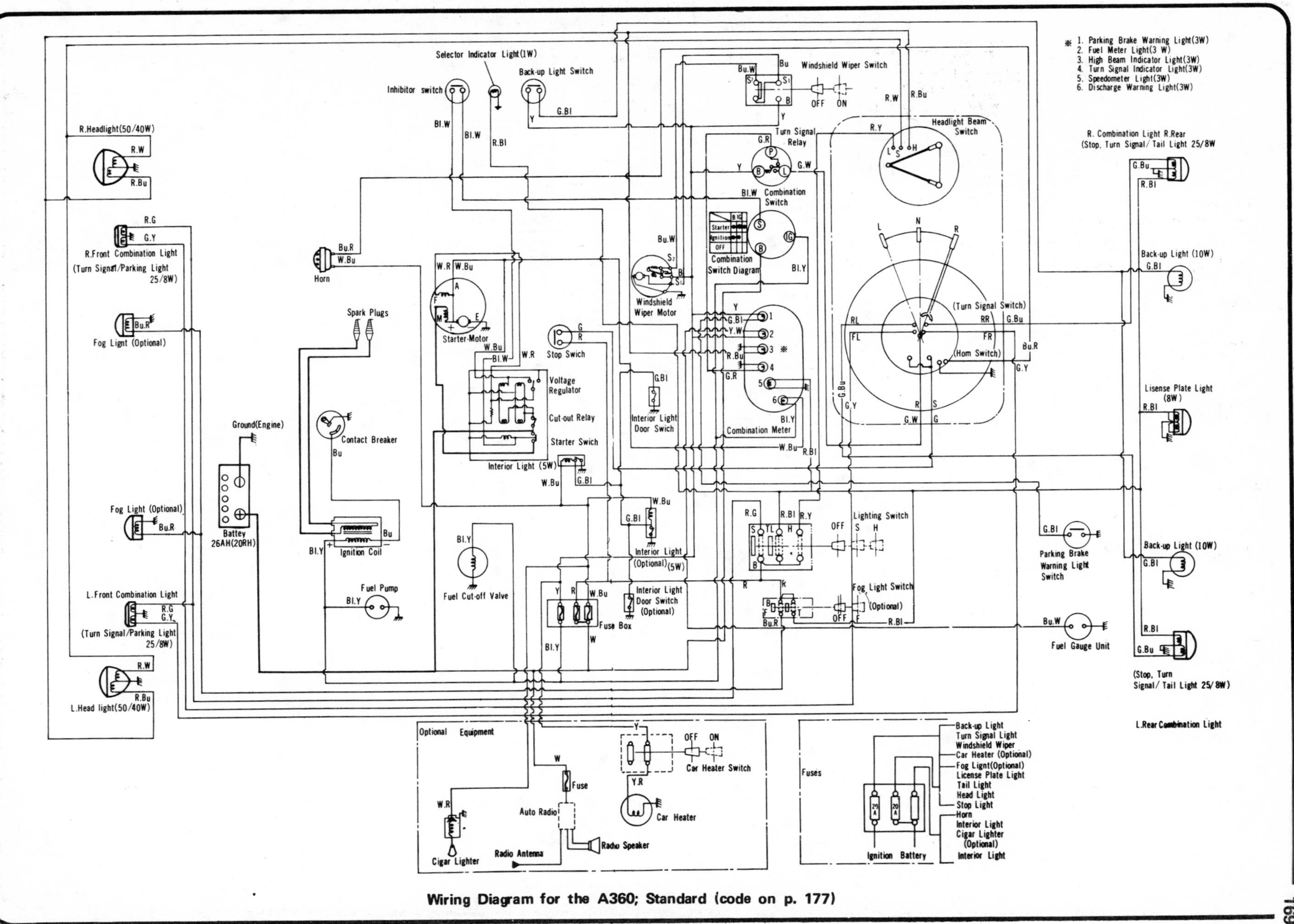

Wiring Diagram for the A360; Standard (code on p. 177)

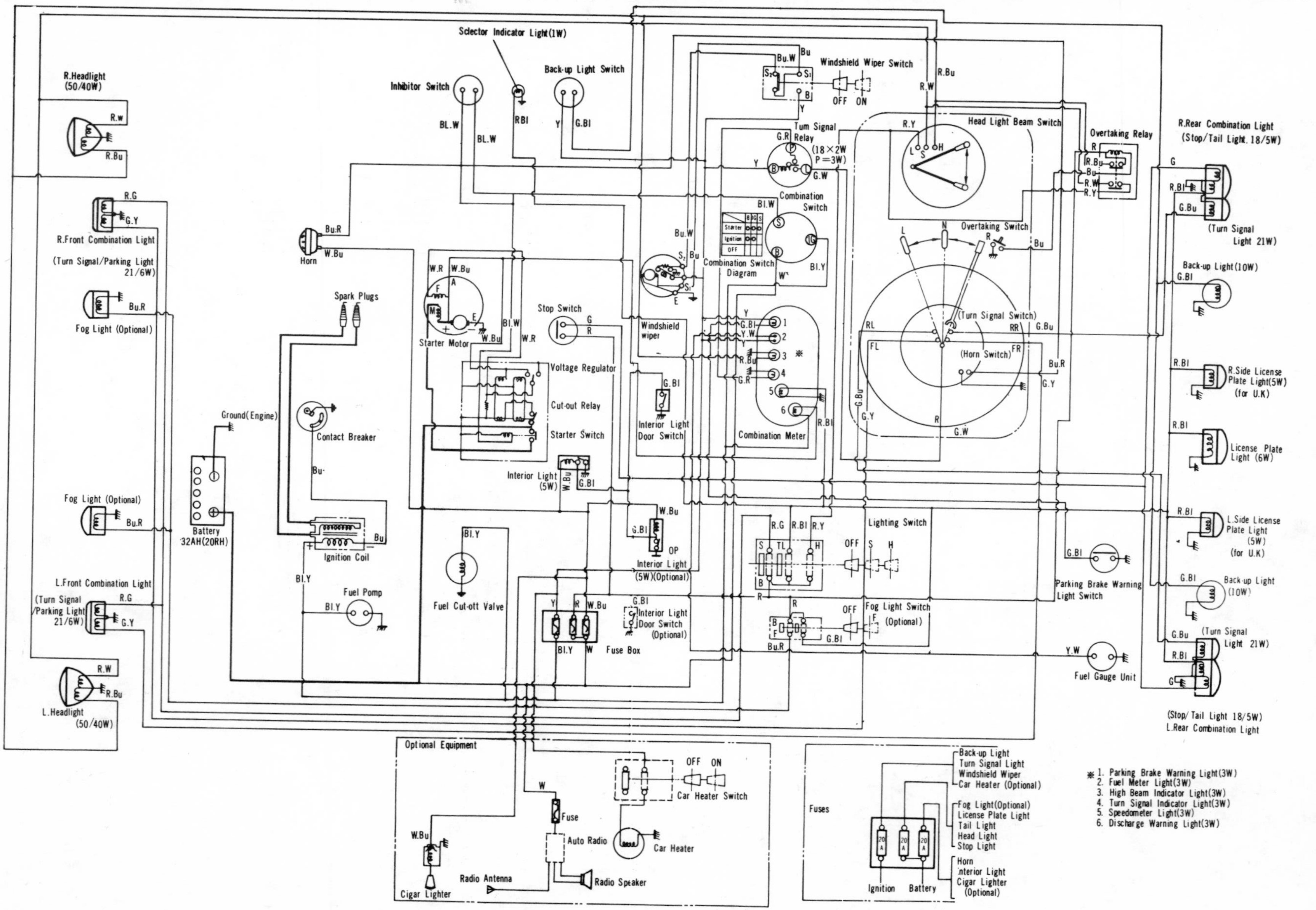

R.Headlight (50/40W)
R.Front Combination Light (Turn Signal/Parking Light 21/6W)
Fog Light (Optional)
L.Front Combination Light (Turn Signal /Parking Light 21/6W)
L.Headlight (50/40W)
Horn
Spark Plugs
Contact Breaker
Ground(Engine)
Battery 32AH(20RH)
Ignition Coil
Fuel Pump
Selector Indicator Light(1W)
Inhibitor Switch
Back-up Light Switch
Starter Motor
Stop Switch
Voltage Regulator
Cut-out Relay
Starter Switch
Interior Light (5W)
Fuel Cut-off Valve
Fuse Box
Windshield wiper
Interior Light Door Switch
Interior Light (5W)(Optional)
Interior Light Door Switch (Optional)
Windshield Wiper Switch
OFF ON
Turn Signal Relay (18×2W P=3W)
Combination Switch
Combination Switch Diagram
Combination Meter
Head Light Beam Switch
Overtaking Switch
Overtaking Relay
(Turn Signal Switch)
(Horn Switch)
Lighting Switch
OFF S H
Fog Light Switch (Optional)
Parking Brake Warning Light Switch
Fuel Gauge Unit
R.Rear Combination Light (Stop/Tail Light 18/5W)
(Turn Signal Light 21W)
Back-up Light(10W)
R.Side License Plate Light(5W) (for U.K)
License Plate Light (6W)
L.Side License Plate Light (5W) (for U.K)
Back-up Light (10W)
(Turn Signal Light 21W)
(Stop/Tail Light 18/5W) L.Rear Combination Light

Optional Equipment
Cigar Lighter
Radio Antenna
Fuse
Auto Radio
Radio Speaker
Car Heater
Car Heater Switch

Fuses
Back-up Light
Turn Signal Light
Windshield Wiper
Car Heater (Optional)
Fog Light(Optional)
License Plate Light
Tail Light
Head Light
Stop Light
Horn
Interior Light
Cigar Lighter (Optional)
Ignition
Battery

※ 1. Parking Brake Warning Light(3W)
2. Fuel Meter Light(3W)
3. High Beam Indicator Light(3W)
4. Turn Signal Indicator Light(3W)
5. Speedometer Light(3W)
6. Discharge Warning Light(3W)

Wiring Diagram for the A360; U.K. and Australia (code on p. 177)

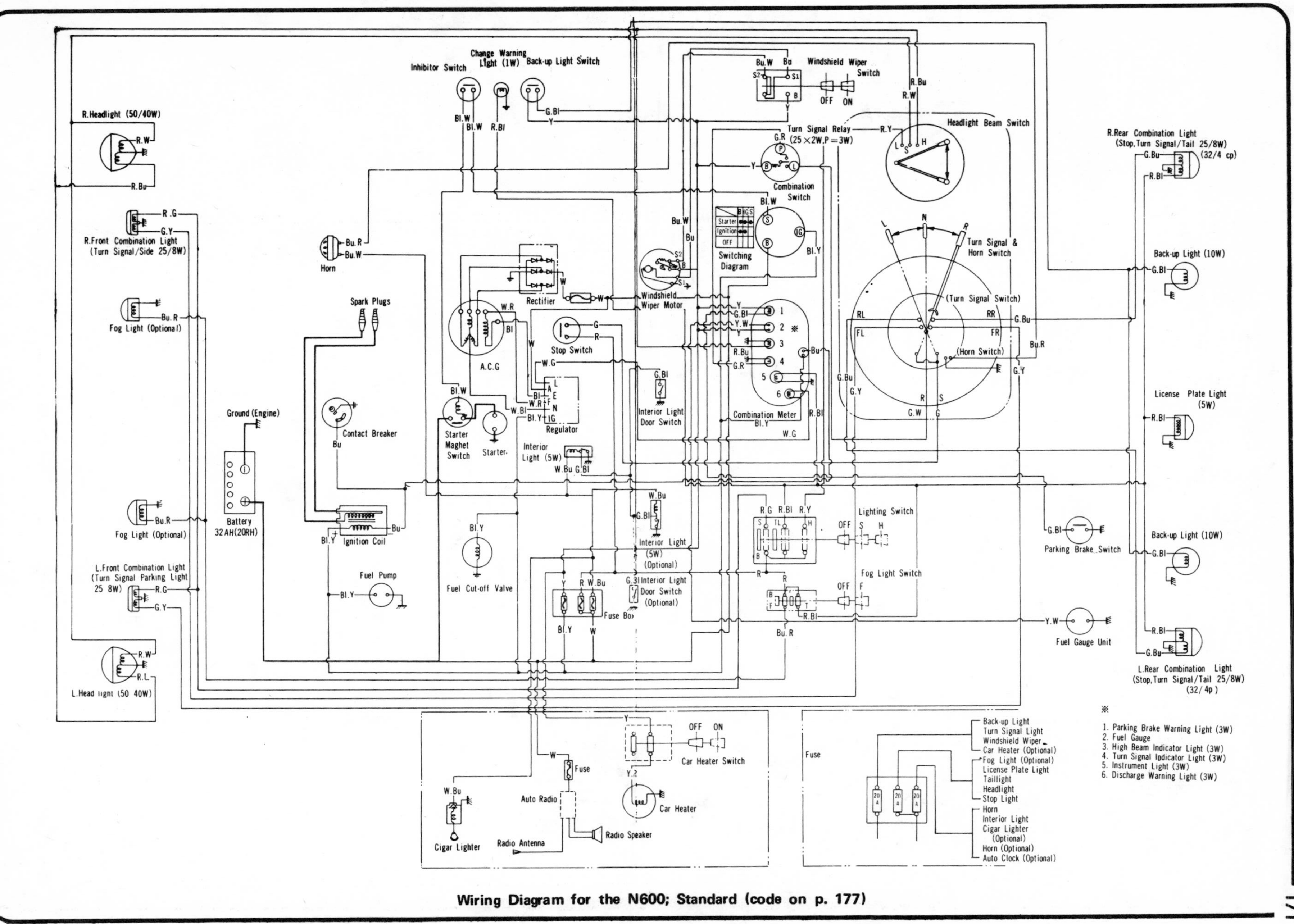

Wiring Diagram for the N600; Standard (code on p. 177)

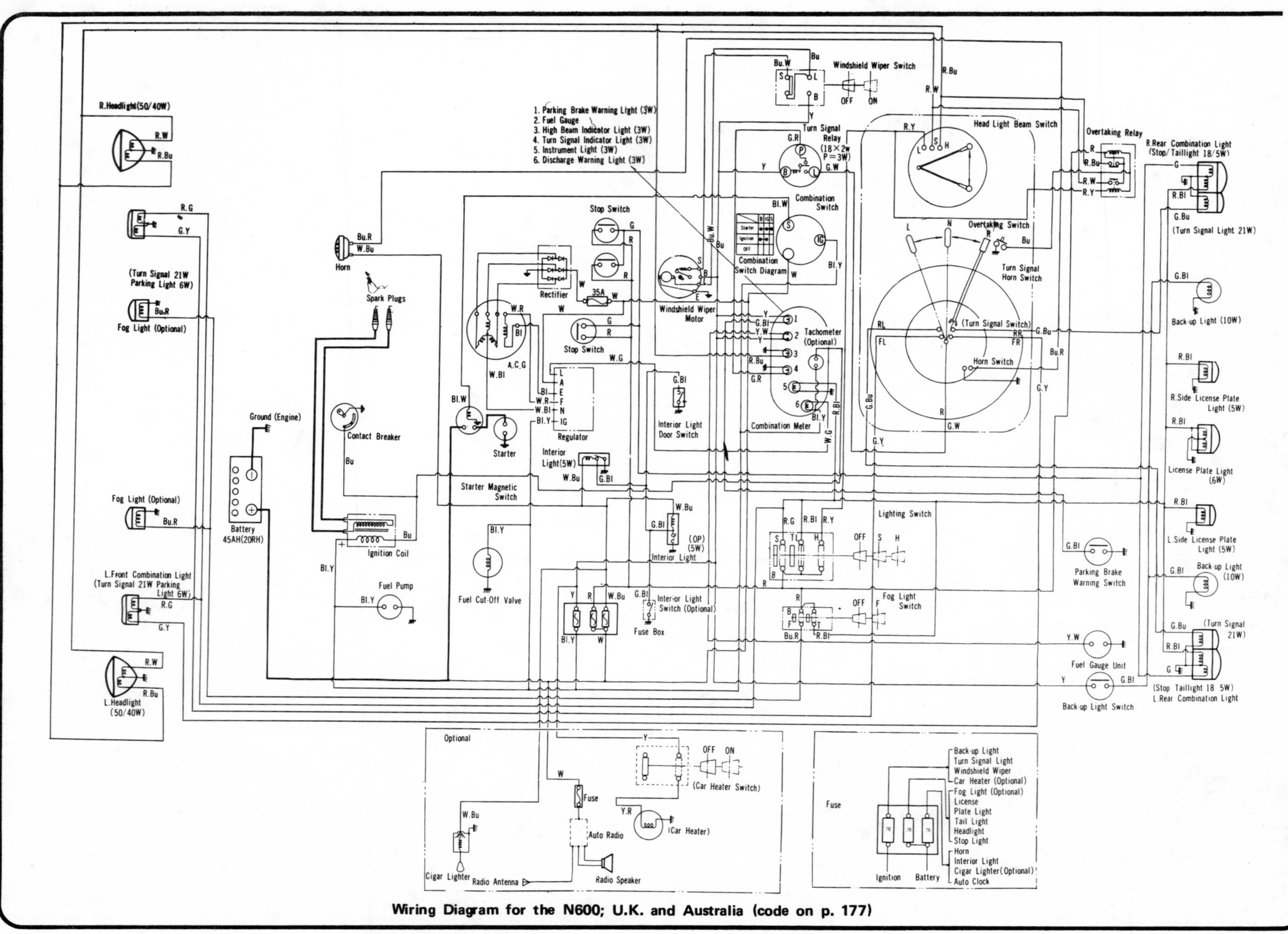

Wiring Diagram for the N600; U.K. and Australia (code on p. 177)

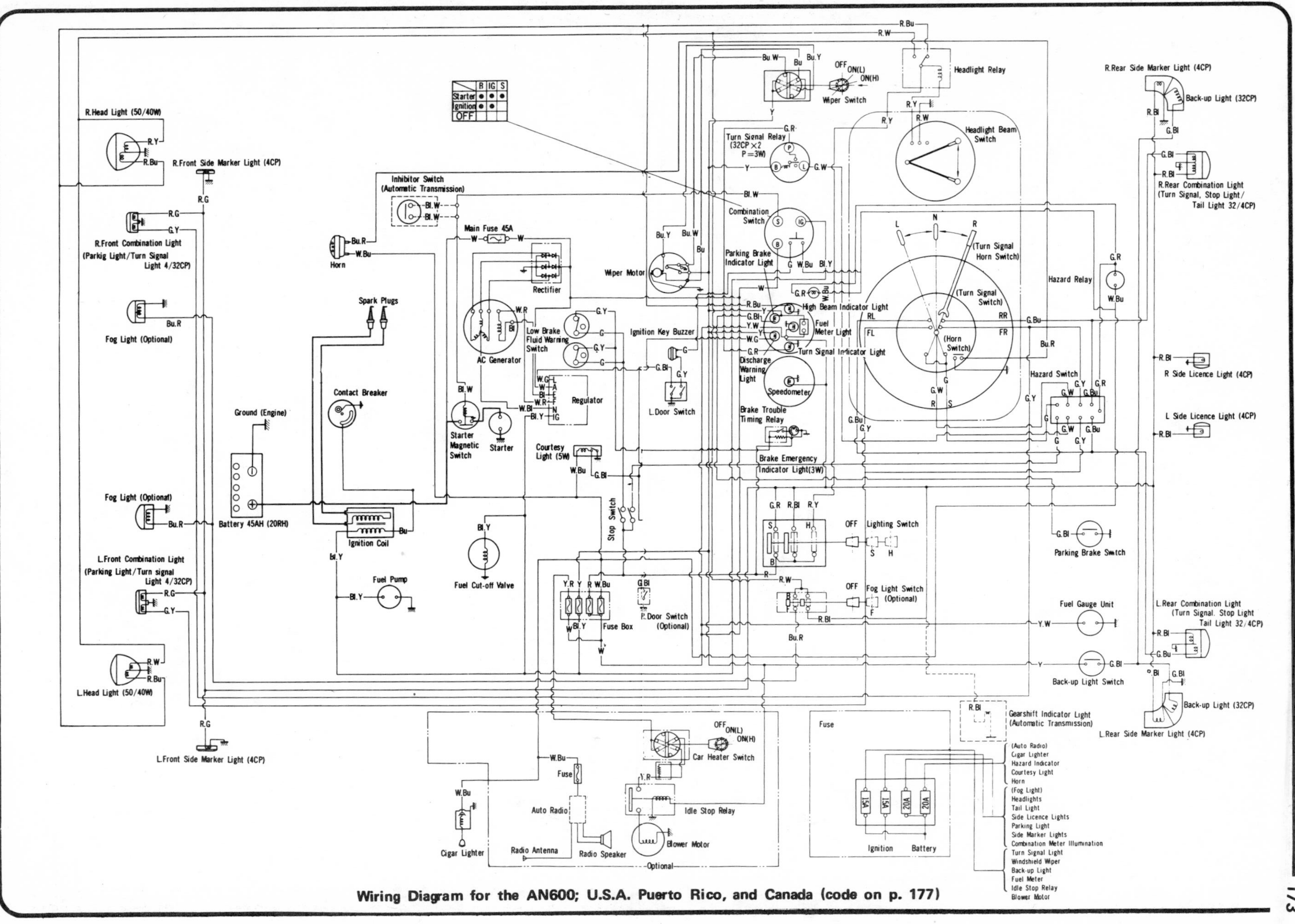

Wiring Diagram for the AN600; U.S.A. Puerto Rico, and Canada (code on p. 177)

R.Headlight (50/40W)
R.Front Combination Light (Turn Signal Light 21W, Parking Light 6W)
Fog Light (Optional)
Fog Light (Optional)
L.Front Combination Light (Turn Signal 21W, Parking Light 6W)
L.Head light (50/40W)
Horn
Ground(Engine)
Battery 40AH(20RH)
Spark Plugs
Contact Breaker
Ignition Coil
Fuel Pump
Inhibitor Switch
Change Warning Light (1W)
Back-up Light Switch
Stop Switch
Rectifier
A.C.G
Stop Switch
Regulator
Starter Magnetic Switch
Starter
Fuel Cut-off Valve
Fuse, Box
Windshield Wiper Motor
Interior Light Door Switch
Switching Diagram
Combination Switch
Combination Meter
Headlight Beam Switch
Overtaking Switch
Turn Signal and Horn Switch
(Turn Signal Switch)
(Horn Switch)
Overtaking Relay
Parking Brake Switch
Fuel Gauge Unit
R.Rear Combination Light (Stop/Tail 18/5W)
(Turn Signal 21W)
Back-up Light (10W)
R.Side License Plate Light (5W)
License Plate Light (6W)
L.Side License Plate Light (5W)
Back-up Light Switch (10W)
(Turn Signal Light 21W)
L.Rear Combination Light (Stop Tail 18 5W)
Cigar Lighter
Radio Antenna
Auto Radio
Fuses
Radio Speaker
Car Heater Switch
Car Heater

Ignition Coil — Back-up Light, Turn Signal Light, Windshield Wiper, Car Heater (Optional)
Fog Light (Optional), License Plate Light, Taillight, Headlight, Stop Light
Battery — Horn, Interior Light, Cigar Lighter (Optional), Horn (Optional), Auto Clock (Optional)

1. Parking Brake Warning Light(3W)
2. Fuel Gauge
3. High Beam Indicator Light(3W)
4. Turn Signal Indicator Light(3W)
5. Instrument Light(3W - 2)
6. Discharge Warning Light(3W)

Wiring Diagram for the A600; U.K. and Australia (code on p. 177)

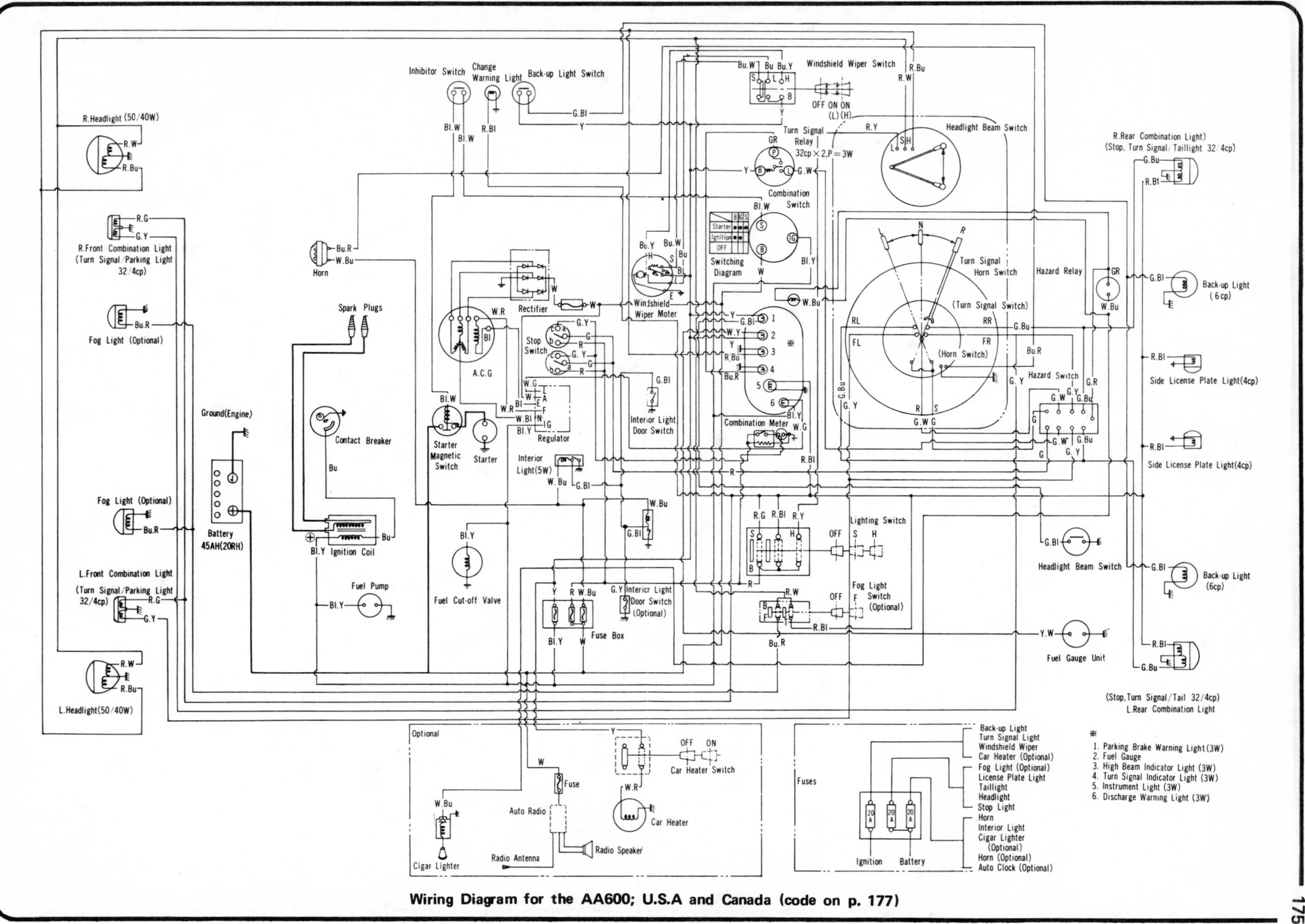

Wiring Diagram for the AA600; U.S.A and Canada (code on p. 177)

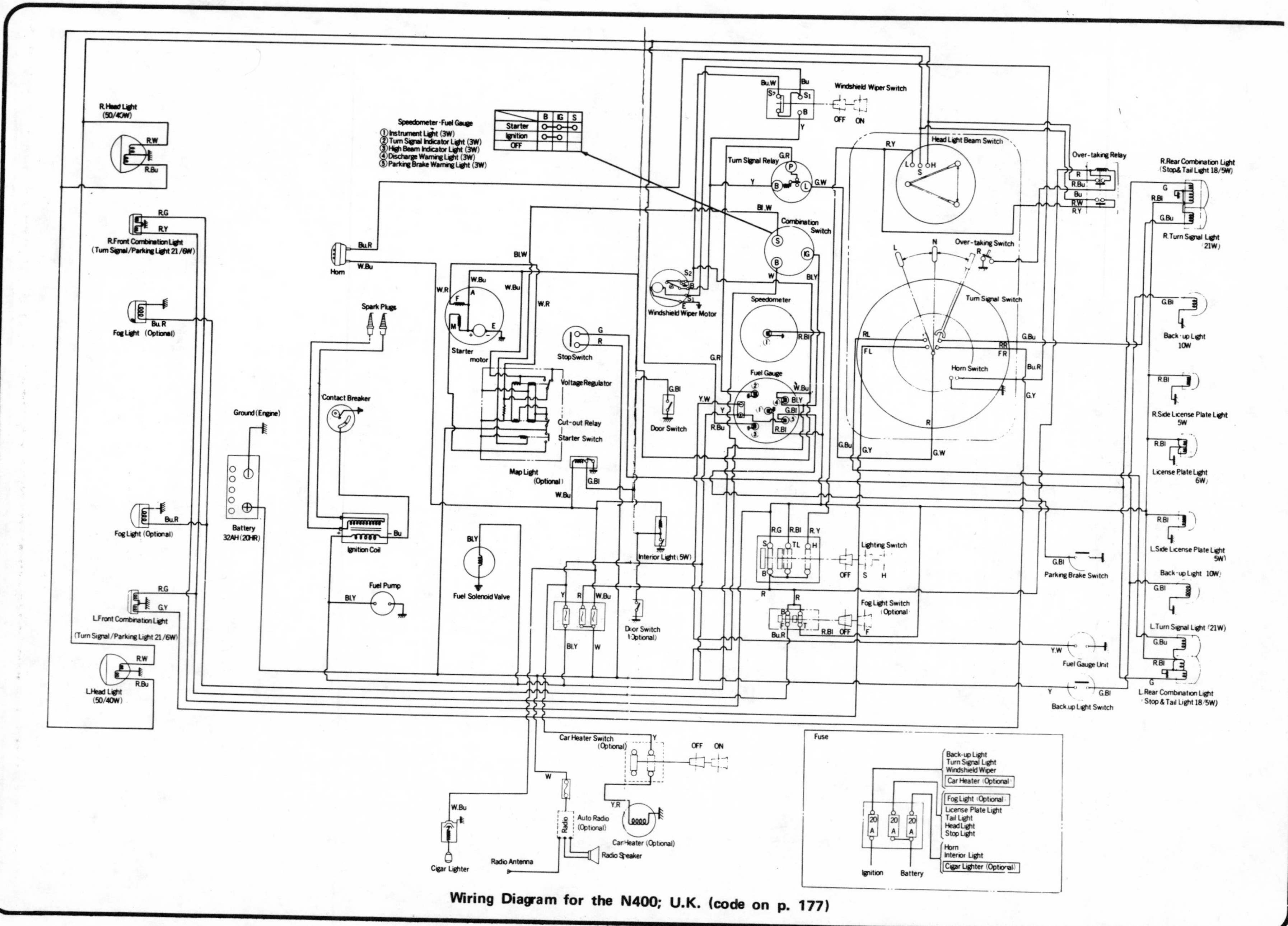

Wiring Diagram for the N400; U.K. (code on p. 177)

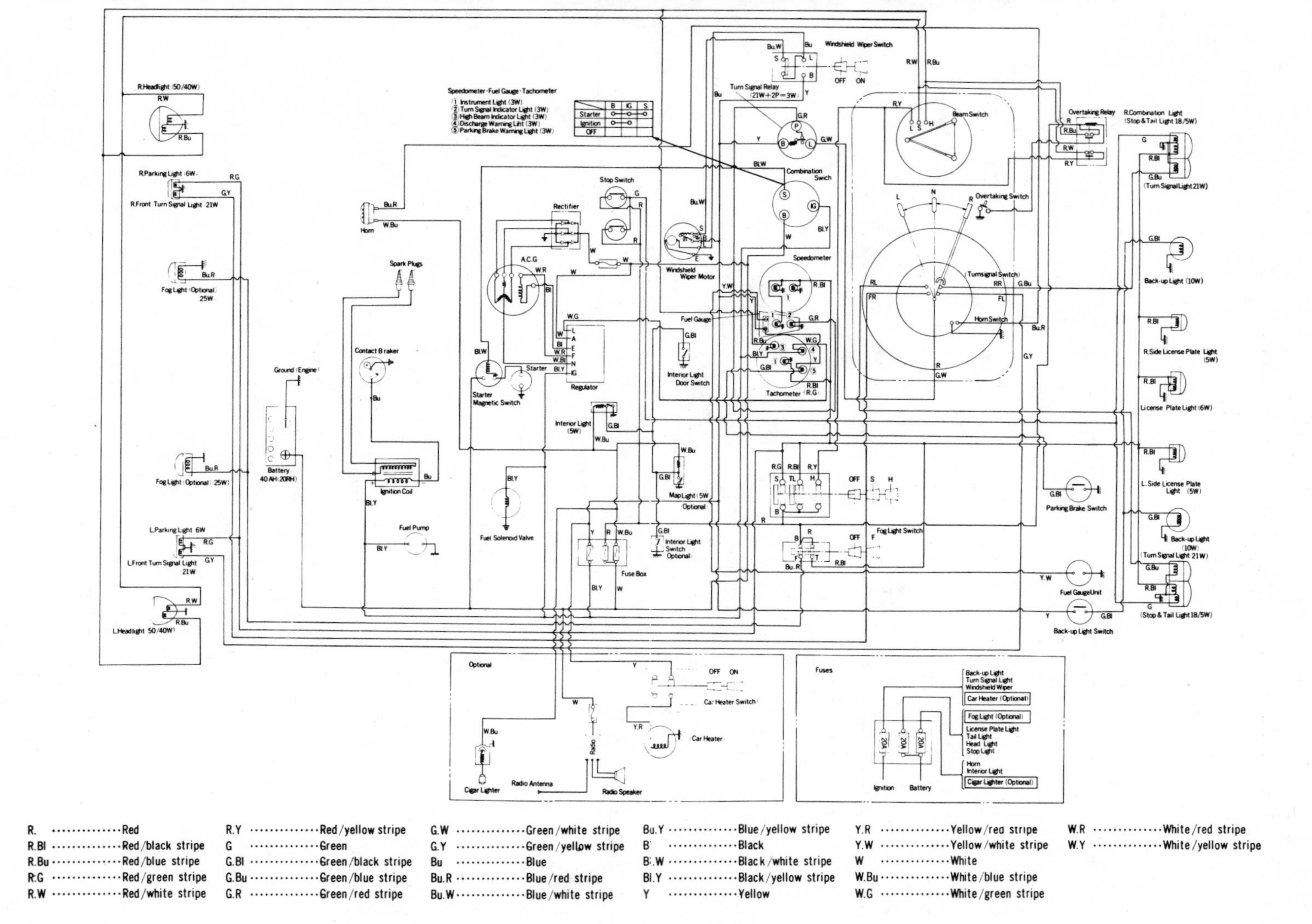

R. ......Red	R.Y ......Red/yellow stripe	G.W ......Green/white stripe	Bu.Y ......Blue/yellow stripe	Y.R ......Yellow/red stripe	W.R ......White/red stripe
R.Bl ......Red/black stripe	G ......Green	G.Y ......Green/yellow stripe	B ......Black	Y.W ......Yellow/white stripe	W.Y ......White/yellow stripe
R.Bu ......Red/blue stripe	G.Bl ......Green/black stripe	Bu ......Blue	B.W ......Black/white stripe	W ......White	
R.G ......Red/green stripe	G.Bu ......Green/blue stripe	Bu.R ......Blue/red stripe	Bl.Y ......Black/yellow stripe	W.Bu ......White/blue stripe	
R.W ......Red/white stripe	G.R ......Green/red stripe	Bu.W ......Blue/white stripe	Y ......Yellow	W.G ......White/green stripe	

Wiring Diagram for the N600G; U.K.

Chapter 12 Bodywork

Contents

Specifications

Body length (overall):

360 cc/21.5 cu in. models	119.1 in. (302.5 cm)
600 cc/35.5 cu in. models	122.0 in. (310.0 cm)
600/(Z) coupe	122.83 in. (312.0 cm)
600 cc/35.5 cu in. (North America)	125.0 in. (317.5 cm)

Body width (overall):

All models (except North America)	51.0 in. (129.5 cm)
North America	52.6 in. (133.5 cm)

Height (overall):

All models (except Coupe (Z))	52.4 in. (133 cm)
Coupe (Z)	50.4 in. (128 cm)

Ground clearance (minimum): ... 6.3 in. (160 mm)

Weight (ready for road):

Model N360	1114 lb (505 kg)
Model A360	1213 lb (550 kg)
Model LN360	1201 lb (545 kg)
Model N600	1213 lb (550 kg)
Model A600	1279 lb (580 kg)
Model 600 (Z) Coupe'	1312 lb (590 kg)
600 cc (North America)	1356 lb (615 kg)

Wheelbase (all models): ... 78.7 in. (200.0 cm)

1 General description

The body is of welded all-steel construction and is available in two door Saloon/Sedan, Estate/Wagon and Coupe (2) versions. The front wings are bolted into position in the interest of ecomonical repair of the front end.

2 Maintenance - bodywork and underframe

1 The general condition of a car's bodywork is the one thing that significantly affects its value. Maintenance is easy but needs to be regular and particular. Neglect - particularly after minor damage - can quickly lead to further deterioration and costly repair bills. It is important also to keep watch on those parts of the bodywork not immediately visible, for example the underside, inside all the wheel arches and the lower part of the engine compartment.

2 The basic maintenance routine for the bodywork is washing - preferably with a lot of water from a hose. This will remove all the loose solids which may have stuck to the car. It is important to flush these off in such a way as to prevent grit from scratching the finish. The wheel arches and underbody need washing in the same way, to remove any accumulated mud which will retain moisture and tend to encourage rust. Paradoxically enough, the best time to clean the underbody and wheel arches is in wet weather when the mud is thoroughly wet and soft. In very wet weather the underbody is usually cleaned of large accumulations automatically and this is a good time for inspection.

3 Periodically, it is a good idea to have the whole of the underside of the car steam cleaned, engine compartment included, so that a thorough inspection can be carried out to see what minor repairs and renovations are necessary. Steam cleaning is available at many garages and is necessary for removal of accumulation of oily grime which sometimes collects thickly in areas near the engine and gearbox.

If steam facilities are not available there are one or two excellent grease solvents available which can be brush applied. The dirt can then be simply hosed off. Any signs of rust on the underside panels and bracing members must be attended to immediately. Thorough wire brushing followed by treatment with an anti-rust compound, primer and underbody sealer will prevent continued deterioration. If not dealt with the car could eventually become structurally unsound and therefore unsafe.

4 After washing the paintwork wipe if off with a chamois leather to give a clear unspotted finish. A coat of clear wax polish will give added protection against chemical pollutants in the air and will survive several subsequent washings. If the paintwork sheen has dulled or oxidised use a cleaner/polish combination to restore the brilliance of the shine. This requires a little more effort but is usually because regular washing has been neglected! Always check that door and ventilator drain holes and pipes are completely clear so that water can drain out. Brightwork should be treated the same way as paintwork. Windscreens and windows can be kept clear of the smeary film which often appears if a little ammonia is added to the water. If glasswork is scratched a good rub with a proprietary metal polish will often clean them. Never use any form of wax or other paint/chromium polish on glass.

3 Maintenance - body interior

Mats and carpets should be brushed or vacuum cleaned regularly to keep them free of grit. If they are badly stained, remove them from the car for scrubbing or sponging and make quite sure that they are dry before replacement. Seat and interior trim panels can be kept clean with a wipe over with a damp cloth. If they do become stained (which can be more apparent on light coloured upholstery) use a little liquid detergent and a soft nailbrush to scoure the grime out of the grain of the material. Do not forget to keep the headlining clean in the same way as the upholstery. When using liquid cleaners inside the car do not over-wet the surfaces being cleaned. Excessive damp could get into the upholstery seams and padded interior, causing stains, offensive odours or even rot. If the inside of the car gets wet accidentally it is worthwhile taking some trouble to dry it out properly, particularly where carpets are involved. **Do not** leave oil or electric heaters inside the car for this purpose. If, when removing carpets or mats for cleaning, there are signs of damp underneath, all the interior of the car floor should be uncovered and the point of water entry found. It may only be a missing grommet, but it could be a rusted through floor panel and this demands immediate attention as described in the previous section. More often than not both sides of the panel will require treatment.

4 Minor bodywork damage - repair

The photograph sequence on pages 182 and 183 illustrate the operations detailed in the following Sections.

Repair of minor scratches in the car's bodywork

If the scratch is very superficial, and does not penetrate to the metal of the bodywork - repair is very simple. Lightly rub the area of the scratch with a paintwork renovator (eg; Top-Cut), or a very fine cutting paste, to remove loose paint from the scratch and to clear the surrounding bodywork of wax polish. Rinse the area with clean water.

Apply touch-up paint to the scratch using a thin paint brush; continue to apply thin layers of paint until the surface of the paint in the scratch is level with the surrounding paintwork. Allow the new paint at least two weeks to harden; then, blend it into the surrounding paintwork by rubbing the paintwork in the scratch area with a paintwork renovator (eg; Top-Cut), or a very fine cutting paste. Finally apply wax polish.

Alternative to painting over the scratch is to use Holts "Scratch-Patch". Use the same preparation for the affected area; then simply, pick a patch of a suitable size to cover the scratch completely. Hold the patch against the scratch and burnish its backing paper; the patch will adhere to the paintwork freeing itself from the backing paper at the same time. Polish the affected area to blend the patch into the surrounding paintwork.

Where a scratch has penetrated right through to the metal of the bodywork, causing the metal to rust, a different repair technique is required. Remove any loose rust from the bottom of the scratch with a penknife; then apply rust inhibiting paint (eg. "Kurust") to prevent the formation of rust in the future. Using a rubber or nylon applicator fill the scratch with body-stopper paste. If required, this paste can be mixed with cellulose thinners to provide a very thin paste which is ideal for filling narrow scratches. Before the stopper-paste in the scratch hardens, wrap a piece of smooth cotton rag around the tip of a finger. Dip the finger in cellulose thinners and then quickly sweep it across the surface of the stopper-paste in the scratch; this will ensure that the surface of the stopper-paste is slightly hollowed. The scratch can now be painted over as described earlier in this Section.

Repair of dents in the car's bodywork

When deep denting of the car's bodywork has taken place, the first task is to pull the dent out, until the affected bodywork almost attains its original shape. There is little point in trying to restore the original shape completely, as the metal in the damaged area will have stretched on impact and cannot be reshaped fully to its original contour. It is better to bring the level of the dent up to a point which is about 1/8 inch (3 mm) below the level of the surrounding bodywork. In cases where the dent is very shallow anyway, it is not worth trying to pull it out at all.

If the underside of the dent is accessible, it can be hammered out gently from behind, using a mallet with a wooden or plastic head. Whilst doing this, hold a suitable block of wood firmly against the outside of the dent. This block will absorb the impact from the hammer blows and thus prevent a large area of bodywork from being 'belled-out'.

Should the dent be in a section of the bodywork which has a double skin or some other factor making it inaccessible from behind, a different technique is called for. Drill several small holes through the metal inside the dent area - particularly in the deeper sections. Then screw long self-tapping screws into the holes just sufficiently for them to gain a good purchase in the metal. Now the dent can be pulled out by pulling on the protruding heads of the screws with a pair of pliers.

The next stage of repair is the removal of the paint from the damaged area and from an inch or so of the surrounding 'sound' bodywork. This is accomplished most easily by using a wire brush or abrasive pad on a power drill, although it can be done just as effectively by hand using sheets of abrasive paper. To complete the preparations for filling, score the surface of the bare metal with a screwdriver or the tang of a file, or alternatively, drill small holes in the affected area. This will provide a really good 'key' for the filler paste.

To complete the repair see the Section on filling and respraying.

Repair of rust holes or gashes in the car's bodywork

Remove all paint from the affected area and from an inch or so of the surrounding 'sound' bodywork, using an abrasive pad or a wire brush on a power drill. If these are not available a few sheets of abrasive paper will do the job just as effectively. With the paint removed you will be able to gauge the severity of the corrosion and therefore decide whether to replace the whole panel (if this is possible) or to repair the affected area. Replacement body panels are not as expensive as most people think and it is often quicker and more satisfactory to fit a new panel than to attempt to repair large areas of corrosion.

Remove all fittings from the affected area, except those which will act as a guide to the original shape of the damaged bodywork (eg. headlamp shells etc.,). Then, using tin snips or a hacksaw blade, remove all loose metal and any other metal badly affected by corrosion. Hanner the edges of the hole inwards in order to create a slight depression for the filler paste.

Wire brush the affected area to remove the powdery rust from the surface of the remaining metal. Paint the affected area with rust inhibiting paint (eg. Kurust); if the back of the rusted area is accessible treat this also.

Before filling can take place it will be necessary to block the hole in some way. This can be achieved by the use of one of the following materials: Zinc gauze, Aluminium tape or Polyurethane foam.

Zinc gauze is probably the best material to use for a large hole. Cut a piece to the approximate size and shape of the hole to be filled, then position it in the hole so that its edges are below the level of the surrounding bodywork. It can be retained in position by several blobs of filler paste around its periphery.

Aluminium tape should be used for small or very narrow holes. Pull a piece off the roll and trim it to the approximate size and shape required, then pull off the backing paper (if used) and stick the tape over the hole; it can be overlapped if the thickness of one piece is insufficient. Burnish down the edges of the tape with the handle of a screwdriver or similar, to ensure that the tape is securely attached to the metal underneath.

Polyurethane foam is best used where the hole is situated in a section of bodywork of complex shape, backed by a small box section (eg. where the sill panel meets the rear wheel arch - most cars). The usual mixing procedure for this foam is as follows: Put equal amounts of fluid from each of the two cans provided in the kit, into one container. Stir until the mixture begins to thicken, then quickly pour this mixture into the hole, and hold a piece of cardboard over the larger apetures. Almost immediately the polyurethane will begine to expand, gushing frantically out of any small holes left unblocked. When the foam hardens it can be cut back to just below the level of the surrounding bodywork with a hacksaw blade.

Having blocked off the hole the affected area must now be filled and sprayed - see Section on bodywork filling and respraying.

Bodywork repairs - filling and re-spraying

Before using this Section, see the Sections on dent, deep scratch, rust hole, and gash repairs.

Many types of bodyfiller are available, but generally speaking those proprietary kits which contain a tin of filler paste and a tube of resin bardener (eg; Holts Cataloy) are best for this type of repair. A wide, flexible plastic or nylon applicator will be found invaluable for imparting a smooth and well contoured finish to the surface of the filler.

Mix up a little filler on a clean piece of card or board - use the hardener sparingly (follow the maker's instructions on the packet), otherwise the filler will set very rapidly.

Using the applicator, apply the filler paste to the prepared area; draw the applicator across the surface of the filler to achieve the correct contour and to level the filler surface. As soon as a contour that approximates the correct one is achieved, stop working the paste - if you carry on too long the paste will become sticky and begin to 'pick-up' on the applicator. Continue to add thin layers of filler paste at twenty-minute intervals until the level of the filler is just 'proud' of the surrounding bodywork.

Once the filler has hardened, excess can be removed using a Surform plane or Dreadnought file. From then on, progressively finer grades of abrasive paper should be used, starting with a 40 grade production paper and finishing with 400 grade 'wet-and-dry' paper. Always wrap the abrasive paper around a flat rubber, cork or wooden block- otherwise the surface of the filler will not be completely flat. During the smoothing of the filler surface the 'Wet-and-dry' paper should be periodically rinsed in water - this will ensure that a very smooth finish is imparted to the filler at the final stage.

At this stage the 'dent' should be surrounded by a ring of bare metal, which in turn should be encircled by the finely 'feathered' edge of the good paintwork. Rinse the repair area with clean water until all of the dust produced by the rubbing-down operation is gone.

Spray the whole repair area with a light coat of grey primer - this will show up any imperfections in the surface of the filler. Repair these imperfections with fresh filler paste or bodystopper, and once more smooth the surface with abrasive paper. If bodystopper is used, it can be mixed with cellulose thinners to form a really thin paste which is ideal for filling small holes. Repeat this spray and repair procedure until you are satisified that the surface of the filler and the feathered edge of the paintwork are perfect. Clean the repair area with clean water and allow to dry fully.

The repair area is now ready for spraying. Paint spraying must be carried out in a warm, dry, windless and dust free atmosphere. This condition can be created artificially if you have access to a large indoor working area, but if you are forced to work in the open, you will have to pick your day very carefully. If you are working indoors, dousing the floor in the work area with water will 'lay' the dust which would otherwise be in the atmosphere. If the repair area is confined to one body panel, mask off the surrounding panels; this will help to minimise the effects of a slight mis-match in paint colours. Bodywork fittings (eg., chrome strips, door handles etc) will also need to be masked off. Use genuine masking tape and several thicknesses of newspaper for the masking operation.

Before commencing to spray, agitate the aerosol can thoroughly, then spray a test area (an old tin, or similar) until the technique is mastered. Cover the repair area with a thick coat of primer; thickness should be built up using several thin layers of paint rather than one thick one. Using 400 grade 'wet-and-dry' paper, rub down the surface of the primer until it is really smooth. While doing this, the work area should be thoroughly doused with water, and the wet-and-dry paper periodically rinsed in water. Allow to dry before spraying on more paint.

Spray on the top coat, again building up the thickness by using several thin layers of paint. Start spraying in the centre of the repair area and then, using a circular motion, work outwards until the whole repair area and about 2 inches of the surrounding original paintwork is covered. Remove all masking material 10 to 15 minutes after spraying on the final coat of paint.

Allow the new paint at lease 2 weeks to harden fully; then, using a paintwork renovator (eg., Top-Cut) or a very fine cutting paste, blend the edges of the new paint into the existing paintwork. Finally, apply wax polish.

5 Major bodywork damage - repair

Major repairs are required after accident damage or where rust has attached and eaten away large areas of panelling. Where rust has attached and weakened structural stress points - such as the front suspension top mountings and rear spring attachment points - and after accident damage, metal work repairs are essential. Accident damage means that the whole structure must be checked for alignment. Damage to one part may affect the whole, due to the principle of construction. If the bodywork is left misaligned the car will be dangerous due to bad-handling properties - and uneven stresses will be placed on steering and transmission causing abnormal wear or total failure. Rust damage stress points may be repairable - it depends on the extent and how much has to be cut away before reaching sound metal to which new pieces may be satisfactorily and safely welded. All such metalwork is beyond the scope of most owners and should be left to professionals.Where large patches of wings or door sills or other non stressed panels need patching, it is possible to use resin filler supported on a wire mesh frame. Here again the deciding factor is whether there is sufficient sound metal in the nearby area on which to hang the repair. In any event all the surrounding area must be thoroughly cleaned of rust and treated otherwise any repair will eventually be once more surrounded with rusted metal and liable to fall away. Much also depends on the age and overall condition of the car as to what sort of repair is economically suitable.

6 Hinges, catches and locks - maintenance

The hinges and door latches should be wiped clean of grease and grime and a few drips of light oil applied occasionally. An oil with a graphite additive is particularly good. Do not over-oil as the excess merely runs out and collects more dirt. Wipe over after oiling. Other places which often stiffen up unnoticed and need a drop of oil are the bonnet and boot lid hinges and the bonnet release and safety catches.

7 Door - tracing and silencing rattles

Having established that a rattle does come from the door(s) check first that it is not loose on its hinges and that the latch is holding itfirmly closed. The hinges can be checked by rocking the door up and down when open to detect any play. If the hinges are worn at the pin the whole hinge will need renewal. When the door is closed the panel should be flush with the pillar. If not then the hinges or latch striker plate need adjustment. The door hinges are held to the door and frame by two bolts on each hinge plate.

The fitting of new hinges requires assistance if damage to the paintwork is to be avoided. To adjust the setting of the door catch first slacken the screws holding the striker plate to the door pillar just enough so that it can be moved but will hold its position. Then close the door, with the latch button pressed, and then release the latch. This is so that the striker plate position is not drastically disturbed on closing the door. Then set the door position by moving it without touching the catch, so that the panel is flush with the bodywork. This will set the striker plate in the proper place. Then carefully release the catch so as not to disturb the striker plate, open the door and tighten the screws. Rattles within the door will be due to loose fixtures or missing anti-rattle pads.

8 Front wings - removal and refitting

1 Raise the bonnet and unscrew the four bolts which secure the wing along its top edge.

2 Remove the two bolts from the rear flange and the two from the front flange directly below the headlamp.

3 If the wing is difficult to remove, cut along the seam to release the sealing mastic.

4 Refitting is a reversal of removal but clean the mating surfaces of old sealing compound and place a fresh fillet of mastic before bolting up the new wing. Insert the bolts only finger tight initially so that the alignment of the wing surfaces may be checked with adjacent body panels.

5 A splash guard plate is fitted to vehicles equipped with an engine warmth type heater.

Fig. 12.1. Front wing attachment bolts

Fig. 12.2. Location of splash guard (engine warmth type heater only)

This sequence of photographs deals with the repair of the dent and scratch (above rear lamp) shown in this photo. The procedure will be similar for the repair of a hole. It should be noted that the procedures given here are simplified - more explicit instructions will be found in the text

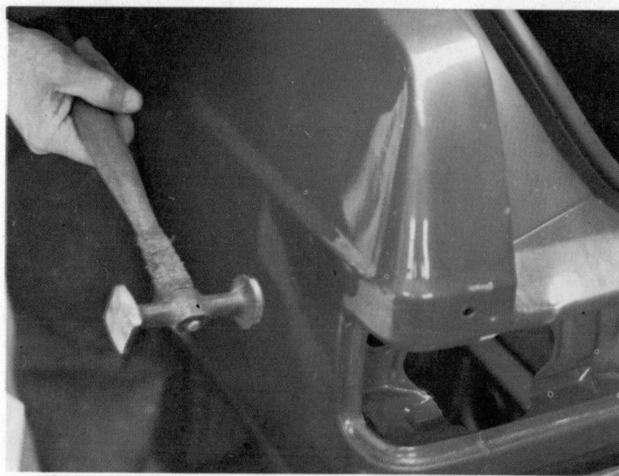

In the case of a dent the first job - after removing surrounding trim - is to hammer out the dent where access is possible. This will minimise filling. Here, the large dent having been hammered out, the damaged area is being made slightly concave

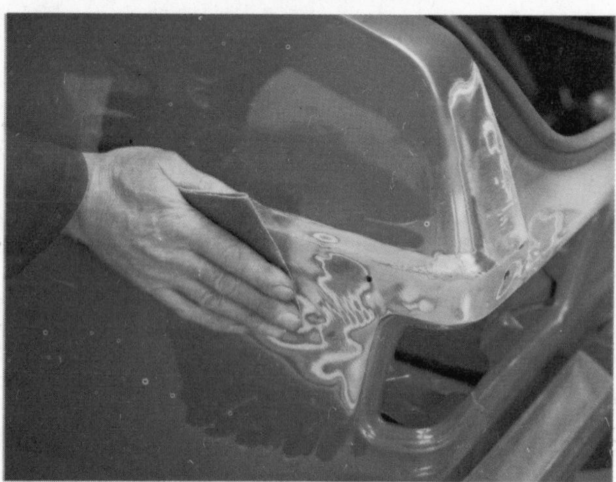

Now all paint must be removed from the damaged area, by rubbing with coarse abrasive paper. Alternatively, a wire brush or abrasive pad can be used in a power drill. Where the repair area meets good paintwork, the edge of the paintwork should be 'feathered', using a finer grade of abrasive paper

In the case of a hole caused by rusting, all damaged sheet-metal should be cut away before proceeding to this stage. Here, the damaged area is being treated with rust remover and inhibitor before being filled

Mix the body filler according to its manufacturer's instructions. In the case of corrosion damage, it will be necessary to block off any large holes before filling - this can be done with zinc gauze or aluminium tape. Make sure the area is absolutely clean before ...

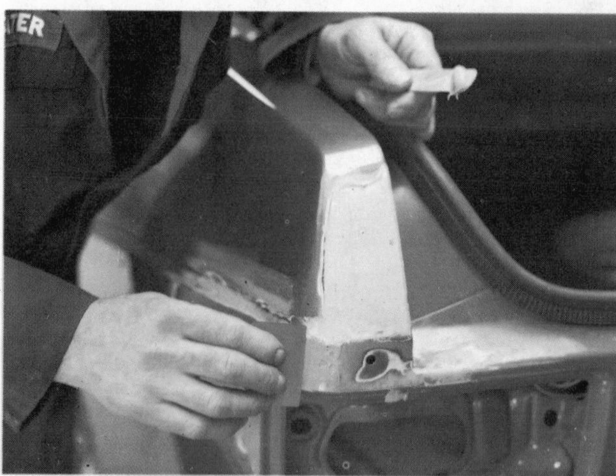

... applying the filler. Filler should be applied with a flexible applicator, as shown, for best results: the wooden spatula being used for confined areas. Apply thin layers of filler at 20-minute intervals, until the surface of the filler is slightly proud of the surrounding bodywork

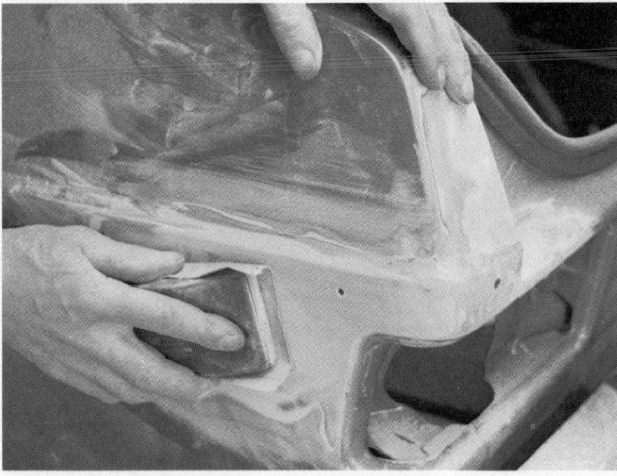

Initial shaping can be done with a Surform plane or Dreadnought file. Then, using progressively finer grades of wet-and-dry paper, wrapped around a sanding block, and copious amounts of clean water, rub-down the filler until really smooth and flat. Again, feather the edges of adjoining paintwork

The whole repair area can now be sprayed or brush-painted with primer. If spraying, ensure adjoining areas are protected from over-spray. Note that at least one-inch of the surrounding sound paintwork should be coated with primer. Primer has a 'thick' consistency, so will fill small imperfections

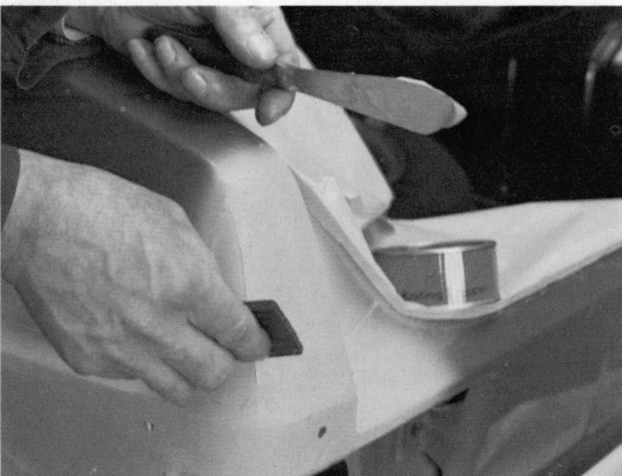

Again, using plenty of water, rub down the primer with a fine grade of wet-and-dry paper (400 grade is probably best) until it is really smooth and well blended into the surrounding paintwork. Any remaining imperfections can now be filled by carefully applied knifing stopper paste

When the stopper has hardened, rub-down the repair area again before applying the final coat of primer. Before rubbing-down this last coat of primer, ensure the repair area is blemish-free - use more stopper if necessary. To ensure that the surface of the primer is really smooth use some finishing compound

The top coat can now be applied. When working out of doors, pick a dry, warm and wind-free day. Ensure surrounding areas are protected from over-spray. Agitate the aerosol thoroughly, then spray the centre of the repair area, working outwards with a circular motion. Apply the paint as several thin coats.

After a period of about two-weeks, which the paint needs to harden fully, the surface of the repaired area can be 'cut' with a mild cutting compound prior to wax polishing. When carrying out bodywork repairs, remember that the quality of the finished job is proportional to the time and effort expended

9 Grille and bumpers - removal and installation

1 The front grille may be removed after withdrawal of the five securing bolts.
2 The expanded metal screen behind it can be removed by bending back the securing tabs.
3 The front and rear bumpers are held in position by four mounting bolts. Cars operating in North America are fitted with an additional tubular guard at each end of the front bumper.
4 Refitting is a reversal of removal but ensure that the screen has its convex side facing forward to avoid contact with the exhaust downpipes.

10 Windscreen glass - removal and refitting

1 Two people are needed when working on the windscreen, one inside and one outside the car. The screen or window is held solely by the rubber sealing strip but the lip of the seal is treated with sealing compound where it contracts the glass surfaces and the body aperture flange on the outside.
2 First remove the windscreen wiper arms, rear view interior mirror and the sun visors. Then, using a blunt edge, such as the handle end of an ordinary nail file, ease the outer lip of the sealing rubber away from the glass in order to break the sealing compound adhesion.
3 Using a similar blunt instrument next ease the inner lip of the rubber (inside the car) over thebody flange at one of the top corners. Once this is started, firm hand pressure applied from inside will force the windscreen out. Make sure someone is ready outside to support the glass when it becomes free.
4 When the screen (or window) is out, remove the weatherstrip and clean away all traces of sealer. In cases of a broken windscreen make sure all broken pieces are removed (if the same strip is being re-used).
5 When fitting a new screen, first make sure that the edges of the new screen are ground bevelled and that no chips or cracks in the edge are apparent. They are potential starters for future cracks across the screen. This must be watched, particularly if you are getting a secondhand screen from a broken car. Next support the screen on a stand, suitably padded against scratching, front side upwards, so that the edges are not obstructed. Then fit the weatherstrip to the screen. Next, the outer face of the strip against the glass should be treated with sealer injected from a flat nozzle that may be inserted under the lip. Such nozzles are usually provided with a good proprietary sealer.
6 Next find a piece of strong cord which is long enough to fit into the weathstrip body flange groove with two long ends left over. **Do not** use thin string as this could cut through the rubber. Put this into the groove - a piece of small bore tube through which the cord can be fed often helps to get it in position easily. The loose ends should cross at the centre of the bottom edge. After the string is in position a further application of sealer should be made to the side of the channel which will bear against the outside face of the body flange.
7 The screen should next be placed centrally in the aperture with the ends of the cord hanging inside the car. The inner edge of the strip can then be pulled over the flange with the cord. If difficulty is experienced in keeping the weatherstrip in position on the glass after fitting the string use self adhesive tape over it onto the glass. This will tear away when the cord is finally pulled out.
8 Finally fit the retaining clips into the groove in the rubber surround onto which the moulding can then be attached.

11 Door locks - removal, refitting and adjustment

1 Remove the screw from the centre of the door lock interior handle.
2 Remove the spring retainer from the window regulator

Fig. 12.3. Front grille securing bolts

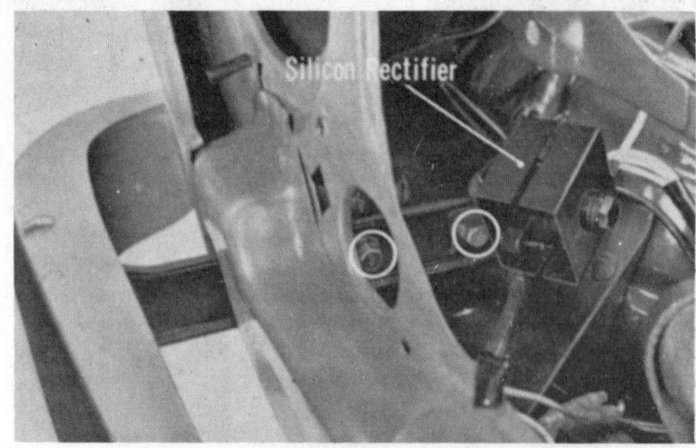

Fig. 12.4. Front bumper mounting bolts

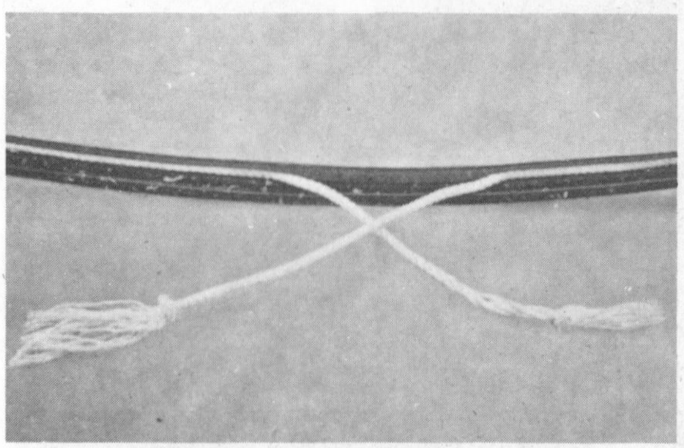

Fig. 12.5. Windscreen rubber surround fitting cord

handle escutcheon and remove the handle.
3 Insert the fingers under the edge of the door trim panel and jerk its clips out of their holes in the door frame. Peel back the vinyl, damp-resistant, membrane.
4 Remove the three bolts which secure the lock mechanism within the door edge, the two nuts which secure the exterior door handle in position and then the two bolts which retain the interior door handle remote control assembly, Fig. 12.9.
5 Disconnect the exterior handle from the lock assembly by removing the exterior handle push-button holder.
6 Withdraw the lock mechanism and remote control rod from the door cavity.
7 Refitting is a reversal of removal but remember to locate the foam rubber cushion behind the remote control rod.
8 When the lock mechanism has been refitted, check the closure of the door and locking action. If necessary adjust the position of the striker plate on the door pillar or in extreme cases, fit an adjusting shim behind the striker plate to ensure that the door closes and locks positively.

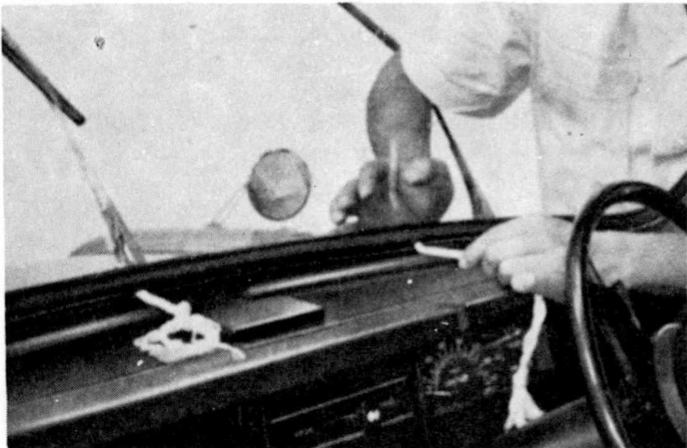

Fig. 12.6. Fitting a windscreen

12 Window regulator and glass - removal and refitting

1 There are two types of door glass regulator mechanism. Both types are removable from within the door cavity after removing the door interior trim and control handles as described in the preceding Section.
2 Disconnect the regulator linkage from the glass bottom channel.
3 Unbolt the glass vertical channel guides at their lower ends also the ventilator securing screws. Detach the weather sealing strips from the upper edge of the door panel and then withdraw the window glass/frame and ventilator assembly from the top of the door.
4 At this time check the opening and closing resistance of the ventilator. This can be adjusted by rotating the adjusting nut on its lower pivot.
5 Refitting is a reversal of removal but check the movement of the glass in its guide channels by temporarily refitting the regulator handle. Adjustment to ensure smooth operation can be made by altering the position of the glass channel securing bolts.

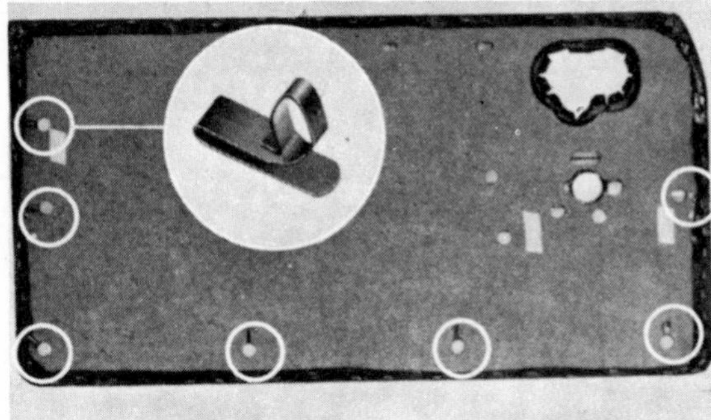

Fig. 12.7. Door trim and clips

13 Quarterlights - removal and refitting

1 The quarterlights are hinged at their top edges by two corrugated springs located in slits in the body.
2 Removal of the bottom opening catch will permit the window to be swung upwards and detached from the body.
3 Refitting is a reversal of removal.

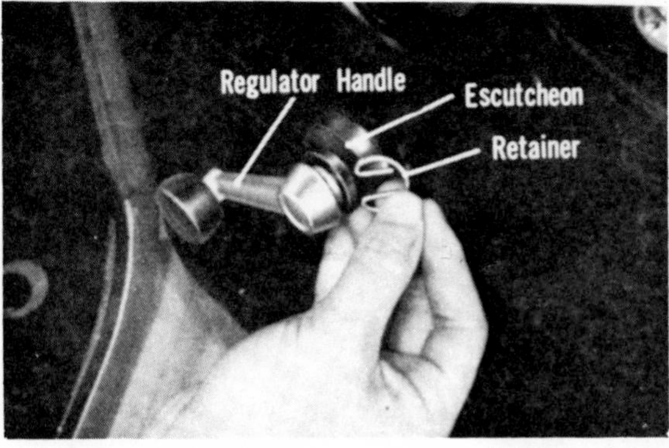

Fig. 12.8. Window regulator retaining clip

14 Doors - removal and refitting

1 Open the door to its fullest extent and support it under its lower edge with a jack or blocks.
2 The door may be removed by either withdrawing the bolts which secure the hinge plates to the door frame or by removing the bolts which secure the hinge plates to the body pillar. The latter method will require removal of the interior body trim below the fascia to gain access to the lower bolts. Before removing the hinge bolts, mark carefully round the hinges to assist refitting.
3 When refitting the door, adjust the position of the hinges by only tightening the bolts finger tight initially. If necessary fit adjusting shims behind the hinge plate.
4 When the door is finally located correctly within the body frame, check the adjustment of the striker plate.

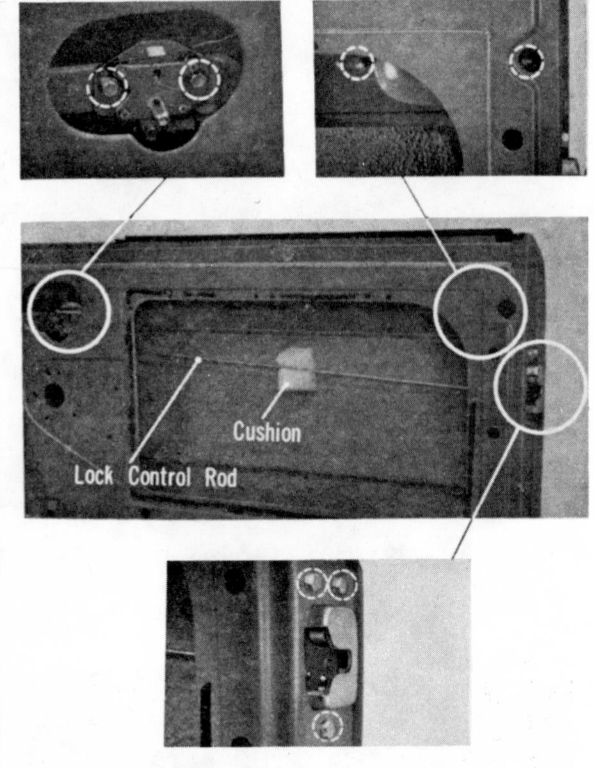

Fig. 12.9. Door lock securing bolts

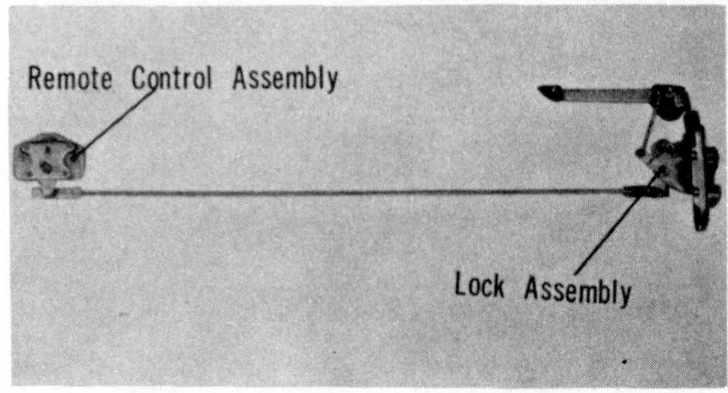

Fig. 12.10. Door iock and remote control mechanism

Fig. 12.11. Adjusting position of door striker plate

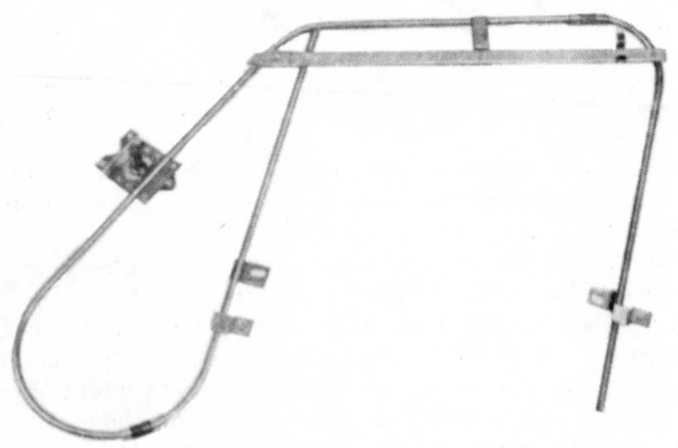

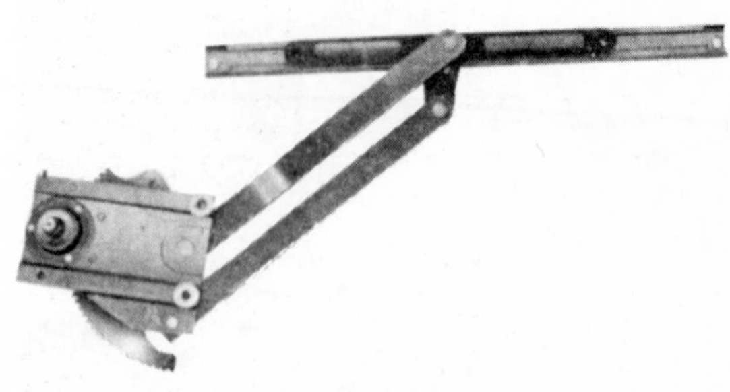

Fig. 12.12. Both types of window winder mechanism

Fig. 12.13. Window winder mechanism securing bolts

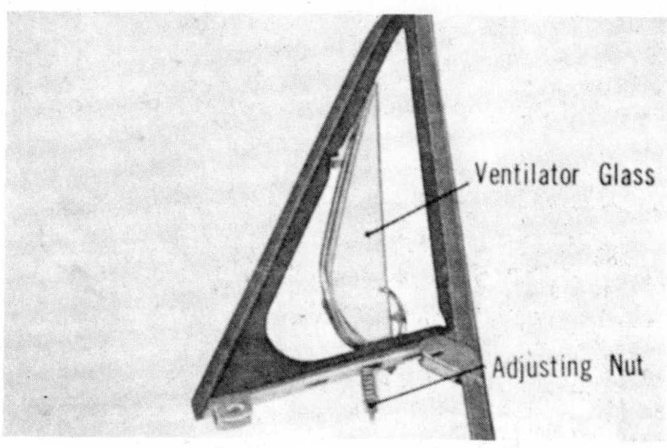

Fig. 12.14. Ventilator pivot adjusting nut

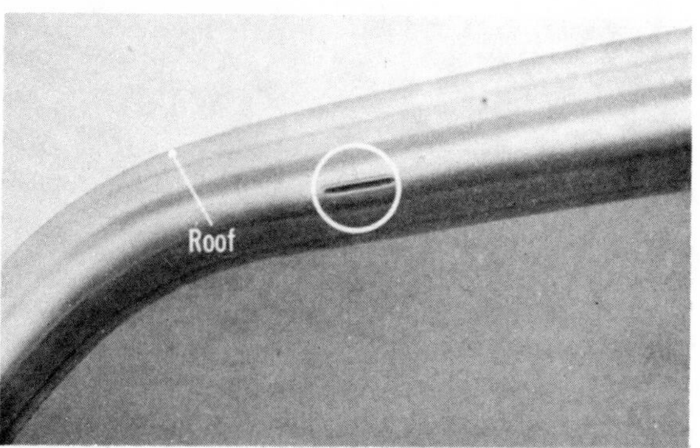

Fig. 12.15. Quarterlight hinge slot

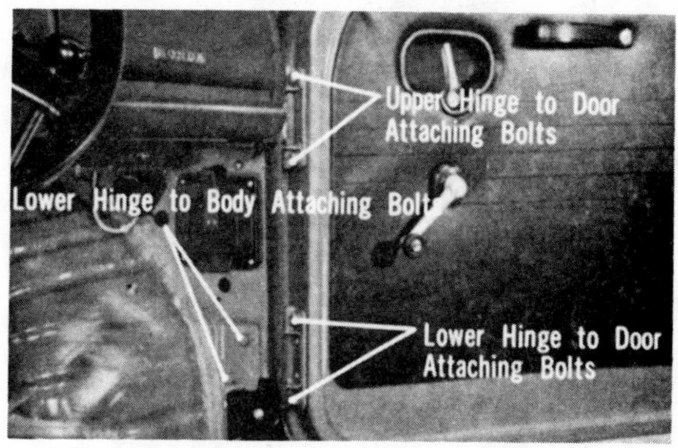

Fig. 12.16. Location of door hinge bolts

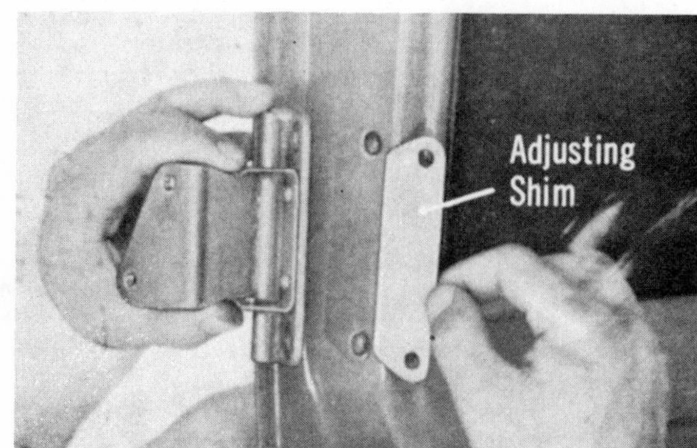

Fig. 12.17. Fitting an adjusting shim to a door hinge

15 Bonnet and luggage boot lids - removal, refitting and adjustment

1 The bonnet and luggage boot (plastic) lids are both rear hinged. Adjustment is provided for by means of the elongated bolt holes.

2 Adjust the bonnet lock dowel so that the bonnet will close securely without rattling or undue tension. Always keep the conical nose of the dowel well greased.

3 The opening stay of the luggage boot lid can be removed by pinching the two rods of the stay together.

4 Keep the luggage boot lock well greased and adjust the position of the striker plate by loosening the two bolts and moving the plate within the range of the elongated bolt holes.

5 Removal and refitting of both lids is simply a matter of removing the hinge bolts. Always mark round the hinges first to facilitate refitting and engage the help of an assistant when removing the lids to prevent damaging or scratching the surfaces of the bodywork.

6 Removal of the luggage boot lid lock is carried out by first withdrawing the lock assembly bolts and then prising out the setting spring from the groove in the lock cylinder.

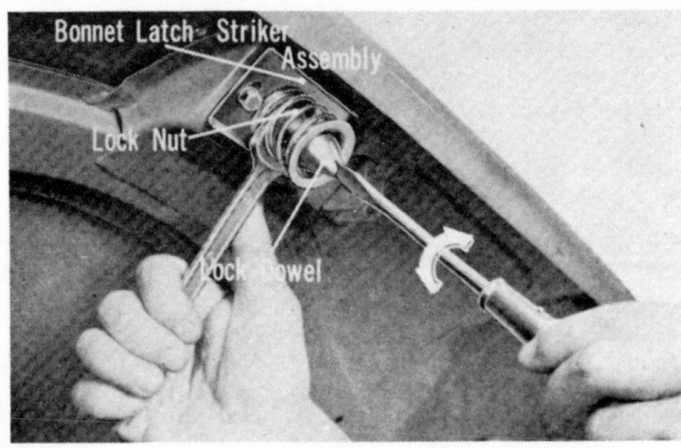

Fig. 12.18. Adjusting a bonnet lock dowel

Fig. 12.19. Removing luggage boot stay

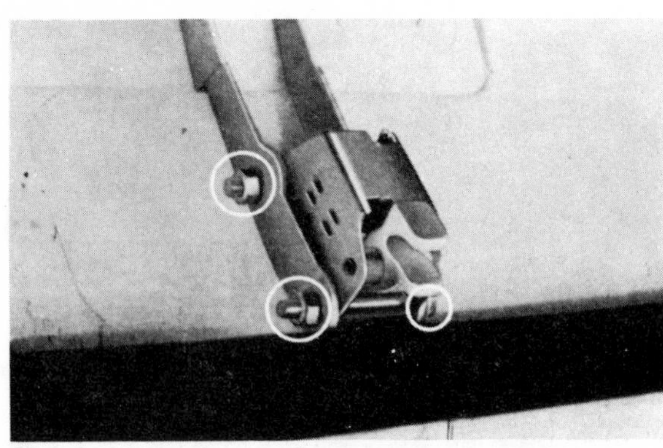

Fig. 12.20. Luggage boot lid lock securing bolts

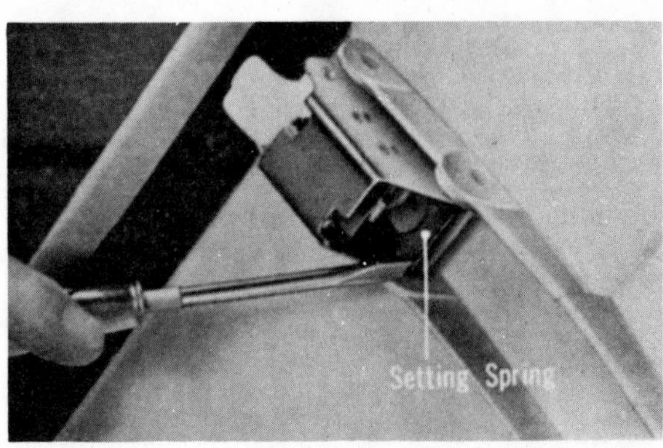

Fig. 12.21. Prising out luggage boot lock setting spring

16 Estate/Wagon tailgate - lock and striker plate adjustment

1 The horizontally split type of tailgate fitted to Estate/Wagon models incorporates hinges with elongated bolt holes to permit precise adjustment of both tailgate sections.
2 Closure of the lower tailgate can be adjusted by moving the striker plates as necessary.
3 Where the gate lock is out of adjustment and will not engage with the striker plates or will not release from them then remove the lower tailgate panel (8 bolts) and adjust the length of the lock control rods.

17 Heating and ventilation system - general description

The fresh air ventilation system takes in air from the area around the headlamps and discharges it into the passenger compartment through the air outlets which are located on either side and below the fascia panel.

Air is finally extracted from the vehicle interior through a slot into the luggage boot and then to atmosphere through the outlet grilles.

One of two types of interior heaters may be encountered, an engine warmth type in which the air which is forced over the cylinder block for the purpose of cooling, is fed into the passenger compartment and an exhaust heated type which incorporates a heat exchanger and blower.

18 Fresh air ventilator flaps - removal and refitting

1 The front flaps are secured by self-tapping screws and are immediately accessible from below the instrument panel.
2 The rear extractor plate can be prised from its location after removing the body interior trim panel.

19 Engine warmth type heater - removal, servicing and refitting

1 Disconnect the heater control rod by withdrawing the joint pin located just above the steering gear.
2 Remove the control lever bracket and withdraw the control rod assembly.
3 Loosen the pinch bolt and detach the control cable from the flap valve operating arm.
4 Remove the single retaining screw from the flap valve shaft and withdraw the shaft.
5 Remove the retaining screw and detach the heater interior/defroster control knob from its lever on the fascia panel.
6 The control lever support bracket may be removed from the

Fig. 12.22. Estate/Wagon split type tailgate

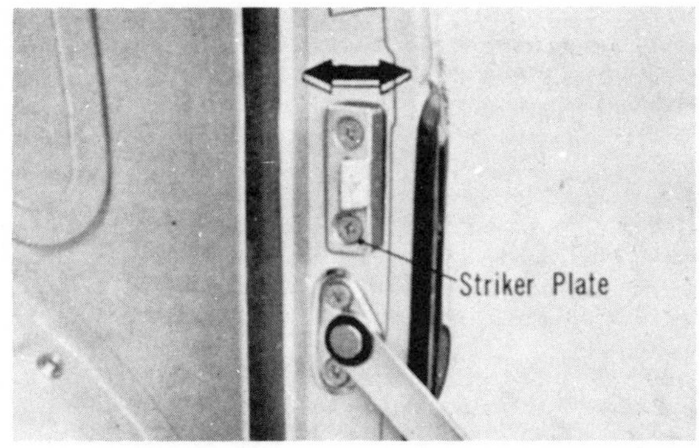

Fig. 12.23. Estate/Wagon lower tailgate striker plate

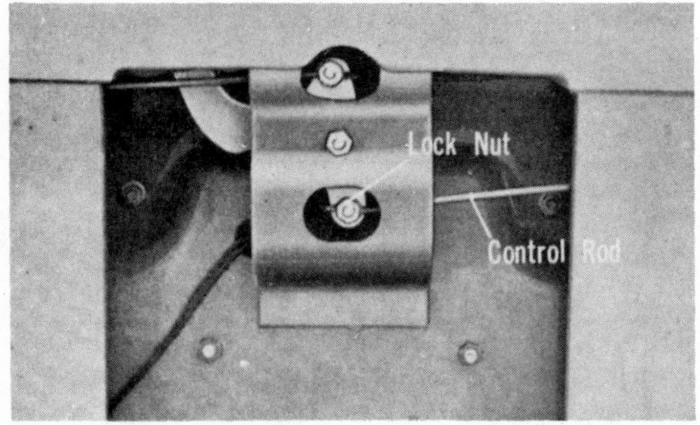

Fig. 12.24. Estate/Wagon lower tailgate lock control rods

Fig. 12.25. Location of a front ventilator flap

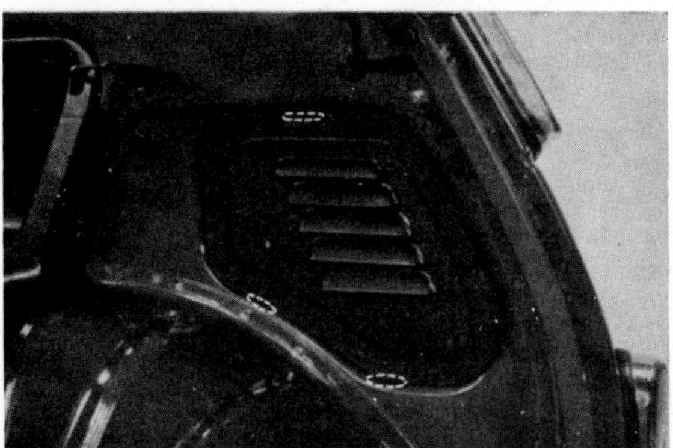

Fig. 12.26. Location of rear ventilator extractor plate

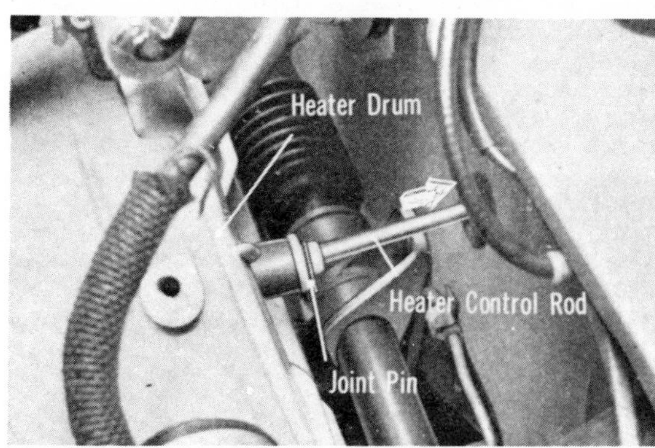

Fig. 12.27. Removing control rod joint pin (engine warmth type heater)

reverse side of the fascia panel after withdrawing the two securing screws.

7 A full description of the fan assembly and drive from the crankshaft pulley is given in Chapter 2 which covers removal, servicing and adjustment and to which reference should be made.

20 Exhaust type heater - removal, servicing, refitting

1 The heat exchanger of this type of heater is flange mounted to the exhaust pipes behind the front grille.

2 Removal is carried out by unscrewing the flange nuts and bolts.

3 To remove the blower from the engine compartment, disconnect both air ducts from it, and detach the positive electrical lead.

4 If there is a leak in the heat exchanger due to corrosion, renew it. If the blower motor will not operate, check the security of the connecting leads particularly the earth connection and then if necessary exchange it for a new assembly.

5 Removal of the heater controls is similar to that described for the engine warmth type heater in the preceding Section.

6 Before refitting the heat exchanger, discard all old gaskets and fit new ones, also renew the lower exhaust pipe flange.

7 Assemble the components with the retaining nuts and bolts finger tight only and check the alignment of the mounting flanges to ensure that there will be no undue strain between them when the bolts are fully tightened (small bolts and nuts 18 lb/ft 2.5 kg/m - large nuts 30 lb/ft 4.1 kg/m).

8 Connect the flap control cable so that with the control at 'shut' the flap is held closed by hand while the pinch bolt is tightened.

9 With this type of heater, an idle stop relay is fitted adjacent to the battery. Its purpose is to break the blower motor circuit whenever the main fascia mounted heater switch is turned off as otherwise the ram effect of the air due to the forward motion of the car, makes the blower motor rotate and act as a generator. This would cause electrical current to flow back to the system.

Fig. 12.28. Removing control rod bracket (engine warmth type heater)

Fig. 12.29. Disconnecting flap valve control cable (engine warmth type heater)

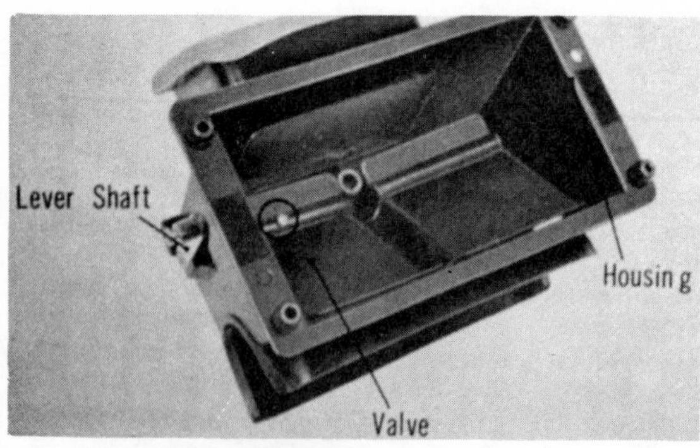

Fig. 12.30. Flap valve shaft retaining screw (engine warmth type heater)

Fig. 12.31. Exhaust type heater mounting flanges

Fig. 12.32. Exhaust type heater blower connections

Fig. 12.33. Exhaust type heater control cable connection

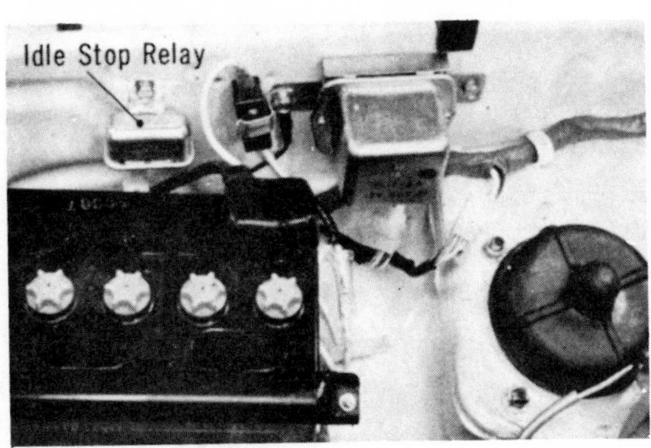

Fig. 12.34. Location of exhaust type heater blower idle stop relay

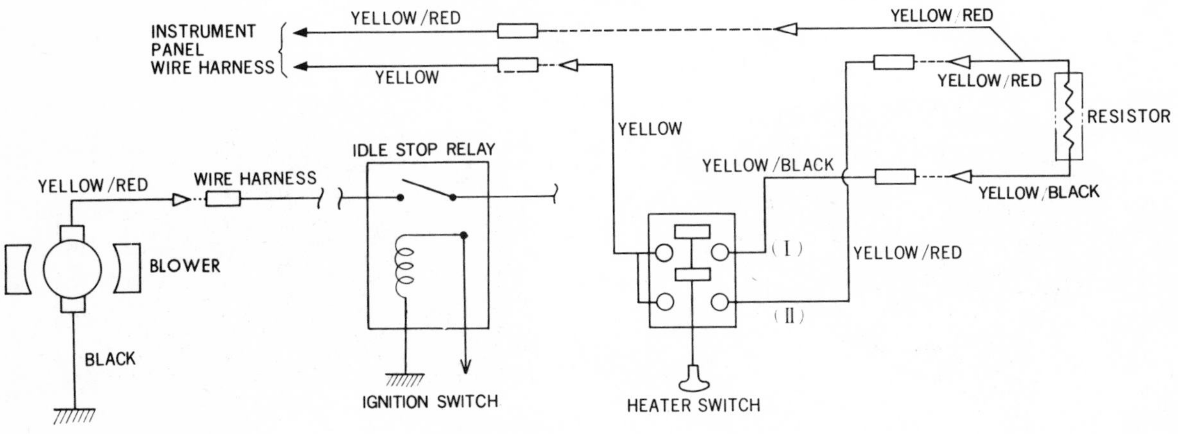

Fig. 12.35. Exhaust type heater wiring diagram

Glossary of terms

As this book has been written in England, it uses the appropriate English component names, phrases, and spelling. Some of these differ from those used in America. Normally, these cause no difficulty, but to make sure, a glossary is printed below. In ordering spare parts remember the parts list will probably use these words:

Glossary

English	American	English	American
Accelerator	Gas pedal	Leading shoe (of brake) ...	Primary shoe
Alternator	Generator (AC)	Locks	Latches
Anti-roll bar	Stabiliser or sway bar	Motorway	Freeway, turnpike etc.
Battery	Energizer	Number plate	Licence plate
Bonnet (engine cover) ...	Hood	Paraffin	Kerosene
Boot lid	Trunk lid	Petrol	Gasoline
Boot (luggage compartment)	Trunk	Petrol tank	Gas tank
Bottom gear	1st gear	'Pinking'	'Pinging'
Bulkhead	Firewall	Propellor shaft	Driveshaft
Camfollower or tappet ...	Valve lifter or tappet	Quarter light	Quarter window
Carburettor	Carburetor	Retread	Recap
Catch	Latch	Reverse	Back-up
Choke/venturi	Barrel	Rocker cover	Valve cover
Circlip	Snap ring	Roof rack	Car-top carrier
Clearance	Lash	Saloon	Sedan
Crownwheel	Ring gear (of differential)	Seized	Frozen
Disc (brake)	Rotor/disk	Side indicator lights ...	Side marker lights
Drop arm	Pitman arm	Side light	Parking light
Drop head coupe	Convertible	Silencer	Muffler
Dynamo	Generator (DC)	Spanner	Wrench
Earth (electrical)	Ground	Sill panel (beneath doors) ...	Rocker panel
Engineer's blue	Prussion blue	Split cotter (for valve spring cap)	Lock (for valve spring retainer)
Estate car	Station wagon	Split pin	Cotter pin
Exhaust manifold	Header	Steering arm	Spindle arm
Fast back (Coupe)	Hard top	Sump	Oil pan
Fault finding/diagnosis ...	Trouble shooting	Tab washer	Tang; lock
Float chamber	Float bowl	Tailgate	Liftgate
Free-play	Lash	Tappet	Valve lifter
Freewheel	Coast	Thrust bearing	Throw-out bearing
Gudgeon pin	Piston pin or wrist pin	Top gear	High
Gearchange	Shift	Trackrod (of steering) ...	Tie-rod (or connecting rod)
Gearbox	Transmission	Trailing shoe (of brake) ...	Secondary shoe
Halfshaft	Axle-shaft	Transmission	Whole drive line
Handbrake	Parking brake	Tyre	Tire
Hood	Soft top	Van	Panel wagon/van
Hot spot	Heat riser	Vice	Vise
Indicator	Turn signal	Wheel nut	Lug nut
Interior light	Dome lamp	Windscreen	Windshield
Layshaft (of gearbox) ...	Counter shaft	Wing/mudguard	Fender

Miscellaneous points

An "Oil seal" is fitted to components lubricated by grease!

A "Damper" is a "Shock absorber" it damps out bouncing, and absorbs shocks of bump impact. Both names are correct, and both are used haphazardly.

Note that British drum brakes are different from the Bendix type that is common in America, so different descriptive names result. The shoe end furthest from the hydraulic wheel cylinder is on a pivot; interconnection between the shoes as on Bendix brakes is most uncommon. Therefore the phrase "Primary" or "Secondary" shoe does not apply. A shoe is said to be Leading or Trailing. A "Leading" shoe is one on which a point on the drum, as it rotates forward, reaches the shoe at the end worked by the hydraulic cylinder before the anchor end. The opposite is a trailing shoe, and this one has no self servo from the wrapping effect of the rotating drum.

Metric conversion tables

Inches	Decimals	Millimetres	Millimetres to Inches		Inches to Millimetres	
			mm	Inches	Inches	mm
1/64	0.015625	0.3969	0.01	0.00039	0.001	0.0254
1/32	0.03125	0.7937	0.02	0.00079	0.002	0.0508
3/64	0.046875	1.1906	0.03	0.00118	0.003	0.0762
1/16	0.0625	1.5875	0.04	0.00157	0.004	0.1016
5/64	0.078125	1.9844	0.05	0.00197	0.005	0.1270
3/32	0.09375	2.3812	0.06	0.00236	0.006	0.1524
7/64	0.109375	2.7781	0.07	0.00276	0.007	0.1778
1/8	0.125	3.1750	0.08	0.00315	0.008	0.2032
9/64	0.140625	3.5719	0.09	0.00354	0.009	0.2286
5/32	0.15625	3.9687	0.1	0.00394	0.01	0.254
11/64	0.171875	4.3656	0.2	0.00787	0.02	0.508
3/16	0.1875	4.7625	0.3	0.01181	0.03	0.762
13/64	0.203125	5.1594	0.4	0.01575	0.04	1.016
7/32	0.21875	5.5562	0.5	0.01969	0.05	1.270
15/64	0.234375	5.9531	0.6	0.02362	0.06	1.524
1/4	0.25	6.3500	0.7	0.02756	0.07	1.778
17/64	0.265625	6.7469	0.8	0.03150	0.08	2.032
9/32	0.28125	7.1437	0.9	0.03543	0.09	2.286
19/64	0.296875	7.5406	1	0.03937	0.1	2.54
5, 16	0.3125	7.9375	2	0.07874	0.2	5.08
21/64	0.328125	8.3344	3	0.11811	0.3	7.62
11/32	0.34375	8.7312	4	0.15748	0.4	10.16
23/64	0.359375	9.1281	5	0.19685	0.5	12.70
3/8	0.375	9.5250	6	0.23622	0.6	15.24
25/64	0.390625	9.9219	7	0.27559	0.7	17.78
13/32	0.40625	10.3187	8	0.31496	0.8	20.32
27/64	0.421875	10.7156	9	0.35433	0.9	22.86
7/16	0.4375	11.1125	10	0.39370	1	25.4
29/64	0.453125	11.5094	11	0.43307	2	50.8
15/32	0.46875	11.9062	12	0.47244	3	76.2
31/64	0.484375	12.3031	13	0.51181	4	101.6
1/2	0.5	12.7000	14	0.55118	5	127.0
33/64	0.515625	13.0969	15	0.59055	6	152.4
17/32	0.53125	13.4937	16	0.62992	7	177.8
35/64	0.546875	13.8906	17	0.66929	8	203.2
9/16	0.5625	14.2875	18	0.70866	9	228.6
37/64	0.578125	14.6844	19	0.74803	10	254.0
19/32	0.59375	15.0812	20	0.78740	11	279.4
39/64	0.609375	15.4781	21	0.82677	12	304.8
5/8	0.625	15.8750	22	0.86614	13	330.2
41/64	0.640625	16.2719	23	0.90551	14	355.6
21/32	0.65625	16.6687	24	0.94488	15	381.0
43/64	0.671875	17.0656	25	0.98425	16	406.4
11/16	0.6875	17.4625	26	1.02362	17	431.8
45/64	0.703125	17.8594	27	1.06299	18	457.2
23/32	0.71875	18.2562	28	1.10236	19	482.6
47/64	0.734375	18.6531	29	1.14173	20	508.0
3/4	0.75	19.0500	30	1.18110	21	533.4
49/64	0.765625	19.4469	31	1.22047	22	558.8
25/32	0.78125	19.8437	32	1.25984	23	584.2
51/64	0.796875	20.2406	33	1.29921	24	609.6
13/16	0.8125	20.6375	34	1.33858	25	635.0
53/64	0.828125	21.0344	35	1.37795	26	660.4
27/32	0.84375	21.4312	36	1.41732	27	685.8
55/64	0.859375	21.8281	37	1.4567	28	711.2
7/8	0.875	22.2250	38	1.4961	29	736.6
57/64	0.890625	22.6219	39	1.5354	30	762.0
29/32	0.90625	23.0187	40	1.5748	31	787.4
59/64	0.921875	23.4156	41	1.6142	32	812.8
15/16	0.9375	23.8125	42	1.6535	33	838.2
61/64	0.953125	24.2094	43	1.6929	34	863.6
31/32	0.96875	24.6062	44	1.7323	35	889.0
63/64	0.984375	25.0031	45	1.7717	36	914.4

Metric Conversion Tables

1 Imperial gallon = 8 Imp pints = 1.16 US gallons = 277.42 cu in = **4.5459 litres**

1 US gallon = 4 US quarts = 0.862 Imp gallon = 231 cu in = 3.785 litres

1 Litre = 0.2199 Imp gallon = 0.2642 US gallon = 61.0253 cu in = 1000 cc

Miles to Kilometres	
1	1.61
2	3.22
3	4.83
4	6.44
5	8.05
6	9.66
7	11.27
8	12.88
9	14.48
10	16.09
20	32.19
30	48.28
40	64.37
50	80.47
60	96.56
70	112.65
80	128.75
90	144.84
100	160.93

Kilometres to Miles	
1	0.62
2	1.24
3	1.86
4	2.49
5	3.11
6	3.73
7	4.35
8	4.97
9	5.59
10	6.21
20	12.43
30	18.64
40	24.85
50	31.07
60	37.28
70	43.50
80	49.71
90	55.92
100	62.14

lb f ft to Kg f m	
1	0.138
2	0.276
3	0.414
4	0.553
5	0.691
6	0.829
7	0.967
8	1.106
9	1.244
10	1.382
20	2.765
30	4.147

Kg f m to lb f ft	
1	7.233
2	14.466
3	21.699
4	28.932
5	36.165
6	43.398
7	50.631
8	57.864
9	65.097
10	72.330
20	144.660
30	216.990

lb f/in^2 : Kg f/cm^2	
1	0.07
2	0.14
3	0.21
4	0.28
5	0.35
6	0.42
7	0.49
8	0.56
9	0.63
10	0.70
20	1.41
30	2.11

Kg f/cm^2 : lb f/in^2	
1	14.22
2	28.50
3	42.67
4	56.89
5	71.12
6	85.34
7	99.56
8	113.79
9	128.00
10	142.23
20	284.47
30	426.70

Index

Printed by
Haynes Publishing Group
Sparkford Yeovil Somerset
England